D1327849

Understanding Marcel Proust

Understanding Modern European and Latin American Literature

James Hardin, Series Editor

volumes on

Ingeborg Bachmann

Samuel Beckett

Juan Benet

Thomas Bernhard

Johannes Bobrowski

Heinrich Böll

Italo Calvino

Albert Camus

Elias Canetti

Camilo José Cela

Céline

Julio Cortázar

Isak Dinesen

José Donoso

Friedrich Dürrenmatt

Rainer Werner Fassbinder

Max Frisch

Federico García Lorca

Gabriel García Márquez

Juan Goytisolo

Günter Grass

Gerhart Hauptmann

Christoph Hein

Hermann Hesse

Eugène Ionesco

Uwe Johnson

Milan Kundera

Primo Levi

John McGahern

Robert Musil

Boris Pasternak

Octavio Paz

Luigi Pirandello

Marcel Proust

Graciliano Ramos

Erich Maria Remarque

Alain Robbe-Grillet

Joseph Roth

Jean-Paul Sartre

W. G. Sebald

Claude Simon

Mario Vargas Llosa

Peter Weiss

Franz Werfel

Christa Wolf

UNDERSTANDING

Marcel Proust

Allen Thiher

The University of South Carolina Press

© 2013 University of South Carolina

Published by the University of South Carolina Press
Columbia, South Carolina 29208

www.sc.edu/uscpress

Manufactured in the United States of America

22 21 20 19 18 17 16 15 14 13   10 9 8 7 6 5 4 3 2 1

Library of Congress Cataloging-in-Publication Data

Thiher, Allen, 1941–
    Understanding Marcel Proust / Allen Thiher.
        pages cm. — (Understanding Modern European and Latin American Literature)
    Includes bibliographical references and index.
      ISBN 978-1-61117-255-3 (hardbound : alk. paper) —
    ISBN 978-1-61117-256-0 (epub) 1. Proust, Marcel, 1871–1922—Criticism and
    interpretation. I. Title.
      PQ2631.R63Z934 2013
      843'.912—dc23

                                                                    2013005008

This book was printed on a recycled paper with 30 percent postconsumer waste content.

To Irma

Contents

Series Editor's Preface   *ix*

Acknowledgments   *xi*

Chronology   *xiii*

Abbreviations and Editions   *xviii*

Chapter 1   Life and Career   *1*

Chapter 2   What Proust Published before *In Search of Lost Time*   *26*

Chapter 3   What Proust Did Not Publish   *69*

Chapter 4   *Swann's Way:* Intimations of Paradise and Paradise Lost   *112*

Chapter 5   *Within a Budding Grove* and *The Guermantes Way:*
             Intimations of the Fall   *154*

Chapter 6   *Sodom and Gomorrah, The Captive,* and *The Fugitive:*
             Intimations of Hell   *200*

Chapter 7   *Time Regained:* Intimations of the Resurrection   *246*

Notes   *291*

Bibliography   *299*

Index   *309*

Series Editor's Preface

Understanding Modern European and Latin American Literature has been planned as a series of guides for undergraduate and graduate students and nonacademic readers. Like the volumes in its companion series, *Understanding Contemporary American Literature,* these books provide introductions to the lives and writings of prominent modern authors and explicate their most important works.

Modern literature makes special demands, and this is particularly true of foreign literature, in which the reader must contend not only with unfamiliar, often arcane artistic conventions and philosophical concepts, but also with the handicap of reading the literature in translation. It is a truism that the nuances of one language can be rendered in another only imperfectly (and this problem is especially acute in fiction), but the fact that the works of European and Latin American writers are situated in a historical and cultural setting quite different from our own can be as great a hindrance to the understanding of these works as the linguistic barrier. For this reason the *UMELL* series emphasizes the sociological and historical background of the writers treated. The philosophical and cultural traditions peculiar to a given culture may be particularly important for an understanding of certain authors, and these are taken up in the introductory chapter and also in the discussion of those works to which this information is relevant. Beyond this the books treat the specifically literary aspects of the author under discussion and attempt to explain the complexities of contemporary literature lucidly. The books are conceived as introductions to the authors covered, not as comprehensive analyses. They do not provide detailed summaries of plot because they are meant to be used in conjunction with the books they treat, not as a substitute for study of the original works. The purpose of the books is to provide information and judicious literary assessment of the major works in the most compact, readable form. It is our hope that the *UMELL* series will help increase knowledge and understanding of European and Latin American cultures and will serve to make the literature of those cultures more accessible.

J.H.

Acknowledgments

I want first to thank the series editor, James Hardin, for his encouragement and for the work he has done for modern literature in general with this series, which he has edited through the years. That is the most recent help I have received. My thanks for the earliest help would go to Proust scholars who, as teachers, introduced me to Proust many years ago: first the late Roger Shattuck, with whom I read Proust as an undergraduate at the University of Texas, and then the late Germaine Brée, who allowed me to take her strictly limited Proust seminar for graduate students at the University of Wisconsin. Thanks also go to the indefatigable Proust scholar J. Theodore Johnson, with whom I had discussions of Proust many years ago at Madison and again more recently via e-mail as I have worked on this book. I can also give thanks to the many students and colleagues who through the years have interacted with me in reading Proust, especially at Middlebury College and at the University of Missouri.

I thank again the University of Missouri Research Council for financing a stay at Cambridge University and Clare Hall, where some years ago I began to work toward publishing my views on Proust. Cambridge's library facilities—with their unparalleled resources in French literature—and conversations with fellows at Clare Hall played their role in the genesis of this book. For a more recent stay at Cambridge, I also give thanks to the University of Missouri Research Board and the University of Missouri's Arts and Humanities Center.

Finally many thanks to Irma for help and patience.

Chronology

1871
Marcel Proust born July 10 to Jeanne Proust, née Weil, and the doctor Adrien Proust, in the house of maternal uncle Louis Weil, in the Parisian suburb of Auteil.

Baptized in August at the Paris church Saint-Louis d'Antin.

1873
Birth of Proust's only sibling, the future doctor Robert Proust.

1880
Proust's first attack of asthma, which plagues him, at times severely, all his life.

1882
After home schooling, enrolls at the Lycée Condorcet in *cinquième,* or approximately the seventh grade.

1888–89
Initiated into philosophy at Condorcet by the neo-Kantian professor Alphonse Darlu. In 1889 Proust receives his baccalaureate and the honor prize in philosophy.

1889
Begins one year of military service in an infantry regiment. Friends in service with Robert de Billy and Gaston de Caillavet.

1890
Enrolls at the École libre des sciences politiques. Publishes texts in a journal, *Le Mensuel,* of which he appears to be an editor. Has an active social life.

1891
Spends the first of many summers on the Normandy coast, at Cabourg or at Trouville.

Matriculates in law school in November.

1892

Publishes texts in *Le Banquet,* of which he is a member of the editorial committee. Passes his exams for a diploma in political science.

1893

Publishes in *La Revue blanche.* Vacations in Saint Moritz, where he works on texts for his first book, *Les plaisirs et les jours (Pleasures and Days).*

Passes his law exams in fall and receives a law diploma dated October 10, 1893. Confronting a father who wants him to embrace a career, Proust keeps him at bay by matriculating for a degree in philosophy. Meets the Baron Robert de Montesquiou.

1894

Studies philosophy and becomes engaged in social life in high society, cultivating contacts with many artists and aristocrats. Involved romantically with musician Reynaldo Hahn.

1895

Gets a diploma in philosophy. Accepted for a nonremunerative position, never occupied, at the Bibliothèque Mazarine. Reads Ralph Waldo Emerson, Thomas Carlyle, Honoré de Balzac, and Gustave Flaubert.

1896

Begins writing a novel, published posthumously under the editor's title *Jean Santeuil.*

Publishes an essay, "Contre l'obscurité" ("Against Obscurity"), in *La Revue blanche.*

In December publishes *Pleasures and Days,* with a preface by Anatole France. Proust becomes friends with Lucien Daudet.

1897

Proust duels with the critic Jean Lorrain because of an insult to him and Daudet in a review of *Pleasures and Days.*

1898

Is an active Dreyfusard at the moment of Zola's trial for pro-Dreyfus activity. Travels to Holland in October.

1899

Takes a fourth and final leave of absence from the Bibliothèque Mazarine. Abandons his project to write *Jean Santeuil.* Reads Émile Mâle on Gothic architecture and begins to translate the English art historian John Ruskin.

1900

Publication in *Le Figaro* of "Pèlerinage ruskiniens en France" ("Ruskinian Pilgrimages in France") and, in *Le Mercure de France,* "Ruskin à Notre-Dame d'Amiens" ("Ruskin at Notre-Dame d'Amiens"). Two trips to

Venice, the first with his mother. Family moves from boulevard Maleherbes to rue de Courcelles, near the elegant parc Monceau.

1902

Proust in Belgium and Holland, accompanied part of the time by Bertrand de Fénelon. Pastiche of Saint-Simon published in *Le Figaro*.

1903

Begins publishing a series of "salons" in *Le Figaro*. Death of his father.

1904

Publishes in *Le Figaro* a call for the preservation of medieval churches, "La mort des cathédrales: Une conséquence du projet Briand sur la séparation" ("The Death of the Cathedrals: A Consequence of Briand's Law on the Separation of Church and State"). Publication of his translation of Ruskin's *The Bible of Amiens*.

1905

Publishes "Sur la lecture" ("On Reading"), preface to his forthcoming translation of Ruskin's *Sesame and Lilies*. Death of Proust's mother, beginning months of mourning. Proust is now financially independent. At end of the year, he enters a sanatorium for a "cure" of his asthma.

1906

Publishes his translation of *Sesame and Lilies*. Moves into 102 boulevard Haussmann, the former apartment of his deceased maternal uncle. Covers walls of the bedroom with cork.

1907

Publishes an article on a matricide in *Le Figaro*, "Sentiments filiaux d'un parricide" ("Filial Sentiments of a Parricide"). Publishes other articles in *Le Figaro*. Gives a dinner at the Ritz at which Gabriel Fauré, taken ill, was to perform his First Sonata, op. 13. Travels in Normandy with his chauffeur, Alfred Agostinelli.

1908

Publishes in *Le Figaro* a series of pastiches of famous French writers. Works on manuscripts posthumously published as *Contre Sainte-Beuve* (*Against Sainte-Beuve*).

1909

Begins the life of a recluse, devoting himself entirely to *A la recherche du temps perdu* (*In Search of Lost Time*). Hahn and Georges de Lauris are enthusiastic about the first version of *Du côté de chez Swann* (*Swann's Way*).

1912

Now listens to music in his apartment on the "théatrophone"—a telephonic music service. Agostinelli becomes his secretary.

1913

Céleste Albaret becomes Proust's housekeeper. Bernard Grasset publishes *Swann's Way* at the author's expense.

1914

Death of Agostinelli in April. World War I begins. During the winter Proust learns of the death of Fénelon and later of Caillavet. Revises the novel throughout the war.

1916

Gives publication of the novel over to publisher Gaston Gallimard and the journal *La Nouvelle Revue française* (NRF). Renews social life, encountering writers such as Jean Cocteau and Paul Morand.

1917

Frequently at the Hotel Ritz. Gallimard publishes a new edition of *Swann's Way.*

1918

Paris is bombarded.

1919

Receives the Goncourt Prize for *A l'ombre des jeunes filles en fleurs* (*Within a Budding Grove*). Also publishes an anthology of earlier writings, *Pastiches et mélanges* (*Pastiches and Miscellanies*). Proust's aunt sells his apartment, obliging him to move to temporary lodgings, then to a fifth floor flat at 44 rue Hamelin, where he works on *In Search of Lost Time* until his death.

1920

Publishes the first volume of *Du côté de Guermantes* (*The Guermantes Way*). NRF publishes essay "A propos du style de Flaubert" ("On Flaubert's Style").

1921

Publishes the second volume of *The Guermantes Way* and the first of *Sodome et Gomorrhe* (*Sodom and Gomorrah*). The essay "A propos de Baudelaire" ("On Baudelaire") appears in *NRF.* Proust becomes ill while visiting an exposition in Paris of Dutch painting, where he sees again Vermeer's *View of Delft.*

1922

Publishes the second volume of *Sodom and Gomorrah.* Works intensely to complete the novel, and then tells Céleste Alberet that he has written the word *end* on the manuscript. Catches viral pneumonia and dies on November 18, 1922.

1923

Proust's brother, Robert, oversees publication of the remaining manuscripts. Publication in two volumes of *La prisonnière* (*The Prisoner*).

1925

Publication of *Albertine disparu*, first called *La fugitive* (*The Fugitive*) in the manuscript but changed at the time to avoid confusion with a work of the same title by Rabindranath Tagore. (In the first translation called *Sweet Cheat Gone*.)

1927

Publication of *Le temps retrouvé* (*Time Regained*) in two volumes. Robert Proust selects occasional pieces and essays for publication as *Chroniques* (*Chronicles*).

1930–36

Publication of a selection of Proust's letters as his *Correspondance générale* by Robert Proust and Paul Brach.

1952

Bernard de Fallois publishes a reconstruction of Proust's abandoned novel, which Fallois titles *Jean Santeuil*.

1954

Fallois collates a group of manuscripts written before *In Search of Lost Time* and publishes them as *Contre Sainte-Beuve*, to which Fallois adds a selection of earlier texts, "Nouveaux mélanges" ("New Miscellany"). First publication of an authoritative edition of *A la recherche du temps perdu* by the Bibliothèque de la Pléiade.

1970

Philip Kolb begins publishing Proust's letters in the multivolume series called *Correspondance*.

1987

Publication of a revised and greatly enlarged Pléiade edition of *A la recherche du temps perdu*.

Abbreviations and Editions

I use the following abbreviations in citations for quotations from *In Search of Lost Time:*

BG   *Within a Budding Grove*
C   *The Captive*
GW   *The Guermantes Way*
P   *The Prisoner*
SG   *Sodom and Gomorrah*
SW   *Swann's Way*
TR   *Time Regained*

All citations for this work come from the Moncrieff translation. Unless otherwise noted, all translations from Proust's other works are my own.

Chapter 1

Life and Career

Marcel Proust was born in 1871, at the very outset of the Third Republic, which Proust's school friend Daniel Halévy later called the "Republic of Dukes."[1] Proust knew no dukes as a child, but he was born into a prosperous bourgeois family of mixed religious background. His mother, Jeanne née Weil, was from a Parisian Jewish family, whereas his father, Adrien, was of provincial Catholic background. The father's hometown of Illiers, not distant from Paris, is partly the basis for the village of Combray, the setting of the imaginary childhood Proust created in his novel, *In Search of Lost Time*. But equally important for the creation of that village was undoubtedly Auteil, then a village, now a suburb adjoining Paris, in which was located the Weil family summer house where Proust was born. Proust regularly spent time in Auteil during his youth, though his family took up permanent residence in Paris in 1873 in an apartment on the boulevard Malesherbes, not far from the Madeleine Church. One can say that Proust began life in the center of Paris and in many important respects never left it. The world of the Parisian upper classes is the setting for his novel; his first contact with it was with the world of the prosperous bourgeoisie, notably the world of his mother's family. Her family was part of the assimilated French Jewry that had been successful in commerce during the preceding century, after the first French Republic had granted full citizenship to Jews in 1791.

Religion is an important theme in Proust, though neither of Proust's parents actively practiced their forebears' religion. They appear in fact not to have had any strong religious beliefs, though Proust was baptized. His family appears to have been liberal and secular in outlook, consciously holding up Enlightenment values. This was especially true of his father, a doctor, who was a nearly model representative of a man of science during the Third Republic. He came from an old but impecunious family, and one may suppose that he was not averse to his wife because there was money in her family. They seem to have been a happy couple. Moreover Adrien

Proust became quite wealthy on his own through his medical practice. In his youth he had to rely on a scholarship to pay for his secondary school studies in Chartres. Leaving the provinces, he studied medicine in Paris and, after receiving his diploma in 1862, quickly occupied a series of prestigious positions while receiving public recognition for his work on contagious diseases. In 1879 he was elected to the Académie Nationale de Médecine. Working as a clinician, he also became a professor and well-published specialist in public health and, subsequently, a diplomat who, as a representative of France, attended international medical conferences dealing with preventive measures for such maladies as cholera and bubonic plague. In short Marcel's father was a very successful doctor, and a strong presence in the life both of Marcel and his younger brother, Robert, who himself became a doctor. In fact Marcel had to resist his father's influence and his desire to see his son pursue a career in one of the accepted professions.

Proust's mother was a cultivated woman who introduced her son to the classics of Western literature, especially writers of the seventeenth century such as Molière, Racine, and Madame de Sévigné, as well as later writers such as Honoré de Balzac and Johann Wolfgang von Goethe. Music was also important in the Proust household, as was the study of languages. When Proust began school at the age of eleven, he already knew some German and Latin, taught to him by his mother and grandmother and perhaps by tutors. Thus he was ready to enter classes in Greek, French, and natural sciences at the Lycée Fontanes, which became the Lycée Condorcet in 1883. When he was not too ill to attend classes, Proust did well in his studies. He had his first asthma attack as a child, and he was frequently subject to its debilitating effects. He rarely enjoyed good health for long periods of time.

Proust's commitment to literature was already evident at the Lycée Condorcet. This is partly demonstrated by his choice in friends there, many of whom later became part of the intellectual and creative elite of the belle époque, as the end of the nineteenth and the beginning of the twentieth century is called with nostalgia. However Proust's secondary studies were almost compromised by his asthma, and because of absences, he was obliged to repeat *seconde*, roughly the tenth grade. He was, however, much more successful in the following year's class, then called *rhétorique*. There, at around age sixteen, he discovered the joys of literary creation, and probably sex, with friends such as Halévy, Robert Dreyfus, and Jacques Bizet.

Proust sent one of his first poems, the unpublished "Pédérastie," to Halévy. Deploring the need for virtue in a repressive world, this early poem reads like a pastiche of the nostalgia for the Latin Golden Age that Proust would have encountered in his literary studies. More interesting for his biography, however, is the fact that in it Proust was more forthright about his desires at an early age than ever in later life. First evoking his desire to flee from the present time, the young poet goes on to write: "Free from rustic irritations, wasps dew or frost / I want to sleep with, love or live for ever / With a warm boy, Jacques, Pierre or Firmin. / Be gone the timid scorn of Prud'hommes! / Doves, send down your snow! Sing, young elms! Ripen, apples! / I want to breathe his scent until I die! Beneath the gold of red suns, / beneath the pearl of moons / I want . . . to faint away and believe I am dead / Far from the mournful knell of importunate Virtues!"[2] These lines suggest that Proust was often captivated by more than one young man. In fact among others at this time, he was infatuated with Bizet, which led him to cultivate the acquaintance of the boy's mother, Geneviève Straus (née Halévy), widow of the composer Georges Bizet. This contact with the Halévy-Straus family was of major importance, since it gained the young poet entrance into select circles.

During these years at the lycée, science and mathematics were complemented by rhetorical and language studies. At the same time, with schoolmates having a comparable literary bent, Proust founded literary reviews with such mildly decadent names as the *Revue verte* (Green Review), which changed color to become the *Revue lilas* (Lilac Review). In Proust's final year in school in 1888, in the class called *philosophie*, he encountered a first-rate mind in his philosophy professor, Alphonse Darlu, a neo-Kantian who founded the influential *Revue de métaphysique et de morale*. The positivism of Marcel's father met a critique in the Kantian idealism that Darlu brought to his teaching. Proust was so taken with Darlu that he later sought out the professor for tutoring during his university years. A letter Proust wrote to Darlu shows that the young man wanted his professor to be a personal mentor to whom he might appeal for intellectual guidance while, as it were, confessing himself. In the letter Proust describes for his professor the *dédoublement,* or divided consciousness, that characterizes him when he examines his inner life. He says that this self-scrutiny is affecting his "supreme joy," that is, his literary life. Proust gives the following example: "When I read for example a poem by Leconte de Lisle, while I am tasting in it the infinite voluptuous pleasures of times gone by, my other *self* looks at me and is amused to consider the causes of my pleasure, looks at them with regard to a certain relationship between me and the work, and thereby destroys the *very* beauty of the work, and above all, by immediately imagining conditions for beauty that oppose it, it manages to kill almost all my pleasure."[3] Proust complains in effect about this constant observation directed toward his inner life—or as he described it in this letter, "ce regard sans cesse ouvert sur ma vie intérieur" (this unceasing stare inspecting my inner life). One suspects that this split consciousness is of romantic provenance—of which Charles Baudelaire is a prime example. This does not detract from the seriousness of Proust's sense of paralysis. In fact the letter suggests that, at sixteen or seventeen, he had full consciousness of the labile nature of his self-consciousness, an involuted consciousness that observes itself as it examines the grounds for believing or feeling or even perceiving anything. In brief Proust was early aware that consciousness itself was a kind of problem and believed that only literature offered a means of living with that consciousness.

By the summer of 1889, Proust had earned a baccalaureate degree with honors for his last year at the lycée. That summer he gained entrance into the salon of Arman de Caillavet, another select Parisian literary circle, where he met the then-celebrated writer Anatole France. Social life receded somewhat into the background after Proust signed up for early military service. This type of volunteer service, available for the last time in 1889, reduced considerably the amount of time the army demanded of a draftee, so that Proust spent only a year in the army, instead of the three that recently passed legislation had mandated. He spent his year mainly in the provincial city of Orleans, close enough to Paris that he could take the train home on weekends to be with his parents or Madame de Caillavet and her son Gaston. At this time Proust manifested a form of behavior that recurred several times in his life. He apparently pretended to be in love with the son's girlfriend so as to distract from the attraction he felt for the son. The imaginary triangle was thus a subterfuge, too successful in the case of Gaston, who got quite angry with Proust.

Proust's experience as a soldier did not seem to make much of an impression on him. He never took to riding horses or gymnastics. He did come away, however, with some experience with firearms—which perhaps served to bolster his courage for dueling. After the year of military service, Proust returned home and was obliged to make a choice of university curriculum. Formal university education was, from his father's viewpoint, the prelude to a choice of a career. Probably under paternal orders, Proust subsequently enrolled, as was not unusual, in two degree programs, first at the École libre des sciences politiques and then, at the same time or perhaps a year later in November 1891, at the university faculty of law. (Sources conflict on this; I follow the biographer Jean-Yves Tadié, who says it was a year later.)[4] Law was not a demanding curriculum, and Proust undoubtedly learned a great deal more from the professors of political science, such as Albert Sorel, a diplomat, historian, and political philosopher who, in the wake of Montesquieu and Alexis de Tocqueville, attempted to explain the logic of history and those laws behind its unfolding. But Proust's academic year was not just devoted to the history of diplomacy and politics. He also went to the theater and continued his social life, meeting notables such as Edmond de Goncourt in salons held by women such as Mme Alphonse Daudet, wife of the famous writer, or the aging Princess Mathilde, daughter of Jerome Bonaparte and a cousin of Napoleon III, who once received writers such as Gustave Flaubert, Charles-Augustin Sainte-Beuve, and Alexandre Dumas.

Nor did university studies preclude literary activity. Sometime in late 1890 or early 1891, Proust was involved in the publication of a student literary journal called *Le Mensuel* in which he published some texts of various sorts. In fact it is possible that he wrote a good bit of what appeared in it. It was a journal with a heterogeneous content, ranging from pieces on art and fashion to music-hall chronicles and literary criticism. What is perhaps Proust's first published poem appeared here, one dedicated to Gustave Laurens de Waru, the nephew of countess de Chevigné, another of several aristocratic women whom Proust frequented and who would contribute much to his understanding of them and their class. The poem is perhaps most notable for being such a patent imitation of Baudelaire that one might call it Proust's first published pastiche.

At the end of 1891, Oscar Wilde arrived in Paris, and Proust may have met him. Legend has it that the notorious Irishman met Proust at his home with his parents; and then Wilde walked out, not mindful of Proust's parents, with the comment, "How ugly it is here."[5] Other celebrities whom he met in these years include the philosopher Henri Bergson, who married Proust's cousin, Louise Neuburger. This marriage did not bring about a rapprochement between the philosopher and the novelist, and Proust seems to have had relatively little contact with his cousin by marriage, the most famous French intellectual of the early twentieth century. There are undoubtedly intellectual grounds for this relative indifference: as Bergson before him, Proust studied at the university with the influential neo-Kantian Émile Boutroux; but whereas he continued to be attracted to a neo-Kantian belief in rationality as an ultimate criterion for knowledge, Bergson rejected it. And though they read each other's works—and early critics made much of their relationship—there is little reason to conjoin the names of Proust and Bergson.

In early 1892 Proust joined again with lycée friends and others to start another literary journal, *Le Banquet*. The title of the journal is redolent of a Platonic dialogue, and the young men undoubtedly picked it in a gesture of respect for the classical origins of Western culture. Fernand Gregh was the editor. Collaborators included Gaston de Caillavet, Léon Blum, and

Henri Barbusse; the editorial committee consisted of Proust, Halévy, and Dreyfus—in short it was published by a group of future philosophers, writers, and even a scholarly future prime minister. The journal was open to foreign writing, with essays on writers as diverse as Henrik Ibsen, Alfred, Lord Tennyson, Dante Gabriel Rossetti, Percy Shelley, and Friedrich Nietzsche. (Halévy later wrote the first book published in French on Nietzsche, one that remained in print into the twenty-first century.) The journal's Platonic title also pointed out that *Le Banquet* was opposed to poetic hermeticism and symbolism. In fine its editors wanted to propagate a classicism that respected tradition—in Proust's case this desire culminated in his essay "Against Obscurity" published a few years later. As was the case with his writings for *Le Mensuel,* Proust wrote on a great variety of things, with much erudition, although that is not always apparent in the few of these texts from *Le Banquet* that he recycled in 1896 in his first published book, *Les plaisirs et les jours* (usually translated *Pleasures and Days*). *Le Banquet* lasted but a year and ceased publication after eight issues.

Writing for a literary journal did not keep Proust from preparing for his political science and law exams, though literary activity, as well as a lack of motivation, may have obliged him to retake some law exams in the fall of 1892. His lack of success at his first go-round of law exams did not seem to perturb him—he did pass them later in the fall—for he hardly had his heart set on becoming a lawyer. The fact that, right before his examinations, he published five "studies" in *Le Banquet* in May shows clearly where his interests lay. Nor did he neglect his social life, either at the seaside resort Trouville in the summer or during the next academic year in salons, where, among other encounters, he met the Baron Robert de Montesquiou at the home of the artist Madeleine Lemaire, a woman with whom Proust had a lifelong friendship.

Proust's friendship with Montesquiou was also of long duration, though their relationship was not always easy. Montesquiou was an aristocrat, a poet, and a notorious homosexual dandy who enjoyed fame at the time as an exemplary fashionable decadent, such as befitted a poet who had been an acquaintance of Paul Verlaine and Stéphane Mallarmé. Proust's relation with him, with its ups and downs, came to an end only with Montesquiou's death in 1921, a year before Proust died. Proust learned to keep a calculated distance vis-à-vis this eccentric and demanding personage, but there is little doubt not only that Montesquiou was a friend, but also that the baron, related to aristocrats throughout Europe, provided much fodder for Proust's imagination as the years passed. He also initiated Proust in an appreciation of various artists ranging from Gustave Moreau and James McNeill Whistler to El Greco and Antoine Watteau—while granting an aperçu of the kinkier sides of the gay scene in Paris that would be central to Proust's vision of Sodom and Gomorrah.

In addition to the world of the plastic arts, Proust's social contacts brought him into contact with the world of music, which, in Paris at the time, was extremely rich. Music often trumped Proust's other activities. For example indicative of Proust's priorities in this regard is the fact that in lieu of preparing for his law exams, immediately before he was to take them, he went to hear Richard Wagner's opera *Die Walküre,* the second opera in *Der Ring des Nibelungen,* of which Proust was a partisan all his life. Music was also linked to his more amorous inclinations, especially when in 1894 he met Reynaldo Hahn, a young musician and composer of mixed Latin American Catholic and German Jewish background, who had studied in Paris with Jules Massenet. Their relationship was passionate for a time, perhaps a long time, and their affectionate friendship lasted off and on until the end of Proust's life. (This is reflected in Proust's letters to Hahn in which he writes something like the baby talk lovers often use.) Music and passion are of course interrelated themes throughout Proust's work.

Le Banquet ended in 1893, and *La Revue blanche* then became the journal to which Proust and his friends began to send their writings. While spending the summer vacation of this year in the Swiss mountain resort of Saint Moritz, Proust worked out his ideas about a book in which he would collect some of his short texts—some he had already published, some yet to appear—in an anthology of his prose work. In ironic homage to Hesiod's *Works and Days,* Proust titled his book *Pleasures and Days.* There is something Voltairean, or indeed Ovidian, in the title's playful suggestion that pleasures have replaced the work of those earlier, unfortunate times that did not enjoy the beneficent, luxurious culture of contemporary France, a culture in which pleasure is held in the highest esteem, and the title says much about Proust's attitude toward society at the time. Apparently the summer pleasures offered that year by a resort frequented by high society did not prevent him from doing some academic work, for he later passed his final law exams and was awarded what would be, for him, a useless law diploma in October 1893.

Proust returned to Paris to enroll in the faculty of letters that autumn with a specialization in philosophy. He was undoubtedly deeply interested in philosophy, though one suspects that his desire to garner another diploma was also part of a strategy designed to keep his father from putting more pressure on him to make a career choice. His main energy went into writing texts that he wanted to appear in *La Revue blanche.* He was also reading widely. For example he, like many other writers at the time, was caught up in enthusiasm for Leo Tolstoy, whose work became a synonym for a commitment to selfless ethical sacrifice. (Tolstoy's influence is notable in Proust's early work, especially the first narrative in *Pleasures and Days*.) Of course nineteenth-century Russian literature was becoming well known in the fin de siècle Western Europe, and a young would-be writer such as Proust felt obliged to know both Tolstoy and Fyodor Dostoyevsky as the century came to an end.

Proust's perseverance at writing, not to mention an active social life, meant that he put off his philosophy exams scheduled for that year. In the fall of 1894 he began actively to look for a publisher for *Pleasures and Days*. His literary activity was briefly put on hold, however, when he took and passed his philosophy exams in the spring of 1895. In commenting on the importance that his education in philosophy had for Proust, biographer Tadié stresses that professors such as Darlu transmitted to him a version of Kantian idealism. It combined the doctrine that the human mind creates knowledge through its innate categories with a belief in "the thing in itself" or a reality hidden behind phenomenal appearances. However this university teaching was based on rigorous analysis that rejected the vaporous imprecision that symbolists and sometimes Bergson favored. Tadié adds, "From Darlu, Marcel also inherited the spiritualism without God that was the faith of the Sorbonne at this time. . . . In brief, ethics, not religious faith, is the heart of philosophical convictions."[6] The philosophical idealism taught by the university did not reject religion out of hand, however, and hence was not committed to the often radical anticlericalism that characterized Third Republic political life.

It is noteworthy that in the university examinations of this year, Proust wrote essays on themes that would prove germane to his novelistic work. The epistemologist Émile Boutroux asked him to write on Descartes's opinions about certain ancient writers; and Paul Janet (the uncle of the famous psychologist) gave him the topic "Unity and the Diversity of the Self." The unity of self, or lack thereof, is of course central to *In Search of Lost Time*. And Descartes's use of subjectivity as the starting point for certainty was never far from Proust's mind. It is important to note that the professor who proposed Descartes as a subject for Proust's exams, Boutroux, was undoubtedly another major influence on his development. For his critique of materialism and determinism, Boutroux was highly influential in French intellectual circles throughout the latter part of the nineteenth century and well into the twentieth. (He also lectured in the United States.) In a work such as *De la contingence des lois de la nature* (*The Contingency of the Law of Nature*) of 1874, Boutroux paved the way for more radical notions about the conventionality of scientific laws as formulated by his friend Henri Poincaré, probably the best-known French scientist at the century's end. These names both suggest the context in which Proust began to think about science and knowledge. For example he read Boutroux's edition of Gottfried Wilhelm Leibniz's *Monadologie,* to which Poincaré appended an essay on mechanics showing that Leibniz, not Descartes, had a protomodern version of the mechanics of motion. And later, significantly, Boutroux showed that Poincaré was the most important thinker about relativity in the nineteenth century.[7]

But all was not science and philosophy in Proust's life in these years: in May 1895 he took what he undoubtedly deemed the disagreeable step of taking an examination to get a nonpaying position as librarian at the Mazarine Library in Paris. He was third on the list of those examined, which meant he would receive a position, though not in a library where he wanted to be placed, if indeed he wanted to be placed at all. Subsequently he took a series of leaves of absence from the position. It seems he never worked one day at any library and was finally dismissed after some four years of nonappearance. Unlike the Argentine writer Jorge Luis Borges, who found the universe in a library, and more like the Austrian novelist Robert Musil, who could not stand working in such a dreary place, Proust never took up work among dusty tomes. The young Proust preferred to find the universe in those social relations he cultivated with the enthusiasm of both a socialite and, increasingly, an anthropologist studying a tribe that quickly adopted him as one of its own. He had no intention of allowing a working career to interfere with his literary life, which in these years also meant his social life. The pretense of working at a nonremunerative job at a library probably allowed him to maintain the fiction that he had some intention of taking up ordinary work. It is dubious that his father was fooled.[8]

To conclude this discussion of Proust's education, I note that much of what he was introduced to at the university countered what he could have learned from his father. Moreover through his father Proust had immediate contact with luminaries of the political and scientific world, and it was through the elder Proust that he first met scientists as well as politicians, pillars of the Third Republic, in whom positivism joined with anticlerical liberalism. Proust's university education in philosophy made him acquainted with reservations about the dominant scientific epistemology that his father espoused. This kind of intellectual opposition undoubtedly sharpened his sense of the way knowledge is first of all a question of questioning. And if the young Proust contested, but finally by and large accepted, the positivist scientific worldview his father held, it is also true that he was willing to consider sympathetically the idealist and even spiritualist alternatives that were offered elsewhere in the Third Republic. This meant that if he never seriously questioned a secular understanding of reality, he also never stopped pondering religious questions, and here the importance of thinkers such as Darlu and Boutroux is central. Moreover even before being educated, so to speak, by John Ruskin and Émile Mâle, Proust was already attentive to and receptive of the great wealth of religious art and myth that permeates French culture. His home milieu offered a grounding in secular positivism, but the world of Christian art around him led him to conceive of art as a way of dealing with the meaning of death and resurrection. In fact at one point the young Proust actively rejected what he saw as materialism and even extravagantly praised Christianity.[9]

However if the medical materialism of his father's milieu had not convinced him of the primacy of matter over spirit, his own suffering body probably would eventually have done so. Proust's severe asthma attacks, which often left him bedridden, also made a medical expert of him. Much of what was considered eccentric in his later behavior can be explained by his attempts to deal with his asthma. For example the famous cork-lined room Proust later maintained in his residence at boulevard Haussmann for sleep and work could be considered a reasonable attempt to keep allergens out his respiratory tract. It seemed eccentric in 1900 when little was known about allergies or asthma, and doctors often treated these afflictions as nervous dispositions. In light of contemporary medical knowledge, it does not appear that Proust was a greater than normal hypochondriac or more psychologically unstable than the average overprivileged child with a domineering father and a succoring mother. Indeed his physical vulnerability might explain why he was extremely attached to his mother. Many biographers and critics have seen in his never leaving home a sign of a pathological attachment to her. I think this evaluation is wrongly accented. Proust did love his mother with an attachment that gives Freudians facile fodder with which to explain his homosexuality. But Freudian speculation aside, it should be noted that in the nineteenth century, young bourgeois men, homosexual or not, often stayed with their families until they married and set up their own household. This was the case of Proust's younger brother, Robert, who left home in 1903 when he married the woman his father apparently selected for him, nearly ten years after he had done his medical internship. Proust of course did not get married.

Dependent upon his parents for an allowance, Proust stayed at home. After his parents died, he was then obliged to make his own way. This was not difficult with the considerable inheritance his family left him, which he managed in a rather slipshod way as he dedicated himself single-mindedly to being a writer. Proust's single-mindedness after, and even during, his years of education suggests the most fruitful perspective for considering how he shaped his life from his adolescence on. Early in life he knew that he wanted to be a writer. Consequently he did whatever it took to realize that goal. This, too, meant staying at home and not dispersing his limited energy on pursuing tasks extraneous to literature, such as giving in to his father's desire that he choose a career. Not unlike the other great modernists—Franz Kafka, Musil, James Joyce, Thomas Mann—Proust came to conceive of writing as something like a sacerdotal commitment, a secular task to be sure but one with a nearly religious dimension. Thus with his education finished, and with a first book of texts ready for publication, in 1895 Proust began to work on a long novel. He never finished it, though he left behind manuscripts that sketch out various projected episodes in it. Biographers speculate that he worked on the novel until at least 1897 and returned to it at least once later, eventually to abandon it probably in 1899. These manuscripts were first published in 1952 under the title *Jean Santeuil*. Some critics saw this as a major "new" work by Proust, while others thought that it simply made available manuscripts that show how long it took for him to find his literary voice. At the very least these manuscripts show that he never stopped writing, and at most they show him experimenting with possibilities for self-expression.

Publishing essays and short fiction in reviews, Proust was acquiring a minor literary reputation in fashionable circles and the reputation of a snob among others. His quest for literary fame was furthered when Anatole France wrote a preface for *Pleasures and Days,* the selection of stories and poems of 1896 that had taken Proust almost two years to get published. In the same year, his maternal grandfather and his uncle died six weeks apart, though grief at these events does not seem to have caused Proust to slacken in his literary work. In fact in this year he published one of his most important critical essays, "Contre l'obscurité" ("Against Obscurity") in *La Revue blanche*. In it he assumes the role of the brash young writer who, in the name of the clarity exemplified by classical and the best modern literature, harshly criticizes the work of the elder generation of symbolist poets. Some critics think that the critique sufficiently irritated the senior statesman of symbolism, Stéphane Mallarmé, that he answered Proust in his "Le mystère dans les lettres" ("Mystery in Letters"), also first published in *La Revue blanche*. Mallarmé hardly heeded Proust's strictures about clarity, for his text is sufficiently obscure that one is hard pressed to say if Proust is the target or not. However, Proust's implicit criticism notwithstanding, Mallarmé remained a favored reference for him throughout his life, ranking with Baudelaire and Balzac.

Perhaps the most notable event caused by the publication of *Pleasures and Days* was that, in the following year, Proust challenged a critic, Jean Lorrain, to a duel for having made a slighting reference to his friend Lucien Daudet. With Anatole France in mind, the critic scoffed at Proust's use of influence to get a preface for his book, and then suggested that he would use Lucien to get his famous father, Alphonse Daudet, to preface some future book. In his informative biography, William Carter puts the event in a perspective that points up the complexity of Proust's relationships. Carter says the critic in question was also a homosexual, apparently a bruiser who liked tough boys, and that, in trashing *Pleasures and Days,* he actually wanted to hurt the pretty and effeminate Lucien.[10] The duel came about as Proust was working on his first long piece of fiction. Some critics think that the whole episode with the duel may have so depressed him that he let the novel drop. Before the duel Proust had in fact told the publisher Calmann-Levy that he would have a manuscript ready for them. After the duel no manuscript was forthcoming. It is also true that no manuscript was even close to being ready.

Nobody was hurt in the duel, and one may wonder what its point was. Tadié says the duel was followed by another in 1901 and two in 1920.[11] Duels were part of upper-class masculine culture in nineteenth-century Europe, and it would seem that Proust availed himself of duels in order to establish a macho identity. However since it appears he was only minimally adept at the use of arms, and since nobody was ever hurt, one may speculate that some, if not all, of these duels were either invented or staged. In any case they were used to create an image. One can look ahead a number of years to see this image in writing. In 1920 after the publication of the third volume of *In Search of Lost Time, The Guermantes Way I,* an offended Proust wrote a reply to the critic Paul Souday, who by this time was something of a friend. Nonetheless he rebuked Souday for his use of the term *feminine* to describe Proust's writing in a review appearing in *Le Temps.* Proust wrote to the critic, "At the moment when I am going to publish *Sodom and Gomorrah* and in which I am going to speak of Sodom, nobody will be courageous enough to take my defense, in advance you are opening the way (without bad intentions, I am sure) for all the evil dispositions, by calling me 'feminine.' From feminine to effeminate there is just one step. Those who have served as my seconds in duels will tell whether I have the softness of the effeminate."[12] Proust's apparent readiness to fight duels is also borne out by the testimony of Lucien Daudet's more famous brother, Léon, who recalled his request that Daudet find out if an elderly diplomat, an expert in weapons, meant to insult Proust by calling him a Dreyfusard. Apparently this incident ended with the diplomat's disclaimer of an intent to offend and a recognition of Proust's valor.[13] In short Proust did not want to see pinned on him or his work the label "effeminate"— undoubtedly because it could be taken as a euphemism for homosexual or pederast, labels that the would-be masculine Proust rejected.

In the 1890s plastic arts and architecture began to occupy Proust's imagination as he matured into a writer who was looking for his literary voice. It was at this moment when he was floundering with the project to write a long novel that he discovered the work of the English art critic and historian John Ruskin. His discovery of Ruskin probably occurred when he read an essay about the critic in 1897 in *La Revue des deux mondes*, notably, Robert de la Sizeranne's "Ruskin et la religion de la beauté." One hesitates to say that "the religion of beauty" was about to seize Proust's imagination, but certainly his interest in art grew rapidly at this time, for he a made a trip to Holland the next year explicitly to view art. He saw a Rembrandt exposition in Amsterdam that made a tremendous impression upon him. This was surely a seminal moment for Proust: viewing Rembrandt's work, he realized that the power of art is found in the individual's vision and not in the subject matter. Rembrandt's example showed that the individual artist privileges certain subjects, as one sees in his limited repertory of themes; but what is essential is the artist's power to convey a personal vision through them.

Ruskin's theories about art were a kind of catalyst for Proust's development, especially the Englishman's views about the superiority of medieval architecture, which were seconded in their effect by the work of the French art historian Mâle. In works such as *L'art religieux du 13e siècle* (translated as *The Gothic Image: Religious Art in France in the Thirteenth Century*), Mâle virtually invented modern iconography studies. Proust relied on both Ruskin and Mâle not only as guides in his travels to view architecture but also as guides for seeing the meaning of the past found existing in the present. All in all Proust's encounter with Ruskin, Dutch art, and especially medieval architecture was a turning point in his imaginative and intellectual life. He was sufficiently taken by Ruskin that, despite his rudimentary knowledge of English, he began to translate two of Ruskin's works into French and to write essays inspired by Ruskin, which he published and then used as prefatory material to the translations he published of *The Bible of Amiens* and *Sesame and Lilies*.

The question of Proust's ability to translate English has been a vexed one for some biographers and critics, though it hardly seems it should be. Proust was an autodidact in English, undoubtedly received much help with the translations from his mother, and got further help from Hahn's English cousin Marie Nordlinger. Thus he became an expert on Ruskin. It is obvious from Proust's references to other works by the critic that he was eventually able to read Ruskin in English as well as in French translations. Therefore what is of interest in Proust's encounter with Ruskin is not that he managed to learn some English but that Ruskin helped him to discover the past dimension of the artwork as an essential part of the ontology of the past so to speak. As the translation of Ruskin's works progressed slowly, Proust published essays on him in 1900, the year of the Englishman's death. For example in the *Mercure de France* appeared pieces such as "Pèleringages ruskiniens en France" ("Ruskinian Pilgrimages in France") and "Ruskin à Notre-Dame d'Amiens" ("Ruskin at Notre-Dame d'Amiens"). With Ruskin's *The Stones of Venice* in hand, Proust also made two trips to Italy and Venice that year, the second one alone while his parents moved into their new apartment in the rue de Courcelles, in a wealthy area not far from the fashionable and beautiful parc Monceau.

In these final years of the nineteenth century, a series of vituperative debates broke out over the Dreyfus affair. The controversy unfolded after a military officer of Jewish extraction, Alfred Dreyfus, was falsely accused of selling secrets to the Germans. Dreyfus was summarily tried and found guilty, stripped of rank, and deported for life to Devil's Island. Calls for a new trial enflamed ideological passions that threatened to bring down the Third Republic. The discrediting and the eventual overthrow of the secular Republic was indeed the goal of many in the anti-Dreyfus movement, a heterogeneous group that wanted to use Dreyfus's putative guilt as a way of furthering various reactionary agendas ranging from reestablishing the power of the church to overthrowing the Republic and restoring the monarchy. For his part Proust was among those who knew early on that Dreyfus had been framed and was active on his behalf in demanding a new trial and acquittal. He also supported Émile Zola after the famous novelist was condemned to a year in prison for his 1898 open letter in support of Dreyfus, "J'accuse" ("I Accuse"). That Proust should have been a supporter of Dreyfus is not surprising. Nearly all the liberal elements of French society were pro-Dreyfus, both in the name of elementary justice and in defense of republican values, and one hardly needed to be Jewish to oppose the use of anti-Semitism to discredit republican institutions.

What is puzzling in Proust's case, however, is that after the affair was more or less settled in 1906, he maintained friendly relations with some of the most notorious anti-Semites of the time: not only anti-Semitic aristocrats who were notably bereft of sympathy for republican values, but also intellectuals such as Charles Maurras and Léon Daudet, writers later associated with the monarchist—and protofascist—movement known as Action Française. Personal friendship was involved with the Daudet family, which explains Proust's relationship with Daudet; and he appears genuinely to have admired the notorious Maurras. It seems that Proust was a liberal who was able to tolerate and even get along with those who were opposed to his values. Moreover as some remarkable pages in *Jean Santeuil* show, he was able to attribute honorable motivation to anti-Dreyfusards such as those army officers for whom the "honor" of the army or the homeland trumped questions of truth and justice—perhaps an example of how anti-Semitism was more or less socially acceptable in the upper classes before the Holocaust.

Stays at the Normandy seashore aside, Proust's travels during these years were largely undertaken with a view of directly acquainting him with works of art. In 1902 he went again to Holland to visit museums. He saw in the Hague what was to be one of the most important paintings for him and his meditation on the nature of art, Vermeer's *View of Delft*. The next year Proust traveled in southern France, making a trip to Vézeley to visit one of the most important Romanesque churches in France. Proust was gaining firsthand acquaintance with the major monuments of Christian culture as well as the works of the great painters.

Proust published his translation of Ruskin's *Bible of Amiens* in 1904. The following year he published an essay, "Sur la lecture" ("On Reading"), that he then used to preface the translation of Ruskin's *Sesame and Lilies* he published in book form in 1906. "On Reading" shows that Proust was developing a theory of poetic reminiscence tied to reading. Indeed parts of the essay offer a description of a child's memory of reading resembling the descriptions found in the "Combray" section of *Swann's Way*. There is probably no point in trying to locate exactly the chronological moment when Proust first conceived of *In Search of Lost Time*, but if we ignore this stricture, it does no harm to say that "On Reading" is not a bad candidate for that precursor moment in which he shaped a theory of art and finally found the voice that led to the novel after several more years of looking for a structure.

But before Proust found that voice, he went through changes in his family life. In 1903 his brother married, and in November of the same year his father died. Proust lived alone with his mother after 1903, though not for long: she died in 1905. Her death left him in a state of deep mourning that stopped him from writing for at least a year. In fact he entered a sanatorium at the end of 1905 in hope of finding some relief from asthma and, most likely, from grief. Six weeks in the sanatorium did little for the former, however, and only time could release him from the latter. He returned home, and then he moved into a new apartment, one more suitable to his needs. He explained the choice of domicile when he wrote to Mme Straus to say that, because he could not resolve himself to live in a house that "Maman" had not known, he decided to sublet his deceased uncle's apartment in the building on boulevard Haussmann. He had frequently gone there with his mother to dine, and indeed there they had seen his uncle die. Proust apparently considered this apartment to be a mere "transition," since he made light of his bad decision to live in a place where, he recognized, he was subject to awful dust from the street, bothersome trees under his window (a source of allergens, perhaps), and constant noise coming from the boulevards.[14] In the meantime while work was going on in the building, he temporarily moved in August 1906 into a hotel in Versailles, from which he apparently did not move until the end of the year—almost literally, since he said in his correspondence that he did not visit anything in Versailles during this entire time.[15] His immobility seems to have been due to bad health.

In the spring of 1907, he went to his first social engagement since his mother's death, and in the fall he began giving dinners for friends at the Ritz: with his inheritance Proust was wealthy enough to entertain wherever he liked. He also began to write again. His first published text after his mother's death was "Sentiments filiaux d'un parricide" ("Filial Sentiments of a Parricide"), a macabre article about a matricide that appeared in *Le Figaro* in February 1907. Writing about a distant acquaintance who murdered his mother and then committed suicide, Proust offered an almost lyrical apology for the universality of parricide. Central to Greek tragedy, to the stories of Ajax and Oedipus, he writes, the tragic vision of parricide shows that the assassin is not a criminal brute but rather a noble example of humanity who is the victim of an ineluctable destiny—today called pathology. The article concludes with lines that sound almost as if Proust is confessing guilt he felt for his mother's death and acknowledging symbolic participation in it. What else to make of his claim that we always kill those who truly love us and that every loving mother could indict her son with this fact? With this strange journalistic performance, Proust apparently cleared his conscience and was then able to write again.

Proust began touring again in France, visiting Gothic churches, driven about by a handsome chauffeur, Alfred Agostinelli, with whom he had a tortured and apparently one-sided relationship. One result of this travel was his essay, published in *Le Figaro* in the fall of 1907, titled "Impressions de route en voiture" ("Impressions of the Road while Driving," republished with changes in 1919 in *Pastiches et mélanges* as "Journées en voiture"). This essay shows, among other things, Proust's enthusiasm for the new era of the automobile; it is noteworthy that he refers in it to his real chauffeur, Agostinelli, but otherwise describes a fictional scenario of traveling to see fictional parents. More important, it also contains Proust's first description of movement that deals with the relativity of motion: as his automobile races toward Caen, constantly changing its position on the road leading toward the city, three church steeples seem themselves to move, almost as if in an orchestrated dance. The framework is constantly shifting as the automobile shows that all spatial reference is relative to a perspective. Christian monuments and modern epistemology are conjoined here.

In 1908 Proust published in *Le Figaro* a series of pastiches of famous French writers. Some critics have seen these stylistic exercises as key to the development of his literary voice. There is perhaps some truth to this; Proust himself thought so, since he said that writing pastiches liberated him from the bewitching influence of the writers whose style he imitated. Each text uses a famous writer's style to narrate the same scandalous event: the "Lemoine affair." This well-publicized affair began in 1907 when a swindler, Henri Lemoine, claiming to be able to manufacture diamonds got a large sum of money from Sir Julius Wernher, the head of the De Beers diamond mines. It ended in 1909 with Lemoine being sentenced to prison. Proust's pastiches narrate reactions to the events, already well commented upon by the press, as they might have been narrated in a novel by Balzac or Flaubert; a critical article by Émile Faguet or Sainte-Beuve; in the Goncourt brothers' journal; in a historical piece by Jules Michelet; and others. All turning on the same event, the pastiches are a self-conscious demonstration that theme and style are quite different things. One narrative event can give rise to a hundred styles—as Raymond Queneau later showed in his *Exercices de style*—which suggests that style, or what Proust came to call the artist's vision, is what we really read when we read a major writer.

Proust's renditions of the same event in different styles might be compared to a musician's practicing major and minor scales before undertaking a major performance. The major performance to which the pastiches are a prelude was indeed beginning: Proust had begun to debate with himself about the shape his work would take. At first it seems he could not decide whether the work should be a critical debate, set in a fictionalized context, or if he should create a fiction containing a critical and theoretical component. With the latter he would explain the nature of the work of art in which the theory is embedded. Without being too clear about its shape, Proust expected to publish this work in the near future, telling the director of the *Mercure de France* in August 1909 that he was getting ready to offer him a novel called "Contre Sainte-Beuve. Souvenirs d'une matinée" ("Against Sainte-Beuve: Memories of a Matinée").[16] Possibly by this time Proust had in mind the basic outline for the opening and closing of the structure of a novel, intending that when one finishes reading it one sees that the entire novel demonstrates the principles of art expressed at its conclusion. This circularity means, as Proust put it, that the novel's conclusion is a kind of preface coming at the end to explain what precedes it. The *Mercure de France* declined the project. After a stay at the sea at Cabourg, Proust returned to Paris, resolved to write more before seeking a publisher, and he did indeed write more. By the end of 1909, Reynaldo Hahn and Georges de Lauris could read, with enthusiasm, the beginnings of the work that Proust would publish in 1913 as *Swann's Way*.

The manuscripts published by Bernard de Fallois in 1954 under the title *Contre Sainte-Beuve* show that at one point Proust had begun to write a critical study or, more precisely, a series of studies that are framed as a fictional conversation with his mother. Undoubtedly it was in rejecting the idea of writing a critical or theoretic work that he then conceived of a novel that illustrates his aesthetic ideas. After a period of trial and error, he found the overall plan for *In Search of Lost Time*, where it would begin and, equally as important for its organization, where it would end. Thanks to his having the novel's overall architecture in mind, Proust was able to persevere writing the work, through bad health and a world war, until the end of his life.

Though some critics have expressed doubts about the preceding scenario, Proust was adamant, after the novel had grown by several volumes and the titles had changed, that he had conceived the novel as a totality. For example he wrote to Paul Souday in December 1919 to assure him, well before most of the novel had been published or even finished, that the conclusion was already in place, since the last chapter of the last volume had been written right after the first chapter of the first volume. Everything between the two volumes, Proust went on to say, had been written afterward.[17]

Once he had conceived the novel's structure, Proust worked on the beginning and the end of the novel more or less at the same time. In 1911 he was apparently correcting the beginning section of *Swann's Way*, called "Combray," while having a secretary type some seven hundred pages of the concluding section, *Le Temp retrouvé* or *Time Regained*. Thus by 1911 it appears that at least the first section of the novel was finished. The following year Proust was still looking for titles and for a way of dividing up the novel as he then conceived it—"Lost Time" and "Time Refound" were the first working titles for two projected volumes, these to be grouped together under a general title "Les Intermittances du Coeur," or roughly "The Irregularity of the Heart." In the fall of 1912, the optimistic Proust told Mme Straus that he had thought he would publish his novel three years earlier, but that now he planned for it to have three volumes instead of two and that the putative publisher, Fasquelle, would certainly want to publish each with a separate title at intervals of six months.[18] Then, in one of the most famous episodes in the history of French letters, three publishers rejected *Swann's Way*—most notably the editorial committee (including André Gide) at Gallimard's *Nouvelle Revue française* apparently did not want to consider work by that "snob" Marcel Proust. Thus rebuffed, Proust finally decided to finance the publication himself. *Swann's Way* appeared at his expense, published by the editor Bernard Grasset in 1913, with the promise of two more volumes to come.

By late 1914, however, France had been invaded, and there existed the possibility that Paris might be occupied by the German army. Proust had begun to publish his novel at the same time the European powers were undertaking mutual slaughter. Publication was put on hold. Not surprisingly the novel's development was significantly influenced by the war. The war not only offered new experiences for Proust, but it also meant that little was published during the years of privation that the war effort imposed from 1914 through 1918. The war thus allowed him to add to the novel with no sense of urgency about publication. And the novel expanded, acquiring many more pages than it would have had he met his own earlier goals. Of course he might not have met those goals, for he was notorious for adding greatly to his supposedly finished typescripts and proofs. With regard to the war itself, Proust experienced it from the viewpoint of a civilian behind the lines, since his health was far too bad for the army to consider him. Of course he knew many people, friends and acquaintances, who did their duty, and he saw many of them die in the war, including several men who were close to him.

There is one event in Proust's personal life right before the war's beginning that many biographers and critics think had a singular influence on the development of *In Search of Lost Time* during the war. That event was the death of his chauffeur, Agostinelli. Having become Proust's secretary in 1913, Agostinelli had moved in with him. This living arrangement did not last long, for Agostinelli left him at the end of the year. Accompanied by the woman he called his wife, he went to southern France, intending to learn aviation—apparently under the name of Marcel Swann. Proust tried to lure him back to Paris, going so far as to offer to buy him an automobile and an airplane. It appears that he was ready to do nearly anything he could to get Agostinelli to return. Agostinelli died in an airplane accident in southern France in the spring of 1914, however, and Proust was left alone to find his own consolation. The death inflicted upon him an experience of loss and sorrow that, given the vacation from publishing the war imposed, may have played a role in the way the novel developed far beyond the limits foreseen in 1913. Biographically minded critics have required little imagination to attribute to this loss the creation of the female character Albertine, the beloved who escapes in death from the narrator's grasp. Agostinelli, in their opinion, became Albertine.

It is true that lengthy development involving Albertine and the volumes now called *The Captive* and *The Fugitive* were not part of Proust's conception of the novel in 1909. However it is also obvious that, because of the free time created by the war, Proust would have in all likelihood published a longer version of the novel than he originally planned with or without Agostinelli. The structure of the novel allows for indefinite expansion from within through the intercalation of events that take place before the foreseen conclusion. Would Proust have expanded the novel in a different way had Agostinelli not died? Counterfactuals are of little interest here, but it should be noted that Albertine existed as an important character before Agostinelli died. There is little doubt that the chauffeur's death was a tremendous blow to the ailing Proust. Suffice it to say that Albertine became a major figure during the war years after Agostinelli's airplane crash.

By suggesting that Albertine is a surrogate for Agostinelli, critics say in effect that Proust's biography offers keys to an interpretation of the novel. That is not my intention here, however, and I note that Proust reacted strongly against this mode of interpretation. For example after the publication of *Swann's Way,* he wrote to tell Mme Straus, who liked the novel very much, that the characters she admired in the first volume will reappear in the yet-to-be published second and third volumes of the novel. To this information he added the commentary that the fictional character Swann, whom she identified with their mutual acquaintance Charles Haas, was not Haas, because, as Proust stressed, there are no *clefs* (keys) or portraits anywhere in the novel.[19] This indeed seems to be largely the case.

In 1916 Proust decided not to continue publishing with Grasset (who could not publish at the time in any case) and accepted an offer from the now contrite Gallimard to continue the publication of the novel with the editions of the *Nouvelle Revue française* (NRF), which was managing to publish a few things. Moreover the editor of the *NRF,* the perceptive Jacques Rivière, had read Proust with care and was among the first to understand the importance of what he was undertaking. Rivière was ready to push forward with the project. Nonetheless Proust published nothing during the war. He received the galleys for *The Guermantes Way* after signing the contract with Gallimard and the *NRF*, but he kept adding to them until 1920. During the war years, Proust clearly regained some energy, for not only did he write at a rapid rate, but he also began socializing again. Elegant places such as the hotels Le Crillon and Le Ritz were his chosen venues as he worked on *Sodom and Gomorrah*, conceived as including *The Captive* and *The Fugitive* (the latter first published as *Albertine disparue* in order to avoid confusion with a recent book of the same title by Indian writer Rabindranath Tagore, whose Nobel Prize of 1913 had made him a conspicuous presence).

One of the most telling, and bizarre, episodes in Proust's life took place during the war in 1917, when he helped a rather louche character named Albert Le Cuziat to acquire a hotel in the rue de l'Arcade. Le Cuziat set up a bathhouse for homosexuals in which sadomasochism was apparently a usual part of the trade. Proust seems to have used his personal visits to document the practices there, which provided firsthand documentation for the novel's final sections. It is almost as if he financed this hotel in order to create the setting for the scenes in which the Baron de Charlus goes to indulge in his favored forms of masochism. If, as claimed, Proust never wrote about anything that he had not personally seen, by 1917 this now included the war and the whip.[20]

After the war started, Proust did not leave Paris. If he no longer traveled to see the Gothic churches that, as he later wrote, were under senseless attack, the fragility of churches was on his mind, as was the religion embodied by them. And while his friends were dying on the front, he had a strong sense that he was precariously close to death himself. For these reasons and undoubtedly for others, religion was never far from his thoughts, as one sees in a poignant letter he wrote during the war to Lionel Hauser to explain his views on religion:

> I do not have faith . . . on the other hand religious concerns
> are never absent for a single day from my life . . . but the more
> religious one is, the less one dares to make an affirmative statement,
> going beyond what one can reasonably believe; now, I don't deny
> anything, I believe that everything is possible, and objections [to
> religion] based on the existence of evil are absurd, since Suffering
> alone seems to me to have made and continues to make of human
> beings something more than brutes. But, to go from that viewpoint
> to affirm any certitude, even to affirm Hope, that requires going
> a great way, and I have not yet gone that distance. Will I ever go
> so far?[21]

It seems Proust remained a rationalist until the end of his life. He was sensitive to suffering, which was omnipresent during the war, and perhaps his most affirmative statement here is to find some meaning in that distress.

Proust retained his sense of humor even in these trying times. For example in a letter from the war years he described, with much irony, a spiritualist séance at which he was present. (Readers of Thomas Mann may recall that even a great ironist such as Mann could take seriously the hocus-pocus of the séances popular in the first decades of the century, as is clear from a key chapter in his *Magic Mountain*.) The medium (*magnétiseur*) presiding over the séance was inept, as Proust notes, for when the hypnotized Princess Murat woke out of her trance before she was supposed to, the charlatan had to hurry to make the appropriate wake-up gestures so as to pretend to stay ahead of her. Proust notes in deadpan that the princess, just like everybody else, had a good many things to request from the séance, but nonetheless, in spite of her absolute faith in the hypnotist, all she could think up to ask for was that she not grind her teeth in the future. A modest request, notes Proust, and then goes on to say, "Il est du reste incroyable à quel point le contact avec le mystère rend insignifiant"—which one might loosely translate as "It is unbelievable how trivial people become when they start dealing with mystery."[22]

The war's conclusion did not offer Proust a trouble-free time for writing, since shortly after the Armistice, in January 1919, he learned that his aunt had sold to a bank the building in which he was living. Proust had to find new lodgings. He first moved into temporary quarters in the apartment of his friend the actress Gabrielle Réjane. His quarters were uncomfortable in several respects. He was obliged to listen, for example, through thin walls to his neighbors' making love every day with a "frenesy" that made Proust jealous, or so he wrote. As Tadié has noted, Proust's description of this noisy lovemaking in a letter to an acquaintance seems to have been directly transposed into a description, given by the novel's narrator listening through a wall, of the noise made by the Baron de Charlus and Jupien in *Sodom I*.[23] If, as some critics maintain, a male character from Proust's life could become a female in his plastic imagination, I note that he could also transpose heterosexual moaning into homosexual cries of pleasure. To be sure Proust wrote about not only what he saw and tasted but also what he heard and smelled.

Proust moved again in the same year to what was to be his last apartment, situated in the rue Hamelin. He continued to work on the novel, oversaw the publication of its second volume, *A l'ombre des jeunes filles en fleurs* (literally "In the Shadow of Young Girls in Flower"; first translated by C. K. Scott Moncrieff as *Within a Budding Grove*). He also put together an anthology of earlier writings, *Pastiches et mélanges,* in which he republished some of his pastiches and some earlier essays. And motivated by the debate about Flaubert's significance, he also took out time from completing the novel to update some old notes, probably from the time of his work on Sainte-Beuve, in order to write in 1920 a brilliant critical essay on Flaubert. The essay made clear that, for Proust, Flaubert was as important as any writer in the literary canon.

Moreover, in the spirit of civic duty he wrote a letter protesting a literary manifesto, published in *Le Figaro,* concocted by right-wing writers like Paul Bourget, Jacques Bainville, Edmond Jaloux, Maurras—in which Proust rejected their idea that literature should be in the service of nationalism. On the contrary he maintained that art and science have no end but themselves, and therefore they cannot be in the service of political causes. In this letter Proust made clear that he stood squarely in opposition to the nationalist movements that in France, as in Germany, were continuing during the 1920s in what the noted German historian Ernst Nolte has called Europe's ongoing civil war. The year ended with Proust's first literary triumph when, supported by Léon Daudet, he was awarded the Prix Goncourt, then as now, the most prestigious of the dozens of literary prizes awarded each year in France.

In 1920 Proust, ill now and feeling that death might be imminent, published *The Guermantes Way I* as well as the critical essay "On Flaubert's Style" in the *NRF.* And in the following year he published *The Guermantes Way II, Sodom and Gomorrah I,* and his last literary essay, the splendid "On Baudelaire." During the spring of 1921 he went to the museum Le Jeu de Paume to see an exposition of Dutch painting. He again had the chance to see Vermeer's *View of Delft.* This visit is undoubtedly the inspiration for the scene of the death of the writer Bergotte in *The Prisoner*—such was the effect of viewing again what Proust called the most beautiful painting in the world.

Proust's international reputation was not slow to develop. *Swann's Way* was reviewed in the *Times Literary Supplement* the year it was published; and, after the war, the writer Aldous Huxley reviewed *Within a Budding Grove* in the same year Proust received the Prix Goncourt. All of Bloomsbury would soon be reading Proust. But the most important reception abroad came in the remarkable critical study, published in *Der Neue Merkur,* by the great German literary scholar Ernst Robert Curtius. In a study that remains one of the best, Curtius showed a remarkable grasp of the novel's totalizing project to grasp human psychology. Curtius's review meant that in the 1920s German readers had a better guide to Proust than anybody else, and this before Proust had even finished the novel. Of course given the way Proust was working on the novel virtually until the moment of his death, one may legitimately ask whether the novel was ever really completed. Those who think it was finished point to the fact that Proust's housekeeper Céleste Albaret said that he told her in the spring of 1922 that the novel was completed. However those who think it really was not point out that through the month of October Proust's last remaining energy went into making substantial corrections of the manuscripts and typescripts of *The Prisoner* and *The Fugitive*. Proust's health deteriorated rapidly at this time, and he died of what was probably pneumonia on November 18, 1922.

There is something moving about the thought of this sick man dedicating his life to completing his novel, motivated by his unrelenting faith that what he was writing was a great work of literature. His dedication paid off, even if Proust did not see the final volumes into print. In fact five years passed before the novel was finally published in the error-filled edition that the *NRF* produced. *The Prisoner* was published in 1923; *The Fugitive* next in 1925 under the title *Albertine disparue*; and *Time Regained* in 1927. Proust's brother oversaw these posthumous publications, as well as the editing of a volume of occasional pieces and essays, *Chroniques*, in 1927. Robert Proust also began to gather and publish an edition of Proust's voluminous correspondence that today, after years of dedicated work by the scholar Philip Kolb, contains more than twenty volumes.

After Proust's death scholars began to go through the many manuscripts he left behind, both of works abandoned and of manuscripts representing various stages in the development of *In Search of Lost Time*. In 1952 Bernard de Fallois brought out, under the title *Jean Santeuil*, the manuscripts of Proust's first attempt at writing a novel; and in 1954 he published, under the title of *Contre Sainte-Beuve*, manuscripts containing critical studies and narrative sketches that appear to be early stages of the author's finding his literary voice. Critical editions of these manuscripts and other texts have been published in the canonical series of the Editions de la Pléiade, which is perhaps a bit misleading, since these publications might suggest that the books are works that Proust finished in some sense, which is not the case. In fact the Pléiade version of *Contre Sainte-Beuve* is quite different from Fallois's version (and not necessarily better). More recent scholarly work has aimed at making available manuscripts presenting various stages of *In Search of Lost Time* for those who want to follow in detail Proust's development as a writer. This work will continue to occupy "genetic" critics for the next few decades. Interested readers can get a sense of this work by looking at the current Pléiade edition of *A la recherche du temps perdu*, now published in four volumes, which includes many early manuscript versions of episodes. This edition has not been received with unanimous approval, but paperback editions based on it make a more or less definitive version of the novel inexpensively available. After all the "definitive" edition of the novel is only a normative ideal that can never be fully realized. But what we now have is very close, and Proust would undoubtedly be happy to see that an edition resembling what he wanted to write is now available.

Chapter 2

What Proust Published before
In Search of Lost Time

Proust published only one book of his own before *In Search of Lost Time*. This was the 1896 collection of his writings *Les plaisirs et les jours* (*Pleasures and Days*). Despite this paucity of publication, he wrote much, some of it appearing in journals and reviews, leaving much for scholars to find after his death. Readers beginning Proust with *Pleasures and Days* are probably not encouraged to continue reading the author's oeuvre. This self-selected anthology offers a series of sketches, stories, and prose poems that may be alien to the contemporary reader. With a little readjustment of perspective, however, the book can be very rewarding. As in many of the occasional pieces Proust published, in it he shows himself to be a beginning writer steeped in the French classical tradition but attempting to renew that tradition by linking it to modernist currents that surrounded him in the Paris of the late nineteenth century. The book also sets out a configuration of themes and motifs that serves as a prelude to Proust's later writing, and for this initiation alone, this early book, as well as many of his early writings now available in anthologies and online, are worth reading.

A useful perspective on this early writing by Proust is provided by the eighteenth-century *moraliste* the Marquis de Vauvenargues (1715–1747). In his commentary on the works of the seventeenth-century classical writers Jean de La Bruyère and François de La Rochefoucauld, Vauvenargues noted in *Réflexions* that "La Bruyère was a great painter, but was perhaps not a great philosopher," whereas "the Duke de La Rochefoucauld was a philosopher and not a painter." For the classical mind, these two favorites of young Proust appear to offer mutually exclusive literary practices. La Bruyère's often comic portraits of individuals drawn literally from court society seem to offer a different type of representation from that found in the ironic maxims that La Rochefoucauld enunciated in nearly lawlike generalizations. Proust was certainly concerned with this kind of opposition, for he was uncertain as to whether he was a La Bruyère whose task was to create portraits of social types or a La Rochefoucauld ferreting out the truth via abstract generalizations about the usually bleak human condition. If La Bruyère is a dominant influence in *Pleasures and Days*, it is also evident that neither pole of the opposition sketched out by Vauvenargues encompasses all that Proust expected of literature. He intuitively knew that abstract generalizations may not adequately account for individual truth, but he also knew that the portrayal of contingent in-dividuals might not reveal those seemingly universal laws that preside over human fate. Moreover the recent renewal of poetic language by Baudelaire and Mallarmé opened up vistas to Proust that were simply not within the ken of the classical imagination.

In meditating upon this opposition of the general and the particular, Proust also seems to have been uncertain as to whether he wanted to be a critic and perhaps a theorist of aesthetics or a creative writer. His waffling reflected his uncertainties about the epistemological dichotomies underpin-ning literary representation. Educated in the philosophical tradition that draws upon the thought of Plato, Benedict de Spinoza, Immanuel Kant, and Arthur Schopenhauer, he could not help wondering if the abstract es-sence is to be preferred to the particular truth that might be embodied in the individual. The perennial Platonist in Proust wondered if all individual cases submit to a universal law, whereas the contemporary scientist in him wondered if the statistical average takes epistemological priority over the random case. This all came down to Proust's asking, after the examples of fictions by Balzac and Flaubert, if the aim of literary representation should be the recurrent pattern or the exceptional case. Proust perhaps did not systematically set out to solve the problems these questions bring up, though by the time he was writing the unpublished texts now available as *Against Sainte-Beuve,* it is not an exaggeration to say that his thinking about literature was dominated by them.

Writing as a critic, theorist, or philosopher of art, Proust reacted against some of the dominant views about literature current around 1890. As he was drawn to essentially classical views about the truth function of art, it is not surprising that, in looking for his way as a writer, he worked through models provided by seventeenth-century French literature, such as Racine, La Bruyère, La Rochefoucauld, Madame de Sévigné, and Henri de Saint-Simon. However he was equally attentive to the great nineteenth-century novelists who, a generation or two before him, had redefined the novel. Influenced by Balzac, Flaubert, Tolstoy, Dostoyevsky, Charles Dickens, and George Eliot, he finally came to consider the novel as the vehicle with which he could incorporate all aspects of literature into one work. But the development of this project required much time. Beginning with the kinds of texts published in *Pleasures and Days,* writing as critic or poet, theorist or novelist, Proust worked slowly toward the conception of a *Gesamtkunstwerk,* a total work of art—to take a term from the aesthetics of Richard Wagner, whose operas influenced Proust deeply. Wanting to overcome the polarities of the particular and the general, of the philosopher and the novelist, he finally conceived of *In Search of Lost Time* as a work that could reconcile mind and emotion in the presentation of the world understood through individual interiority and the objective existence of law-bound phenomena. From the perspective of Proust's final achievement, one sees that the early publications testify to how, from his lycée writings onward, he moved back and forth between maxim and portrait, theory and illustration.

One of Proust's earliest narrative texts illustrates well the dual thrust of his writing, characterizing the creator of portraits and the explorer of psychological laws. In 1893 he published in *La Revue blanche* a short story, "Avant la nuit" ("Before the Night"). He did not republish it later, not only, perhaps, because he dealt openly in it with homosexuality—for he does not avoid the theme later—but also because he deals with homosexuality in apologetic terms. In this short narrative, a young man, Leslie, listens to a widow whom he loves, Françoise, confess to him why she has not given herself to him. Her confession is also a revelation as to why she has suffered a gunshot wound. It is self-inflicted, and she is dying from it. But before she dies, she reveals that she is a lesbian. In self-defense she recalls to Leslie a justification of homosexuality that he had made to her with regard to a lesbian relationship. Leslie had told Françoise that one could not condemn what Socrates himself had approved and that, moreover, there is no difference between men and women. He reasoned, in addition, that once sex is no longer used for procreation, then there is no hierarchy among the "sterile forms of love." It is thus no more immoral for a woman to enjoy pleasure with a woman than with a man, since "the cause of this type of love is found in a nervous alteration that is so exclusively a question of the nerves that it cannot bear with it a moral content."[1] In other words homosexual desire is a natural phenomenon explainable by neurophysiology.

In this publication the twenty-two-year-old Proust set out at once a vague but nonetheless scientific explanation of homosexuality that rejects ethical condemnation as unreasonable. This rejection results from his application of a general law to a specific description. Sexual desire can no more be called wrong, Proust argues, than can the vision of people who see violet where others see red. Therefore the woman's sexuality is a neutral fact morally—even if social opprobrium has apparently driven her to kill herself. If sex illustrates natural law, it is nonetheless subject to individual variation, and accordingly the function of a literary text is to offer an individual portrait. Here it is the portrait of a woman who asks for compassion from the man who has loved her so that he can understand that, unable to bear the world's judgment, she has shot herself. Finally the text ends with metaphor showing that, for Proust, poetry was an essential part of this unique portrait. He portrays the star-crossed lovers in a world transformed metaphorically into a musical moment: at the end their world becomes a chord with a sad and broad harmony.

This narrative's concluding musical metaphor shows that Proust was seeking rhetorical means to individualize the space of literary representation. The metaphor equating the characters' world with music also suggests that young Proust considered music to be a mode of representation that literature could use, that somehow literature and music overlap as art forms. This is not an idea suggested by Racine or Molière. Rather Baudelaire and Paul Verlaine were sources for this view and practice. Resonant with the physical music of sounds, Baudelaire's poetry illustrates that tropes can perhaps imitate nonliterary modes of representation. Comparable for its play with sonority, Verlaine's verse frankly proclaims music to be the goal of poetry: "De la musique avant toute chose" (roughly "Music before all else"). Proust's borrowing from Baudelaire is apparent, for example, in an early prose poem, "Choses normandes" (published in *Le Mensuel* in December 1891 and translated as "Norman Things" in *The Complete Short Stories*), in which he describes a Norman landscape. In "Norman Things" the narrator says he envies those who can spend autumn on the coast near Trouville. They can hear the music of the sea, which he "listens to as it seems to accord rhythmically its sobs to the human soul."[2] For Proust, much as for Baudelaire, the sea is the music of the created world, and hence like music, having nothing material and describing nothing, it is the "monotonous chant of ambitious, but defective willpower [*volonté*]."[3] Ironically modifying Schopenhauer's description of music as the expression of the will, the text projects onto nature Proust's pessimistic feelings about his own capacity for willpower. He equates the tragic music of nature with his own sense of inadequacy. The sea can also be confounded with the sky in a visual metaphor. (This is an image that returns in *In Search of Lost Time* to characterize a Monet-like painting by Elstir, the novel's exemplary painter.) The metaphor unites sea and heaven so that the narrator sees a ship that seems to sail in the sky. All in all the world is a great store of metaphors, wherein the sea is what Baudelaire called the mirror of the soul (in "L'homme et la mer" ["Man and the Sea"] of *Les fleurs du mal*). The sea reproduces the music that is the language of the soul and is hence somehow truer than words to the soul's need.

Proust could also take comic distance from the pathos of this symbolist poetizing of the world. Four years later in "Un dimanche au conservatoire" (originally published in *Le Gaulois* and translated in Sturrock's version of *Against Sainte-Beuve* as "A Sunday at the Conservatoire"), he describes the effect of Ludwig van Beethoven's Fifth Symphony by which audience and music are united when the music commands the listeners' souls. Once in the midst of his rapture, however, Proust hears a female voice nearby loudly asking, "Do you want any candy?" This banality causes the narrator to reflect on the transitory power music has, since it is only for a fleeting moment that the listeners' hearts were "disobstructed" so that they could perceive truth and beauty resembling that found in Sophocles or Spinoza.[4] The transcendence attributed to art by idealist philosophy is a chancy matter at best—and the vicissitudes produced by the aleatory nature of things is not the least interesting of Proust's future themes, nor is the inevitable deflation of the ideal that accompanies chance happenings.

In addition to texts of pure narrative or pure theory, along with articles on fashion, music hall singers, and salons, the young Proust also wrote some poetry in regular verse. The most interesting of these poems offer portraits of artists and musicians. Their importance is underscored by the fact that he placed them near the center of *Pleasures and Days*. They are not included in all translations, however, undoubtedly because they are poetically rich and show a mastery of French versification that is translated only with difficulty. (The poems are available in translation on the Marcel Proust Ephemera website). These poems can serve as an introduction to Proust's first book, again to emphasize that he was combining the individual portrait with theoretical considerations of art. In each poem the poet directly addresses himself to an individual artist. Proust borrows this rhetorical stance from Baudelaire's poem "Les Phares," in which the poet addresses himself directly to "Lighthouses"—the artists, painters, and musicians who have been "witnesses unto eternity" of human tribulation. And as in Baudelaire, the poet's juxtaposition of an artist's name with a descriptive phrase transforms the opening vocative into a metaphor by apposition. For example in the first portrait of the series portraying musicians, Proust addresses himself to Frédéric Chopin: "Chopin, a sea of sighs, of tears, of sobs / That a flight of butterflies crosses without landing / Playing on sadness or dancing on the waves."[5] "Chopin" is at once the object of the poet's direct address and set in apposition to a sea of emotion: the composer thus becomes a sea of sighs. His name becomes a metaphor for a world of emotions that, as the poem unfolds, are set against each other, like the antithetical forces characterizing Chopin's musical compositions. Simultaneously the poet continues to address himself to the musician, telling him, "your grief is the accomplice of your joy." The address continues using antitheses depicting the sick artist who exalts and grows pale as the sun inundates his room: "Smile of regret and tears of Hope!" Chopin's portrait is created through opposing metaphors—Chopin is both smile and tears—setting forth contradictory feelings. And all of this undoubtedly reflects Proust's reading of Mallarmé's description in the poem "Les Fenêtres" ("The Windows") of human existence through the metaphor of a hospital room in which the patient feverishly desires the blue sky. Comparably Proust's Chopin lies sick in a room inundated with sunshine.

The play of oppositions characterizes most of the texts Proust published in *Pleasures and Days*. For example in another poem Proust addresses Christoph Willibald Gluck (1714–87), the German composer who drew upon classical literature to renovate opera in the eighteenth century. In his portrait of the musician, Proust refers to several of Gluck's operas. The poet says that the musician sculpts a world in which the hero Heracles enters the garden of the enchanting witch Armida—referring to Gluck's *Alceste* and *Armide* (as well as his *Iphigénie en Aulide* based on Racine's adaptation). Proust ends the poem with the assertion that through these works Gluck has overcome death, much like Alcestis, who offers to enter the realm of the dead in place of her husband, Admetus. As in Euripides's tragedy *Alcestis*, love overcomes death, so that Gluck himself stands metaphorically as the "august temple of courage, on the ruins / of the small temple of love." This trope seems to affirm that opera is allied with classical literature as an artistic monument enduring against time. This affirmation is perhaps a young writer's optimistic version of the eternal nature of art that one finds ironically portrayed in the writer Bergotte's death in *In Search of Lost Time*.

Proust makes a rather enigmatic portrait of the romantic composer Robert Schumann. He refers to a number of Schumann's *lieder* and compositions in order to portray the contradiction, I think, between the successful compositions and the composer's mental anguish, his near insanity, that nothing could assuage. Proust's antitheses find their culmination in the poetic portrait of Wolfgang Amadeus Mozart. This poem is set in a landscape in which an Italian woman strolls on the arm of a Bavarian prince. The prince gives himself over to love as the poem evokes Cherubin and Don Juan, characters from Mozart's operas *The Marriage of Figaro* and *Don Giovanni*. These operas are set in the gardens of Andalusia and Tuscany and become part of the scene of love. At the poem's conclusion, it turns out that the Italian woman with the German prince is the Queen of the Night, the triumphant queen of the opera *The Magic Flute,* who now uses her flute to create an earthly paradise uniting the freshness of sorbets, kisses, and heaven. In fine Proust's poem conjures up a world in which Mozart's operas uniting the supposedly opposite worlds of German and Italian culture, unfold in a garden of paradise. Access to this paradise of reconciliation is to be found in works of art.

The nostalgia for paradise is an important motif throughout Proust's work. It serves to contrast the fallen world of reality with the splendor of what has been lost. For example the first two portraits of artists in *Pleasures and Days* are sonnets paired like antithetical pendants contrasting a portrayal of bliss, found in the utopian world of the ideal, with the anguish characterizing the fallen world of spleen—to recall the Baudelairean term for *ennui* that Proust has in mind. Proust presents this contrast of spleen and ideal in two sonnets about paintings by seventeenth-century Dutch landscape painters now in the Louvre: the first sonnet depicts Albert Cuyp's *Le Départ pour la promenade à cheval* (*Departure for a Ride on Horseback*) and the second, Paulus Potter's *Deux chevaux de trait devant une chaumière* (*Two Workhorses in Front of a Thatched Hut*). The ideal is found in Cuyp's world, bathed in limpid sunlight, in which young male riders—well dressed, groomed, blond—are part of a colorful landscape whose harmony is troubled by nothing. The youths belong to the ideal world of an aristocratic elite that Proust had notable trouble finding in reality. By contrast the landscape Potter portrays is gray, dismal, and dominated by images bound up with the grind of daily toil: a peasant is seen returning home, bearing buckets of water on his shoulders, while a horse in front of the hut raises its head in a gesture to which Proust attributes inquisitiveness, disquiet, and anxiety. Potter's is the fallen world of daily reality, which stands in quiet but resolute contrast to the utopia inhabited by the aristocratic riders who deeply inhale moments of profundity redolent of bliss as Proust understands it.

The next portrait of a painter is that of Antoine Watteau, the eighteenth-century artist whose portrayals of eros suggest a transitory utopia in which the pleasures of love are uncertain at best. Proust underscored this viewpoint in an unpublished essay on Watteau (by contrast in the poem "Lighthouses," Baudelaire suggests that Watteau's work is a carnival illuminated by lights pouring out madness). The ephemeral nature of erotic bliss Proust sees in Watteau complements his portrait of Anthony Van Dyck, whom Proust also interprets as depicting the transitoriness of all beauty, quite specifically the beauty of aristocrats. In this somewhat longer poem, the poet explicitly refers to Van Dyck's painting of the Duke of Richmond, James Stuart; he may also have in mind Van Dyck's famous portrait of

King Charles I, as well as the portrait of the two young Palatine princes, German nephews of the king, all of which are on view in the Louvre. Meditating on the transitory nature of all that is superior, Proust says that, in "all these beautiful beings who are going soon to die," Van Dyck triumphs by contrasting their beauty with our knowledge of their death to come. Actually our precise knowledge of a death to come is limited to that of the king beheaded by Puritan republicans in Proust's beloved seventeenth century, for in fact the handsome young men portrayed in the paintings lived fairly long lives, however certain their death may have been. The point is that these aristocrats are utopian beings who present the "noble grace of things / which shine in their eyes, the velvet and the woods; / beautiful elevated language of conservation and of poses" (133). Aristocrats conscious of their precarious existence, they have souls "too elevated" to allow tears to come to their eyes. The young Duke of Richmond is an especially poignant figure, for at the poem's end he stands contemplating a piece of fruit he holds in his hand, and the poet cannot decide if this "detached fruit" is a sign of wisdom or madness and concludes: "I always come back to you: a sapphire, on your neck, / Sparkles with fire as soft as your tranquil gaze."

With this bejeweled image, Proust associates Van Dyck's beautiful nobles with a realm in which the dream of transcending the trivial might be realized. And with this association, Proust is, perhaps unconsciously, elegizing the demise of what he admires: the ideal that existed at least once in art. The social backdrop for *In Search of Lost Time* is already in place.

The themes found in these portraits of artists are touched upon in the dedication of *Pleasures and Days*. (The dedication is omitted in one translation of the collection, though it can be found in *The Complete Short Stories*.) Proust dedicated the book to a deceased friend, Willie Heath. Significantly in this dedication he makes reference to the Van Dyck paintings. Proust says his dead friend resembled one of the lords painted by the Dutch painter. In comparing Heath with the Duke of Richmond, he seems to imply that in his own life he momentarily had seen reality coincide with the ideal proposed by art. He goes on to say that he and his friend entertained "the dream, almost the plan of living more and more with each other, in a circle of select and magnanimous women and men, sufficiently distant from stupidity, vice, and evil so as to feel that we were secure against their vulgar arrows" (40). Their dream was to found a moral aristocracy. The friend's death ended this project, and Proust says that his own illness has forced him to reduce his activity. However his illness has also brought him into contact with the "au-delà de la mort" (realm beyond death). What Proust means by this is not clear, but it is certain that his friend's death and his own illness had brought him up against limits: these limits are strongly illuminated by the contrast between, on the one hand, a yearning for a utopian realm of aristocratic self-realization and, on the other hand, the tragic recognition that death limits every attempt at transcendence in life.

Proust's description of his pact with his friend sounds as if it were inspired by the Renaissance utopia Rabelais created with his project for Thélème Abbey. In this utopia beautiful people live in complete harmony with each other as they realize a perfect life of play, meditation, and aesthetic enjoyment. They keep themselves distant from the rabble, exemplified for Rabelais by nuns and monks, whereas Proust's ideal world delimits itself by excluding the vulgar and the stupid. The great difference between Rabelais and Proust is that the younger man's reverie includes the recognition that every utopia is subject to the fall brought on by human frailty, vice, and death. A comparable pessimism is demonstrated in nearly all the texts of *Pleasures and Days*. Whatever be the mode of writing Proust uses in them—narrative, poem, portrait, essay, pastiche—most of them portray the flaws of individuals and of society that destroy the possibility of an aristocratic mode of being. Hence a fair resumé of the book is that it is a series of portraits and prose poems grounded in a demonstration of recurrent moral and, indeed, ontological laws, presiding over deflation, deception, and the fall.

Proust organized the texts in *Pleasures and Days* as a series of polarized symmetries. Bernard Gicquel first proposed this idea some sixty years ago in an ingenious essay purporting that there is a geometry at work in the texts' arrangement, as shown by a diagrammed circle. This geometry is rather hard to apply.[6] Suffice it to say that Proust's arrangement of the texts appears generally to be a reflection of geometric oppositions. For example in the narration of two exemplary deaths, the book's opening and concluding tales entertain a symmetry borne of resemblance. Comparably other narrative texts in the first and second half of the collection show similar themes, with the poems about artists and painters occupying approximately the middle position. The notion of complementary symmetries is also useful to describe how, in the first half of *Pleasures and Days*, Proust pays homage to La Bruyère and Flaubert with an objective comedy of social life; and, drawing upon Baudelaire, Mallarmé, and Verlaine, in the second half he offers prose poems portraying the intricacies of subjectivity. The prose poems usually turn on the realization that the present moment is irrevocably a moment of decline and that only the past and the future can escape deception—perhaps because they do not really exist. The texts in the first half (as well as the final story) by and large explore comic and ironic narrative modes of writing about society and the individual, whereas the prose poems of the second half explore the inner world of reverie and meditation. Taken together in their symmetrical contrast, they suggest the path that Proust follows for the structure of *In Search of Lost Time,* a novel combining the social and the subjective in its epic exploration of the narrator's subjectivity set against the world of social comedy.

The narratives that open and close *Pleasures and Days* are framing tales in that each narrates the death of an exceptional individual or noble being. Critics have commented on Proust's indebtedness to Tolstoy for these stories, and nowhere is that debt more apparent than in the Russian novelist's portrayals of death. Proust was hardly alone in the interest he took in Tolstoy's view of death, for an anthology of Tolstoy's death scenes was published in France in 1886.[7] Tolstoy portrays death not simply as the cessation of animal faculties as a naturalist might; rather he uses realistic narration that, as in the case of the death of Ivan Illych or of Prince Andrei in *War and Peace,* does not exclude hope for a spiritual dimension. Moreover it can be argued that Tolstoy and, after him, Proust were reacting in their work to what was probably the most famous death scene in nineteenth-century fiction, the grotesque suicide of Flaubert's Madame Bovary, whose agony marks the beginning in fiction of a naturalistic view of death. Though not rejecting physiology as the ultimate explanation of death, Tolstoy rebutted Flaubert by exquisite descriptions of scenes of deaths that were ultimately not bereft of hope. Young Proust drew upon Tolstoy's narration as a way of preserving the aristocratic nature of his heroes even in death. In the framing tales of *Pleasures and Days,* his heroes, like Tolstoy's, come to their end without conventional religious belief but also without undergoing the convulsions that shake Madame Bovary in her last moments. (Later, in the case of the grandmother's death in *In Search of Lost Time,* Flaubert may seem to have the last word when the narrator sees the ravages that time has worked upon his grandmother—though perhaps Tolstoy returns when the narrator sees that, in her final serenity, she finds a youthful appearance.)

"La mort de Baldassare Silvande Vicomte de Sylvanie" ("The Death of Baldassare Silvande, Viscount of Sylvania") is the first story of *Pleasures and Days.* It deals with the aesthetics of death. The viscount lives in an imaginary land, a somewhat allegorical realm, perhaps a flawed utopia, since in it one can die of a real malady, which has a real historical existence. He suffers from a syndrome discovered earlier in the nineteenth century: the general paralysis that only later was recognized as the tertiary stage of syphilis. The story follows the stages of the disease's crippling development, marked by one brief period of remission. The narrator has a clinician's eye, such that one wonders whether he could know that general paralysis is the last stage of syphilis (since the treponema involved in the disease's etiology was not identified until the early twentieth century). However, the frequency with which free-living individuals died in the nineteenth century from general paralysis surely led some in the medical milieu of Proust's father to suspect the venereal cause for the malady that causes the progressive dysfunction of the viscount's nervous system. Proust's Baldassare, musician as well as aristocrat, has had a life of free love. Significantly his great regret in dying is that he will have no more control over a lover who refuses to skip a society ball in order to spend time thinking of him as he dies. She only promises to think of him each day afterward, which in effect assures him a rather minimal afterlife. This is more, however, than some of Proust's later characters are willing to do in *In Search of Lost Time,* for neither a Guermantes nor a Verdurin lets a relative or friend's death interfere with their pleasure. Early in Proust's work, the dying find out that the living prefer to satisfy their vanity before all else.

Proust presents an alter ego to the viscount in the presence of his nephew, Alexis, aged thirteen at the tale's outset. The boy observes in bewilderment that his dying uncle, like all those around him, continues to pursue trivial distractions even when about to die—such as a seventy-year-old duchess who dyes her hair and pays for newspaper articles that will flatter her for her appearance, her salon, and her mind. Like a young Blaise Pascal, Alexis resolves to avoid trivial distractions, the need for which Pascal saw as the ultimate sign of humanity's fall from grace. Alexis envisages fleeing society and retiring, like the ancient prophets, into a desert with some of his friends. And so he informs his parents. This project, Proust suggests with perhaps his own failed utopia in mind, will come to nothing once Alexis has drunk more fully from the milk of life. But it is noteworthy that Alexis, like Proust and the narrator of *In Search of Lost Time,* set the emptiness of society in opposition to the fullness of solitude.

During his moment of remission from general paralysis, the viscount entertains the illusion that he may not die. In this moment he experiences nostalgia for death and for the exile to that strange country that he was beginning to know. General paralysis does not relent, however, and the sick aristocratic musician is soon delirious. He comes briefly to consciousness and finds himself prepared for exile: through a window he watches a ship depart and imagines the passengers, much as in Baudelaire's "Le Voyage," leaving on a voyage with their thirst for the unknown. Proust is clearly in debt to Tolstoy, however, for the portrayal of the musician's serenity with respect to death, even though the narration takes on a specifically Proustian cast when, at the moment of dying, the musician recalls time past. The past floods his mind, bringing with it scenes from his childhood, centered upon his mother and his sister, memories all tinged with regret, for the aristocrat has not fulfilled the promise he held out to his family: he has not been the great musician they and his nanny expected, nor has he married as his mother wanted. In significant contrast to his regret, as he dies he sees the departing ship and a young cabin boy standing on its deck, perhaps as a hopeful sign that life may yet be ongoing. The voyage continues for the young.

Proust ends this first story of *Pleasures and Days* with this ambiguous suggestion of resurrection or renewal, contrasting with the way the viscount's past seems to be resurrected through memory precisely to point up its unfulfilled promise. The scene sets out a fundamental Proustian configuration: the past recalled in the present is overlaid with a patina of regret about the way the present has not fulfilled the promise of the past. This regret is part of living in time, a fall from innocence that is Proust's version of original sin, visited upon all those who live. The viscount dies knowing that one can never realize the plenitude promised by the past, which, recalled in the present, perversely continues to reverberate. The ship leaves the viscount behind, after all.

The concluding tale of *Pleasures and Days* has the title "La Fin de la Jalousie" ("The End of Jealousy"). It stands in symmetrical opposition to the first story by setting love in opposition to death. It deals with love, which in Proust means that it deals with jealousy. It seems that from a young age he accepted as axiomatic that jealousy is a precondition for love to exist. Without jealousy there is no desire for a possession that can never be realized, and vice versa, if one prefers, for love and jealousy exist in a circular condition of one causing the other. In "The End of Jealousy," Proust's presentation of love sets out the coordinates for the "laws" of love illustrated at length in *In Search of Lost Time* and, before that, in *Jean Santeuil*.

At the story's beginning, the main character, Honoré, is conscious that he loves Françoise, an aristocratic widow, in part because he knows that his love will come to end. He knows that he is subject to the psychological law of inconstancy and that it would be as difficult to violate that law as it would be to disobey the law of gravity or that of death ("laws" also paired up in Tolstoy). A nominally religious aristocrat, Honoré prays to God to suspend this law but with little hope, for the passage of time inevitably brings about the end of any form of plenitude. Yet his love, perhaps nearly pathological, continues to exist when, and because, it is threatened. This occurs after an acquaintance, ignorant of Honoré's liaison with the widow, tells him that he has heard that Françoise is of loose morals. As in the case of Swann, who loves a loose woman, the *cocotte* Odette, the torments of jealousy descend upon Honoré. Not unlike jealous husbands in Boccaccio's tales or William Shakespeare's version thereof in *Cymbeline*, Honoré dreams of proving his lover's fidelity. He imagines hiding in her boudoir and viewing her when she faces the lovers he would send to test her. With jealousy in his soul, he now prays to God to grant him release from his love for Françoise.

The narration makes a leap forward in time to relate that Honoré's beloved Françoise, née princess of Galaise-Orlande, has had a prestigious salon for the past two years, though during the three years before that time her social life had been greatly reduced after Honoré's death. The flash-forward in time then necessitates a flashback to fill in the narrative: the couple's affair had come to an end after Honoré was run over by a horse and both of his legs were broken. Up until that point it seems he had been living his love as an experience in unhappiness, even though Françoise loved him unceasingly and society had accepted their liaison.

Through the accident Proust pays homage to Tolstoy's belief that the brotherhood of love is the only possible basis for the creation of a just or good society. The homage unfolds in the following manner. Proust portrays love's taking the shape of forgiveness, but only after Honoré's crippled body begins to disintegrate and unceasing jealousy torments him. He imagines the pleasure other men can give Françoise. This morbid self-torture is accompanied by his recall of Proust's equivalent of the primal scene: Honoré could not abide it as a child when his mother dressed to go out to dinner and he had to relinquish her to others and go to sleep. This memory of bedtime trauma suggests, much like what the narrator undergoes in "Combray," that the lover's desire for possession finds its roots in the boy's impossible desire to possess his mother. However Honoré differs significantly from later Proustian characters. He is religious and feels the presence of a God who judges his attitude. He realizes that his broken body has made him jealous of the pleasures that healthy bodies are capable of experiencing. With this recognition he gradually accepts that Françoise can receive pleasure from other men, so that, nearing death, he embraces all around him in a unifying love. Jealousy, as the title promises, comes to an end, and Honoré finds his realm in the sky and the earth. If the story ends as an homage to Tolstoy's idealism, it is one that uses Proust's favored motifs of jealousy and time past to suggest that Tolstoy's unorthodox Christian vision might even work in Parisian society. Proust's portrayal of this forgiving love is unusual in its lack of skepticism.

The two framing narratives offer individual portraits that also illustrate "laws" of love and death. For his narration of these portraits, Proust drew upon Baudelaire and Tolstoy. In the other texts in *Pleasures and Days* he used a great variety of literary, philosophical, and scientific ideas, trying them out in various narrative modes in a search for the proper mix of La

Bruyère and La Rochefoucauld, so to speak. For example the story "Violante ou La Mondanité" ("Violante or High Society") is a secular allegory, drawing directly upon the medieval Christian mystic Thomas à Kempis in depicting the polarity between, on the one hand, the ideal of personal development and, on the other, the acceptance of hypocrisy demanded by existence in society. Proust prefaces each of the story's four chapters with an epigraph from Kempis's *Imitation of Christ*. Proust was greatly attracted to this work, also divided into four parts, which offers homilies about what one must do to live a truly Christian life. Each epigraph serves ironically to underscore that if Thomas aims at the salvation of the reader's soul through union with God, by contrast Proust's tale of Violante's life in high society depicts the destruction of her as a moral being. She experiences in effect moral death when she accepts being comfortably integrated into the kind of society that Thomas pointedly says to avoid.

Born in the bucolic paradise of Styrie, Violante receives an education from her beneficent tutor, Augustin. After disappointments in love, she leaves the earthly garden to go into the real world, the court of Austria (though no Hapsburgs are encountered). Her life is then essentially a process of becoming vain and shallow while losing her capacities to understand art and nature. Her decline is such that when "goodness no longer pleased her except as a form of elegance," she can only dream or read "in order to admire herself in voluptuousness and coquetry as though she were looking at a mirror" (78). The departure from the garden is a process that cannot be reversed, though Proust saves his explanation for the girl's fall for the end. Violante never went back to the garden because she was overcome by a force that "can defeat disgust, scorn, and even boredom: it was habit." Habit is another overriding Proustian theme; indeed it is another law. Samuel Beckett wrote, in paraphrasing Proverbs 26:11, that in Proust's work the force of habit is the ballast that chains a dog to its vomit.[8] In Violante's case the ballast drags her along after her leaving paradise. Habits must be extirpated if one is to find salvation, though doubts about that possibility are certainly allowed. Proust's pessimism in "Violante or High Society" overlaps Christian belief, not only in the portrayal of the Fall but also in the story's view of human weakness: for him, now and later, vanity is habit, and habit is a universal law limiting freedom in the fallen world of time present. Few characters in Proust have the strength of character to overcome habit, though it might be argued that this is what the narrator does at the end of *In Search of Lost Time*. It appears that he may free himself from the ballast.

The indictment of society continues in "Un Dîner en ville" ("A Dinner in High Society"), though in a more satirical mode. Proust prefaces the story with an epigraph from the Roman satirist Horace. The lines from Horace link Proust's portrayal of a festive meal to a tradition of social satire beginning with the Romans, though his satire aims at late nineteenth-century decadence as well as the eternal, all-embracing vanity found everywhere at any time. His satire also has an ironic, self-reflective dimension, for in obvious self-commentary the description of the dinner party includes a humanist who, speaking with a "wearying elegance," also quotes from Horace in order to "poeticize in his own eyes, and to excuse in the eyes of others, his gluttony and drunkenness" (155). In this way Proust satirizes his own socialite desires, as represented by a "banquet" that hardly corresponds to the festive banquet in which Socrates held forth with his admirers. In fact after becoming inebriated, the Honoré of "A Dinner in High Society" goes wandering in the streets so tipsy that he thinks wine has disclosed to him a realm of exaltation beyond reality. However his Baudelairean artificial paradise, created by intoxication, lasts but a moment, and normal ennui reasserts itself in his subsequent recognition that life is idiotic. Proust's self-directed irony in this social critique might seem nihilistic if it were not for the self-conscious homage to classical satire: literature has the capacity to redeem the worthless precisely because the latter can be the subject of literature. The strategy of *In Search of Lost Time* may appear at times to be not greatly different.

The writer most frequently mentioned in *In Search of Lost Time* is the seventeenth-century tragedian Racine. Racine is well known for having transposed Euripides's use of psychology in tragedy in order to give a personal expression to a Jansenist vision of the Fall. Like some Protestant doctrines, Jansenism was a seventeenth-century French Catholic version of that strain of Christianity holding that the damned are condemned by God from the beginning of time. Such pessimism comes inevitably to mind when Proust evokes Racinian tragedy to suggest a parallel for his ill-fated heroine, Madame de Breyves, as depicted in "Mélancolique Villégiature de Madame de Breyves" ("The Melancholy Summer of Madame de Breyves"). Proust begins the story in fact with an epigraph taken from Racine's tragedy *Phèdre,* namely, the lines in which Phèdre remembers that her sister Ariadne was abandoned by Theseus after she had saved his life. Such antique heroics are not part of modern life. The modern counterpart to Phèdre's blind, irrational passion is Madame de Breyves's overbearing love for a man she finds neither especially attractive nor intelligent but who, in his absence, obsessively dominates her thoughts. She seems condemned to love him despite her own common sense. The strength of her passion is also in direct proportion to the man's lack of availability, which is perhaps Proust's way of translating for modernity the passion born of interdiction that Phèdre feels for her son-in-law, Hippolyte—a near-incestuous desire that she tries unsuccessfully to deny. Madame de Breyves, too, is consumed by a love that is not to be boasted of—though mainly because it is ridiculous. Her passion is, as she knows, a product of her imagination. It is a kind of disease that she cultivates at the same time she curses herself for listening to music that encourages passion, such as a certain phrase from Wagner's *Die Meistersinger*. Proust was drawn at times to the idea that music *is* emotion, indeed at times an emotion resembling a drug one cannot do without. Love, injected into the soul by music, as it were, becomes an addiction that one can curse and bemoan but, as is the case with most habits, one can do little about. Thus this tale of the unhappy summer spent by Madame de Breyves illustrates a concrete case of passion from which one can infer several psychological generalizations; for example that music can be a form of diseased passion, not unlike the melancholia of classical psychiatry.

In contrast with Madame de Breyves's irrational passion, a purely psychic state, stands the physical demands of eroticism and concupiscence as portrayed in "La Confession d'une jeune fille" ("A Young Girl's Confession"). The girl's confession, redolent of a request for absolution, is narrated as she is dying. It appears she shot herself after being seen by her mother in an erotic act, which caused her mother to have a stroke. Two aspects of the confession are striking. First the girl begins it by recalling past scenes in which she knew anguish, caused especially by her mother's leaving her alone at bedtime and thus depriving her of the pleasure associated with the mother's kisses. This recurrent drama of bedtime anguish in Proust's work suggests that eroticism is a substitute for the passionate pleasure the child got from the mother's presence, more so in this story than later in "Combray." The girl's anguish is also bound up with sensual associations in which the world of childhood, again an earthly paradise, is recalled through "the matinal odor of lilies"—a sensual image that also seems symbolic of purity and resurrection, of matins and the first morning of the world (143). These associations evoking childhood are found in a layer of the girl's self where she is always fourteen years old. Second Proust shows that sexual pleasure is subject to the law of habit. The girl in "La Confession d'une jeune fille" has become addicted to erotic practices while a teenager. The girl knows she has in some sense become corrupt and that her corruption has become a habit. Losing contact with art and nature, like Violante, she has fallen into what she considers a state of depravity about which she can do little. She can no longer find the childhood plenitude once offered by art and nature. Thus her fall signifies a rupture with the original childhood paradise. The story much resembles "Before the Night," though

Proust has filled in the background for it so that we can construct a kind of etiology not unlike what we may construct for the narrator of "Combray."

Religion is indirectly present throughout *In Search of Lost Time*. In *Pleasures and Days* the narratives show that the young Proust considered religion important at the very least for the way it informs characters' evaluation of experience. In "A Young Girl's Confession," the girl had turned to religion for help with the "convalescence" of her soul and, she says, to recover the lost chastity that would allow her to satisfy the desires of the conventional fiancé she planned to marry. Habit is too strong, however. A few glasses of champagne and the presence of a former lover reawaken her desires, and she sneaks away with him for sadomasochistic pleasure: in the sexual act, even before her mother actually sees her convulsed in pleasure, the girl imagines that she is "making her mother's soul cry" (151). Like the sadomasochistic Mlle Vinteuil of *In Search of Lost Time,* the girl stages a ritual of mental profanation by imagining her mother watching her physical writhing, at once "voluptuous and guilty," that causes "pure angels" to be martyred, as she puts it. Her pleasure seemingly demands profanation of the body, which is completed by the imagined presence of the watching mother. In "A Young Girl's Confession," the sadism differs mainly from the rituals performed before Vinteuil's picture in that Proust caps this sexual scene with the mother's accidentally seeing what is happening, with catastrophic results.

The longest section of the first half of *Pleasures and Days* is called "Fragments from Italian Comedy." In these fourteen putative fragments, Proust borrows directly from seventeenth-century modes of narration—though not really from the Commedia dell'arte to which the title seems to make reference. The evocation of La Bruyère and La Rochefoucauld is fully justified by these texts, most of which read like a pastiche of one writer or the other. Proust's pastiches are undertaken as a humorous way of bringing them up to date, at least as up-to-date as the epigraph from Ralph Waldo Emerson that Proust appends to suggest that we can entertain our own vices if we see them symbolically represented. (Emerson was extremely popular in Europe at the end of the nineteenth century.) La Rochefoucauld gets perhaps less emphasis in these fragments, though the tenth fragment, a maxim reminiscent of that writer, sets the tone for Proust's moral criticism of society throughout these fragments: "An elegant society is one in which the opinion of each is made up of the opinion of everybody else. If people take a point of view opposing the opinion of everybody else? It is a literary society" (92). Such is life among the elegant and the creative.

Most of these "fragments" offer sketches of characters who embody a typical social vice. They may appear to be embodiments of moral abstractions or, indeed, portraits of Proust's friends. In any case they often resemble the pastiches of La Bruyère, who wittily portrays varied character types. Not surprisingly Proust has a predilection for types that he knows, mainly snobs, social climbers, and inept lovers. For example Fabrice finds one mistress too overtly intelligent, the next too dumb, and a third who ideally combines wit with tact has only one fault: she does not love him. Countess Myrto pursues her friend Parthénis as a means to increase her own status; she receives the lowly Cléanthis because it shows her magnanimity; and she hates the slightly inferior Doris because Doris, in wanting to be received, shows her the image of her own social climbing vis-à-vis Parthénis. This fragment sets out a geometrical diagram of the relationships created by snobbery.

Among other snobs perhaps the most interesting is the woman of the fourth fragment, whom the narrator directly addresses, saying, "Your soul is, as Tolstoy says, a dark forest," and noting that the trees in that forest are all genealogical trees (88). However Proust finds in his female snob a wealth of imagination that suggests a degree of self-portraiture: "The genealogical trees you cultivate with so much care and whose fruits you gather each year with so much joy have roots that delve into the most ancient French earth. Your dream makes the present have solidarity with the past. The soul of the crusades animates for you the most banal of contemporary faces and if you reread feverishly visiting cards you receive, isn't it because that at each name you feel awakening, quivering, and almost singing like a dead person rising from her blazoned tombstone, sumptuous ancient France?" (89).

The desire for a poeticized resurrection of the historical past is part of the boy's ideal in "Combray" and continues even later, even after he learns that his banal contemporaries have little to offer of past glory other than a name. The snobs of *Pleasures and Days* are thus superficial prototypes for the egomaniacs richly portrayed in *In Search of Lost Time*. While wasting their time and hence their lives, these early versions use their social station to practice vices mechanically, as indicated by the theatrical characters in "Comédie mondaine" ("Comedy of High Society"), the fourteenth fragment. Vice is always cleverly hidden. It suffices in society to "reprove one person's snobbism, another's libertinism, or the harshness of a third" so that, having paid tribute to benevolence, modesty, and charity, "one can go give oneself over without remorse, with a tranquil conscience that has just proved itself, to the elegant vices that one practices all at one time" (103). This fragment is a longer illustration of La Rochefoucauld's maxim 218: "L'hypocrisie est un hommage que le vice rend à la vertue" (Hypocrisy is an homage that vice pays to virtue). For Proust and La Rochefoucauld, the socialite is immoral though not unmindful of the pleasures of a good conscience.

One of the "fragments" differs notably from the others, largely because Mallarmé's shadow seems to hover over it. We shall see presently that young Proust criticized obscurity in literature, and in his critique he could only have Mallarmé in mind; but it can also be argued that Proust's own aesthetics echoes the symbolist's belief that the only thing that can redeem existence is to write "Le Livre"—the total book Mallarmé dreamed of creating, what he conceived as an Orphic explanation of life on earth. Proust's admiration and critique of Mallarmé point up an ambivalent attitude on his part concerning the function of literature. With regard to *Pleasures and Days,* the sixth fragment, "Cires perdues" ("Lost Wax") reads like an homage to Mallarmé, though, for this relation to be clear, it should be pointed out that "Lost Wax" refers to the lost process of casting bronze or, in other words, to art objects. In this fragment in two parts, Proust writes a text whose title itself is a metaphor equating the writing in it with an artwork. The first part of "Lost Wax" concerns a woman, Cydalise, a blond whose stature suggests an ancient princess. She resembles a living museum piece. With convoluted self-reflexivity the narrator says that he would like to have placed in her hands a vase recalling the historical past she seemingly embodies. In the text's second part, the narrator describes another woman, Hippolyta, whose unique beauty is of mythological provenance. She resembles a fabulous bird. These lost wax bronzes offer a contrast between icy beauty, born of past mythology but present today, and the dominant theme in *Pleasures and Days,* which is that of the ongoing delusions born of the present moment. Proust's preciosity is obvious, though perhaps less evident is that he seems here to be trying to outdo Mallarmé with these portraits of existence transformed into sumptuous bibelots—a word used by Mallarmé himself in his sonnets about the impossibility of the transformation of existence.

Proust's bent for pastiche underlies the section in *Pleasure and Days* called "Mondanité et mélomanie de Bouvard et Pécuchet" ("Social Ambitions and Musical Tastes of Bouvard and Pécuchet"). The two texts composing this section supposedly offer a continuation of Flaubert's satirical novel *Bouvard et Pécuchet* (1881), in which two benighted but likeable provincials attempt to master the total encyclopedia of all that can be known. In his sequel to Flaubert's novel, Proust has considerably reduced the range of Bouvard and Pécuchet's interests. Desirous of being received in high society, they find it necessary to have opinions on only two topics: literature and music. Thus they pass in review all the writers and musicians current on the Parisian scene. They offer a catalog of contemporary clichés about writers and musicians from the perspective of would-be socialites. (Flaubert's *Dictionary of Received Ideas* also stands in the background here.) Discussing literature in "Social Ambitions," they parrot received ideas, according to which Verlaine is too sensitive, Mallarmé's disciple Henri de Régnier (actually admired by Proust) is either a hoax or a madman, and Mallarmé himself has no talent, though he is a brilliant conversationalist. Having mastered these clichés, they must decide which milieu they will frequent. They weigh the pros and cons of being with aristocrats, financiers, protestants, artists, theatrical people, and, in conclusion, even with Jews, since Bouvard and Pécuchet endorse the cliché that "one must be liberal"—in spite of their antipathy for these social interlopers who once were all "lorgnette salesmen in Germany" (110). The anti-Semitic clichés of the day, though used with irony, take on added relief when set against the Dreyfus affair then at hand.

The second section, "Musical Tastes," follows the same pattern as the section on "social ambitions," with Proust here giving nods of recognition to his friends Reynaldo Hahn and Robert de Montesquiou. Bouvard and Pécuchet are willing to recognize the latter for his extravagant poems but not for music, for they foresee he may soon do a "Requiem for Kangaroos." Proust's friends are thus mentioned along with famous composers such as Wagner, Charles Gounod, Giuseppe Verdi, Beethoven, Johann Sebastian Bach, Camille Saint-Saëns, and Jules Massenet, as well as a few others whose names history has discarded. All in all, then, in his continuation of Flaubert's satire, Proust renders homage to Flaubert while writing the kind of expurgatory pastiche that he believed would free him from the anxiety of influence.

The comedy found in some of the texts in the first half of *Pleasures and Days* may have appeared to young Proust to offer a possible solution to the problem created by the impossible transcendence of which he dreamed. Comedy demands for its existence the recognition of imperfection, indeed the necessity of imperfection. Imperfection redeemed by comedy lies at the heart of several of these fragments that turn on the foibles of the character types that Proust finds throughout Parisian society, not to mention the clichéd world of Bouvard and Pécuchet. Comic, too, is the contrast of the world of La Bruyère, re-created in a sense by Proust's language, and the social world of the triumphant nineteenth-century bourgeoisie, in which aristocratic values were making their final stand against the combined onslaught of Enlightenment values and the power of money. The historical context is diffuse, however, for the narrative perspective in these texts usually suggests a kind of timeless allegory in which snobs are perpetually victims of their own delusions and lovers try to live in the illusion that their love is lasting. Only Bouvard and Pécuchet belong squarely to the clichéd world of the late nineteenth century.

In symmetrical contrast with the portraits and critique in the narratives of the first part of *Pleasures and Days* stand the prose poems in the second part of the book (with the exception of "The End of Jealousy," placed at the end of the book). This section is titled "Regrets et rêveries, couleur du temps" (translated as "Nostalgia—Daydreams under Changing Skies" as well as "Regrets, Reveries the Color of Time," since *temps* means both "time" and "weather"). In this section Proust sketches out scenes of regret and moments of reverie in thirty texts portraying subjective states that compose "the color of time." The notion of "the color of time" is puzzling. It implies that time itself can be perceived directly through the senses, though the texts also underscore the malleability of memory and its relation to sensual perception. In these explorations of subjectivity, Proust also depicts dreams and regrets as they take on specific shapes. In short, states of regret and reverie, of loss and imagination, can be portrayed in precise moments in psychic life, with color constituting a specific flavor, so to speak, bound up with time. Like several of the narrative texts, these regrets and reveries also illustrate the inevitable fall into time and hence the impossibility of plenitude—except when it is imagined for the past or the future, which do not exist. As in the case of Olivan, the literary man of the thirteenth fragment, "you can take pleasure [*jouir*] only through regret and expectation, which is to say, the past and the future" (100).

In general, then, these prose poems depict the loss and deception characterizing all human desire. With regard to Proust's gloom about desire and its realization, some critics have spoken of the influence of that dour pessimist Arthur Schopenhauer on Proust. Admittedly Proust's pessimism in these prose poems is so omnipresent that one can indifferently call it an outgrowth of a romantic Weltanschauung or attribute it to the Christian sense of misery, of which Pascal makes the emblematic description. What is determining is that an abstract law of existence decrees that it is universal fate to be condemned before one is born. And all question of influences aside, it is hardly to be doubted that some of these texts show that at times as a young man Proust did feel genuine despair. However, others are ironic and wittily flippant, which suggests that Proust, like Nietzsche confronting Schopenhauer, knew the value of ironic comedy and sardonic wit in overcoming the temptation of nihilism. Like Nietzsche, Proust was seconded in his resistance to decadent pessimism by his masters in irony, the moralist classics, such as La Bruyère, La Rochefoucauld, Nicolas Chamfort, and Vauvenargues.

Text 25 is a good starting point in reading Proust's poetical musings on pessimism, the essence of which is given by its title, "Critique de l'espérance à la lumière de l'amour" ("Critique of Hope in the Light of Love"). Directing readers to contemplate their belief in hope by the disasters they know in love, the text asserts that, as masters in despair such as Beckett or Emil Cioran would have appreciated, we fail to suspect that the very essence of the present moment is that it harbors within it an incurable imperfection. This is why we rationalize circumstances to account for our misery and do not relinquish our never-disabused confidence in some dream, like love, which will always eventually turn out to be a disappointed dream. Nonetheless we make constant appeal to a dreamed-of future, which also serves to condemn our present moment. The present is forever tawdry in comparison to what the future once promised, precisely for having become the present (205). The narrator recalls that he once foolishly declared to his beloved that he loved her. The declaration meant that his love was immediately ruined, for the present immediacy of love can never match what the dream of it in the future promises. At the narrative's end, the narrator hopes that he might make amends for his fault if he can lead the beloved to approach him and, keeping some distance, to look at the fires of love that illuminate the past. In the past he imagines the existence of some hope: "I believe that indulgent and powerful Memory wishes us well and is undertaking to do us much good, my dear" (206). The past is equal to the future as a kind of compensation for the relentless misery of the present. Such is the sardonic search for lost time here—which reads at times like an anticipatory parody of the Proustian narrator's later desire to re-create time past.

The attempted satisfaction of desire must lead to dissatisfaction, and hence, as the opening lines of the untitled sixth text put it, it is best to seek refuge from the dream life: "Desire makes flower, possession makes wither all things; it is better to dream one's life than to live it, although to live one's life is also to dream it, but at once less mysteriously and less sharply, in a heavy and dark dream, comparable to the dream dispersed in the feeble consciousness of a ruminating animal" (170–71). Is it an ironic moralist who pens these opening lines or a decadent metaphysician? The latter seems to be at work in the sixth text's illustration of the impossibility of realizing desire. The narrator tells of a boy who loves a girl from afar, admiring her from his window, but once he can actually speak to her, once he compares "with despair this blemished perfection with the absolute perfection on which he lived" up to that point, he then throws himself from the window (172). The boy survives his fall in a ruminant-like coma. Nonetheless the girl marries him, and their life is a slow process of degradation in which it is permitted to see the symbolist aesthete's vision of bourgeois life—or a parody thereof.

Recurrent in these prose poems is that love manifests itself as emotion in the present moment of consciousness, and as such it is inevitably condemned by the degradation inherent in the present itself. In the untitled seventh text, for example, an aging sea captain suffers a heart affliction that will soon kill him. Therefore he decides to experience again, in the present, the loves he has known in the past, using all the accumulated letters, albums, and "relics" that he has in his possession: "He began . . . to adore these shadows and lent them a dear existence in contrast to the absolute oblivion that was soon to come" (173). But these mirror images of his heart soon become tarnished, and to his surprise the captain finds that he cannot even hold on to his sorrow in the present: "And he felt sorrow about having less and less sorrow, and then even that disappeared" (174). The ongoing moment destroys even the shadow of shadows, the reflection of a reflection, a feeling about feelings. Such is the first version of what Proust later calls the intermittences of the heart or the misery of the fallen man who cannot even remain faithful to his misery.

Once one grasps this pattern of desire and fall in most of these regrets and reveries, one can take pleasure in pursuing the variations on a theme that Proust develops in a nearly musical sense. For example the opening text, "Les Tuileries" illustrates imperfection simply in the bad weather that accompanies a visit to the titular Parisian gardens. More grandiosely the prose poem "Versailles" points out that the extravagant quest for beauty undertaken in the construction of the gigantic palace ended up creating a "royal graveyard." It has hence served less to create joy for an earlier historical period than to produce a sense of sadness in us now. Even the garden's ponds are redolent of sadness, for they resemble "urns offered up to the trees' melancholy" (165). Versailles is an enormous stone monument to depression.

In fine imperfection is omnipresent, and its power is increased by the fact that the subjective world is subject to delusion. Subjectivity lends itself all too easily to manipulation by treacherous external circumstances. For example in the fourteenth text, a brief narrative called "Rencontre au bord du lac" ("Encounter by the Lake"), the narrator resolves to do without a beloved who, leaving on vacation, shows that she does not care for him. He then mistakes a woman he happens to see for the woman he loves, believing she has greeted him in a friendly way. This case of mistaken identity transforms his attitude toward her so that he believes briefly again in her love. Even after he knows he is a victim of a delusion, the memory of the mistake continues to haunt his mind with the same power as if it had been based on reality. But the intellectual recognition that one is victim of a delusion does little to modify one's emotional response, for, as Proust often asserts, intellect and emotion operate in different spheres.

Dreams, too, participate in this creation of delusions and false beliefs. The seventeenth text, "Rêve" ("Dream"), illustrates dream-formed delusion in the case of a man who falls in love with a woman whom he finds uninteresting—without charm or intellect. She attracts him, however, after she appears to him in a dream in which together they know "a great miracle of happiness and glory" (191). The woman, viewed first by the narrator as insignificant, is transformed by the dream so that he is irresistibly attracted to her even while expecting disenchantment. But he is powerless to react against his emotion even when he knows that love has passed over him "like this dream, with the same mysterious power of transfiguration" (193). This text illustrates a Proustian law of the mind that he later uses to great effect: the subjective world constantly works to change the objective world by reconfiguring it to make it conform to the delusions that the mind entertains, sometimes even when the mind knows it is delusional. Desire wants to construe reality.

Nature, music, and dream—these are sources of emotion that induce delusional states that at times are comic and at other moments are almost intimidating in the way they border on real madness. For instance in the fourth text, "Famille écoutant la musique" ("A Family Listening to Music"), the first-person narrator declares that he finds in music the "vast and universal beauty of life and death." Then addressing himself to his absent beloved, he says that he experiences in music what he experiences as unique about her charm. Not unlike the Swann of *Swann's Way* with his belief that he finds his love embodied in music, this narrator thinks that if music can be emotion, it can be love. Hence, he reasons, music is superior to the love induced by an earthly creature, since music exists in a realm that cannot be impinged upon by the imperfections of the present moment. (Later, in meditating on the music of Vinteuil in *In Search of Lost Time*, the Proustian narrator calls this realm "the real.") In "A Family Listening to Music," the narrator concludes that, transfigured by music, becoming music, love is then an imaginary state that can be perhaps best be experienced in the absence of the beloved. Swann is not so perspicacious.

In the eighth text, "Reliques" ("Relics"), delusion is fostered by relics, the holy presences left from the past, by which the batty narrator means the playing cards and novels that once belonged to the deceased woman he still loves (and who apparently would not speak to him when she was alive). He collects these relics, mementos impregnated with the past, which allow him to reconstitute her world and thus to love her in dream. Hence, he madly concludes, the beloved's real beauty is still to be found in his desire; or as he reasons, "She lived her life, but perhaps I alone dreamed it" (176). Delusion again believes it is superior to objective reality. Another type of borderline sanity is illustrated in the twenty-second prose poem, ironically titled "Présence réelle" ("Real Presence"), ironic because by all normal standards the narrator goes beyond the limits of sanity when he speaks to his absent beloved. He orates about the passion he feels for her when inspired by the beauty of nature in the Engadine Valley of the Swiss mountains, especially at the village Sils-Maria (where Nietzsche spent several years). The ecstatic lover tells his beloved they would have been "mad" together had she been there. Her absence apparently does not prevent him from indulging in madness. Only a grudging recognition that he misses the mere "material" presence of the woman suggests that the narrator has any grip on reality.

In contrast to the imperfections of love in these reveries stands the nonhuman natural world. For example, in the twenty-eighth text, "La mer" ("The Sea"), Proust develops a theme found in Baudelaire's poem "L'homme et la mer" ("Man and the Sea"), in which the sea is declared to be a mirror to the human soul. (Proust also alluded to this poem in his poem portraying Chopin.) In the sea the soul contemplates its own deceptive nature in the infinite play of the waves, for as Baudelaire puts it, the human spirit is no less "a bitter abyss" than the ever-restless ocean. Proust rephrases Baudelaire by declaring that the sea will always fascinate those who find that "the disgust with life" and "the attraction of mystery" have preceded their first sorrows. For them the sea offers a foreshadowing of reality's insufficiencies (209). The sea fills the soul with joy because it, like the soul, is "an infinite and impotent aspiration, an élan forever broken and falling, an eternal, soft lamentation," which imitates the movements of the soul (210).

This text proclaiming romantically the harmony existing between nature and the poet's inner world is at odds, however, with Proust's twenty-sixth text, "Sous-Bois" (meaning "undergrowth" and translated as "Forest Scene"). Finding himself in a forest setting, the narrator tries to force his mind to espouse the contours of the trees' branches, but they offer him no human resonance. Unlike the sea's invitation to union, the trees of the forest invite one "to sympathize with a life at once antique and young, so different from ours, of which it seems to be the inexhaustible, dark reserve" (207). This is not an invitation the mind can entertain, and the woods can only separate the viewer from a world standing aloof in its otherness. This impression of otherness is also the result of Proust's attempt at anthropomorphizing trees in the prose poem "Les marronniers" ("Horse-Chestnut

Trees"). The trees first exist for the poet as "greenish and mysterious grottos" that become, with the arrival of autumn, creatures whose branches appear more solid and darker for being shorn and that "thus joined to the trunk seem to hold back, like a magnificent comb, the soft blond waves of hair they spill forth" (208). This personification does little to bring nature into human ken, for the disheveled trees continue to remain distant, daunting, and incommensurably other.

To conclude these considerations of Proust's prose poems in *Pleasures and Days,* let us turn to two of the most ambitious texts, which pull all these motifs together in anticipation of the dominant themes of *In Search of Lost Time.* First the ninth text, "Sonate clair de lune" ("Moonlight Sonata"), the title of which seems to allude to Beethoven as well as Verlaine. The music of this sonata is produced as much by nature as by art, and both exist in a dream in which the narrator finds·that moonlight alleviates his pain so that his melancholia leaves him. A female friend awakens him, and in a state in which he is now transfigured by the tears shed by the moon itself, he enters into communion with her. Proust did not need to read Ruskin (which he soon would do) to know that this crying moon is an example of what Ruskin called the pathetic fallacy, for the narrator recognizes that this moon is a projection of his own self and is thus unreal (179). The narrator is in a delusional state in which the moon receives unto itself "the woods, the fields, the sky which again reflected itself in the sea," so that his heart sees at last clearly into the woman's heart (180). This communion conjures up a cosmic vision of sadness that eliminates nature even as it evokes Verlaine's lines from his "Clair de lune" ("Moonlight"). In this poem Verlaine identifies the landscape of a moonlit night with "votre âme" (your soul), wherein the moon makes the fountains sob in a garden of the heart. In Proust's text, as in Verlaine's, the self has interiorized everything, including the other's soul, in a delusional state that is far more unsettling than Verlaine's raptures. In depressed lucidity the narrator knows that he is incapable of mastering his own dreams and inner states.

Finally with regard to the fall into time, the twenty-ninth text, "Marine," presents a striking example of the desire of the return to childhood that lies at the heart of the narrator's later quest for resurrection in *In Search of Lost Time.* In this prose poem, Proust draws on Baudelaire and Plato to embroider upon a myth accounting for the present state of fallenness as well as a mystic version of salvation from it. In "Marine" (which can be translated "Seascape") the narrator muses that the soul, upon being embodied in the present world, loses its contact with the paradise it knew before or perhaps immediately after birth, which is to say, before life began its dreary unfolding in time. The fall has meant the loss of the original language used by the soul when it existed in a prelapsarian paradise. The poet thinks that for him to recover the meaning of all the words he has lost, these words would have to be said again by the things he has left in the past, which for him would be found at a seaside in Normandy. Were he there he would need to demand nothing more from these "natal things," for they would speak to the adult the language they spoke to him when he was a child. He then is able to remember the things that he would perceive if, walking, he were to approach the sea and were to see "the old melancholy queen," perhaps broken by waves, perhaps glistening and smooth. The text ends inconclusively, though the implication is that the narrator could thus recover the language of his natal things upon returning to a place of origin. This recovery is not quite what Proust found in Baudelaire's Platonic "La vie antérieure" ("Previous Life"), a poem describing a prenatal paradise in which the soul once spoke an original language that was lost upon birth, after which the fallen world obscures the soul's knowledge of its previous disincarnate state. In "Marine" Proust uses Baudelaire's version of Plato's myth with the additional hope that perhaps paradise could be restored through contact with the things found in and attached to childhood: "They are generous to the child they saw born, of themselves they would teach him forgotten things" (211). So "natal things" retain the language that could resurrect the past and end the alienation in the present. The childhood paradise of Combray is not distant.

The texts in *Pleasures and Days* show Proust concerned with trying out various narrative techniques and types of poetic imagery. In addition he was also thinking about aesthetics and literary theory when he put these texts together for his anthology. The best example of his concern with aesthetics at the time is found in an essay, "Contre l'obscurité" ("Against Obscurity"), published in 1896 in *La Revue blanche,* a journal receptive to the then-current generation of symbolist writers. (Proust himself had published several pieces in it.) In publishing what is something like a manifesto in this journal, Proust picked in effect a symbolist venue to bid adieu to the older symbolist generation. Wanting to announce a moment of historical change, he vaunts his youth as he attacks the older generation for its lack of critical understanding as shown by its pursuit of hermetic writing. Proust attacks these poets for their obscurity and defends the value of clarity in writing. He finds the clarity he defends embodied in a tradition going from the Greeks through Shakespeare and Racine and culminating in the type of fiction he most admired, exemplified specifically in his essay by Tolstoy's *War and Peace* and Eliot's *Mill on the Floss.* According to Proust this Western tradition has produced works that achieve depth in clarity and offer metaphysical truths drawn from the visible world but also respect the demands of language and what he calls the laws of art.

With exemplary clarity Proust's manifesto criticizes four strategies, or arguments, used by the current generation of writers to justify their obscurity. Presenting their strategies as affirmative propositions, he then turns the propositions against themselves by demonstrating their incoherence, which in turn allows him to elaborate his own aesthetic program. First Proust says that the symbolists claim that their obscurity is typical of all great art, which the public cannot understand when it first appears. This point is especially interesting since the narrator of *In Search of Lost Time* elaborates a theory about the transformation of vision necessary for new art to be understood, and thus it might appear that Proust later agrees with the idea he attacks here. This is not really the case, since in neither case does Proust argue in favor of obscurity. In the essay he says that Racine and Hugo caused a malaise when their works first appeared, but the difficulty their works offered is not because of unintelligibility, which is the meaning of obscurity that Proust uses to characterize the work of the current generation. Racine and Hugo are perhaps difficult at times, but they are intelligible, and in their innovations they respect the necessity for communication imposed, as the young Proust maintains, by the "laws of the universe and of thought." His rationalist side comes to the fore with this argument. This side does not disappear in the later theorizing.

Against the rationalist viewpoint arguing for universal laws governing communication, Proust says today's poets contend that all difficult systems of thought are obscure because they are profound. With Kant, Spinoza, and G. W. F. Hegel as examples, these poets claim that they, too, are offering systems of deep thought that are perforce obscure. In this context *profound* seems to mean philosophical. Probably with his own impulse toward abstraction in mind, Proust retorts that stuffing philosophy into a novel or poem is as erroneous in practice as it is in theory. Literature is not philosophy, though, as *Macbeth* demonstrates, literature can communicate metaphysics through a style that conveys nonrational truth. However, "since the poet does not address himself to our logical faculties, the poet cannot benefit from the right to appear obscure that every profound thinker initially enjoys."[9] Making a distinction he held throughout his life, Proust declares that the truths of poetry derive from the artistic use of language in which words are not simply pure signs. Rather the writer uses them at times musically and at times plays upon their range of associations in order to communicate the latent meanings by which they may, for example, conjure up meanings bound up with a historical past (97). This means that the sensations that the poet communicates may be obscure, but, as Proust observes, obscurity should not characterize the language with which they are communicated.

The symbolist's third justification for obscurity that Proust formulates surely derives from the aesthetics of the senior statesman of symbolism, Mallarmé, though the poet is not named. Proust notes that the symbolist says, as Mallarmé indeed proclaimed, he must use obscurity to keep the vulgar reader at bay. He rejects this argument, noting that if the poet tries to take account of the plebian nature of some readers, then the poet is actually paying homage to such a reader, since every attempt either to please or to displease the crowd can only delight second-rate readers (97). The fourth justification for obscurity in "Against Obscurity" reflects the debate in Proust's own mind about the relative weight to be given to the general and the specific in artistic representation. The symbolists, he ironically observes, wish to neglect the "accidents" of space and time in their representations of "eternal truths" (98). In commenting on this neglect of the accidents that happen to make up the real world—which one might criticize in Proust's own reveries in *Pleasures and Days*—he underscores that the desire to escape the contingent determinations of space and time shows a failure to understand the "law of life" that decrees that the universal and the eternal can only be realized and represented in the individual case, as well exemplified by the fictions of Tolstoy and Eliot. Much like a modern biologist, Proust interprets this "law" to mean that the universal has no existence apart from the specific case exemplifying it. This argument is in fact an anti-Platonism. Indeed Proust's aesthetic is an anti-Platonism, which explains his view that, in their pretense to represent the "universal soul," most symbolist texts are simply "cold allegories." This is not to say that the Platonist and anti-Platonist do not often debate in Proust's bosom, but here the anti-Platonist will have no truck with Mallarmé's symbolist dream that the goal of literature is to write "The Book" incarnating the Ideal.

Some critics think that Mallarmé reacted to Proust's essay with his piece published in September in *La Revue blanche*, "Le mystère dans les letters" ("Mystery in Letters"). If so this event confirms that young Proust had more presence on the Parisian literary scene that one might be inclined to think. But that is a secondary issue. More important is the fact that "Against Obscurity" shows how Proust wanted to liberate himself from the power that Mallarmé had exerted over him and an entire generation of poets and that he was able to write an important essay to argue the point.

To conclude this consideration of Mallarmé and his presence in Proust's imagination, it is revealing to return to *Pleasures and Days* to look at a text called "Eventail" ("Fan")—one placed, or seemingly misplaced, in the "Fragments from Italian Comedy" discussed above. First published in 1893 in *La Revue blanche,* "Eventail" shows that Proust could emulate Mallarmé, who had written poems with the same title. In his text Proust implicitly contrasts the paradise of art hinted at in Mallarmé's poems with a description of society as a place where banality runs rampant. To this end his prose poem describes a handheld fan of the sort popular among women in the nineteenth century. They were often painted and hence minor works of art. Metaphorically, then, Proust's prose text presents itself as a painted fan, offering through description an iconic representation while also taking the form of homage directly addressed to the deceased Madame de Saussine, the woman whose salon Proust describes in the text as if it were painted upon the fan. Not unlike what one finds in some of Mallarmé's occasional verse, Proust first describes in glowing terms the social ideal that was once realized in this woman's salon. In lines that echo the wish for utopia evoked in the dedication of *Pleasures and Days,* Proust says that on the fan she will see, in the foreground of the painting, noble lords, beautiful women, and men of talent who created in her salon a more harmonious universe than found in the world outside. Amazingly enough, in her salon could be found dukes without arrogance and novelists without pretensions (97). Proust then undermines the description of the ideal by going on to describe other scenes on the fan with a more "realistic pessimism." One sees a great writer, with the appearances of a snob, who listens to a noble lord perorating on a poet about whom, as the noble's expression shows, the nobleman understands nothing. With this portrayal Proust anticipates the salon life of the Guermantes and its radical fall from the ideal the young narrator dreams of. This split between a possible ideal world once realized in the past and the real, present world sets out the configuration that leads Proust to the structure of *In Search of Lost Time.* Thus, while it may seem that he had by the writing of "Against Obscurity" broken the spell Mallarmé had cast upon him, the similarities between "Eventail" and *In Search of Lost Time* suggest that the older symbolist remained a major presence in Proust's life: even after 1896 he continued to share Mallarmé's anguish about the impossibility of the ideal, but he expressed it in clear and often comic prose.

Proust's description of a high-society salon in "Eventail" points to another facet of his early published writings, namely, his journalistic coverage of social life. The text's praise of a deceased woman's salon is similar to other occasional pieces in which poetic paeans of flattery and passages of journalism are not always separate. Covering social events or reviewing books by friends, Proust wrote many such occasional articles, sometimes as part of a desultory effort to make money and more often because he wanted to frequent high society, study it, and draw lessons from it—while ingratiating himself to some of its notables. These writings, published in *Le Figaro* and elsewhere, did little to enhance Proust's reputation. On the contrary: because of these occasional pieces, Proust apparently acquired a rather negative reputation as a snob. Not surprisingly he did not republish these society pieces (though his brother republished a few in *Chroniques* after Proust's death). He pertinently observes in several of these texts that snobbism is the artist's enemy, as if he wanted to remind himself, while rubbing shoulders with socialites and aristocrats, of the destruction that intoxication with rank could inflict on his artistic ambitions—a recurrent theme in *Jean Santeuil* as well as *In Search of Lost Time*. From this perspective it is not surprising that, despite his unstinting praise of aristocratic friends, Proust feels at times the need to defend his integrity in writing these occasional pieces. For example in a journalistic text written in 1903 for *Le Figaro* and republished in *Chroniques,* about the salon of the Princesse Mathilde, he observes: "An artist should only serve truth and have no respect for rank. He must simply take it into account in his portrayals, insofar as rank is a principle of differentiation, much like, for example, nationality, race, background. Every social condition presents its own interest, and it can be just as curious for an artist to show the manners of a queen as the habits of a seamstress."[10] In such statements Proust's conscience appears to be bothering him a bit. After all he had been an assiduous reader of Tolstoy and the Bible, neither of which would suggest that the rich and famous are a source of great wisdom. However it is also clear that by observing the world of high society, Proust was, in fact, finding the material for his own artistic vision.

Society reporting overlaps at times with literary criticism in Proust's occasional writings, even when it borders on nearly comic flattery in reviews of the work done by friends, such the dandy aristocrat Montesquiou or the poet Anna de Noailles. In lavishing fulsome praise, Proust was nonetheless developing his critical categories. For example in a review of a book of Noailles's poems for *Le Figaro* in 1907, he uses critical categories that he was to elaborate in his texts about Sainte-Beuve, then in *In Search of Lost Time,* to wit, the distinction of the social self (*le moi social*) and the deep self (*le moi profond*). About Noailles he wrote: "Nothing that constitutes the contingent social self of Mme de Noailles, this self that the poets sometimes try so hard to make us know, is spoken about a single time in the course of these four hundred pages" (*Chroniques,* 180–81). Noailles meditates on her ancestors, but Proust claims, with the hyperbole typical of his journalistic pieces, that this recall is filtered through her sensibility, so that there is no book in which the social self has such a small place and in which the deep self has so much. Then with no hyperbole he defines the poet's deep self as the locus that individualizes a work of art, in contrast with the social self, about which one can say, paraphrasing Pascal, that it is detestable (182). The deep self is the grounds for the unified artistic vision that Proust finds in the individual works—paintings or poems—of all authentic artists.

In this same review, Proust underscores the importance of metaphor. Namely the poet's use of metaphor is a means by which the past can be restored to the present: "And these charming and quite lively comparisons which substitute for the recognition of what is, the resurrection of what we have felt (the only interesting reality) disappear themselves when set beside really sublime images" (188). This somewhat contradictory appraisal of the poems—in which the only reality of interest is that which has been, except when set beside the sublime—leads Proust to conclude that Noailles's work is the masterwork of literary impressionism (189). *Impressionism* was already Proust's shorthand term for the artist's capacity to create an image that renews vision. Painting is clearly on his mind when, in praise of Noailles and other poets or a painter such as Monet, he imagines a book of gardens he would like to write in which all their gardens would find a place. One sees that the way toward the earthly garden of Combray leads through Monet's gardens of delight.

Proust's forays into high society, written up for *Le Figaro* and other journals, show that, despite his revels in pessimism, he never stopped being fascinated by the idea of a utopia, as sketched out in the dedication and some of the poems of *Pleasures and Days*. In his journalism—self-seeking obsequiousness aside—he projects at times onto his aristocrats a brilliant light to show that they represent an ongoing historical continuity of the best that society once had to offer, always something like a resurrected utopia, as if only the past harbored the conditions of possibility for the ideal. Thus in depicting how grandly the present Count d'Haussonville inhabits the château of Coppet that belonged to his great grandmother, the celebrated Madame de Staël, Proust describes a scene, again reminiscent of Rabelais's Thélème Abbey, in which the then-contemporary aristocrats indulge in ideal play:

> It is divine to arrive at Coppet on a day softened and gilded by autumn, when the vines are golden and the lake still blue, to come into this rather chilly eighteenth-century residence, both historic and lively, inhabited by descendants who possess both "style" and life.
>
> It [the château] is a church that is already an historic monument, but in which mass is still celebrated. Mme de Staël's room is

occupied by the Duchesse de Chartres, Mme Récamier's by the
Comtesse de Béarn, Mme de Luxembourg's by Mme de Talleyrand,
the Duchesse de Broglie's by the Princesse de Broglie. They chat,
they sing, they laugh, they go out for motor car excursions, they
have supper, they read, they do things their own way and without
the affectation of imitating the behavior of those of a bygone era,
they live. And in this unconscious continuation of life among the
things to which they are accustomed, the perfume of the past is
emitted more acutely and strongly than in those "reconstructions"
of "old Paris" where in an archaic setting the "characters of
the period" have been set out and costumed. The past and the
present rub shoulders. In Mme de Staël's library we find M.
d'Haussonville's books of choice.[11]

There is a "divine" quality to this life deriving from the way in which the
past is resurrected in the present as a utopian idyll. We suspect that Proust
knew well that most of this utopian vision was of his own creation and
that, whatever the degree of truth in this portrayal, Proust could not resist
his urges to resurrect paradise lost, especially when the portrayal would
also flatter those to whose society he wanted to belong.

Suffice it to say about the available journalistic writings that, if Proust
was not also the author of *In Search of Lost Time*, they would probably be
totally forgotten. The same can probably be said about the posthumously
published *Jean Santeuil*, the novel he began but abandoned around the
time he fell under the sway of the works of John Ruskin. Having given
up on writing this novel, and with some prodding and certainly much
help from his mother, Proust began reading Ruskin. His next published
work took the form of essays on Ruskin and annotated translations of the
English critic's *The Bible of Amiens* and *Sesame and Lilies*. *The Bible of
Amiens* offers Ruskin's views of the development of Christian civilization,
especially as mirrored in the cathedral of Amiens. It is also an initiation
into how to "read" the biblical figures represented on Amiens's Gothic
cathedral. The version of *Sesame and Lilies* Proust translated consists of
two didactic lectures Ruskin gave on how and what to read, one for workingmen, the second for women. (Proust did not translate the third lecture
found in a later edition of *Sesame and Lilies* of 1894.) Before publishing
these translations, however, he published essays on Ruskin in 1900, the
year of Ruskin's death. Proust subsequently used these essays in the preface
to his translation, *La Bible d'Amiens*, published in 1904.

In the first essays on Ruskin, Proust is by and large positive about
Ruskin's work. By contrast he is quite critical of the Englishman in the

"Post-Scriptum" that concludes his preface to *La Bible d'Amiens* and in the lengthy footnotes he appended to the translations. In fact at no point did Proust accept all of Ruskin's views on aesthetics, nor did he acknowledge the important role Ruskin had taken on in England as a social and economic reformer. He focused on Ruskin's views of art and especially medieval architecture, and there is no doubt that his views on art history were an important springboard for Proust's finding the aesthetic vision—or the vision of aesthetics—that underpins *In Search of Lost Time*. In fact, as suggested earlier, the prefatory essay he wrote for *Sesame and Lilies* (*Sésame et les lys*), "On Reading," shows that, while translating the works, Proust found the literary voice he uses in "Combray." In this prefatory text recalling memories of reading as a child, he leaves behind the poetizing texts and ironic portraits of *Pleasures and Days* as well as the third person narration he used in *Jean Santeuil*. He was able to do this after roughly six or seven years during which he meditated on Ruskin's views of art, ethics, and history—until, having absorbed the English critic's views on aesthetics and history, he abandoned him and returned to his own creative endeavors.

In 1944 the literary scholar L. A. Bisson wrote an essay about the publication of the letters Proust had sent to Madame Riefstahl, the married name of Proust's near co-translator, Marie Nordlinger. In it Bisson asked, as does nearly every reader puzzled by Proust's development, the following question, "Where, then, does Ruskin come into this maturing vision?" His elegant answer to this question has been mirrored in much subsequent criticism: "In Proust's admiration for Ruskin in general two elements are worth isolating here. The first is the warmth of his response to Ruskin's theme of the survival of men, unknown or long-forgotten, in the houses or churches they built, in the work of the craftsman's hand and tools; and blended, often identified with this, is his ardent insistence that Ruskin's truest memorial is in the objects he loved and praised."[12] Then, in the second part of his answer, Bisson stated that Ruskin's views of writing and reading were instrumental in Proust's finding his own style: "It was Ruskin's remarks on reading that inspired him to write the essay *Journées de lecture* [*sic*], published as a preface to his translation of *Sesame and Lilies*. That essay is the first draft, the first sure promise of the tender recording of early experience, that gives the exquisite picture of family life at Combray that is one of the loveliest and truest things in all his vast work. . . . The direct influence on him of Ruskin's individual thought and particular theme had waned; but part of its function had been to arouse the Muse of Memory who inhabited Proust's mind and claimed him for her own."[13] Bisson did not know about *Jean Santeuil,* so he could not know that the themes of memory were in Proust's mind before the encounter with Ruskin (and he confused the title of the essay introducing the translation with a later version of the essay Proust published in *Pastiches et mélanges*). However it is accurate to say, as does Bisson and a host of later critics, that Proust's encounter with Ruskin was fundamental for his development of the concept of memory as embodied in material objects, especially in art and architecture. It could be argued, in fact, that Proust's sense of history is largely derived from Ruskin's historical work, seconded by his reading of Émile Mâle's studies of gothic iconography.

Upon opening *La Bible d'Amiens*, the reader first finds that Proust has written the preface to it in four parts (available on more than one Internet site as well as in translation). First there is an "avant-propos" (foreword) written for the translation and then a travel essay about "Notre-Dame d'Amiens according to Ruskin," after which there is a separate essay on Ruskin drawing on the previously published essays, and finally the above-mentioned "post-scriptum," the previously unpublished essay testifying that in 1904 Proust had already taken his distance from Ruskin. Turning to the *Sésame et les lys* of 1906, the reader finds the aforementioned preface, "Sur la lecture" ("On Reading"), which is a longer version of the "Journées de lecture" ("Days of Reading") that Proust later published in 1919 in his anthology *Pastiches et mélanges*. (Bisson's mistaking "Journées de lecture" for the essay prefatory to *Sésame et les lys* is indicative of the difficulty keeping straight Proust's early texts.)[14] The reworking of this prefatory material in 1919 for *Pastiches et mélanges* shows that, rapidly acquiring a reputation, Proust wanted his writings on Ruskin to be considered part of his opus. This desire distinguishes them notably from the occasional pieces he published in *Le Figaro* and other journals. To avoid confusion, however, one should bear in mind that when Proust reworked these prefaces for *Pastiches et mélanges*, he published the second text of the preface "Notre Dame d'Amiens selon Ruskin" as "Journées de Pèlerinage, Ruskin à Notre-Dame d'Amiens" ("Days of Pilgrimage, Ruskin at Notre Dame of Amiens"), and that he melded together into one essay the texts published in the preface as "John Ruskin" and the critique contained in his postscript. (Proust seems not to have been overly concerned about confusing his readers: not only did he publish a version of "Sur la lecture" in the anthology as "Journées de lecture," he also used the latter title for a review of the *Mémoires* of the Countess of Boigne.)

In the foreword to *La Bible d'Amiens*, a philosophical Proust emerges as he sketches out what he wants to do for Ruskin's work in his essays and in footnotes. In so doing he actually writes less on Ruskin and more on his own theory of literary criticism, based on a theory of art he has worked out in some detail. He writes that the critic's task is to go through a writer's work and find those essential characteristics or traits that acquire meaning through recurrence. In general terms, Proust says, meaning in art is ultimately not bound up with a work's explicit subject matter but is found in the recurrences that create style and hence an artistic vision. Just as viewing one painting by Rembrandt will not allow the viewer to understand Rembrandt's vision, so a reading of one poem is insufficient to grasp the poet's vision. Only after a viewer or reader has experienced a series of works can he or she grasp the recurrent traits that make up the artist's singular vision. This holds true for all types of artists, which in Proust's view includes a critic and historian such as Ruskin. In this regard he argues that Ruskin was a writer with a specific vision. In his foreword Proust makes a longer exposition of what he had only suggested in his critical comments on Anna de Noailles, to wit, that the recurrent motifs in a work represent the expression of the artist's deep self.

Two dominant themes thus emerge in the foreword to *La Bible d'Amiens*. First, for an artwork to be truly meaningful, the viewer or reader must grasp the singularity of the recurrent forms or motifs in an artist's work. Proust long grappled with the problem of singularity. There is no doubt that he was tempted by a Platonic universalism, which is precisely what he rejected in "Against Obscurity." In the foreword he spells out his views that an artist's vision is always singular and unique to the artist in question. Second Proust employs the concept of vision to underpin his view of the unity of art, indeed of the unity of knowledge, for he goes on to suggest, in a not altogether clear comparison, that the artist's new singular vision, embodying specific recurrent traits, is like a scientific instrument that allows a physicist to undertake an experiment. One might be tempted to say that Proust is using *vision* in a metaphorical sense to characterize both painting and literary text, though the notion seems to have a nearly literal intent if we understand that the literary text resembles something like a scientific optical instrument. Perhaps sensing that he is being equivocal with the notion of vision, Proust draws back from pursuing his theory with the recognition that, within the limits of his translation of Ruskin, he cannot really reconstitute the singular spiritual/intellectual life of the writer haunted by "special realities." The reconstitution of these special realities is nonetheless the critic's ultimate task if he is to be successful in showing where meaning lies in the work. With this task in mind, Proust justifies his long footnotes to Ruskin's text, for he hopes they will allow the reader to get an approximate sense of the recurrent features that constitute Ruskin's vision.

In *Pastiches et mélanges,* Proust republished the next parts of the preface to *La Bible d'Amiens* in a more inclusive section titled "En mémoire des églises assassinées" ("In Memory of the Assassinated Churches"). With this title Proust calls attention to the state of the Gothic cathedrals damaged or destroyed by artillery fire during the world war that had just ended. This somber title, grouping together four essays, suggests that Proust's belief in the lasting nature of art had been severely shaken. (He revised *In Search of Lost Time* to place Combray in the war zone so that the church at Combray could be appropriately destroyed.) After the war Proust undoubtedly recognized that his prefatory texts to Ruskin's works were rooted in a nineteenth-century worldview, by which I mean his concern with art was rooted in an era for which the destruction of cities and churches was not part of its historical experience. Before the war Proust, with Ruskin, viewed the Gothic cathedrals, whose existence spanned centuries, as nearly everlasting monuments in which the historical past lived into the present. It was with the sense of the sublimation of history into the present that Proust had wanted the tourist to be able to use the essay "Ruskin at Notre-Dame d'Amiens" as a guide to the cathedral. "Ruskin at Notre-Dame d'Amiens" is Proust's preface to Ruskin's reading the church as the Bible, quite literally, since the Bible is translated into the cathedral's statues, telling the Judeo-Christian narrative. From this perspective the Bible is not an archaic text but lives on in full presence in the stones and statues found in Amiens. This is what Ruskin taught Proust, he says, at a time when he did not understand that medieval sculpture contains within it the living soul of those artists who believed the Bible's words. Comparably in Ruskin's text itself, as in the stones it evokes, Ruskin's soul also lives on, by which we may understand Proust means the deep self that read these stones. Through Ruskin he finds in the church a perpetually resurrected past that is not dead.

In these writings on Ruskin, Proust's attitude toward Christianity is positive, however much he distrusts what he sees as Ruskin's brand of aestheticized Protestantism. Young Proust was drawn to the church not only for its aesthetics but also for its role as a cultural institution. This attraction animates an early essay published under a pseudonym in *Le Banquet* in 1892. In it he had attacked his era's "materialism," asserting that France owed to Christianity all that it had accomplished of value, be it in the domain of action or of speculation. His examples of Christian action and speculation were, respectively, France's exporting Christianity to its colonies and its having given birth to Descartes and Pascal.[15] And later, though saying goodbye to Ruskin, he drew upon him again, as well as Mâle's study of Gothic architecture, to make a critique of an anticlerical project to disenfranchise and nationalize the cathedrals. In the essay "La mort des cathédrales" ("The Death of the Cathedrals"), he criticized the government in 1904 for failing to understand the symbolic beauty of the Catholic liturgy. Proust went so far as to say that it is a spectacle superior to Parisian theater or Wagnerian opera. He was ironically restrained but obviously disheartened at the prospect that the Gothic cathedrals—considered by him to be the highest and most original expression of France's genius—might be converted into casinos or lecture halls.[16]

In the prefatory piece "John Ruskin," Proust shows that he was drawn to Ruskin's idea that nothing seemingly dies in history, at least in the Western tradition that concerns him. This view significantly inflected Proust's view of Christianity, for it meant that religion was permanently a part of the living past in French culture. He largely accepted Ruskin's thesis that art makes the past live into the present, in this case the Christian art that encapsulates centuries of European and French cultural development. If Proust could not accept the literal truth of resurrection—though he seems to have been tempted by it—he was apparently willing to endorse Ruskin's neo-Christian belief that in art nothing dies. In developing these ideas, Ruskin himself sets out the thesis that two great streams of tradition, which he defined as the Greek and Gothic cultures, have constantly entertained fruitful mutual oppositions throughout European history. Ruskin finds the Greek strain running from Homer to St. Mark's Basilica in Venice and then manifesting itself in Ruskin's favorite painter, J. M. W. Turner; whereas the Gothic culture, springing from the Frankish tribes, underlies the Gothic cathedrals. Proust may have noticed that rather little in the way of the Gothic seems to be present in most modern painting. In any case he certainly noticed the role played by St. Mark's in Ruskin's history of Western culture. The upshot of this opposition Ruskin found perennially at work in Western culture is the affirmation that certain "eternal realities" continue to exist in the present. It is the quest for these realities that Proust finds at the heart of Ruskin's writings. As he sees it, Ruskin's is a quest for a reality that is neither exclusively material nor intellectual. This is because the reality art encompasses involves both, which means that the artistic genius can perceive reality in different material forms. Hence it is a matter of indifference whether the reality is expressed in painting, music, or poetry. All cultural forms are equal expressions of the eternal reality the thinker or artist embodies in them.

Proust makes a mild critique of Ruskin on this point, saying that the English critic does not sufficiently differentiate specific art forms. To illustrate this point, he asserts that painting can be great only when it does not try to be literature. How true that assertion is can be debated. What is important for Proust is that the general argument he attributes to Ruskin is one that he illustrates in *In Search of Lost Time* by means of its triad of artists, each developing a different art form, each form giving rise to a body of works characterized by a commonality of embodied vision.

Proust melded the postscript of 1904 with "John Ruskin" in the republication in *Pastiches et mélanges* in 1919. In either version he makes a pointed critique of Ruskin. He indicts Ruskin for the idolatry of art that Ruskin found in those hedonistic aesthetes who believe that the ultimate justification of art is sheer pleasure. For example the influential contemporary writer and critic Walter Pater, himself influenced by Ruskin, maintained that art should be valued for its enhancement of each present moment spent with it. A generation of aesthetes such as Oscar Wilde took this idea to heart. A neo-Puritan such as Ruskin could only scorn this viewpoint. Proust approved Ruskin's rejection of aestheticism but then doubted that art is motivated or justified by ethics. He points out, in fact, that if Ruskin's criticism of aestheticism turns on his belief that art has a fundamentally moral role, Ruskin's real reason for choosing the artworks whose moral worth impresses him is actually how beautiful these works are. Proust recognizes that Ruskin seems not to have been aware that he practiced the very "idolatry" he denounced. Idolatry is an important notion for Proust's later work. However, in his definition of idolatry, he goes beyond Ruskin to conflate the hedonism defended by the aestheticism Ruskin attacks and the social snobbery that caused Proust's Parisian coevals to adore, modishly, certain works of art. For him aestheticism and snobbery are two sides of the same coin. He sees idolatry of art as a form of the self-worship attendant upon snobbism. In attacking idolatry that includes both aestheticism and snobbery, Proust is engaging in self-defense and is perhaps guilty of projecting onto Ruskin some of his own sins. What is most relevant for reading Proust, however, is to see that, in coining his notion of idolatry, he is in effect laying the ground for his future writing: he is defining an often comic trait of his novel's characters. Incapable of understanding art, they use it narcissistically to surround themselves with an aura that should redound to their credit.

Resurrection is a key theme in Proust, and it is not a matter of indifference that he concludes the postscript with a valedictory expression of regret about a resurrection that now cannot occur: the passion he once felt for Ruskin is now gone and not to be recalled. Or rather it can be recalled only by using the type of memory that retrieves dead facts. It is the type of memory that "tells us, you were such and such, without allowing us to become it again, that affirms that reality of a lost paradise instead of restoring it to us in a memory."[17] This categorizing of memory anticipates the fears and anguish the narrator feels in *In Search of Lost Time*, fears about the possibility that time consigns to nothingness what he holds most valuable.

The postscript concludes with a powerful image conveying this anguish. He compares the lost paradise of the past he is powerless to reenter with an image drawn from classical antiquity: in trying to recall Ruskin, he resembles Antigone, the tragic heroine who, as Proust sees it, wants to restore a desolate tomb. Underscoring the death of Ruskin as a living presence for Proust, this final juxtaposition of Greek and Christian motifs, of lost paradise and tragic impossibility, is in fact a fitting homage to the Ruskin who believed the ongoing life of culture is determined by the interplay of the Greek and the Gothic-Christian.[18]

The comparison of the passion Proust felt for Ruskin with a lost paradise again shows that the Judeo-Christian image of the utopian garden is never far from his mind when he thinks about time. Notably the image recurs in "On Reading." Paradise is glimpsed in Proust's recollection of reading during his childhood. His description of childhood reading is supposedly a critique of the views of reading Ruskin propounds in the two lectures in *Sésame et les lys,* though it is obvious that Proust is only superficially interested in those views. The reader who reads only "On Reading" will not know that Ruskin offers, in the first lecture for workingmen, an exemplary reading of John Milton's "Lycidas" in order to demonstrate how the truth can be found in the text of a great poet. Proust is actually dismissive of Ruskin's point that the poet offers truths that ordinary men cannot find in their own minds—and thus according to Ruskin they must become attentive readers of great literature. (Ruskin's second lecture for women is of much less interest: it outlines the type of reading lower-class women should undertake to fulfill their subservient roles in Victorian society.) In "On Reading" Proust especially criticizes Ruskin's idea that one reads a book to "discover" some truth within, like a hidden Platonic essence waiting to be revealed. Proust charges that Ruskin's view of reading reveals that at heart he is a neo-Platonist. One may suspect that Proust is having a debate with himself about the nature of essence and the place Platonism has in his own thought. In any case a philosopher of literary theory comes to the fore when Proust claims that reading is an initiation in a process leading to truth. Reading is a means by which the self develops its own truth. In effect he is reading Emerson against Ruskin, and in so doing undertakes a description—almost an enactment—of the lost paradise lurking in the reading he did as a child, which also demonstrates what he means by reading.

In his demonstration of reading, Proust writes scenes that are ready to be transposed to "Combray" and its description of the narrator's childhood. He describes a typical day of the recurrent pleasures of reading, experienced by a boy during vacation. In this description Proust uses the imperfect tense, the *imparfait*, which in French describes the open-ended repetition in the past of an act, so as to portray scenes of recurrence that would happen (in the sense of *were recurring*) each day. (Romance languages have this tense, English and German do not.) For example he describes how reading fills up the boy's morning until lunch, followed by the recurrent rituals of the family meal, then followed by reading again in the seclusion of fields of flowers; and finally the boy would read each night while hiding under the bedcovers. The description of objects in the boy's bedroom linked with religious practices complements the image of the ever-present church at the center of the village. All of this permeates the rituals of childhood with a religious aura, so that the ideal day of reading seems resurrected in the repetition, narrated in the imperfect tense, and the past is restored as an unfolding plenitude of which the child with his book was scarcely aware—but which Proust recalls in melancholy.

Proust calls attention to his melancholy in a strange footnote to "On Reading." Pondering his own sadness, he suggests that his emotion is due to the imperfect verb tense he uses. He experiences this tense, he says, as one designating the incompleteness of recurrent actions in the past. Thus he experiences it as a cruel tense presenting life as something ephemeral. Proust advances the singular idea that the imperfect is a past tense that characterizes the action it narrates as an illusion, so that in the very act of narration it annihilates the experience. He contrasts the destruction worked by the imperfect with the "perfect" (*parfait*) tense, about which he says that it leaves us with the consolation of "activity." This is indeed a strange usage of *perfect*, which is not often used in French to describe French verbs. *Perfect* in French can apply in fact to both the absolute or historical past tense and the present perfect tense or the *passé composé*, which is also used as the past tense, or preterit, in conversation. (The absolute or historical past, the *passé simple*, is a literary tense used only in writing.) Perhaps the use of the *passé composé* as a preterit is why Proust thinks the compound "perfect" keeps activity alive by presenting it as past while suggesting its relation to the present (as when we say in English with the present perfect tense that "something has taken place"). I will later discuss the implications of verb tenses for *In Search of Lost Time*. With regard to "On Reading," Proust's idiosyncratic interpretation of the implications of the imperfect tense strongly implies that the resurrection the tense enacts is not really a cause for joy. It does not seem that he always thinks this way; or perhaps the imperfect tense plays a preponderant role in his later work, precisely because, for Proust, it at once restores a plenitude and commemorates melancholy disappearance.

After his critique of Ruskin's concept of reading, Proust proposes the idea that all great writers and artists are readers of the past. In concrete terms this means that ordinary mortals read mainly their contemporaries, but truly great writers read Horace, Molière, and Shakespeare. Or with regard to painters, Proust says the contemporary public went in 1900 to see expositions of Édouard Vuillard and Maurice Denis, whereas these artists themselves go to the Louvre to view the classic artists on display there (so that today, I add, Vuillard and Denis are included in collections of modern classics). Proust's point here is that the artist who is successful is committed, like Proust himself, to maintaining a unified cultural tradition, both as a reality and an ideal. This tradition is necessary for the genesis of a living contemporary culture. The descriptive and the prescriptive overlap in his vision of what is the basis for culture: empirically he argues that the canonical tradition is in fact the basis for contemporary artistic creation; and he argues prescriptively that it is imperative that tradition be respected. In this regard he endorses Ruskin's historicism that makes of the canonical past the source of the present. Before reading Ruskin young Proust had, as we have seen, already outlined a view of tradition in literature, and Ruskin broadened his perspective so as to include the world of art and architecture.

Proust develops this historicism with his own nuances. He greatly values the fact, for example, that past works of art bring about the resurrection of the past, not only referentially through their themes and situations but also in their very material substance. Time lost is restored, for example, by the historically marked syntax and semantics of the language in a play by Racine or by the aging stones set in two medieval columns on the piazetta next to St. Mark's Basilica, about which Ruskin writes in *The Stones of Venice*. From Proust's perspective the Venetian columns intercalate concrete moments of the twelfth century into the present; whereas Racine's syntax restores the materials of speech existing at the time of Louis XIV. Proust cut the final part of "On Reading" when he republished it 1919 in *Pastiches et mélanges*, undoubtedly because its vision of the past surging forth into the present greatly resembled what he was going to publish in *Time Regained*, the final volume of *In Search of Lost Time*. In that volume the narrator ponders the resurrection that art enacts, even after the religious underpinnings of the belief in resurrection no longer command assent. Despite Proust's cuts from "On Reading," the later truncated version of the essay still bares resemblance to the novel. The very act of the recollection of reading is a way of acceding to the past, one central to the strategies Proust develops in *In Search of Lost Time*.

The notion of process and slow accession to truth may seem to be apt notions for describing Proust's own career. His career shows that his writing was a process in that he kept up a constant quest to find what eluded him for years as the right form for his own vision—to apply to Proust his own metaphor, if metaphor it is. In dealing with the writings he actually published, one sees some of the important steps in that process—imitation, pastiche, narrative and poetic forms, journalism about the ways of society, and theoretical and historical writing on art. We can deal with other steps in this process by turning now to the fragmentary writings that Proust left in the tomb of forgetfulness—buried steps in the process of reaching the truth he sought. Editors have brought them to light and, one might say, resurrected them. I refer primarily to manuscripts now published as *Jean Santeuil* and *Contre Sainte-Beuve,* though there are also numerous other shorter texts. This resurrection is not without interest, since whatever their intrinsic value, these projects were essential parts of the process characterizing Proust's constant writing as he sought the literary form that would finally take the shape of *In Search of Lost Time.*

Chapter 3

What Proust Did Not Publish

Proust wrote much that he did not publish before beginning *In Search of Lost Time*. That he did not publish these texts does not mean they are insignificant, as is perhaps shown by the great interest critics have taken in them, especially in the manuscripts published as *Jean Santeuil* (1952) and *Contre Sainte-Beuve* (*Against Sainte-Beuve*, 1954), as well as some of his unpublished essays. *Jean Santeuil* is usually considered a novel, though it might just as well be considered a title grouping together narrative texts written mainly before Proust's work on Ruskin; whereas *Against Sainte-Beuve* contains both critical and narrative texts written after the Ruskin project. Proust was undoubtedly at one time looking for a unifying schema to turn these groups of manuscripts into books, and one can argue that he finally found the schema when working on *Against Sainte-Beuve*, though he did not complete that project. Rather he then began to write *In Search of Lost Time*. In both groups of manuscripts are found versions of themes and situations that surface again in the novel. I stress this point, since it is misleading to privilege one group of manuscripts or the other in looking for a starting point for the elaboration of *In Search of Lost Time*. All the manuscripts were part of Proust's process of development leading to that novel. But I also stress that the books one can read today are the inventions of their editors, including their titles. Both *Jean Santeuil* and *Contre Sainte-Beuve* were first edited by the talented Bernard de Fallois, and one can give him credit for their titles. Even though they bear Fallois's titles, later editions of the manuscripts differ from his versions. In the case of the *Against Sainte-Beuve* published by the authoritative Editions de la Pléiade in 1971, I believe that Fallois's earlier edition is to be preferred to the later. The Pléiade version was edited tendentiously to prove that these manuscripts did not have a role in the development of *In Search of Lost Time*. That viewpoint is very difficult to accept. The Fallois version is still in print, and it has been used for the most widely available translation in English, though the Pléiade version has also been translated.

Jean Santeuil and *Against Sainte-Beuve* call to mind again the earlier noted distinction Vauvenargues made about the type of writing that characterizes the classical moralists La Bruyère and La Rochefoucauld. With La Bruyère and La Rochefoucauld in mind—the first a painter of characters, the second a philosophical writer of maxims—one can say that after *Pleasures and Days* Proust remained uncertain as to whether he wanted to be a creative writer or an aesthetic theorist, a painter of character or perhaps a philosopher-scientist looking for general laws. It seems that these polarities were always present in his mind. On the one hand, the manuscripts published as *Jean Santeuil* reveal the fragments of a more or less realist novel in which Proust was looking for an aesthetic philosophy to ground it. The novel depicts characters that the young protagonist encounters as, rising in the social world, he tries to become a writer. On the other hand, in the case of the manuscripts published as *Contre Sainte-Beuve,* Proust apparently began a critical treatise that might have taken the shape of a novel, one perhaps unfolding as a conversation about literature between the narrator and his mother. In these texts Proust exposes the flaws in the critical practice of the nineteenth-century critic Sainte-Beuve while making critical comments on writers such as Baudelaire, Balzac, and Gérard de Nerval— major writers neglected by Sainte-Beuve. Both sets of manuscripts contain arguments about aesthetics that could be set in a novel, so that, while portraying the novelist and the society in which he lives, they illustrate theories about art. Judged as such both *Jean Santeuil* and *Against Sainte-Beuve* appear to have been useful, and probably necessary, experiments for Proust to undertake in order to become a complete writer—combining, as it were, La Bruyère and La Rochefoucauld—a portraitist and critical theorist who portrays both the unique and the universal.

Jean Santeuil and *Against Sainte-Beuve* are hardly the only works Proust did not seek to publish. He tried his hand at many types of writing, including poems, essays, reviews, and society pieces, and much of it did not appear in print. Today some of these abandoned texts are of interest as markers along his way to formulating the aesthetics that led him beyond *Pleasures and Days.*[1] For example an early unpublished essay on Chardin and Rembrandt offers an especially good example of Proust's thought as he developed his ideas about aesthetics. In this essay, probably written around 1895, he meditates on what he could learn from Chardin, an eighteenth-century French realist painter in the Dutch tradition of realism. To this end he creates a seminarrative that presents an older man imagining a hypothetical younger man who, his head full of images of cathedrals, the sea, and mountains, is disgusted with the disorder of daily life he sees about himself, especially the mess of his humble dining room. (Like Proust the young man has clearly been reading Baudelaire.) In his romantic re-fusal of limits, the young man is disgruntled with real life and the tawdry necessities it imposes. The older man's remedy for this case of spleen, he says, would be to send the young man to the Louvre and direct him not to Paolo Veronese's sumptuous Venetian palaces nor to Van Dyck's handsome princes but to the realist representations of daily life found in the paintings by Chardin. These works, in which, for example, a cat strolls on top of oysters and a dead ray hangs from the wall, represent the same disordered trivia found in the boy's kitchen. In a still life by Chardin portraying daily banality, nothing is "dead"—as is suggested by the French term *nature morte* (dead nature) for "still life." Quite simply Chardin found beauty in the messiness of daily dirt. A still life shows that affinities exist between people and things so that inanimate objects in the painting play a living, active role. Chardin teaches that "a pear is as living as a woman" and that a piece of kitchen pottery can be as beautiful as jewels, all of which makes vivid "the divine equality of all things before the mind that contemplates them."[2]

Young Proust seems resolutely modernist in his rejection of any hierar-chy in the determination of the beauty of objects. This position seems to derive from the way he uses the tradition of philosophical idealism, or at least its basic epistemological postulate, to describe the nature of percep-tion. Reality, he declares, is enhanced by the mind that views it. Beauty is not intrinsic to the object. Rather the painter's mind interacts with the objects it perceives to create beauty. Aesthetic categories are hence part of the structure of the mind. An important consequence of this viewpoint is that things can be as much a source of enchantment as are people.

Proust wrote a few other texts on painters, at undetermined dates, in-cluding one on Watteau that shows, as does his poem on the painter, that Watteau's wistfully questioning the possibility of love played a role in Proust's querying love. Proust infers from Watteau's work that the painter's poor health kept him from entering into the world of pleasure that his erot-ically suggestive paintings seem to portray. For Proust, however, the wistful lack of permanence portrayed in Watteau's work suggests something quite different. He considers Watteau to be the poet of love's impossibility. Or as Helen O. Borowitz has argued, in Watteau's paintings Proust discovered an expression of disenchantment with love and hence with people; whereas in Chardin he discovered the revelation that could be offered by a chance encounter with inanimate things: it was this type of revelation that could lead to his vocation as a writer.[3] Borowitz proposes that behind the rev-elation of the past, discovered in the pastry called the *petite madeleine* in Proust's "Combray," lies the discovery that Chardin's paintings can reveal beauty in the trivial. Proust's meditation on the aesthetic power unleashed by banal objects sets the stage for his idea that things can transform experience, indeed that redemption might be found in the quotidian. In brief the essays on Watteau and Chardin show that painting, from Proust's early days, offered ideas and motifs that, transformed by his own sensibility, he would use in constructing the fictional world of Combray.

Proust's first attempt at embodying a fictional world in a long narrative is *Jean Santeuil,* a work conceived of, in part, as a fictional biography. Among its most interesting pages are those in which Proust seeks the style and narrative structure to introduce redemption into a world bereft of transcendence. Because of these pages, some critics maintain that he was able to formulate his aesthetic philosophy in its mature form in these manuscripts.[4] I would modify this viewpoint by pointing out that in these texts Proust is at times more openly a philosophical romantic, at times more dramatically nihilistic, than in *In Search of Lost Time.* Complementary to his romanticism is a quest for redemption that is directly inflected by those Christian beliefs that he could defend but not accept. As his essay on Chardin, not to mention *Pleasures and Days,* points up, Proust was hungry for something that could redeem his experience of the decline and fall with which time besets all human activity. For this reason alone, it is not surprising that in the 1890s he was drawn to Christianity, for its myths and for its social value, even before he read Ruskin.

In his search for redemption from his own philosophical nihilism, young Proust began to write in *Jean Santeuil* what most critics consider an incipient bildungsroman: the story of the education and development of a boy, a would-be poet, who, as he grows into a man, must in his writing confront the nothingness underlying existence. But aside from the chronological schema for a laying out a fictional life, Proust did not find a temporal framework to unite the disparate incidents narrated by these manuscripts that seek to illuminate the past from the perspective of the future. Despite the fragmentary nature of these manuscripts, there is little doubt that with them Proust wanted to write something more substantial that what he had written to date. In fact after his less than successful literary debut with *Pleasures and Days,* it is understandable that he should set out to write a real novel—which is to say, a long, unified narrative work, taking as its model novels by nineteenth-century writers such as Goethe, Tolstoy, and Flaubert, writers who represented one summit of literary art for Proust.

With these models in mind, Proust first intended to write a realist novel narrated by an objective third-person narrator. However, having written a number of disparate scenes, it appears he then decided to try to unify the work with the eighteenth-century ploy of the "found manuscript" that is framed by an editor's commentary. Thus he wrote an opening section for the projected novel, telling the reader that the novel itself is a manuscript entrusted to the first-person narrator, who is the book's editor. Specifically the opening section, titled "Preface," narrates in the first person that the novel's editor came to Brittany and there made the acquaintance of a writer called C. Subsequently after C. died the narrator decided to publish a manuscript by C. that he had received from the writer when he was still alive. The "found" manuscript written in the third person constitutes the rest of *Jean Santeuil*. By imposing this framing narration, taking place after the time of the novel's action, Proust probably hoped to create an appearance of unity for the various scenes he had already written.

It is with self-reflexive irony that the narrator offers his impressions of the writer C.—irony alluding at once to the text and to its writer. Not unlike what Proust claimed about himself, C. writes only about what he has experienced. And not unlike Proust, C. is something of a socialite—in spite of himself. Teasingly the book's editor, like a biographical critic, wonders what exactly the relations were between C. and the characters in the novel. But he cannot really answer the question, since he had not dared to ask it while C. was alive. The editor says he would have liked to study the question so as to learn "the secret relationships, the necessary metamorphoses, that exist between a writer's life and his work, between reality and art, or rather . . . between the appearances of life and the very reality which makes up its durable background and that art has disclosed" (53). Proust's editor muses on a potentially self-reflexive relationship in which the novel, had it been completed, might have disclosed the grounds for its own existence. He wonders if the work might have included theories about the act of metamorphosis lying at the heart of art's autonomy, which is to say, its transformative relation to life. Proust has developed here his typical, playful ironic stance in these lines in which the theorizing editor steps into the reader's position to wonder about the truth of the truth revealed by the potential writer—Proust or C., as the irony allows—and to deflect it by declaring it finally a moot point.

After the preface the manuscripts are grouped under eleven headings, following roughly the chronology of a bildungsroman narrating Jean's life. This is true of all editions, though the Pléiade edition as well as Tadié's update of it use a different ordering of the manuscripts from that found in the Fallois edition. In any case all the arrangements of the manuscripts begin with descriptions of Jean's childhood and youth in Paris, with vacations in the provincial village of Illiers, where he has relatives. The narration's cycle of events is centered upon the gardens of Illiers and its church. It is of no little interest that much of it is later used again in "Combray," such as the description of the anguish the boy knows when he is separated from his mother upon going to bed. Also transposed into "Combray" is the description in *Jean Santeuil* of the boy's love for a little girl named Marie Kossichef whom he met in the park on the Champs-Elysées. Jean's youthful passion for this little Russian girl anticipates the love Gilberte inspires in the narrator of "Combray" as a boy, and the girl's parents exert the same kind of fascination on Jean that Gilberte Swann's parents exert on the narrator when a boy.

There are significant differences, however, between *Jean Santeuil* and *In Search of Lost Time*. For example formal education in *Jean Santeuil* plays a much greater role than it does in *In Search of Lost Time*, in which it is barely mentioned. For his secondary education, Jean attends the Lycée Henri IV, where he is greatly influenced by his philosophy professor, Beulier. Beulier initiates him into philosophical learning. In the course of this initiation, Jean is astonished to learn that one can speak meaningfully about good, evil, and truth and that science is not an enemy of the "kingdom of spirit," as he had imagined it to be (137). In Beulier, Jean encounters a man whose discourse is always in the service of truth. The idealized realm of learning aside, the other most powerful influence on Jean is his schoolmate Henri de Réveillon, a young nobleman who, becoming his friend, introduces Jean to aristocratic society. Friendship is thus given a more positive role in *Jean Santeuil* than in *In Search of Lost Time*. Thanks to his friend, Jean is received at the Réveillon family château, and many pages are devoted to life there and to the family of the Duke of Réveillon. The latter is an eccentrically prejudiced aristocrat who has little use for members of the bourgeoisie—Jean notably excepted. In the scenes narrating life at the château, a novel almost takes shape, for Proust develops in these texts the rhetorical means for narrating social comedy, first involving members of the aristocratic family and then dealing with Jean's social life, with members of the social register—the so-called *figures mondaines*.

After the portrayal of Jean's initiation into social life, the reader learns of his later travels as well as military service. Perhaps more interesting, however, are two substantial developments of narration centered on political events that Jean witnesses in Paris, one dealing with the Panama scandal and another involving the Dreyfus affair. Nothing like them is found in later work by Proust. These two narrative lines focus the narration on ethical questions brought up by the contrasting way public figures conceive of their duty in public service. A substantial part of the manuscripts also deals with Jean's later social life, with his love affairs and their vicissitudes, all this in theme and event anticipating Proust's later work. Finally *Jean*

Santeuil ends with descriptions of Jean's parents as, in old age, they prepare for death. In these texts Proust portrays Jean's revolt against his father but also his tenderness as he comes to terms with his parents' demands. The passage of time has transformed the demands, for his parents have, with regret, modified their expectations of Jean. He has failed to live up to their ideal for him. The failure to live up to parents' expectations is another leitmotif in Proust and is linked to the meaning of the passage of time: the boy's development in time is a form of fall from that ideal his parents once held up for him. Time is almost a character at the conclusion of *Jean Santeuil*, especially when the parents return to Auteil, the village where Proust was born—now become a Parisian suburb—in which the garden of Jean's youth has been covered with six-story buildings. The lost garden at the end of the manuscripts stands in contrasting symmetry to Illiers's opening gardens of paradise, the scene of childhood.

These manuscripts are united mainly by the fact that a character named Jean Santeuil is present in them. Maurice Blanchot argued that they are intentionally written as a series of fragments, since Proust wanted to concentrate the work on a series of epiphanic truths, not on an unfolding narrative. This is a provocative argument, but even Blanchot recognized that most of the manuscripts offer the stuff of a realist novel: a protagonist and his ongoing relationship to characters.[5] To be sure the manuscripts are obvious first drafts that, to say the least, allow a great deal of interpretive latitude about wherein lie their epiphanic truths. Notably names are not constant throughout, nor are events consistently related to each other. Perhaps this inconsistency is no great matter, for their main interest consists in the fact that some of the texts are attractive experiments in which Proust tried out ways of using realistic narration to expound moral and political as well as aesthetic arguments.

I will now discuss several examples of this experimentation, which highlight society and the social comedy, Jean's love life, and his discovery of politics and the ethics of public life, and I will conclude with what is perhaps the most interesting aspect of *Jean Santeuil*: Proust's search for the poetical means of redeeming lost time. Many of these themes will be recast in *In Search of Lost Time*, and their configuration here can throw light on Proust's permanent concerns.

First, life in society: The Tadié edition of *Jean Santeuil*, on which the present discussion is based, groups together sketches dealing with social relations in sections called "La vie mondaine de Jean," "Figures mondaines," and "De l'amour"—roughly "Jean's Social Life," "High Society Characters," and "On Love." Only about half of the manuscripts published under the rubric "On Love" deal with Jean's love life, though coming to terms with love is very much part of the young man's initiation into the ways of the fashionable world. In the sketches of social life and love affairs, often having little narrative development, Proust offers portraits not unlike those found in *Pleasures and Days,* especially of aristocrats, snobs, and jealous lovers. The unnamed third-person narrator has a detached ironic stance so that Jean himself can be the object of a critique. Moreover the narrator's distance allows him to make moral evaluations of the world of upper-class mores, fashions, caprices, and snobbism. This evaluation is the basis for the kind of social comedy that will be a hallmark of Proust's later writing. The starting point for much of this comedy is the narrator's less than utopian perspective on Jean's world. The narrator's perspective is much like that of Proust's nineteenth-century novelistic predecessors. For example he makes at times the same kind of ironic critique of Jean that George Eliot makes when, in *Middlemarch,* she notes that the arriviste Rosamond pursues a marriage offering her the "vistas of the middle-class heaven"— which is found, namely, in social rank.[6] In his frequenting people of rank—like Eliot's social-climbing heroine, who views rising in rank as a way to getting nearer to a "celestial condition on earth"—Jean dreams of a realm in which he would have nothing to do with vulgar people. He is a middle-class social climber who enters, with little effort, into his dreamed-of heaven to find that not all is paradisiacal there, especially after he leaves the sheltered aristocratic paradise found briefly in the château of Réveillon. In this respect the château where he is royally received by his friend Henri resembles, as Jean gets older, another lost paradise.

With the revelation that paradise is always found in the past, the narrator (and eventually Jean himself) recognizes that all human exchange is fundamentally skewed and hence comic. Social intercourse is comic because it is always flawed when judged by elementary norms of civility. This viewpoint is the basis for the creation of comedy in many nineteenth-century novels, especially in England. That Proust explicitly meditated on the comic in fiction is demonstrated in the manuscripts when the nature of the comic is given a philosophical exposition. It is expounded in a scene set in the château, where Jean is most at ease. Into this milieu comes one day another member of the Réveillon elite, a young poetess who can "find something droll in every conversation she heard, in every act or event: for a refined person, whose faculty for sympathy allows her to put herself in the place of every other person instead of remaining always bound to oneself, sees the comical everywhere, since everyone thinks only about himself and thus necessarily says something which, from the other person's viewpoint, is comic." To this exposition of the universal nature of the comic the narrator adds: "But since this observation was not egoistically made from anybody's particular viewpoint, her gaiety, rather central to all, contained nothing that wasn't indulgent and full of sympathy" (381). And as if to clinch this argument with an analogy to science that points up his objectivity, the narrator contends that this gaiety springing from the poetess's capacity to view the comic is "an element fundamental to everything" that anyone can find anywhere without especially seeking it, just as chemical analysis shows that carbon is an omnipresent element so that to find it, there is no need "to go look for it on the moon" (381). This passage elucidates a broader idea of comic vision than is embodied in *Pleasures and Days*. The narrator affirms that the comic does not rely on satire or even irony but that it results when a universal social norm is universally not respected, not even in paradise. The comic is omnipresent, and thus there is no need to seek out exotic domains to find it. Indeed, it cannot be avoided.

In *Jean Santeuil* Proust does not entirely sort this all out, for there are a good many passages set in society in which he forgets his comic perspective. And then Jean is portrayed as an actor in something like an unbelievable medieval pageant in which the noble are truly noble and the fallen snobs and evil parvenus are properly punished for not recognizing that meritorious Jean has entered the elite of the chosen, the paradise of rank, as Eliot sarcastically puts it. The sections dealing with high society in *Jean Santeuil* waver between near adulation of the ideal aristocratic society and Proust's mature comic vision in which the human monad is forever out of sync with its own pretensions and hence is nearly always comic. There is a metaphysical side to this comic vision, something akin to the universal law of inadequacy illustrated in *Pleasures and Days*. In Proust's first stories and prose poems, human inadequacy entails that communication is always marked by a disjuncture between sender and receiver. This inadequacy springs as it were from a basic ontological weakness—one as well described by the doctrine of original sin as by the metaphysics underwriting Schopenhauerian pessimism. However in *Jean Santeuil* the law of inadequacy tempers all ethical judgments brought up in comedy, hence the poetess's indulgence and sympathy. And Jean's recognition of the law of social inadequacy may explain why the increasingly disgruntled would-be poet does not flee a society he finds increasingly reprehensible. There is as little point in condemning a universal condition as there is hope of avoiding it, which means that Jean should expect to find everywhere a comic misfit between all ideals and acts. The narrator of *In Search of Lost Time*, another bildungsroman, also learns this lesson.

Nonetheless because of his stellar qualities, Jean rises quickly to the pinnacle of the paradise of rank, where his qualities can be adequately recognized by the elite capable of appreciating him. The interface between bourgeois Jean and his aristocratic friends has been variously appraised by critics. Looking at the puerile side to the representation of Jean's life in society, biographer Maurice Bardèche opines that in Jean's ascension in society, Proust was engaging in a compensative projection for defeats he may have felt himself. This projection would explain Jean's cocky readiness to fight duels when insulted or the fact that when he is disinvited to dinner by snobs, the snobs are duly punished by being excluded from the Réveillon circle. It is adequate revenge that the evil snobs sorrowfully regret that they had not recognized the power Jean had acquired by his association with the truly elite. It is, in fact, easy to argue that Proust was compensating for something when he makes sure that an unpleasant character like the social-climbing snob Madame Marmet gets her comeuppance at least three times for not recognizing Jean's elite nature. However one need not agree with Bardèche that *Jean Santeuil* is the "défoulement d'un maniaque d'orgueil" (desublimation of a maniac of pride) to recognize that the manuscripts in the book are quite unequal and that, indeed, some of them have an almost comic book quality, which explains Bardèche's ireful outburst.[7] Moreover other critics disagree with Bardèche. For example Serge Gaubert thinks that with Jean's ascension Proust effectively shows that the aristocracy really is disinterested and objective in its judgment of people. This is because the true aristocrat, not interested in social climbing or pecuniary gain, deals with other people without egoistical considerations of self-interest playing any role.[8] That would certainly be Jean's opinion when in a utopian mood. And Germaine Brée, situating the novel in its historical context, argues that Proust is in fact portraying a real historical change in mores and "collective sensibility." This change occurred at a moment when, with the emergence of a common aesthetics born of the new habits fostered by the accumulation of great wealth, the aristocracy and the bourgeoisie were tending to merge.[9] From this perspective Jean is on the cutting edge of historical change insofar as he represents in his ascension the fusion of classes.

However disinterested the truly aristocratic may be—and this is not consistently the case—the narrator's moral evaluation of what this milieu is doing to Jean is explicit in its condemnation. The indirect discourse Proust uses makes it appear that Jean probably shares at least some part of the narrator's negative judgment: "Evil [*le mal*] was for him all that hardened his mind and made it awash with noble names, witty conversations, material facts, mastered formulas . . . ." (657). Social intercourse in this upper-class milieu fills Jean's head with a flotsam and jetsam that takes away suppleness of mind. His desire to please in society causes him narcissistically to seek to be brilliant in frivolous ways—while he worries about his physical beauty. And anticipating the sustained critique of the upper class made by the narrator of *In Search of Lost Time,* Jean finds that he dissipates in chatter what he should have used in silence for his work. Proust's attack on the literary critic Sainte-Beuve is foreshadowed in this negative evaluation of social role playing. In criticizing Sainte-Beuve he shows that the snobbism of social life makes of the writer a chatterbox who talks and does not listen. Sainte-Beuve's great error, according to Proust, was to believe that conversation could be part of literary activity. The idle talk fostered by social life only demonstrates that the social self is in perpetual miscommunication with others in society. Admittedly in *Jean Santeuil* the judgment remains largely an abstract proposition, finding its main demonstration in some of the better comic scenes. But already formulated here, if not well illustrated, is Proust's basic theme that a writer's deep self is not found, or expressed, in aristocratic banter.

Proust outlines a tentative theory of ethics and writing here. On the one hand, Jean believes that the joy attached to certain ideas shows their value. He compares this self-demonstration of value—or aesthetic worth—to Descartes's proposition that self-evidence is the criteria of the truth of clear ideas. Intellectual truth and artistic representations have, for Jean, analogous criteria for validity: they carry with them an intrinsic force of conviction. Moreover all that interferes with the writer's quest for these valid ideas is evil. Jean muses that justification of this ethical truth can only be found in something like a Platonic theory of anamnesis, which is to say, through the writer's recall of ideas existing before birth, since certainly nothing in his life experience suggests the validity of any ethical ideals. As in the case in *Pleasures and Days* and its prose poem on the language of origins, it appears that Proust is not entirely ironic with Jean's reference to Plato (and the argument will recur in the narrator's meditations on Bergotte in *In Search of Lost Time*). For it is clear that neither Proust nor the narrator can easily justify the value they attribute to poetry's creation of ideas endowed with joy nor find in lived experience the grounds for an ethical principle justifying the writer's quest.

Nor is justification of Jean's belief in the ethical mission of the writer to be found in the examples of the two writers encountered in the social world. One writer is called the "old master." He has been able to turn his conventional vices, especially drink, into virtues so that poetry could become the center of his moral life. This writer sounds somewhat like a proto-Nietzschean for whom art justifies the writer's seeking the sources of his work beyond conventional good and evil (660–61). By contrast, in the brief outline of the life of the second writer, Silvain Bastelle, Proust offers a portrait of the stereotypically "successful" writer. Bastelle has everything—wealth, connections with aristocrats, fame—but his health no longer allows him to enjoy the plenitude of sensations that, one supposes, were the basis of his art, not to mention his joy in life (693). Art, along with life, has gone sour. (For reasons not clear to me, these two writers appear to be conflated into one in Fallois's edition of *Jean Santeuil*.) These fragmentary portraits of writers show that Proust was examining various ethical stances deriving from different concepts of the artist, while wondering how one can know what is valid, true, or moral in art. Finally in the Tadié edition of *Jean Santeuil* appears the brief but significant portrait of an anonymous provincial art collector who sets out another ideal about art. He buys Monet's paintings simply because he loves them. This brief anecdote, set in contrast to the dominant snobbism surrounding art in an aristocratic milieu, points up, before *Against Sainte-Beuve,* that an authentic relation to art involves no social relationships at all.

The manuscripts grouped together in the penultimate section of *Jean Santeuil,* called "On Love," begin as a response to Stendhal's theory of love, especially as he expounds it in his treatise *De l'amour* (*On Love*) of 1822. In general Proust's narrator endorses Stendhal's ideas, especially that love unfolds in a preordained series of steps according to a law of development. This acceptance does not preclude a critique of Stendhal's shortcomings, for the two writers are quite opposed when it comes to their understanding of the value of love. Proust's relation to Stendhal is ambivalent. The rationalist side in him could only be attracted to Stendhal, a witty materialist with an Enlightenment commitment to scientific explanation, who suggests in his treatise on love that medicine will finally have an explanation for it in the next century. And Proust certainly meditated on Stendhal's typology of love—with four basic types. According to Stendhal's theory of types, love springs either from pure passion, from physical attraction, from tastes, or from vanity. It would appear that the four types of love are all found illustrated in Proust's work. Physical attraction is found of course everywhere at all times, and as Stendhal notes, it is typified by an encounter with a pretty peasant in the woods—rather much like the narrator's youthful fantasies about meeting a peasant girl in the woods in "Combray." The other three types of love are conditioned by social history and changing mores. In the modern era, if not always, these types follow a programmed development that is initiated by the psychological state of "admiration"—in the seventeenth-century sense of experiencing something extraordinary—after which love proceeds through obligatory stages. After admiration the most important step is what Stendhal calls "crystallization." Drawing upon mineralogy for this metaphor, he means that the lover projects onto the beloved all the perfections that may or may not inhere to her or him, just as crystals form on a stick in the proper environment. (Swann is Proust's case study illustrating this view of the rather mechanical and hence inevitable nature of love.) Yet despite his determinism Stendhal celebrates love as a miracle created by, almost as a justification of, civilization. Proust demurs strongly on this point.

Proust adapts Stendhal's theory to his needs. For example already in *Pleasures and Days,* he portrays concretely Stendhal's idea that art, especially music, can produce the same effect on a lover as the presence of the beloved. But in *Jean Santeuil* Proust is critical of what he considered the crude materialism Stendhal had inherited from the Enlightenment and the concomitant hedonist eudemonism that led Stendhal to believe that love is to be cultivated whenever possible. For Proust love is not a justification of existence. It is a form of servitude that, as the narrator almost angrily says, makes one's inner life dependent upon another (728). Proust and his narrator are really inheritors of a pre-Enlightenment moralist tradition, that of Christian stoicism and the Ciceronian moralizing preceding it, according to which love is indeed involuntary, for it is something like a disease. Stendhal offers an etiology, as it were, of love, for what Proust and his narrator consider a malady requiring diagnosis and amenable to prognosis. Accordingly Proust modifies Stendhal to show that after the crystallization that produces the illusion of the ideal comes jealousy, another form of dependency, producing the pathology known as being deeply in love.

Stendhal had seen jealousy as an inconvenience, painful to be sure, but also as something the clever strategist might even use in making a conquest. It is not for him an essential feature of love's development. Jean discovers, however, that jealousy is the essence of romantic love. It is an inevitable part of the desire to possess. However possession is an illusion. Coveting an illusion, wanting to annihilate the distance that separates the lover and the beloved, the lover becomes sick with jealousy. In *Jean Santeuil* jealousy imposes on the lover an obsessive need to know, as if knowing something about the beloved could grant him possession. The desire for knowledge turns Jean into a near detective, causing him to investigate events and objects that might offer some truth about the beloved without her knowing that he knows. But the desire for possession also turns him into something resembling an interrogator. With this mode of inquest, he submits the beloved to a process that greatly resembles the third degree.

A number of women's names appear in the manuscripts of *Jean Santeuil*. Primarily two are objects of Jean's love, and hence jealousy, Madame S. and Françoise. Seeking knowledge about Madame S., Jean becomes an investigative voyeur, preceding Swann in this regard, trying to look into her lighted window at night and finally knocking on it to learn what is going on behind it, only to discover he has mistaken which window is hers. Like the Swann of *Swann's Way*, Jean is a clumsy detective. But detective he is: for example upon examining a letter she has asked him to mail, he deciphers through the envelope a message suggesting that, as Jean interprets it, she has not been honest with him. His love for this widow hardly abates for all that. Rather it is transformed from a case of love based on taste to one of passionate attraction, or what the narrator calls a passionate curiosity born of the desire to see what only God might know about the other (729). The narrator seems to know, if Jean does not, that this epistemological desire to be God must run aground simply because "it is the case that the reality of events eludes us" (729). Reality is elusive in spite of the most ingenuous hypotheses or calculations—all of which prefigures the repeated discoveries made by the narrator of *In Search of Lost Time* that he can know nothing certain about what others really do and think.

If events cannot be elucidated, Jean can attempt to make the beloved herself reveal the truth. In one manuscript, displaying a mastery of dialogue comparable to that found in *In Search of Lost Time*, Jean interrogates Françoise about what her activities and inclinations have been. Anticipating the epistemological torture dramatized in later scenes with Albertine, the hapless interrogator in *Jean Santeuil* finds that his beloved interlocutor possesses a willfully deficient memory in which neither her sexual activities nor erotic tastes are clear. In his desire to possess the beloved's past—a surrogate for the elusive present——Jean shows himself fundamentally deluded, for he believes, like a police interrogator, that there could be one final answer to one last question that will put his jealous need for questioning to rest. The upshot is that knowledge of the other, garnered from deciphered events or from extorted confessions, is always inadequate, for no knowledge could ever offer anything like the total possession the jealous lover ardently desires.

At one point the narrator of *Jean Santeuil*, resembling a doctor with stoic antecedents, says proleptically that Jean, like most young men, will arise from his "disease," meaning his love, stronger than he was before he was sick (797). From this perspective it seems that Proust conceived the scenes of interrogation as part of a projected narration that would tell how Jean's love, like a disease, plays out its course. For this demonstration of prognosis, the narrator needs to relate Jean's future to the past, which means that the representation of time is essential for the representation of the inevitable course of love. But in *Jean Santeuil* Proust had not found an adequate structure for representing a psychological state unfolding in time. Since the novel's narration coincides by and large with events as they occur, the narrator repeatedly feels the need to recall the past from a viewpoint in the future so that he can draw a lesson that can only be had retrospectively after the end of the love affair. The narrator is obliged rather awkwardly to leap ahead to garner some temporal distance on Jean's love. Thus the narrator tells of a later, future scene in which Françoise plays a sonata by Saint-Saëns. Jean listens to chords composing the phrase that, at the outset of their affair, had embodied their love. Now, after the end of the affair, the phrase contains a "divine memory" of what is disenchanted (797). The musical phrase allows Jean (or the narrator) to measure the nothingness of love, which is emphasized somewhat awkwardly when, again proleptically, the narrator says that years later the phrase would still be imbued with love, even after Jean has forgotten Françoise. In that projected future time, Jean will see that in some way, as an art form, the musical phrase is linked to nature, and hence he will know the sadness one feels because nature is not able to satisfy the desire for love (800). This idea about nature is none too clear but is of more than a little interest in that the narrative meandering shows that Proust had begun to seek temporal perspectives portraying the development, with ruptures and losses, of his character's self and his knowledge of love, with temporal perspectives set against each other. It was by situating the narrator of *In Search of Lost Time* in a time set after all past events that Proust found a narrative structure that obviated this kind of jumping forward in time. We will see presently here that this narrative schema allows the older narrator of *In Search of Lost Time* to live the unfolding of time past, seen from the present, as an uninterrupted series of revelations, not least of all about the disease called love.

In contrast with the texts on love, a quite different narrative experiment underlies the narration of the political events that take shape as the "Marie affair." Marie is a fictional political figure of the Third Republic. He has been identified with more than one corrupt politician who made money in the shady financing surrounding France's attempt to dig the first Panama canal. What is important is that Marie is a typical politician of the new republic. Hardly a malicious evildoer, he simply does not mind taking advantage of his position and connections to enrich himself through dubious financial transactions. Hedonistic and happily powerful, Marie is nonetheless a "good" man who helps people out, has a very virtuous Jewish wife, and is a friend of Jean's father, a political figure working in the diplomatic service. As Marie's wife is dying, she extracts a promise from Jean's mother that she and her husband will not abandon Marie, no matter what happens in the future. It appears she suspects that her husband has been less than aboveboard in his dealings and justifiably fears that the future holds dire consequences in store for him. When it comes to light that Marie is corrupt, left-wing political parties seize upon the occasion in order to prosecute him. Not surprisingly when the elder Santeuil honors the promise made to Marie's wife and stands up publicly for him, Marie's enemies circulate rumors in the press that Jean's father is corrupt, too.

The texts dealing with Marie realistically narrate events involving moral complexity. A complete novella unto themselves, in them Proust experiments in narrative dealing with politics and the type of ethical ambiguity often characterizing the public arena. This ambiguity does not characterize Marie, of course, who is unambiguously corrupt. Rather Proust introduces moral uncertainty by setting him in contrast to the head of the Socialist Party, named Couzon here, a character undoubtedly modeled on the Socialist orator Jean Jaurès. Couzon shows great ethical courage when, like Jaurès, he addresses the Chamber of Deputies and denounces the political compromise leading to France's failure to help the Christian Armenians who are being massacred by the Ottoman authorities. (For a useful comparison, Tadié includes Jaurès's speech in his edition of *Jean Santeuil*: Jaurès is still a strong presence in France.) Jean admires Couzon, and when his father is being persecuted in the press, he naively believes he can go to Couzon and ask him to use his influence to make the newspapers stop printing the slanders. There ensues an ethical debate in which Couzon says that the Marie scandal works to great advantage for the workers' party and that it is in the interest of the Socialists to get as much leverage out of the scandal as possible (544). Moreover left-wing outrage has just been aroused anew since the charges against Marie have been dismissed, precisely at the moment Jean comes to Couzon for help. It is clear that Jean's father is not dishonest and that Couzon could probably stop the press campaign against him. But the Socialist leader chooses not to do so, arguing to Jean that he does not have the right to prefer the happiness of Jean's father to the "happiness of millions of beings" who have their faith in him (552). A young Kantian, it seems, Jean argues against Couzon's type of expedient utilitarianism by stressing, fruitlessly, that the promotion of injustice, in the slander printed by the newspapers, renders those who read them unjust and increases the evil attendant thereupon. In Jean's meeting with the Socialist leader, Proust sets out an ethical dilemma in which two sets of values confront each other: on the one hand, personal honesty and integrity and, on the other, the commitment to promoting the cause of the working class, considered here as a just cause. Proust's sympathies appear to lie on both sides of the weighted scales, for the narrator empathizes with Jaurès and the Socialist cause at the same time that Jean makes a powerful argument against opportunism even if in the service of a worthy cause. After Jean's confrontation with a Couzon willing to countenance injustice—and it strikes me that finally the Socialist leader loses the debate—Proust turns for a final rendering of justice with an ironic portrayal of the unrepentant Marie, who publishes his memoires in *La Revue des Deux Mondes* while awaiting his "rehabilitation" (557). This ironic closure, giving final touches to the portrait of a scoundrel, is not the last time that Proust refers to this fashionable review that, for him, was an emblem of public foolishness and journalistic knavery.

Complementary to Proust's experimentation with the portrayal of moral ambiguities deriving from politics—from the struggle for social justice and the stains of political corruption—are the manuscripts centering on the Dreyfus affair. As mentioned in the introduction, Proust was among the first to be aware that a forgery had been used to concoct the evidence condemning the Jewish officer Dreyfus for supposedly selling military secrets to Germany. The manuscripts published in *Jean Santeuil* show how much he was concerned by the Dreyfus affair—much more directly in fact than in *In Search of Lost Time*, where the Dreyfus affair is used more as a litmus test for characters' beliefs. *Jean Santeuil* directly depicts moments in the judicial proceedings associated with the affair, such as the revision and the trial brought against Zola after he wrote his famous "J'accuse." It is true that the manuscripts dealing with the Dreyfus affair lack the unity of those depicting the Marie affair, but one may infer that at one point Proust probably intended to draw a parallel between the two incidents. Jean's debate with Couzon involves themes parallel to those that the Dreyfus affair illustrates, especially the corruption of those army officers who place their honor or duty above respecting the truth.

A significant difference between the two affairs is, however, that in describing the Dreyfus affair Proust uses the names of the historical figures actually involved. Jean goes on a daily basis to hear the trial against Zola, taking place in 1898. He spends his evenings with a friend passionately discussing the trial, as the narrator says, much like those Florentines or Athenians whose "ardent occupation was to busy themselves with the passionate affairs of the city" (565). Proust's narrator becomes in effect a historian, for example, offering a description of the army chief of staff, General de Boisdeffre, a powerful man who committed his honor to saving the army's honor at any cost. In contrast stands Colonel Picquart, the officer who refused to back down from his conviction that Dreyfus was innocent and, at the moment of narration, is in prison for defending his belief by finding evidence that damns the army's case. In Proust's portrayal of him, Picquart emerges as an extraordinary figure, comparable to the Socrates of the *Phaedo,* who prefers truth to life since, as Proust puts it in a kind of ethical manifesto, life has value only insofar as it can be devoted to the quest for truth and for doing good unto others (586). Plato was never far from Proust's intellectual horizon.

Some critics have problems dealing with the passionate idealism expressed in this historical narrative. They are uneasy with the fact that Proust was experimenting to see if a novel could deal with the highest ethical demands, with a Kantian or Platonic commitment to the ultimate value of the truth. That this is Proust's goal is shown by the way in which he highlights positively other historical figures for their commitment to truth, such as the pro-Dreyfus chemist and senator Scheurer-Kestner, and the experts in medieval manuscripts Paul Meyer, Arthur Giry, and Auguste Molinier. Meyer, Giry, and Molinier used their scientific knowledge to show that Dreyfus could not have written the document used to prove he was a traitor. These scholars motivate the narrator's praise of science, its honor, and its ethical commitment to objective truth. It is truth that exists in itself, as the narrator says, a truth not affected by opinion or human conventions (596). This view of truth is hardly postmodern, nor is the praise of science to the taste of some of our post-Nietzschean contemporaries for whom all scientific truth is opinion. But Proust was not a Nietzschean, and it is with no irony that these texts are a eulogy of the objective ideal of science. However elusive may be the truths characterizing individual human relations, he had a positive belief in science, and as we will see in discussing *In Search of Lost Time,* this lasted until the end of his life.

Both the Marie scandal and the Dreyfus affair involve conflicts of truth and convenience. In the first affair, Jean's father is truly honest, but Couzon allows expediency to determine his course of action. In the Dreyfus affair, on a grander scale, most of the army, and subsequently every anti-Semite in France, felt that the truth should be subordinated to either the defense of the army's honor or the need to inflict a lesson on Jews and, by implication, upon all those who might undermine whatever they took to be the French nation. Standing above these conflicts based upon ideological stances is the Socratic or scientific pursuit of truth, which occupies an ethical position that cannot be grasped by those for whom all belief is a matter of "form," as the narrator puts it in describing the "formalisms" that are the basis of the judgments of those who look only at appearances (571). With the idea that most judgments are based on formalisms or conventions and not a respect for truth, Proust seems to implicate most socialites, politicians, and men of letters. A notable exception is, to be sure, Jean's mother, a woman who with intuitive certainty admires Picquart's courage and generosity.

It must be said that the ideological balance between the episodes involving Marie and Dreyfus is admirable. With the Marie affair, Proust experimented to see how a fiction could form judgments about politics and its ethical debates, whereas with the Dreyfus affair, he drew upon contemporary events to add a historical dimension delving into the nature of truth and ethics. Proust was experimenting to see if fiction can depict history and history in turn can function in fiction, and in both cases to see how these modes of narration can illustrate ethics. He wanted to dramatize, by drawing parallels with ideological equanimity, that both generals and Socialist leaders can overlook truth in the service of self-interested convenience and convention. There is nothing quite like this in Proust's later writing, though these texts do anticipate Proust's use of the Dreyfus affair to point up ideology and ethics in *In Search of Lost Time.* Reaction to the affair in the novel shows who makes of truth a supreme value and who does not. It must also be said that Proust later seems to have lost much of his idealism with regard to political causes, finding apparently that politics were often as much a matter of fashion as are clothes.

For the reader of *In Search of Lost Time,* perhaps the most interesting aspect of *Jean Santeuil* is Proust's attempt in this projected novel to find a narrative strategy conveying a sense of what might be redemption effected through the recall of time past. I use the verb *convey* here, though *create* might better describe this quest for embodied redemption. This quest is narrated in the manuscripts presenting Jean's vacations spent as a boy in the village of Illiers as well as those dealing with Jean's stay, as a young man, at the Réveillon château and then in Brittany at Beg-Meil. In these manuscripts Proust experiments in narrating events that are or will be memory, and the possibility of the redemption of these events. He envisages resurrection through recall of time lost or through the narration of cyclical events that abolishes time. In fine he seeks a strategy that might give the lie to the nihilism of his own belief that all experience is destined to the nothingness that ultimately characterizes, say, Jean's love for Françoise. Ontology and aesthetics merge in this quest: Proust wants to write a novel overcoming the human being's fall into time. This kind of redemption usually presupposes transcendence of some sort, though it is not clear that this is the case in Proust. By setting Jean's experience within a framed narrative, he seems to want to situate the locus for the redemption of experience squarely in the framework of the circumscribed textual world. Therefore one may doubt that the quest can exist outside the text that expresses it. This is to say that redemption must take place in the world within the framework of C.'s putative fictional work. The world to be redeemed is circumscribed doubly by Jean's perception, and the fictional representation of that perception. I stress this complexity to suggest why Proust did not manage to put all this together, for the third-person narrative in *Jean Santeuil,* unfolding as the events take place, is hopelessly welded to the present—even if C. is dead. However, as we will now see, Proust did work out some strategies for narration that he subsequently put to use in the same quest in *In Search of Lost Time.*

In the manuscripts presenting Illiers, the village that is the scene of Jean's childhood, Proust sketches out a cyclical replay of time lived as recurrence by Jean when he is on vacation. The situation is quite close to that in "Combray." An ideal day in the child's paradise unfolds through recurrent scenes, starting in the morning and lasting until night. This sense of a cycle is perhaps not as well developed as in the section set at Réveillon describing the cycle of seasons, where Proust straightforwardly narrates the seasons' unfolding without concern for their being recalled as time past. To create the paradise of Illiers, he aims at the re-creation of the past in an experiment in narrating time-annulling recurrences. To this end he uses the imperfect tense for the narration of events—the tense he described as "melancholy" in a footnote to Ruskin that he wrote after he had started using it in *Jean Santeuil.* Narrated in the imperfect tense, the descriptions of Illiers emphasize the repetitive regularity of natural changes. Manifesting itself in the gardens of Illiers, nature seems to be an animated presence, perhaps in a pantheistic sense. But the garden also takes on a mythical dimension: it inevitably figures the proto-Christian paradise once found in the Edenic garden.

For example Jean wanders in a garden in which flowers are the "blessed, giving to whomever looks at them an unheard of happiness, the idea that the gardener is a blessed one, that this garden is paradise" (181). As a boy he finds himself in the "happy kingdom" embodying the "sweetness of our childhood" (this, I note, set against other texts showing that he had experienced his childhood mainly as a time of anguish). The temporal perspective on the happy kingdom is problematic here, for the narrator, in viewing this sweetness, must state proleptically that an aged Jean will recall this happiness at a moment when a sunbeam re-creates in the future shadows such as he once knew them in the garden (182–83). In other words in order to create the unfolding sense of epiphany lying in the past, Proust is again obliged to create memory by a forward projection: hence the narrator suggests that Jean *will* one day recall the world of Illiers as an immense garden in which he once found, during the month of May (the month dedicated to the Virgin Mary), that flowers naturally figure altars just as altars demand to be covered with flowers. The past is thus proleptically redeemed—the past in which the virgin's own hawthorn, usually with white but sometimes with pink flowers, plays a central role in converting nature into a chapel. The garden of the past is endowed with a sacred aura: "The pink hawthorn caused to shimmer, as reliquaries shimmer in dark chapels, the brightly rose rosary, almost red, of its marvelous flowers" (219). These analogies work back and forth in scenes of future memories to make of nature a church and of the church a flowering garden in which hedges are "finely toothed chapels" and the flowers of the wild rose [*églantines*] form a tabernacle (224). As in "Combray" the text's religious images endow the natural world with religious connotations, and they in turn convert flowering foliage into a chapel or an altar. Childhood and paradise become metaphorically interchangeable.

Not surprisingly, then, Sunday occupies a large place in the cycle of events centered on Illiers. The Sunday Mass is the recurrent event that brings together all the members of the town in a repetition of social rituals. All of this anticipates the village in "Combray" in some detail, though it is also rather disparate when compared to the structural complexity Proust elaborates for his later paradise. The paradise of *In Search of Lost Time* has been lost to the aging narrator through the passage of time, so that the novel exists as a narrated memory, not as a potential or projected one. The paradise of *Jean Santeuil* will be lost in the future, but for most of its narration, as is the case with the narration about Jean's love life, it unfolds concurrently with the instance of narration as something that the young Jean experiences at the moment. In brief Proust's experiment with the childhood paradise of Illiers undoubtedly demonstrated to him that he needed a different narrative structure if the narrated experience is to exist as the paradise of time past and not as a fleeting moment of what is really a yet to be redeemed present.

Another strategy for overcoming time is found in the description of Jean's stay at the château of Réveillon as a guest of his friend Henri de Réveillon. Without concern for the future, Proust experiments with the narration of cyclical recurrence suggesting recurrent activity that transcends linear time. The narration is thus centered on the cycle of the seasons with their repetition marking the passage of time during Jean's stay. (This is not so clear in Fallois's version of the manuscripts, and in this regard Pierre Clarac's and Tadié's ordering is superior.) The cycle depicted in the narration underscores that Jean's stay with his aristocratic hosts lasts off and on over the better part of a year, from spring until winter storms arrive, but the duration of the stay is not the major issue. Proust's rhetoric endows the narration of this sojourn with a sense of recurrence that creates a deeper sense of chronological repetition. He again uses the imperfect tense throughout to suggest the recurrence of the routine marking Jean's stay. His later melancholic evaluation of this tense is no more evident in this part of *Jean Santeuil* than in the description of Illiers's paradise. Proust uses the tense to narrate a cyclical repetition of natural events that hardly seem to want to disappear in their narration, as he put it in the footnote to "On Reading." The repetition created by the imperfect tense, here the fundamental narrative tense to describe seasonal events, suggests on the contrary the eternal return of the events. This recurrence is set off by the occasional reference to an exceptional happening or to events that recur at irregular times, such as rainy days and visits. These singular events are set off by "sometimes" or "one day" and other temporal indicators that underscore the imperfect tense's repetition by interrupting it.

Life in the château—which is to say, in something like utopia—is tied to the cycle of the seasons. To give the "color" of the seasons, Proust excels in describing the flora that recurs in marking each moment of a season's passage, right up to the moment when the trees' bark is in harmony with the lack of vegetation. Jean arrives at the château in the spring to find flowers that are the "creatures of time" (312). They undergo transformation, summer arrives, and Jean goes back to Paris. But he is soon back at Réveillon, despite the duke's reticence at inviting him for the "bad season." Jean returns to pursue the poem of four seasons that leads him to discover the poetry of places. Places are persons, Jean thinks, and they can be desired much as one desires those people who, unlike places, change. As a locus of stability, from young Jean's perspective, places seemingly promise redemption (395). And so Réveillon, like the garden of Illiers, is one of those places the resurrection of which might transcend the fall into time. However at the novel's putative end, Jean learns that even places change, for the Auteuil garden of his childhood has been obliterated, and the garden paradise can only exist as memory. Paradise must be lost to be resurrected, as the narrator says in *Time Regained*.

The narration of the cycle of seasons spent at Réveillon accompanies another version of Proust's vision of the utopia that, in the introduction to *Pleasures and Days*, he says he once entertained. The château of Réveillon represents, almost allegorically, a social cell in which the chosen elite gather—members of the family, neighboring aristocrats, writers—at various moments in the seasons' unfolding. The portraits of some of these characters are comic, to be sure, for Proust was also broadening his narrative palette, here with the development of a form of the comic that eschews the near cynicism of *Pleasures and Days*. In the first part of *Jean Santeuil*, Jean's entrance into utopia is not at odds with this comedy. The Réveillon château is above all the place in which young Jean feels himself at home, no longer alienated in a world in which "the woods, the vines, the stones themselves had harmonized themselves with the light of the sun and the purity of the sky, and when the sky clouded over, as if by a change of tonality, the multitude of leaves, the earth of the roads, the roofs of the town, all remained united in a new world" (348). Initially it seems to Jean that he was in unison with all things, and he felt perfect enjoyment [*jouissance*] resulting from this harmony. This is not an emotion frequently felt by the narrator of *In Search of Lost Time*.

The notion of divine harmony is part of the romantic pantheistic notion of universal analogy in which all parts of the natural world entertain relations with each other. Jean's sense of harmony reflects this notion that unity underlies paradise. There are many sources for this notion of unity. Jean's sense of it surely reflects Baudelaire's vision of correspondences among all parts of the temple called nature. Jean's romantic inheritance also includes the poet Alphonse de Lamartine's desire that nature should perpetually incarnate past experience in eternal memory—as every French lycée student knows from the poem "Le lac" ("The Lake"). And Jean gives exposition to the theory of the romantic philosopher Friedrich Schelling, according to which the artist is the mouthpiece for nature. However any question of "influence" here is subject to a caveat. It is obvious that, in the manuscripts dealing with Illiers and in "Beg-Meil," Proust knows his romantic poets and thinkers. This does not mean that he is trying to be their mouthpiece. Rather a more fruitful perspective on Proust is to consider the young writer to be an experimenter with ideas taken from many sources. And especially in *Jean Santeuil,* he is experimenting with setting aesthetic and philosophical ideas in different texts and contexts to try them out and see if they are adequate forms of response to experience, for instance, the experience of loss and decline. The idea of experimentation is especially fruitful in reading the section called "Beg-Meil," one of the richest texts in *Jean Santeuil*.[10]

What is most engaging about the "Beg-Meil" section is Proust's dealing with the natural world. In it he uses several different seashores as locations for Jean's promenades. Walking by the sea, he discovers that nature knows what the potential writer has to express. Obligingly nature leads him to the place where he can discover it. He discovers nothing less than "the fabulous world of our memories which has become the world of truth" (460). This revelation of truth occurs on the shore of Lake Geneva, an inland lake that awakens in Jean the memory of the Brittany sea he had earlier loved. With a curious shift to first-person narration, Jean recalls the image "of a life lived for a long time" whose beauty and charm "resonate in my heart"; the life is one that lies "beyond the indifferent spectacle of present life," in a place where he encounters "the resurrected image of the past, the feeling that animated it, a charm of the imagination that attached us definitively to life and embodies it in us." Finally he perceives the "transmutation of memory into a directly perceived reality" (462). The "Beg-Meil" manuscripts conclude with this vision of the redemption of experience, conceived as time past emerging when the present moment coincides in some way with a moment in the past (464). It is understatement to say that this leitmotif is one that Proust later develops at length.

These passages praising nature reflect the philosophical viewpoint that the imagination can grasp in nature an "eternal essence," which leads the narrator to the hypothesis that "our true nature might lie outside of time" (465). The romantic belief that self-fulfillment is impossible is perhaps the most immediate source for the idea that the imagination cannot be content with either time present or time past. However Proust enlarges upon this source and draws upon an extended lineage of poets and thinkers who have confronted the dismal prospects of life lived as the fall into time. Not only Baudelaire, Lamartine, and Schelling but Schopenhauer, Plato, and Spinoza seem to lie behind the text as the third-person narrator and Jean, as well as a first-person narrator, orchestrate a consciousness struggling to overcome the inadequacy of the present. A great deal of Western thought resonates in the mind that Proust portrays here. For he shows it at work trying to pin down the proper concepts and images leading to redemption, perhaps through resurrection, perhaps through finding a harmonious relation with nature, and perhaps through a revelation of the atemporal transcendence Proust does not quite believe in. In fine the narrative experiment centers on the mind grappling with its experience—a drama that Proust continues to enact in the narrative quest of *In Search of Lost Time*. In "Beg-Meil" the drama begins with the narrator drawing on what education and tradition offer him for making sense of experience. He studies in effect his own mind and its contents as he seeks perhaps contradictorily to cobble together a general theory to make sense of a unique experience. In the first draft state offered by "Beg-Meil," the orchestration of consciousness is, understandably, not well crafted, for different points of view seem to emerge and even clash at times as Proust seeks a narrative voice.

This brief discussion of Proust's play with ideas and theories cannot really do justice to the empirical riches of the experience narrated in several of the passages of "Beg-Meil," such as the narration of a coastal storm or the scenes describing Jean's anguish at being separated from his mother. The image of the bedroom as a place of exile is also sketched out in this section, again in anticipation, as it were, of the first pages of "Combray." In the later work, the narrator's multiple bedchambers are evoked as the primary locus for recall of the past—but this only after Proust finally resolved the problems of narrative structure for dealing with time past and present by collapsing narrator and protagonist into one being, existing in the undefined present and in multiple past times. Structural differences aside, the overall shape of narration in "Beg-Meil" is nonetheless suggestive of how *In Search of Lost Time* first took form. The narration in this section represents emblematically, in miniature, the shape of the writer's quest: it leads from anguish through deception and finally to a revelation that somehow one might, as the last line in the section says, tear oneself from slavery to the present to be inundated with a feeling of a permanent life (465). Redemption is postulated here as the goal to be realized at the end of the writer's quest.

Redemption does not occur in the manuscripts that seem logically to be the end of *Jean Santeuil*. Jean's parents are destined to die, and the garden at Auteil is lost. Probably with no conclusion in mind, Proust set the work aside and began the work on Ruskin, before returning to the project of finding aesthetic salvation in his own work. After the translations of Ruskin, his next major attempt at writing is in some sense a return to what he did not complete with *Jean Santeuil*. Proust then began his quest for an aesthetics of redemption, however, with a critical liquidation of Sainte-Beuve and his critical and aesthetic legacy. The manuscripts of this new project, abandoned by Proust when he finally conceived the structure of *In Search of Lost Time,* are the second important group of texts that Proust left unpublished. These manuscripts, now published as *Against Sainte-Beuve,* lead directly to the novel that is the reason why we want to understand Proust. In fact readers who have read *In Search of Lost Time* probably find more that is familiar in *Against Sainte-Beuve* than in *Jean Santeuil*—however much there is in *Jean Santeuil* that Proust redeployed in *In Search of Lost Time*. In any case in the following discussion I refer mainly to Bernard de Fallois's version of *Against Sainte-Beuve,* though I do so without endorsing the idea that there is, or could be, any definitive ordering of the manuscripts. Fallois's version has the virtue of clearly showing that Proust, in trying to reconcile theory and poetry, fiction and philosophy, became for a time a literary critic who lectures on literature in texts that might have become a novel. Sometimes his lectures take the form of a conversation with—or discourse directed at—his mother. So we might call this project that falls between the work on Ruskin and the beginning of the great novel, "For *maman* and against Sainte-Beuve."

First some context: after finishing the Ruskin project and, equally important, after his mother's death in 1905, Proust found himself at a turning point. *Jean Santeuil* was a dead project, and he had no more interest in Ruskin or translations. He then apparently thought of writing a critical study that, as several manuscripts suggest, would take the shape of a narrative fiction embodying the theory. In his introduction to *Against Sainte-Beuve,* Fallois says this project began to take shape in 1905, was worked on mainly in 1908, and was abandoned in 1909 when work on *In Search of Lost Time* supplanted it. Fallois cites one of Proust's letters to confirm this viewpoint: he wrote to a friend in November 1908 that he was hesitating between writing an article, something like an critical essay by the literary historian Hippolyte Taine, or undertaking the narration of a morning during which he would tell his mother, while lying in bed, what he wants to write about the critic Sainte-Beuve.[11] With hindsight one sees that the embodiment of aesthetic theory in a fiction was about to become a key for the conception of *In Search of Lost Time*. Of course it would not take the form of the conversations with his mother, even if the bed is a privileged location in the novel.

I want to make a few critical distinctions to clarify the discussion of the texts in *Against Sainte-Beuve,* distinctions that will be useful later in the discussion of *In Search of Lost Time*. First, in these unpublished manuscripts, Proust is concerned with literary theory or *descriptive* aesthetics. He wants to describe objectively what actually takes place in literary texts. Hence he rejects as a matter of fact Sainte-Beuve's idea that a writer's biography can shed light on the aesthetic intent of a writer's work. Biography can only describe the writer's social or exterior self. For Proust it is an empirical fact that the writer's social self is not, nor can it be, the origin of the writer's work. In addition to enunciating this kind of theoretical proposition, he is also interested in *prescriptive* aesthetics, which is to say, in questions about what a work should be in order to be of value. Evaluation of literature also brings up questions of descriptive aesthetics. A critic must know what literature actually is before the critic can have an objective basis for judging whether a writer's work has any value or not. It is from both a prescriptive as well as from a descriptive viewpoint that Proust rejects what he sees as Saint-Beuve's confusing the interest a writer's personality may offer with the value of the writer's work. The boundary line between descriptive theory and prescriptive judgment is not always clear, but when Sainte-Beuve's value judgments are brought up, Proust is never hesitant to judge that the critic failed in his task, both through sins of commission and omission. Sainte-Beuve judged canonical writers, such as Balzac and Baudelaire, with lamentable results, and others, such as Stendhal or Nerval, he failed to judge at all. Because Sainte-Beuve did not understand how a work functions to express the writer's deep, which is to say nonsocial, self, he failed at both descriptive and prescriptive tasks. Proust is adamant: it is for the expression of deep vision that the writer must be judged.

In addition Proust also offers practical criticism in these manuscripts. In his practical criticism, as distinct from his descriptive theory, he shows how literary texts generate meanings. Proust is a critic who, with great insight, describes, in conversations with his mother, the meaning of works by specific writers such as Nerval, Baudelaire, and Balzac. It seems accurate to say that in some texts in *Against Sainte-Beuve,* he wants to do criticism just as much as he wants to write fiction. His staged scenes of a critic-narrator talking to his mother about Baudelaire or Balzac are highly contrived but quite successful for their critical commentary. Proust's critical understanding of these writers (and later Flaubert) is impressive.

Proust's practical criticism thus succeeds qua criticism, that is, as judged by its logical exposition and truth value. Logic and truth values are the criteria by which one judges a normal expository essay. If his criticism is remarkable, then one is prompted to ask why Proust eschews the expository prose that both criticism and theory usually use. Why does he write the criticism by setting it in a fictional framework? This question concerns directly *Against Sainte-Beuve,* but also *In Search of Lost Time* and its elaborate project of theorizing about aesthetics. I would not argue that Proust is not respectful of logic and truth values, but it is true that fiction does not need to respect these criteria insofar as it makes no claims to such value in the sense that expository prose does. Fiction often may include true statements, of course, but it is not obliged to do so, and the freedom granted by fiction may explain why Proust prefers to eschew the use of expository prose and to place his criticism in a fictive discourse. By using a fictive axis of discourse in which a speaker-narrator addresses somebody, either explicitly in the fictional world of discourse or implicitly to an observer of that fictional world, Proust can distance his discourse from claims to truth value. The critical discourse acquires in this way a dramatic value. In several of these texts, for example, the mother is the addressee of the discourse, though in others there is no clear interlocutor, but the context is still a fictive one, and the reader's interest is claimed as much by the drama of the mind at work as by the truth of the ideas expounded. The reader's final impression may be that Proust does not really want to write expository prose in Taine's manner because he is more interested in the dramatic value of ideas than in setting out the absolute truth. He does not want to detract from dramatic tension, elaborated by conflicting hypotheses, by being obliged at each step to defend his ideas in terms of propositional truth. The eventual result of this experimentation will be the pages of fictional theory developed in *In Search of Lost Time,* which is to say, pages of aesthetic philosophy inscribed in the drama of narrative consciousness— what we have already seen tentatively attempted in *Jean Santeuil.*

There is a poignant autobiographical side to *Against Sainte-Beuve.* Mixing fiction and autobiography, Proust uses his now-deceased mother as a sounding board for his critical discussion. In giving her a role in a discussion of Saint-Beuve's "method," Proust can at least symbolically show her that her son has not failed in life. This symbolic enactment is done with affectionate humor. For example the text called "L'article dans 'Le Figaro'" ("The Article in *Le Figaro*") presents Proust's comic considerations of himself as a published writer—at last success. To this end he describes his reaction to receiving the morning newspaper in which appears an article he has written. Indulging in irony about his own vanity, he says it appears impossible to him, now a published writer, that the ten thousand readers who are opening their morning newspaper at the very moment he does do not feel the same admiration for him that he feels for himself. His mother serves largely as a vehicle for moving the fiction along, since she slyly places the journal on his table along with the mail and remains so that Proust, with comic vanity, can try to get information about how well his article has been received.

Once the mother fulfills her role in "The Article in *Le Figaro*," however, she is lost from view. Reverting to poetic association as a principle for composition, the usually nocturnal author sees that, being awake for once to see the morning light, he experiences a desire to travel. A series of associations leads him away from the domestic scene as he imagines that a train carries him away to a place where sensations of beauty give rise to theoretical considerations about what beauty is. At the end of "The Article in *Le Figaro*," the narrator becomes a straightforward aesthetician, lecturing to inform the reader that the effect that beauty has is an individual trait, not a general category. He clinches this argument about beauty by declaring that he is interested not simply in beautiful women but in a specific beautiful girl; comparably not just in beautiful cathedrals but in the unique beauty of the cathedral of Amiens. And so the manuscript ends, drawing upon Proust's encounter with Ruskin and stressing that validity in art can only be found in the experience of the unique, the individual, the singular. The narrative and the critical exposition, if that is the term, encompass at least three disparate modes of writing.

Proust's mother is thus a character used to create the dramatic mode. For instance she shares the stage with him in "Le rayon de soleil sur le balcon" ("The Sunbeam on the Balcony"). This text begins as a potential fiction with Proust the narrator recalling that lunch on Saturday, as in "Combray," was a special ritual, taking place an hour earlier than during the week. The narration again turns away from developing a dramatic fiction as the narrator's attention follows the movement of a sunbeam, which gives rise to another more or less straightforward meditation on the aesthetics of description. The longest dramatic narrative involving the mother is found in the next text, "Conversation avec Maman" ("Talking to Mama"), in which the narrator recalls Venice and contrasts it with the province where he finds himself. He converses with his mother and reflects, in nostalgic recall, on her Jewish face, her Christian sweetness, and what he calls her Jansenist courage. Presaging themes developed in *In Search of Lost Time*, Proust says that his mother's favorite play is Racine's *Esther*, the embodiment of these three traits. He subsequently tells his mother that, having published an article in *Le Figaro*, he now has a topic for his next essay—notably one against Sainte-Beuve. The manuscript comes to an abrupt end with his mother's reply to Proust's question as to whether she knows what Sainte-Beuve's method is. She encourages him to continue by telling him to act as if she did not know. Symbolically this maternal encouragement might seem to be Proust's own spurring himself on to write. However the text that responds to the encouragement is a separate piece, "La méthode de Sainte-Beuve," which does not involve the mother. To be sure "The Method of Sainte-Beuve" could be read as a discourse meant for the mother, who wants to hear her son's ideas about the famous critic, the critic's failures, and, by implication, her son's successes.

Proust's mother also reappears in texts on Baudelaire and on Balzac, writers about whom she apparently had rather negative opinions that were a challenge to Proust's admiration of them. "Sainte-Beuve and Baudelaire" might well be titled "Mother and Baudelaire," for in it Proust wants to convince her that this poet, whom she only "half likes," is a major literary voice. He first upbraids Sainte-Beuve for his lack of sensitivity to Baudelaire's poetry and also for Sainte-Beuve's not helping the poet, his supposed friend, when testimony from a public figure of Sainte-Beuve's stature would have been useful to Baudelaire during the latter's trial for obscenity in *The Flowers of Evil*. Then Proust turns from considerations of Sainte-Beuve's failure to understand the nature of great poetry in order to address his critical discussion of Baudelaire to his mother. More precisely Proust tries to convince her that "cruel Baudelaire" presents suffering in his work with an impassive stance that vouchsafes truth to his portrayals of fate's victims—including the poet himself. Proust calls upon his favored critical categories to frame an argument to convince his dubious mother: Baudelaire's poems are so many fragments of a unified world of associations, tied together metaphorically, possessing their own "colors" that make up the emotive force linking Baudelaire to a greater world of art. In short, as is the case of every authentic artist, underlying all Baudelaire's poems is one vision.

"Sainte-Beuve and Balzac" also involves dramatic tension in its presentation of Proust's critical argument, for he begins by conceding to his mother that she is not wrong to dislike Balzac for the writer's well-known vulgarity. He recognizes that the writer in life was a parvenu and that his vulgarity is reflected in his language. But this concession to his mother is really made so that Proust can establish a context for his laudatory exposition of Balzac's theory that the novel's function is to explore the historical conditions in which a potentially "great man" flounders in anonymity. The theory may be flawed, Proust says, but it suggests the new dimension found in Balzac's work and, consequently, in the historical development of the novel. Proust also concedes to his classical-minded mother that Balzac does not fulfill the expectations one has of great literature, which is, he says, echoing Aristotle, the cathartic function of purging passion. Reversing field, Proust then claims that it is Balzac's lack of style that constitutes his power: Balzac hides nothing; he says everything (248). By this he seems to mean that, unlike Flaubert, who dramatizes through description, Balzac does not show what happens. He simply says what happens, which means that the reader has no choice but to believe Balzac's narrator.

As the essay "Sainte-Beuve and Balzac" develops, Proust's mother again fades out of sight so that when he reaches the point at which he wants to explain Balzac's genius, she does not appear to be in the scene to hear it. Proust may get so carried away by his defense of Balzac's genius that he forgets his mother, but he does not forget Sainte-Beuve, against whom he presses the charge that the critic understood nothing, especially not that Balzac's genius was to invent the novel of recurrent characters in which the individual novel has less importance than the "cycle" in which the characters occur. Pointing up the importance of cycles and recurrence in Balzac, Proust thus defines the total vision underlying all the individual novels. This idea of the cycle of events and characters is certainly not without relevance for the genesis of *In Search of Lost Time*.

In "Sainte-Beuve and Balzac," Proust mixes descriptive and prescriptive notions to stress Balzac's originality, in such a way that the notion of originality is at once prescriptive (originality is good) and descriptive (Balzac is original). This dual thrust of the notion of originality underwrites Proust's description of the history of successful art and literature. Their history is a successive history of originalities, and that is what it should be. Balzac's originality is that he captured reality in such a way that he endowed with literary value a "thousand things" that until his time were considered "too contingent" to be incorporated into a literary work (263). Proust's description of Balzac's historical originality is thus a form of positive evaluation. Perhaps more purely descriptive is his idea that Balzac, in showing that the truth of individual acts is contingent and individual, laid bare a law of contingencies demonstrated by all events in realist fiction. This can be taken as a definition of realism. From Proust's point of view, this is also positive, for realism in this sense is original. Moreover his claim that contingency, not necessity, is demonstrated by the Balzacian novel is a key for understanding Proust's own view of how fiction should function. The belief in the contingency of real events, viewed from the individual's viewpoint, is one of the most important philosophical viewpoints underlying his version of the realist novel. Necessity, as Spinoza has it, is imposed by the view of the totality of being, but of course nobody ever has that view. Implicitly arguing against the Spinoza he read with Daru, Proust argues that the creative imagination's domain can and should be the contingent world of individual details where, as Proust wrote about Chardin's realism, nothing is banal.

The penultimate text of Fallois's edition of *Against Sainte-Beuve* is "Retour à Guermantes" (translated as "The Return," though it should be "Return to the Guermantes," Proust's fictive aristocratic family). In this text the reader encounters names that occur again in *In Search of Lost Time*. Proust's mother is also introduced again as an interlocutor, though the scene with her is entirely fictive. The narrator explains to her the charms of the château of the Guermantes, whose importance for Proust is that their domain is a place in which the past lives on into the present. For instance their eleventh-century chapel is a place in which past time has been concretized in stone. The narrator tells her that upon entering it, he finds a past world sublimated into the present in which, as he puts it, time has taken on the form of space. In the presence of a few stones, he says, it is as if he had walked onto the stage of Shakespeare's theatrical world, where the historical past is resurrected by being illuminated with simple stage directions. He compares this experience to that of entering into the medieval world re-created in images that his mother projects onto the wall with a magic lantern, images that make the Merovingian past come alive through illumination. This same experience of the Middle Ages when projected onto a wall with a magic lantern is much more disquieting for the child of "Combray." As is frequently the case in Proust, a theme that is positive in one context becomes negative in another.

There is a rupture in the narration about the Guermantes as Fallois has constructed it in "Return to the Guermantes." The narrator ceases to address his mother but evokes her, now dead, in the third person and recalls the memory they jointly had of the medieval cathedral at Chartres (which recalls that Proust had originally set Combray in central France, near Chartres, and not in the north so that it would be destroyed during World War I). Tied up with this recall of the cathedral is a fictive memory in which the boy experiences the recurrent drama of separation that occurred when Proust, having now become a child in his own fiction, accompanied his mother on a train from the fictive village of Combray to the real town of Chartres. After visiting the cathedral there, his mother would return to Paris, and the boy would return to Combray for the duration of vacation time. Proust's younger brother gets a role in this fiction: he, too, wants prevent their mother from catching the train for Paris, so that the drama of separation is played out here by two siblings, not by the narrator alone as in "Combray." The brother's career is of short duration in Proust's fiction, perhaps because it is difficult to share anguish.

The narration of the memory breaks off in Fallois's version of "Return to the Guermantes." Then the narrator finds himself again with his mother, and the published text ends when the adult narrator, directly addressing her as his "little mother," remembers the need he felt for her in the very recent past, after viewing Chartres on the horizon as seen from the Guermantes way—one of the two ways that leave Combray and point to the narrator's future in *In Search of Lost Time*. After the sight of the cathedral—and it can in fact be seen from a great distance across the plain—he could not stay away from his mother. Fiction and autobiography are mixed here in various proportions, though the autobiographical seems to dominate when Proust's narrator—his sometime fictional double—tells his mother that his need for her is like the need one has for air when one is suffocating. Proust's suffocation from asthma acquainted him undoubtedly with the kind of psychological anguish that can also stop breathing. The physical and the psychological are frequently united in his world: they are the two ways the sick body and the unsubstantial self experience the fall and loss that characterize life in time. This anguish is recurrent in his fiction—though his anguish about losing his mother was hardly a fiction.

The affection and anguish associated with Proust's mother in the text dealing with Chartres and the Guermantes domain reveal that, as he was writing it, he was still working through his mourning. Her death is explicitly mentioned here in memoriam. However if several of the fictions and most of the theoretical ideas of *Against Sainte-Beuve* are reconfigured in *In Search of Lost Time*, after the opening narration of "Combray," the mother will cease to be the affective presence in the novel that she is in these manuscripts. Perhaps this is because, having overcome his trauma, Proust then ceased writing autobiography. His new self-mastery allowed him to recast and transpose the autobiographical reality involved in the dramas of separation narrated in earlier texts. In fine before he could write fiction, he had to surmount anguish: he did so by becoming a writer of resurrections, motivated by the angst born of separation and dread of annihilation. To those of a Freudian persuasion, I propose, moreover, that Proust's shift from autobiography to fiction was not simply a way of refiguring his Oedipal complex, for the drama involved in his drama of separation is more inclusive than Freud's Oedipal allegory. To lay bare the mechanism of anguish behind the power of love, Proust dramatizes the separation that causes the anguish and then shows that it is concomitant with the need to reclaim and resurrect the past. This is a contingent relation, not necessarily a causal one, however universal may be the human condition in which death entails traumatic separation from what constitutes one's being—such as the mother for the narrator in "Return to Guermantes." In Proust's unique and yet quite general drama of separation, the loss of the wholeness the mother once seemed to guarantee is experienced as the obliteration of the totality of what gave value to existence.

"Return to Guermantes" shows, in addition, that Proust has tapped into the anguish that lies at the origins of much Western religious feeling. It is this anguish about obliteration that creates the need for tradition and the art that creates the tradition keeping alive the past, wherein, as Proust has it, time takes on the shape of space. With this belief he was committed to the proposition that anguish might be overcome by resurrecting the past as a meaningful present—which is of course the basis for Christianity. Proust's genius is to find this need for redemption at the origins of family life, not to mention passionate love affairs. With the resurrection of a present, anguish about annihilation of the past is annulled—and then resurrection overcomes separation in a vision of unity. In that moment, as Proust puts it in the sixth text of *Against Sainte-Beuve,* where he describes a ray of sunshine that calls forth layers of time past, death no longer has any importance (130). And so also reads the conclusion of *In Search of Lost Time.*

Critical considerations of art and redemption are explicitly laid out in what Fallois titled the preface to *Against Sainte-Beuve.* Rejecting abstract theory in this text, Proust minimizes the role of intelligence in art, even though he is also aware that, in the work he was then envisaging, critical intelligence will play a key role. Examining his own attitude toward intelligence, Proust expresses misgivings about his project of writing about Sainte-Beuve—he dismissively says the critic's "method" ultimately does not really seem all that important anyway. But Proust also asserts, with the sense of paradox that characterized him to the end of his life, that it is up to intelligence to judge that intelligence should not receive the crown in the hierarchy of values. Or as he concludes, intelligence is the only faculty empowered to grant to instinct the crown of its superiority. Instinct is a jarring notion here, and I do not think that the term is quite what Proust wants. The preface shows that what deserves the crown in the hierarchy of values are those moments in which something like the essence of the past is restored and the fullness of lost being is recovered. Instinct is a concept taken from nineteenth-century philosophical discourse, opposing nonrational impulse to intelligence, and Proust's own examples show that the overworked concept of instinct is not really what he means, even if it serves to focus attention on whatever stands in opposition to the imperial claims of the rational intellect.

The preface offers in fact three concrete examples of what Proust means, all of which will be used again, with little modification, at pivotal moments in *In Search of Lost Time*. These examples are all moments of pure perception: the taste of toast dipped in tea, the rough feel of paving stones in a courtyard, and the sound of a hammer struck against the wheels of a railroad car. These moments of perception, unfiltered through the intellect, offer sensorial means for effecting the resurrection of the past. Each moment recalls "a past impression, a bit of pure life that has been purely preserved," which has no relationship with intelligence nor with the kind of memory that one uses voluntarily to recall the past (58). The taste of toast brings about remembrance of the summer vacation home of the narrator's childhood; the pavement stones are linked to days he spent in Venice; and the sound of the hammer against a wheel conjures up a day of travel he once undertook. Proust seemingly excludes vision from these sensations, though he admits he often stops and tries to see the past in the outlines of things. The sense of sight functions in dream, however, and Proust implies that there is an equivalency between the past he recalls in vision and moments of anguish, experienced in dream, that are associated with his mother. These moments of dream possess the same reality as the time lived when he was a child, which, as he says, is now already just a dream. In contrast to these moments of perception are truths relying upon his intelligence. These intellectual truths are of little existential value when compared to the essence of one's self revealed in the recovery of the past brought about by its recall caused by present sensations (61). In this prefatory text, Proust's notions about redemption are taking definitive shape, beginning with the disgruntled rejection of the belief that the rational operations of mind can produce much of anything of existential value.

The three texts following the preface are also sketches that anticipate Proust's future novel. "Sommeils" ("In Slumbers") outlines moments of anguish and illumination experienced by the sleeping narrator. "Chambres" ("Bedrooms") offers variations on the same theme of sleep and sleep's demonstration of the mind's malleability. In dreams the mind is cut free from the moorings of intelligence, which allows the mind to experience its potential autonomy from rational constraints. The third text, "Journées" ("The Days"), is a nearly autobiographical description of how

Proust's mind adapts to seasons and weather after he has begun staying up all night and sleeping during the day in his Paris apartment. He describes the meandering of his mind as it entertains travel fantasies. These fantasies in turn lead to meditation on the happiness offered by the presence of beautiful young girls, anticipating the blossoming adolescents of *In Search of Lost Time*. Proust's mind is receptive to all sensations, including the odor of petrol that enters the room. The smell of urban pollution sets off a strangely exuberant meditation on the rural places associated with the odor of gasoline and the joy of being on the road. Proust declares it a delicious sensation, because it sends his mind traveling in the past, for example through the wheat fields of the Beauce plateau, which one crosses when traveling to Chartres from Paris (92–93). Apparently there are no limits to the types of sensations the unfettered mind can use to resurrect the past.

Equally as interesting as Proust's aesthetics and metaphysics, as outlined in *Against Sainte-Beuve,* is the articulation here of his enchantment and disenchantment with the nobility. The treatment of social themes presages the same disabused vision of society found later in *In Search of Lost Time;* and arguably they are not greatly different from those found in *Pleasures and Days.* Resembling his own young narrator in *In Search of Lost Time,* Proust claims he is drawn to the aristocracy because they offer him enchantment through the evocation of the historic past associated with their names. In explaining this enchantment, he broaches something like a theory of poetic language, based on the distinction of utilitarian words and the evocative power of names. Mere everyday words or common nouns stand in opposition to people's names. Words are conveyors of the banally real, whereas proper names function in myth and dream to re-create the past. In the text of *Against Sainte-Beuve* called "Noms de personnes" ("Names"), Proust free-associates proper names and impressions, like Guermantes and others, which, poetically, contain at least a château in the colored space of their syllables—or so the narrator says, without irony, I think. These associations reach their culminating point in a poetic outburst comparing medieval stained-glass windows and the biblical genealogies they portray with the genealogies of aristocratic families, which is to say, those families who donated the stained-glass windows and whose progenitors are represented in them. They offer images embodying the life of tradition that presides over this orchestration of Proust's enchantment with names and similes. The life of tradition is given especially concrete representation by the image of the resurrection illustrated by the tree of Jesse, or the genealogical tree of Christ, with which stained-glass-window makers depicted a biblical lineage extending back to David, Jesse, and Boaz.[12] From Boaz to Jesus, and from Clothide to Guermantes, the genealogical names are linked mythically in stained-glass magnificence to a past restored in the resurrection. In the wake of Ruskin, in "Names" Proust again proposes the idea that, in the medieval artwork, time has taken on the form of space so that the work presents a "figure of Time" (338–39). Moreover the very act of associating aristocrats with these spatial figures made permanent in time presents a strategy for preventing the narrator from being disenchanted with them: by imagining their poeticized history, he can attempt to evade the disenchantment that hovers constantly on his horizon. The narrator of *The Guermantes Way* has recourse to the same strategy.

As in *In Search of Lost Time*, the young hero finally experiences disenchantment once he has learned that aristocratic proper names are really just words like any other. Hence disenchantment again seems inevitable for those who live in time, as illustrated by the fact that even the nobility can become disenchanted with the nobility. In *Against Sainte-Beuve* this is described in "La comtesse" ("The Countess"). In it Proust sketches out a narrative about a noblewoman who was inaccessible to the narrator when he was a boy but who has become a friend of the adult narrator. They spend much time alone together, having both become disenchanted with the aristocratic crowd they once frequented. The narrator says that from her he draws truths that, once expressed, seem to coincide with what his dreams mean. This appears to be something like a unique moment in Proust, when there is momentary communion between two characters. The woman's fantasies offer him fantasies already in himself, though now she is disenchanted with her truths, since "these were just words." Communion is short lived. The countess is alienated from her social world, for it has given the lie to the power that words once seemed to have (104). Deflation of hope is, to be sure, another meaning of the passage of time.

One definition of traditional nobility is that it is a class that embodies superior traits passed on by "blood." Blood means genetic inheritance, and Proust accepts a version of biological determinism to conclude that the past is embodied in the physical presence of aristocrats. This vague genetic determinism justifies his belief in a literal repetition of hereditary traits from generation to generation. In *Against Sainte-Beuve* the narrator of "Names" discusses at length the traits that the Guermantes manifest, their hair, their eyes, and even their intelligence—all determined by the kind of genome that later supposedly manifests itself in the aristocrat Saint-Loup's inborn elegance as described in *In Search of Lost Time*. But not all is elegant in the aristocratic inheritance, and Proust is at times a humorous biologist, for example, with intentionally comic examples of the way the Guermantes family's past can be embodied in the present. To illustrate their intelligence, in "Le Balzac de M. de Guermantes" ("M. of Guermantes' Balzac"), the narrator describes an aunt of the clan, Madame de Villeparisis. She offers a verbatim illustration of what in "Names" is described as the attitude of an intelligent Guermantes: genetic inheritance determines that no Guermantes has any interest in reading books about things they already know. Thus Madame de Villeparisis dislikes Balzac, since she already knows about provincial life and has no need of the novelist's realist descriptions of it. Proust indulges in malicious irony in this portrait: Madame de Villeparisis heartily endorses Sainte-Beuve, a really charming man, she says, who knew how to stay in his place when among his betters, such as her family. Apparently aristocratic prejudice is also a hereditary trait, and genetics brings about the fall as much as it restores the past. The restitution of time past effected by genetics can hardly dissipate disenchantment with the aristocracy, though Proust's attitude is ambivalent. Among its gifts, genetics seemingly offers the elegant manners of the past as well as ingrained stupidity of the present.

Another form of disenchantment underlies "M. de Guermantes's Balzac" and the text's illustration of artistic idolatry, the latter also seemingly a comic product of defective genes. Idolatry is illustrated by the Marquise de Cardaillec, née Forcheville, who has restored a château with all the bric-a-brac necessary to live exactly like an aristocrat in Balzac's early nineteenth-century world (291). The narrator readily calls on genetics to explain that the marquise's mania was due not to the hereditary effects of the Forcheville blood but to the Swann blood. Since Swann has no role yet in these texts and Forcheville later belongs to another aristocratic family, it is clear that Proust was still meditating on how to divide up his fictional gene pool—so that artistic idolatry, like blue eyes and masochistic homosexuality, might find an explanation in hereditary repetition.

Proust's acceptance of what appears today to be nineteenth-century "biologism" is part and parcel of contemporary medical theory, which had no more of a theory about the genetic transmission of traits than, for example, did Darwin. But the patina of medical theory with which Proust overlays these texts, as well as *In Search of Lost Time,* allows him to entertain the idea that gender orientation is determined by hereditary factors. Genetic determination offers a possible explanation of gender behavior, as described by the text bearing the biblical title "La race maudite" ("An Accursed Race"). In it Proust is not adamant about genetic theory; indeed I suspect that his skeptical rationalism made him doubt that there is a scientifically valid explanation of gender determination. However if homosexuality is genetically determined, then one may conclude that it really has no moral component. (Recall the early story, "The End of the Night," in which the narrator considers homosexuality simply as a physiological given no more subject to moral opprobrium than the color of one's eyes.) Genetic determinism notwithstanding, French culture of the early twentieth century was quite intolerant in its moral condemnation of homosexuality (though homosexuality was not a criminal offense in France as in England). This intolerance is reflected in Fallois's choosing the title "La race maudite"—a title not used by Proust, though the notion occurs in the text. The notion of the cursed race has biblical resonances that resound in Proust's argument that the Jew and the homosexual share certain traits, notably that of being the brunt of widespread, if unjustified, intolerance.

"An Accursed Race" begins with a comic anecdote, one later amplified in *In Search of Lost Time*. After the narrator has received an invitation to a social gathering given by a Guermantes, he must overcome his own timid disbelief: he thinks the invitation must be a mistake and that he will be thrown out once the aristocrats see him, an unknown bourgeois, daring to appear in their sacred midst. There has been no mistake, and the narrator attends the gathering, where he discovers that the really great mistake has been made by genetic selection: one of the Guermantes, the Count de Quercy, actually has a woman inside him. He is a homosexual, and in this sense the narrator says he is a woman. This character, precursor to the Baron de Charlus of *In Search of Lost Time*, provides the narrator with an occasion to meditate that such a man is cursed by his desires, since he must desire a sexual partner who, if he really has male sexual orientation, must reject homosexuals (303). In his analysis of the homosexual's paradoxical desires, Proust also draws an analogy between homosexuals and criminals, since both must hide their secret from those they love, out of the fear of hurting their family, of being scorned by their friends, and of being punished by their country. His analogy of the homosexual with the closet criminal is clearly motivated; perhaps less obvious is the subsequent analogy the narrator makes between the homosexual and "Israel."

This analogy is motivated by a common history of persecution. The homosexual, like historical Israel and contemporary Jewry, has fallen into "the common opprobrium of an unmerited abjection" (303). Thus isolated, Jews have taken on the characteristics of a race. Race is a subject that requires caution, and Proust's use of it should not be conflated with racism. (Nor is it reasonable to ascribe to him some putative self-hatred either as a homosexual or as a Frenchman with Jewish blood.) Proust means that so-called normal members of society use the term *race* to justify stereotypes for both homosexuals and Jews. They use these stereotypes to denigrate what is different from themselves. Hence their racism serves to proclaim their own superiority. With Dreyfus undoubtedly in mind, Proust notes that people say that the Jew is naturally a traitor and then says that, by analogy, they say the homosexual is easily an assassin. This is a curious stereotype, suggesting that Proust has some strange sense of the homosexual male as a potential predator. In any case since the Jew and the homosexual cannot usually be identified by their physical appearance—only some kind of flagrant display can show that one is a member of the "race"—the cursed members of each race walk in society hearing insults heaped upon their kind without being able to reply. But, as Proust says, homosexuals, like Freemasons, are invisibly present everywhere, leading their cursed existence.

The rest of this text is a series of notes and sketches for what becomes the representation of homosexuality embodied in the Baron de Charlus. Proust alternates between theorizing and depicting characters, between a natural history of the species, drawing upon biological metaphors, and the history of one fictional aristocrat whose cursed life has been miserable at times. He reconciles his desire to be a scientist with his desire to describe real individuals by drawing up a typology of the gay men found in Paris at the time. There are three dominant types: the elegant dandies, the fearful Levites, and "the sect of bracelet wearers," by which he seems to mean the overtly effeminate. This is just a sketch, witty and insightful but demanding greater development. To be sure the sketches that make up "An Accursed Race" are among the most interesting in *Against Sainte-Beuve* if only because they make clear that Proust pondered the nature of homosexuality and the role it could play in his work at the same time that he staked out the world of heterosexuality for the narrator of *In Search of Lost Time*. It is also patent that he was always aware of the Jewish side of his identity.

The two other literary essays Fallois included in *Against Sainte-Beuve* are the aforementioned "The Method of Sainte-Beuve" and "Gérard de Nerval." Only three of the titles Fallois uses for the manuscripts are Proust's own, but of the invented titles, certainly an apposite one is "The Method of Sainte-Beuve," given to the eighth text. Critical discussions of the book *Against Sainte-Beuve* often focus on this essay outlining Proust's critique of Sainte-Beuve's reliance on biography to understand writers. As stated above Sainte-Beuve's reliance led to his failure to see that, as Proust strongly believed, the writer's deep self, embodied in a literary work, is not the same self that the writer manifests in society. Another of Sainte-Beuve's failures is the scientism Proust attributes to his method. This use or abuse of science irritated Proust, who was a sometime scientist himself. It is true that Sainte-Beuve was often viewed as wrapping himself in the mantle of an objective scientist doing a "natural history" of the human mind. For example it was for this attempt to apply science to understanding literary culture that the even more scientifically minded critic Taine praised Sainte-Beuve—the same

Taine that Proust thought he might imitate in writing a critical essay. Taine notwithstanding, Proust undoubtedly felt that in claiming to imitate natural history, Sainte-Beuve was trying to borrow a method on the cheap. He was hardly alone, since borrowing, at least metaphorically, from biology was probably as common in the nineteenth as the twentieth century, as Proust's own example shows. Most famously in the preface to his series of novels, *La Comédie humaine*, Proust's favorite, Balzac, had claimed, with more pomp than Sainte-Beuve, to rival the biologists Georges Cuvier and Geoffroy Saint-Hilaire in his novelistic natural history. At the end of the century, the naturalist novelist Zola entertained comparable hopes. Apparently Proust had nothing against writers using science, just critics.

Proust is against critics who believe that they can explain art with science—which is not the same as using science as part of art. His irritation with Sainte-Beuve is thus formulated with the blanket judgment that "philosophers have not been able to discover what in art is real and independent of science" (153). By raising a major question about the nature of knowledge, Proust, well versed in epistemology, contends that science cannot account for the contingent and nondetermined realm of the particular that the artwork takes as its object. He accuses the scientifically inclined philosophers of desiring to hide their failure by annexing the truths of art and criticism. To accomplish this annexation, he charges that philosophers have come up with the idea that art and criticism resemble science. This means that the philosophical critic can claim, like the scientist, that critical theory and philosophical thought make progress and that each predecessor is "less advanced" than the philosophical critics coming afterward. The march of history means that criticism and theory are characterized by ever-greater progress. This notion of progress Proust rejects totally. There is no progress in art or in criticism. Rather the individual is the locus of artistic truth, and as Proust puts it, the individual artist today is no further along than Homer was.

Proust does not always espouse this view. The reader of *In Search of Lost Time* finds that the narrator there views the history of art as a series of breakthroughs. It is not static. But change does not mean progress; rather the history of art is defined as a series of new originalities, if that is not a redundant formulation. Where Proust does not waver is in defending the position that the individual is responsible for the contingent truths that art reveals. This view that artistic truth is contingent hardly means that Proust rejects science. On the contrary he accepts and uses the truths that science reveals. His views on homosexuality show that Proust can use scientific models both for serious and comic purposes. If he is hostile to the scientism attributed to Sainte-Beuve, he nonetheless accepts that science orders our vision of things in the material world. Proust ruefully accepts in the end that it is physiology, not metaphysics, that opposes religious belief. This is why, in "Return to the Guermantes" ("Retour à Guermantes"), he says that the possibility of some eternal existence—which would bring back his mother—is condemned by the laws of physiology (354). Notably it is his father's discipline, medicine and its allied sciences, that obliges Proust to envisage the loss of what he most valued.

Medical knowledge is thus not opposed to literary knowledge. In fact Proust's medical understanding is the backdrop for his essay on Nerval. Nerval was subject to periodic bouts of insanity, and Proust shows great sensitivity to the role madness played in his creative life. Overlooking Nerval was another of Sainte-Beuve's critical failures, and Proust uses his understanding of the poet's madness to explain why earlier critics failed to understand his work, such as his novella *Sylvie*. The failure was due to their attempt to reduce Nerval's work to a few easily accessible, received categories. Proust maintains that they wanted to find in Nerval some manifestation of French clarity and eighteenth-century rationalism. He dismisses this viewpoint as absurd, recalling that Nerval, a translator of Goethe's *Faust,* was steeped in German romanticism. Proust's medical insight allows him to see that Nerval's madness was not merely a clinical condition, a syndrome having periodical manifestations, but also a condition at the origin of his uncontested literary originality. Comparably he sees madness as a component in Baudelaire's creativity and concludes "Sainte-Beuve and Baudelaire" with commentary on Baudelaire's description of madness in the poem "Châtiment de l'orgueil" ("The Punishment of Pride," poem 16 in Baudelaire's *Flowers of Evil*). Proust interprets this poem's description of madness, inflicted upon a medieval theologian who challenges God with threats, as an anticipatory portrayal of the dementia Baudelaire felt engulfing him. As in Nerval's case, he considered Baudelaire's precarious mental health to be a part of his genius (a view explained at greater length in the essay-letter Proust published on Baudelaire in 1921 in the *Nouvelle Revue française*). In fine both Nerval and Baudelaire offer examples of how the deep self is expressed through a heightening of sensation brought about by near or actual insanity.

Perhaps most interesting about *Against Sainte-Beuve*, at least with regard to the novel that Proust was about to begin, is that it shows that he found in Nerval a way to free his narrative from the constraints of time. He says that Nerval was able, up to a certain point, to document his madness in writing, "like an artist might note while going to sleep the stages of consciousness that lead from waking to sleep, up to the moment where sleep renders the double consciousness [*dédoublement*] impossible" (182).

He maintains that in *Sylvie* Nerval creates the dream of a dream (192). Nerval's example seems to point here toward the narrative tools Proust needed for portraying the mind set free from the restrictions of space and time. Nerval moves in and out of the past, as Proust says, so that in reading *Sylvie* one is obliged in uncertainty to keep turning back to see if the text is describing the present moment or a recalled moment of the past (193). The relations between past and present are sustained in the mind, in this case a mind that cannot always delineate temporal boundaries or be sure about where it may find itself. In brief Proust's analogy between Nerval and a sleeping artist is redolent of his forthcoming writing project, a project using the moments between wakefulness and sleep to free the narrating self from the limits of Kantian space-time. Nerval, like his generation of romantics, understood this project well.

To conclude these considerations of what Proust did not publish, let us turn to something he did publish, late in his career, when as a critic he returned to other texts he had written before beginning *In Search of Lost Time;* Proust's intent in *In Search of Lost Time* is greatly illuminated by them, especially by the ideas he finally published in 1920 as "A propos du 'style' de Flaubert" ("On Flaubert's 'Style'") in the *Nouvelle Revue française.* I think Proust's return to Flaubert at the end of his life was motivated in part by his feeling that, having abandoned his writings on Sainte-Beuve, he had never settled the score with him. Thus recalling his thoughts on Stendhal and Nerval from years earlier, he publicly indicted Sainte-Beuve for his signal failure to recognize the great writers of his time. But along with the attack on Sainte-Beuve, Proust also took to task in 1920 the contemporary critic Alfred Thibaudet for not understanding Flaubert's use of verb tenses, especially the contrast of past and imperfective tenses.

According to Proust, with his contrast of tenses Flaubert created a stylistic revolution that was as important for renewing literary vision as were Kant's categories of the understanding for renewing philosophical discourse. Did Proust have himself in mind in making this comparison? It is certainly arguable that in the essay of 1920 he appears to be talking as much about himself as Flaubert when he describes the writer's use of the imperfect tense. Saying that Flaubert's use of the imperfect tense creates a sense of repetitive duration not often found in earlier literature, Proust selects François-René de Chateaubriand as well as Flaubert as a precursor for his use of tenses. But it is mainly Flaubert who interests him. Proust says that Flaubert's usage of the imperfect tense is "so new in literature" that it "changes entirely the appearance of things and beings, like a lamp whose light one casts about, on the arrival in a new house, or on going into an old one if it's nearly empty when you are moving out."[13] The imperfect tense is, in Proust's metaphor, an illuminating agent, lighting up the vacant past as well as pointing to the now empty future and pulling them together in a privileged space. It may appear that this tense overcomes time by changing one's perspective on it. In this regard, then, the essay on Flaubert can serve as an introduction to *In Search of Lost Time*, the novel to which we will now turn, to see how Proust finally came to grips with, among many other things, the imperfect tense.

Chapter 4

Swann's Way

Intimations of Paradise and Paradise Lost

In Search of Lost Time, a novel composed of seven interlinking and continuous volumes, is best known for its first, *Swann's Way.* This volume itself may appear to be made up of self-contained parts. The first two parts, "Combray" and "Un amour de Swann" ("Swann in Love"), are often read in fact as separate novels, especially in courses on French literature, though these sections should also be considered a prelude to the rest of the novel. This is especially true of the first section, "Combray," with its opening exploration of the narrator's subjectivity and his recall of his childhood. Together "Combray" and "Swann in Love" set forth the major themes of the novel, especially the narrator's quest for his vocation as he, like Jean Santeuil before him, becomes educated in life and love in society. The third part of *Swann's Way,* "Noms de pays: Le nom" ("Place-Names: The Name"), begins the development of the narration that leads sequentially through each subsequent volume to the conclusion in *Time Regained,* which is to say, the third section begins the narrator's account of his education in the ways of the world. Thus if I concede that each section of *Swann's Way* is a remarkable work of literature in its own right and accordingly discuss each of them here for their intrinsic interest, one should bear in mind that upon opening *Swann's Way* one has entered a novelistic world to which these remarkable sections are an overture.

First it is useful to sketch out the interrelationship of the three parts composing *Swann's Way.* "Combray" begins with the presentation of a nameless narrator who recalls scenes of childhood experience. In the narration of these childhood memories taking place during the child's vacations in the village of Combray are found the intimations of paradise that, by contrast, set off the rest of the novel in all its epic sweep narrating the narrator's growth and decline before, in the final volume, he perhaps discovers the means to realize his vocation as writer. This discovery would allow him to recover through writing the paradise he lost after leaving the world of childhood set forth in Combray. In the following section, "Swann in Love," the narrator does *not* continue the ongoing narration of his childhood experiences, turning instead to what he learned of a love affair, concerning a family friend named Swann, that occurred before the narrator was born. Swann's dismal love affair foreshadows much of what the narrator himself later experiences in the deceptions he has with both love and society. He then ends the volume, in "Place-Names: The Name," by beginning the tale of his own first experience of love as a child when he fell in love with Gilberte, the daughter of Swann. One has learned that Swann's unhappy love affair eventuated nonetheless in his marrying Gilberte's mother, Odette, a woman whom he no longer loved. The narrator breaks off the recollection of his own love story with a nostalgic but comic denunciation of the present moment, which is apparently close to the moment at which the narration is taking place. Beyond this the present moment is left undefined, though automobiles have replaced horses. It is characterized by the mature narrator as a period of decline, since the elegance of the past, the elegance he had seen embodied years earlier in Odette, has totally disappeared.

The first question the reader asks upon opening *Swann's Way* is "who is this narrator whose autobiography is narrated not only in this first volume but, with the exception of the tale of Swann's love affair, occupies the entirety of the novel?" The narrator does not name himself, although later in the novel "Marcel" is twice used in reference to him. In the opinion of most critics, "Marcel" is probably an uncorrected lapse on Proust's part, for it seems obvious from the outset of the novel that he intended for his narrator to remain nameless. He is simply "I," and his narrative voice is the voice of a self-reflective consciousness that does not address itself with a name. The voice belongs to a Frenchman who, raised in Paris, vacationed as a child with his family in a small town called Combray. He has, it appears, later traveled in France and other parts of Europe as a young man. References to various locations situate the narrator in a network of geographical places, most real, some fictitious, as the novel unfolds. However what does not become apparent as the novel unfolds is the location of the narrator when he is narrating the story of his life.

The term *narrate* needs some commentary. I use it in a neutral sense with no reference to writing, since the narrator does not claim to be putting pen to paper as he recalls the past. He simply recalls his memories. He seemingly exists as a voice. He makes no claim to write, since throughout the novel's narration he has not yet found his vocation as writer. Rather as the narrator himself puts it, he is "remembering again all the places and people" he had known, what he "had actually seen of them" and what others had told him.[1] The reader may be legitimately puzzled by the fact that the narrator does not claim to be writing down his memories and seems to be thinking out loud. Where does this voice come from? There is no answer given to this question in the novel.

Moreover at times the narrator appears greatly to resemble the third-person narrators of the realist fiction Proust greatly admired, the type of narrator who never or rarely talks about the pen that must be moving if something is being written. This realist convention, effacing reference to the narrative act, means that most of the time the reader faces a written text that is imitating something like a speaking voice. In Proust's case the narrative voice comments at times on its act of narration, though the meta-commentary is usually commentary on the act of remembrance. As such it is part of conventional first-person narration. However Proust does not always respect this convention. He allows his first-person narrator to recall not only his own past but also what other people have remembered and, sometimes, supposedly told the narrator. Sometimes the narrator limits his recall to verbal accounts of what others have told him about things, but at other times he seems actually to remember the memories of other characters. This is true not only in the case of Swann, whose past inner life is an open book to the narrator. With respect to Swann and certain other characters, the narrator enters into their mental world, and at times he remembers both the experience he had of them and what they felt or thought. He can then seemingly remember the experience they have of the world. He knows their thoughts, their perceptions, their real values. It appears on these occasions that Proust endows his first-person narrator with omniscience, usually whenever he wants more than one viewpoint on the experience narrated, often for comic or ironic effects. In these moments the narrator knows what characters are really thinking in spite of the façade behind which they hide their thoughts from others or even themselves. In other words the fact that Proust decided to use a first-person narrator for this novel does not mean that he entirely gave up the rhetorical advantages that he had found in writing *Jean Santeuil* in the third person.

The use of privileged insight is part of the rhetoric of the realist fiction Balzac and then Flaubert developed. Their omniscient narrators can view the depths of their characters' subjectivity, though the omniscient narrator who does so is usually not a character in the novel. By contrast Proust's first-person narrator is at once a character in the novel with a limited point of view and at times an omniscient narrator who can selectively enter into the minds of others. Conventional realism grants this capacity to an omniscient narrator, so perhaps we should speak of unconventional realism in Proust's case. For it must also be said that, at least in my experience of reading Proust, it rarely seems implausible for his narrator to recall the experience that others have had or to know what is truly on their mind. Perhaps we all confront the hidden world of others' consciousness with something like a working belief in our power to enter that world. The philosopher Ludwig Wittgenstein mused on what it would be like to experience somebody else's pain or remember somebody else's memories. Proust offers us something like an experiment with that experience in the recollection of Swann's love and in other moments throughout the novel when the narrative viewpoint opens up well beyond the confines of a single narrator's subjectivity. His consciousness impinges then on others' consciousness—though admittedly the narrator has a very limited viewpoint when he wonders what the women he loves are thinking and doing. There are no privileged insights when one is blinded by passion.

Yet it is an individual narrator's singular subjectivity that establishes the framework for all the experience narrated, with the exception of "Swann in Love." Throughout the novel this subjectivity undergirds the perception of all the experience narrated, though it offers a flexible framework. This flexibility is obvious from the first reference to *I* found in the first sentence in the novel. Before opening the narration up onto the historical world of the novel, the narrator situates himself by suggesting that he might be in bed. In the widely read, twice-revised Moncrieff translation, this first sentence reads, "For a long time I would go to bed early." The translation suggests a habitual act in the past, for which a French writer would normally use the imperfect tense about which I have made some commentary. However this is not the tense Proust's narrator uses in the first sentence. Rather he speaks using the *passé composé*, or the compound present perfect: "Longtemps je me suis couché de bonne heure." The English translation does convey some of the syntactical awkwardness of this admittedly strange French sentence, without, unfortunately, conveying the temporal relationship that the French compound past tense suggests.

Here in fact the narrative voice is located by the compound tense in the present moment. As the novel's development in the first few pages makes clear, the English present perfect tense would be a better translation, something like "For a long time now I have been going to bed early" or "I've been an early bed-goer for some time now." The narrator is situating himself in the present moment with his use of the *passé composé*, a compound past tense that in conversation can be the equivalent of the English present perfect as well as the preterit. However since the narrator often uses the literary preterit (the *passé défini*) for singular past events, by contrast the compound past tense designates here a relation of the speaker to the present moment, which in English usually takes the present perfect tense.

In effect in the novel's first sentence, the narrator is telling the reader that he is speaking from a moment in the present. Moreover this present moment is evoked each of the relatively few times the narrator uses the *passé composé* tense to refer to himself or to events. It evokes a present moment that is, however, never situated.[2] I stress: the equivalent of the present perfect is notable because it does not occur very often in the novel.

After the first sentence, the *passé composé* tense is used only infrequently but at key moments. One such example is when the narrator says that Combray has (now) emerged from a cup of tea: "Tout Combray . . . est sorti . . . de ma tasse de thé"—which we should take to mean that the narration the narrator is now undertaking has sprung forth into the narrative present from the recent taste of a cup of lime tea. In Proust the *passé composé* derives its meaning, moreover, not only through contrast with the definite past tense but also through contrast with the imperfect tense, the dominant tense used by the narrator throughout the novel. As in *Jean Santeuil,* the narrator uses this tense not only in its iterative and descriptive senses but also for events that happened only once or only infrequently. His use of the imperfect tense is a rather unusual stylistic fact. So used, it seems to express more than simply the open-ended repetition of acts in the past or to describe states of indefinite duration. As we saw in his footnote to Ruskin, Proust commented explicitly and perhaps contradictorily on what the imperfect meant to him. According to the footnote, it is the tense of infinite sadness. However in his commentary on Flaubert's use of the imperfect tense, he says that it can be used to illuminate those privileged spaces in which the past moves into the future. The latter is closer to the meaning the tense acquires in *Swann's Way.* Translation of Proust's tenses is not easy. In English his imperfect tense can often be translated to the effect that "something used to happen" or "something would regularly happen," such as "I used to go to bed early." But to correct the translation's first sentence once more, this is not what the narrator is saying about his bedtime habits.

Proust makes another commentary on the imperfect tense when in "Combray" the narrator says the voice of his mother was able, in reading a novel to the narrator as a boy, to endow "the imperfect and the preterit with all the sweetness to be found in generosity" (*SW,* 57). Proust's crediting the mother with the power to endow the past with fullness explains, in part, why the imperfect and the preterit are the tenses of choice in the novel—not least of all for the "generosity" with which they can restore time past. From this perspective in Proust's idiosyncratic reading of tenses, it would seem that the mother's presence is thus never absent whenever the narrator reads literature written in these usual literary tenses. However this may be, Proust mainly uses for the novel the imperfective tense, with its suggestion of ongoing duration, and the preterit that expresses the so-called simple past: this tense designates that an event took place, and that is it. When the narrator uses the tense, he does so quite self-consciously to stress that he is recalling a single event that took place usually on "one day" in the unfolding and repeating past narrated in the imperfect tense. Contrasting with the preterit and the imperfect, then, the occasional but revealing *passé composé* should be translated in a way that alerts the reader to the narrator's speaking about or from the indefinite present moment. The narrator uses the awkward phraseology of the first sentence to underscore the fact that the narrative viewpoint is centered on a present moment from which he recalls various moments of the past—layers of the past, as he puts it. Set against the narration—necessarily situated in the present—the narrated event is nearly always in the past, distant or immediate, a past existing in tension with the present moment in which the narrator undertakes the quest for memory.

Of course one may reasonably ask where exactly the narrator is as he remembers. In fact it seems he is nowhere specific; he simply occupies the present instance of discourse necessary so that the past exists in counterpoint to it. His present is the present moment of all enunciation, as linguists put it in making a structural description of the act of enunciation. Nowhere in the course of the novel is the present moment of narration ever located with clear spatial-temporal coordinates, not even at the end of the novel when World War I is over and an indefinite number of years have passed before the narrator returns to society. Context sometimes suggests approximately this or that historical moment, but the narrator never says at the end of *Swann's Way* (pace the translators who suggest in a footnote that he could), "I remember just two months ago standing in the Bois de Boulogne in 1913 on such and such date, I was there remembering what an elegant beauty Madame Swann was when I used to see her there in 1890." This is a sentence that might have only been accurate when *Swann's Way* was published in 1913. But it is not true for a novel continuing beyond World War I. And it is certainly not true of a novel that simply refuses ever to locate its narrator. And if there are no coordinates precisely situating the narrator, it is also true that there are remarkably few precise dates used in the entire novel. The narrator eschews dates, and the exact comparisons in time afforded thereby, so that a lack of precision characterizes not only the his location but also the exact relation among events in the past. The active reader and the zealous critic may construct a temporal framework for the narrator's past by sorting out the allusions and historical references he makes, though ultimately the detail of the historical framework is the reader's and critic's own creation. The foundation of the narration is the narrator's unfolding consciousness.

It is also true that lack of temporal precision springs from the fact that the narrator himself is uncertain as to the temporal relations constituting his past. This is both an epistemological problem—the narrator is not certain about things—and a psychological state: he remembers only what by chance springs into memory. So his mind ranges over a wide field of past events. Existing in something like a vacuum, then, the present narrative moment has no validation of its being except as a repository in which memories are collected. It is as if the narrator's perception of the present moment is a kind of phenomenological emptiness that must be filled by the recalled past if he is to find substance to his being. In this regard the present moment is in itself nothingness, which is symmetrical to the narrator's repeated fear that the past may be nothingness, too. If this commentary sounds like an existentialist phenomenology of the self, then it may well be that existentialist terminology offers, up to a certain point, a useful and not too metaphorical way of understanding the narrative self in Proust. It is a kind of present nothingness, moving into the indefinite future but turned toward the past, seeking to find interiority by something exterior to it. In the narrator's case, the exteriority is made up of the various types of memories that flow into it as it tries to reconstitute itself in the present by recalling what it was in the past. The limits of this phenomenology are given by the fact that the narrator is a speaker needing language: the narration of all perception must be translated into language, hence the importance for understanding the way the verbs function in this seizure of the past. But the enunciation of this seizure is always in a virtual present.

Some critics have argued that the narrative *I* resembles the transcendental ego of idealist philosophy. Perhaps, though I think Proust's ironies about philosophical idealism hardly support that interpretation. In any case the narrative *I* does not transcend his experience through categories of understanding innate to the narrating mind. Rather the narrating mind is constituted by the experience of the past it encounters in an attempt to remember it.

Consider now the early bed-goer who, at the beginning of *Swann's Way,* examines recent memories of what enters his mind during bouts of insomnia. He recalls recent dream images, for example, deriving from his nocturnal reading: "It seemed to me that I myself was the immediate subject of my book: church, a quartet, the rivalry between François I and Charles V" (*SW,* 1). He recalls that at times he is able to go back to sleep, only to awaken to new memories, such as those of his great-uncle who used to pull his curls when he was a child. Reflecting on these memories conjoined with his recollection of dreams, he enunciates in the present tense what seems to be a general law about the self: "When a man is asleep, he has in a circle around him the chain of the hours, the sequence of the years, the order of the heavenly bodies" (*SW,* 4). And when the sleeper awakes, he can read off from this circle "his own position on the earth's surface and the time that has elapsed," though "this ordered procession is apt to grow confused and to break its ranks" (*SW,* 4). When this happens, says the narrator with apparent reference to himself, the self will no longer have a sense of place or time. His view of the self's mobility, of its tenuous connection with the exterior world, is thus the justification for the opening narrative prelude centered on a self that is apparently set free from the normal laws of space and time.

The meandering in the prelude illustrates a law about the self and, as such, sets out a recurrent feature of Proust's narration: the derivation of "laws" from the narrator's immediate experience. The law of the self's power in sleep and the law of its weakness upon awakening are both observations offering general truths. Not unlike a modernist La Rochefoucauld, throughout the novel the narrator frequently enunciates laws in the present tense characterized by no special temporal or spatial location, just by general validity. Laws in the past tense are, of course, not part of what we understand by a law. Thus in using the present tense, the narrator does not speak about his present moment, the moment of enunciation, but about a moment transcending it: the moment of lasting truth. A law, such as the one about the frequent disassociation of self and world, seems here to serve as an organizing principle to justify the order or perhaps disorder of the presentation of space and time in which the narrative self has been involved. The law sets out the difficult conditions for the narrator's quest for memory.

Perhaps now liberated from the normal constraints of objective ordering, the narrating self navigates time according to principles that may not be in accord with the causal laws we sometimes think rule over the entire realm of realty. In practice this disassociated meandering in time means the narrator negotiates the convolutions of memory's movements according to aleatory encounters and chance juxtapositions. The net result is to create a collage of time and place. The notion of collage is useful to describe the type of arbitrary assemblages that modernist art created by juxtaposing things not normally associated. The collages created by the narrator's memory are modeled by his subjectivity into the narrative wholes that may well not take into account the public history the reader knows, especially when the narrator's collage is assembled in anguish and involves traumatic memory. His collage of past memories follows its own "laws" without obeying the ordering principle imposed by official history's dates and exact public chronology.

In brief the narrator narrates a past made up of a collage involving different kinds of memory. I insist on the notion of different kinds of memory in order to encourage the reader to interpret Proust more liberally than some critics do. Critics often use a rigidly binary distinction to categorize all memories in Proust as either voluntary or involuntary. To be sure this distinction applies a priori to all memories, more or less, but it is not an adequate description of memories that may incidentally be voluntary or not. For example traumatic memory is central to *Swann's Way*. It characterizes the narrator's obsessive memories described in the opening scenes of "Combray" and, later, memories characterizing Swann's love and, even later, those of the narrator's love affairs. Traumatic memory is repetitive and involuntary. It can come forth obsessively, especially in periods of the narrator's insomnia, when, as he regretfully says at the beginning of *Swann's Way,* he recalls that he "used to spend the greater part of the night recalling our life in the old days at Combray with my great-aunt" (*SW,* 9). This traumatic memory is involuntary. It hardly offers the plenitude of the resurrected past offered by the kind of involuntary memory elicited by sensory correspondences—as in the case of the resurrection of the narrator's childhood in Combray. The latter comes forth, in a recent past, in the recall afforded by the correspondence of the taste of lime tea and a biscuit with the same tastes the narrator often knew in Combray as a child.

The resurrection of Combray thanks to lime tea and a crumbled cookie is perhaps the most famous moment in the novel. It has become a staple for literary comparisons in the *TLS* and cartoons in the *New Yorker.* But there are other types of memories of Combray as well as this one, and some are as just as central to the narrator's consciousness. The first extended evocation of Combray in *Swann's Way* is in fact associated with the anguish the narrator knew as a boy when the order of his habitual world was threatened by his mother's use of a magic lantern to project an image on the wall of his room: "I found plenty of charm in these bright projections, which seemed to emanate from a Merovingian past and shed around me the reflections of such ancient history. But I cannot express the discomfort I felt at this intrusion of mystery and beauty into a room which I had succeeded in filling with my own personality until I thought no more of it than of myself. The anaesthetic effect of habit being destroyed, I would begin to think—and to feel—such melancholy things" (*SW,* 11).

The adult narrator thus remembers remembering throughout his periods of insomnia the anguish generated by the destruction of his usual perception of his room, a perturbation of habit that the child could not easily cope with. Herein lies another Proustian law: the daily self is a creature of habit. (And for readers of *Against Sainte-Beuve,* herein lies another illustration of Proustian ambivalence, since the magic lantern mentioned there produces the wonder of the past resurrected in the present.)

The central traumatic memory of *Swann's Way* involves the destruction of the child's bedtime routine when, on one occasion, Swann, a family friend, came for dinner, and the boy was sent to bed early without his mother's coming up to see him. The imperfect tense actually first suggests that this routine with guests was a recurring event, in other words, a recurrent misery for the boy. But the routine disrupting his routine is made worse when, on one occasion, he did not even receive a kiss before having to go upstairs to his bedroom. Unable to bear the anguish springing from the destruction of this habit, he decides to contravene his father's rules—or whims—and ask the servant Françoise take a letter to his mother while the adults are still at dinner, saying that he has to see her about an urgent matter. This is a singular dramatic event standing out against the backdrop of the recurrent events of social routine. In narrating this memory, the narrator first presents Swann and the narrator's family to the reader. He uses flashbacks for the background needed to explain the sequence leading to the traumatic moment. Then he focuses on the specifics of the drama of the child's anguish. He has not only been deprived of his mother's affection, but as a result he also has dared to contest his father's authority.

The traumatic memory of this event has been central to the narrator's development. By its very position at the outset of the novel, the memory stands out and demands to be interpreted as a seminal experience. In this light deprivation may appear to be the foundation stone for all future love in the novel and, indeed, for what we can call the Proustian psychology of love. It seems to underlie the obsessive need of characters such as Swann as well as the older narrator. They are driven to overcome separation, so that this desire to overcome deprivation appears to be the dominant drive behind the desire known as love or, alternatively, jealousy. The narrator is quite aware that a lack lies behind his anguish and that something comparable characterizes Swann. He points out the similarity when he compares the anguish he knew as a child with what he later found about Swann: he had gone through years of being forced to accept separation from the woman he loved and hence could have sympathized with the boy's suffering—since in Swann's case "a similar anguish had been the bane of his life for many years" (*SW,* 39). It is a universal suffering, illustrated again when the narrator recalls that his mother does not come in response to the letter. He then makes an implied comparison of himself as a child with "some poor girl" of the type that later, as an adult, he sees more than once stranded on the doorstep of a luxury hotel or gambling club, desperately wanting to contact some man within. The only result of her pleas is to be humiliated by the doorman who scorns her need (*SW,* 41). Picturing himself as a scorned lover—perhaps as one of the women whom Swann had used in his life as a skirt chaser—the narrator projects himself into the world of passive lovers who are rejected, scorned, and damned to separation. Perhaps we might speak of Proust's law of passionate lack with a passing nod to the psychiatrist Jacques Lacan, a contemporary moralist and occasional psychoanalyst for whom all desire is a form of lack.

However most readers are more likely to think of Freud and his universal allegory describing the child's need to possess the parent of the opposite sex. This is not irrelevant, though, as I suggested earlier, I would propose that Proust opens up Freud's allegory by largely desexualizing the origins of love, to make of love a need to overcome the traumatic absence and separation for which the mother is, in the narrator's case, the first instance. This perspective on separation will also prove useful for interpreting Proust's views about resurrection in connection with the need to overcome the anguish about separation from the past itself, a dominant theme throughout the novel. The child's revolt against the father may also seem to have Freudian overtones, though the revolt is presented with wry humor in Proust. The narrator recalls that after he, a mere child, decided against all reason to accost his mother on the stairs, he saw his father approaching, "standing like Abraham in the engraving after Benozzo Gozzoli which M. Swann had given me, telling Sarah that she must tear herself away from Isaac" (*SW,* 49).

Proust invents a work of art and a biblical scene for his ironic comparison, since neither the Italian painter Gozzoli nor the Bible offers exactly that image. The scene is a plausible one: after all Abraham was told to sacrifice Isaac, and as the Danish philosopher Søren Kierkegaard insisted, the father would be able to justify the act of killing his son, Isaac, to nobody, least of all to Sarah, since it defies all reason. Proust seems to have something comparable in mind about the arbitrary sacrifice of the child to the will of the father, since in his description the narrator says that his father's will is, in fact, as capricious as that of the biblical God who demands that Abraham kill his son. The Father decrees, and the child/Abraham should obey to show he is obedient. However in Proust's narrative the child's father capriciously relents and tells the boy's mother to spend the night with him, which is not quite the same as the biblical narrative in which God grants Isaac a last-moment reprieve. The latter reprieve is merited, since Abraham has passed the test. By contrast the narrator's father recognizes the child's weakness and caters to it. The father's suspension of the law is not perceived by the boy as generosity but rather as a more subtle form of condemnation. The reprieve acknowledges the child's fundamental failure, for which he suffers those guilt feelings he will continue to feel until the end of the novel. After this traumatic moment, the narrator recalls his "puberty of sorrow," in which his sobbing tears are not a release but a sign of recognition that he has not lived up to his parents' ideal for him (*SW*, 51). This ideal, something like a superego if one wishes but informed by the mother with tenderness, subtends the novel's unfolding, haunting the narrator during the years in which he fruitlessly seeks his vocation.

This unique night of trauma ends with the boy's mother reading to him from a novel by George Sand. Literature itself is linked to the trauma of separation, though as a promise of plenitude and generosity that might heal the trauma. It is hard to resist the thought that the association of literature and the mother might play a formative role in the narrator's self-image as a would-be writer. Later the older narrator notes that he taught his mother not to value the quality of a voice full of generosity or to believe that moral distinction is the supreme value in literature—as opposed to the value both generosity and moral distinction have in life. But for the child of "Combray," literature and life are not to be separated and reading is part of paradise. There is no separation of life values and the value of literature for the child, whatever lessons the older narrator may have given his mother at some point in time. A curious memory of strictures found in *Against Sainte-Beuve* seems reflected in the narrator's claim to have been so didactic with his mother, as if he wanted to prevent his mother from committing Sainte-Beuve's errors in confusing social values and the deep self the writer expresses in literature. However literature in this posttraumatic scene of reading is itself the communication of maternal concern, and for that reason her generous voice enters into the paradise of Combray, inflecting the very tenses of literary language.

The adult voice of the older narrator intrudes into the narration of the child's trauma to comment on the great distance that now separates him from this scene. Separation is measured by what has perished since the night of that drama; for example even the wall of the staircase his father climbed that night has since been demolished (*SW*, 49). The recurrent memory of trauma underscores the tension created by living with the transience of a past that will not go away and of which seeming nothing remains. Struck by this seeming paradox, the narrator returns to the question of the nothingness that seems to have engulfed the past, wondering if all is "permanently dead"—to which he answers, "Quite possibly" (*SW*, 59). The recognition of time's annihilation of all things must be reconciled with the fact that this past continues to reverberate into the present moment of narration: "But of late I have been increasingly able to catch, if I listen attentively, the sound of the sobs which I had the strength to control in my father's presence, and which broke out only when I found myself alone with Mamma. In reality their echo has never ceased: and it is only because life is now growing more and more quiet round about me that I hear them anew, like those convent bells which are so effectively drowned during the day by the noises of the street that one would suppose them to have stopped, until they ring out again through the silent evening air" (*SW*, 49).

This is a description of another type of memory, a recurrent memory, ready to be acknowledged if the present moment ceases the resistance it opposes to memory. With his simile comparing memories with muffled convent bells, the narrator finds an image for the present, filled with all the noises that usually fill the present moment, until the self reduces them and allows the past to speak with the same sounds it had once upon a time. Perhaps the paradox can be resolved by pure listening.

Commenting on these recurrent memories of Combray, the narrator says that he could of course call forth other memories but denigrates them, since what he would have "recalled would have been prompted only by voluntary memory, the memory of the intellect, and since the pictures which that kind of memory shows us preserve nothing of the past itself, I should never have had any wish to ponder over this residue of Combray" (*SW*, 59). This residue is dead memory, of which the narrator has given but scant example in the first pages dealing with Combray. He introduces this notion of a voluntary memory in contrast to the traumatic memory he has of being deprived of his mother's kiss. In this context voluntary memory is still a rather abstract concept that serves as a foil to the involuntary type Proust wants to introduce in the second part of "Combray," which is the memory embodying the living plenitude of the past restored into the present. This latter type of memory is recalled involuntarily, since it occurs through the chance promptings of sensation in which odors and tastes, colors and sounds, can elicit from the past their exact counterparts and resurrect them by short-circuiting the intellect. This is the event the narrator describes when, concluding the first part of "Combray" with the recollection of his mother's reading to him, he describes a recent event—one set close to the present moment of narration—in which he drank some lime tea and ate a small pastry called a "petite madeleine" (*SW*, 60).

The second part of "Combray" is narrated as an epiphanic memory event. At some recent time in the past, while with his mother, the aging narrator has tasted the "petite madeleine" and the lime tea, which call forth memories that invade him with the force of a revelation. The memory event resembles something like a mystical experience taking him outside the normal boundaries of time. Not only is he inundated with extraordinary pleasure, but, as he says, he arrives at a state of mind in which "the vicissitudes of life had become indifferent . . . its disasters innocuous, its brevity illusory," at least for so long as the experience filled him with what he calls an essence, in effect, the essence of himself locked up in time past (*SW,* 60). After the first explosion of inchoate revelation, however, the complete memory experience requires intellectual effort on the narrator's part. Interrogating this experience, he looks into his own depths, to use his spatial metaphor, one that seems motivated as much by the image of a teacup as by romantic poetry or depth psychology. In any case the narrator has to seek and go after the visual memory that, he says, was attached to the sensorial recall afforded by the tastes and odor of the lime tea and pastry.

After this struggle seconded by the narrator's will and intellect, the entire involuntary memory "has emerged," a memory of Combray and especially of his aunt Léonie in her bedroom, who would give him a bite of a "petite madeleine" before the family went to Sunday Mass. The memory, encoded in the imperfect tense, bursts forth into the present moment of narration. For it is here in the present moment of narration that the act of memory itself is narrated, as I said earlier, in the sentence in the present perfect tense (the *passé composé*) with which the narrator describes his memories' present relation to this past: "Tout Combray et ses environs, tout cela qui prend forme et solidité, est sorti, villes et jardins de ma tasse de thé." Moncrieff's rendering is adequate, though the past tense he used in the translation does not quite allow Combray to spring into the present moment, to wit: "The whole of Combray and its surroundings, taking shape and solidity, sprang into being, town and gardens alike, from my cup of tea" (*SW,* 64). But consider that "Combray has emerged from the tea" and, as the narrator goes on to show, has become present as it once was. And this past springing into the present is what he narrates in the second part of "Combray."

I do not think it is hyperbole to speak of resurrection, or the myth thereof, to describe what Proust wants to do in the second part of "Combray." In it he contrasts intimations of paradise with the memories of trauma that it had been the narrator's lot to remember unceasingly until the experience of memories called forth by the lime tea. It is to be sure a paradise in which there is much foreshadowing that the boy was to be inevitably driven from the earthly garden—the gardens of Combray in this case, like the gardens of Illiers in *Jean Santeuil.* Yet the garden was once there, in its plenitude, before the narrator's fall from grace into a world ruled over by the laws that determine how things unfold with their decline in time. This development in time has led to the total loss of the garden, even, it appears, in the narrator's memory. In the second part of "Combray," the narrator thus takes the reader into a past that had been in effect annihilated before his fortuitous encounter with the lime tea.

In a sense this encounter is Proust's version of grace: something fortuitous but seemingly irrevocably absolute. Like Pascal's fortunate Christian knocking on the door that finally opens onto faith, the lime tea and madeleine open the door onto the resurrection that the aging narrator had supposed impossible. Proust differs from Pascal in that his version of grace does not simply grant hope of resurrection in the future: the tea allows the narrator to experience now in narration what he once was. But like the Christian doctrine of grace, the narrator's experience of recovery is fully grasped only if illuminated by the myth of the Fall and the loss it entails. An important part of this myth concerns knowledge. Though knowledge produced the Fall in the first place, the result is that one no longer knows the presence of the divine. In the fallen world, nobody knows anything with certainty. "Combray" is the first part of the repeated demonstration that Proust and his narrator suffered because of the epistemological dilemma involved in finding certain knowledge in a world in which all empirical knowledge is uncertain. Proust will find a loophole in this law: uncertainty does not always characterize the individual self and the knowledge it has of itself. This is Proust's affirmation in the novel, for in the encounter of the narrator with his own past subjectivity, he finds that there is a realm of certain knowledge. It is the self's unique realm in which the self knows itself. This knowledge of self cannot be put in question. What the self knows uniquely about itself cannot logically be denied. *Time Regained* develops this notion at greater length. But already in "Combray" it is shown that, if the narrator's fall into time entailed the loss of that past self, once it is recovered, the self is what it was: a unique realm that the narrating self can know with no contingency. The narrator claims that this certainty of self-seizing knowledge releases him from the anguish he once knew, the anguish of having been separated from himself and believing his own being to be utterly contingent. Overcoming separation of the present self from the past self is thus a necessity for noncontingent knowledge. Such knowledge is in effect resurrection, the resurrection of Combray and the child's life there.

The doctrine of resurrection Proust proposes can be viewed as something of a mirror-image inversion of Christian resurrection. The latter promises resurrection in the future of bliss that is held out for those who are fortunate enough to know grace (to put a slightly Jansenist and Pascalian cast on the matter). Proust's resurrection is a matter of reviving the past. But both Christians and Proust share the view that if one is to know plenitude, no aspect of one's being can be denied: one must be able to lay claim to every moment of one's existence, especially where it was closest to paradise already, in the family abode and garden wherein lived the adults who were already gods for the child. Proust's insistence on the physical nature of sensorial recall also resembles the medieval Christian belief that the physical body must be resurrected if resurrection is meaningful, which is to say, literal. Or to draw upon popular Protestant hymns and gospel singing, which are redolent of Proust's "Combray," resurrection means the faithful can go home again, can cross over Jordan, and find again the mother and father, not to mention grandmother and aunts, they left behind. In fine no resurrection could be meaningful that denied the total restoration of the past or denied the certainty of knowing what is that past.

The narrator's past is embodied, metonymically as it were, in the village of Combray, where the child spent vacation time, paradisiacal for the free time it offered for walks and reading as well as entering into the routine of the village life, especially routines centered on the church and the celebration of Mass. With his first reference to the lime tea, the narrator also sets out the two poles to his vision of Combray: namely the chamber of the bedridden Aunt Léonie and the village church. If the church is the center of the town, the aunt's room is the spatial center of the network of relations making up family life here. The church also embodies the temporal dimension of life in the village, sublimating the distant and indefinite past into the present while the steeple points up to the future in heaven. Perhaps for its associations with paradise, the church gets first mention when the narrator begins to narrate what the lime tea has recalled to him. He recalls that he would arrive on the train during the week before Easter—precisely before the celebration of the resurrection. Upon arriving in the train, the passenger would view Combray from afar, or as the narrator says, he would see "a church epitomizing the town" with its medieval ramparts "enclosed, here and there, in an outline as scrupulously circular as that of a little town in a primitive painting" (*SW*, 65). In the narrator's memory image, it is noteworthy that paradise is concretely represented in space and time, with real physical existence as pictured in an early Flemish or Italian painting. This is not a neutral comparison, for it suggests a space permeated with religious meanings and invested with eternal presence.

After the church Aunt Léonie's bedroom becomes the center of the painting. Through her windows she peers out into the street and, in moments of great comedy, watches the village routines taking place. The village offers its inhabitants a world of the totally known, so much so that if the narrator's aunt happened "to see a dog go by which she 'didn't know from Adam' she never stopped thinking about it, devoting all her inductive talents and her leisure hours to this incomprehensible phenomenon" (*SW*, 79). The network of habitual acts and events making up life in Combray is viewed in the street from Aunt Léonie's room, such as people's going to Mass on Sunday and known dogs passing by. Habit has its habitual variations, too, such as the Saturday devotions during May, the month dedicated to the Virgin Mary. But all in all Aunt Léonie's world runs as habitually as a well-made clock.

The narrator is fascinated by the concrete presence of time embodied in the physical world of Combray, which is best represented in the church at the center of the village. Proust's study of Ruskin and Mâle comes to the fore here, for in his description the narrator knowingly uses each feature of the Gothic church as a symbol for the presence of the past embodied in the present. For example the abbots of Combray are present in memorial stones composing the choir's pavement, as is the lineage of the Guermantes family represented in the tapestries' biblical story, in which Esther, according to tradition, has the traits of a lady of Guermantes who was once the weaver's lover. Tradition, myth, and history are intertwined in the multiple representations in stone, fabric, and glass found in the church. Remembering how time is (was) embodied in space within the church, the older narrator superimposes his viewpoint upon the boy's vision: "All this made of the church for me something entirely different from the rest of the town: an edifice occupying, so to speak, a four-dimensional space—the name of the fourth being Time—extending through the centuries its ancient nave, which bay after bay, chapel after chapel, seemed to stretch across and conquer not merely a few yards of soil, but each successive epoch from which it emerged triumphant" (*SW*, 83).

Some critics have concluded that Proust is here talking about something like Einstein's theory of relativity in which time and space are conjoined according to the framework of reference selected for perceiving them. Aside from the fact that Proust probably did not know Einstein when he wrote this passage, the passage does not really quite say that time is always measured relative to a spatial framework and vice versa. It does say that all notions of time are embodied in physical objects and hence space, which in effect does eliminate the notion of an absolute metric for measuring time. One might then read the passage to the effect that time is not universally the same everywhere; thus it is in agreement with the Einstein who eliminated absolute time when he made logical deductions about what follows from the fact that the speed of light is the same everywhere. That reading is a bit misleading, however. I think a better reading is that Proust, and hence the narrator, has something in mind not far from what a scientist such as the mathematician Henri Poincaré held at the time: all measures are conventional and relative to a given framework. Poincaré's relativist epistemology preceded Einstein's work and was undoubtedly familiar to Proust, a point I will return to at the end of this study.

From this perspective Proust's refusal to peg the novel's events on a received public chronology takes on another sense. Just as the church's various parts, originating in various times, coexist in a spatial equilibrium, with no internal necessity for one historical memento or period to take precedence over another, so Proust's recall of the past casts various memories in various places with no exterior chronological necessity tying them together. The framework for his collage is the narrator's self, and his memory and voice tie it together. In narrating the second part of "Combray," for example, he recalls the routine of village life centering on chamber and church. This establishes the basic temporal framework. However other memories from other times may enter as associations with Combray. These are mainly memories of events occurring after the time when the narrator used to go to Combray as a boy. All these layers of time recalled unfold in the narrator's consciousness, the center of the narrative, which in turn is centered, like the village's routines, on the church whose steeple "shaped and crowned and consecrated every occupation, every hour of the day, every view in the town" (*SW*, 88). In fine memory is composed of the abiding presence of what gives value to it, of recurrent church services and walks along the river but also of singular events that often pointedly and negatively contrast with this abiding presence—the presence of the past continuing to reverberate in Proust's imperfect tense.

The narrator has ironic distance from his own desire for routine and habitual recurrence, and it is with self-directed humor that he portrays the chamber of the bedridden aunt whose daily routine never knew any variation—unknown dogs excepted. She lives in such a way that apparent deviations from routine are actually "repeated at regular intervals and in identical form" so that they "did no more than print a sort of uniform pattern upon the greater uniformity of her life" (*SW*, 152–53). Habit informs every aspect of her life, as is generally the case with life in the village, so that apparent deviation from the routine can show itself to be another form of recurrence. For example it is the family's habit to lunch one hour earlier than usual on Saturday. This deviation occurs every week, so it is only habitual deviation from the greater uniformity, one that has become ritual. More impressive than this ritual of the family is the regular irregularity of Saturdays in the month of May, when regularly once a year a time of sacred metamorphoses occurs. Nature transforms itself into a chapel, and the church's altar becomes an extension of nature. Hawthorn blossoms are profusely displayed on the altar, so that "it was Nature herself who, by trimming the shape of the foliage, and by adding the crowning ornament of those snowy buds, had made the decorations worthy of what was at once a public rejoicing and a solemn mystery" (*SW,* 156). Displayed in the church every year, the ever-renewed flowers are the emblem of that celebration of resurrection whose essence lies in its unending repetition of the same.

Set against the repetition of meals, reading, and church, the individual events the narrator recalls often have more sinister negative connotations, portending the loss of paradise. Dissent and discord are possible even in the nearly ideal world of childhood. This is certainly one meaning of the singular memory the narrator recalls when he says that, at some time when he was a child, he ceased going into the sitting room once occupied by his Uncle Adolphe, his grandfather's brother. The reference to his uncle needs an explanation, which prompts the narrator to recall a series of events occurring outside the time spent at Combray. He recalls that as a boy he was responsible for the permanent break in relations between the uncle and the rest of the family. In narrating what is a flashback taking place before the eternally present past of Combray, the narrator relates that as a boy he greatly wanted to know what theater is like, a desire encouraged by the fact that his parents allowed him to go out alone in Paris. On his walks he looked at theatrical playbills with great curiosity, since his parents deemed he was not old enough to set foot inside a theater. One day he deviated from this routine: he took advantage of his freedom to go, unannounced, to see his uncle precisely when the uncle was entertaining a "lady" to whom he presented his nephew. The uncle's careless act was a breach of the conventions of the received morality that allowed adult males to consort with ladies of dubious morality but not boys. The boy, however, sees no harm in his being introduced to a charming courtesan and shares his enthusiasm about the attractive lady with his parents, since he assumes they would judge his new acquaintance by the same principles he used to judge her. Unfortunately he discovers that his parents "had recourse to principles entirely different" from those the boy intended for them to adopt (*SW,* 109). The parents are angry, a quarrel ensues, and the resulting rupture with the uncle is permanent. This unique event not only reveals to the boy the radical otherness characterizing the subjectivity of other people and hence the possibility for radical disagreement but also portends the grievous amorous adventures Swann will have, since the uncle's courtesan appears to have been none other than the Odette who becomes Swann's wife. The upshot of this unique event is that it initiates the narrator into the disharmony that rules over the adult world he comes to know when he no longer lives within the harmonious routines of Combray's paradise.

Singular events that first appear positive may also presage the troubles the older narrator comes to know. For example one day Swann, a knowledgeable aesthete, gives the boy a work by the writer Bergotte. This occurs after the narrator heard about this writer from his sometime friend Bloch, a young, unintelligible would-be symbolist with whom Proust continues, comically, the critique of symbolism he began years earlier in the essay "Against Obscurity." Bloch may be nearly a satirical figure, but the boy discovers that his usually obscure friend knew what he was talking about when he touted Bergotte's work. Significantly with the introduction of this fictive author, the narrator begins his explorations of the nature of reading, the importance of literature, and the nature of art, all of which set out coordinates for his future development. Unfortunately, however, the singular event also points toward a future in which the narrator writes but little as he tries to find his vocation as a writer. The event is endowed with a doubly ironic dimension in that the gift of Bergotte comes from Swann, a would-be Ruskin who cannot finish the book on Vermeer he had begun years before. Dilettante Swann thus prefigures the narrator's fate in more ways than one, for his procrastination prefigures the narrator's sloth—as can be figured by the allegorical figure for that vice found in the Giotto frescoes Swann also introduces the boy to. Nonetheless Bergotte's work shows the boy what a successful writer does. It allows the narrator to discover that a certain style—an individual vision independent of theme and subject matter—is what makes up the value of the work. (These same themes about the artist's vision were first elaborated, one recalls, in *Jean Santeuil* and *Against Sainte-Beuve*.) The singular event, the encounter with Bergotte's work, sets the boy on the path toward his vocation—one to be marked by his unending sense of loss and inadequacy. The writer qua writer is to be sought only in his books, and a book is precisely what Proust's narrator spends the novel not writing.

One visit to his uncle suffices to introduce the boy to the murky world of moral uncertainties, and the gift of a book by Bergotte opens a new world of aesthetic vistas that will visit upon the narrator an unending sense of failure. These singular events are paralleled in the world of Combray itself by another portending what the boy's future holds in store for him. In this case the encounter with Legrandin, a fellow parishioner at the church, reveals the multiplicity of social selves embodied by one person. Legrandin offers the boy an introduction into social role playing and therewith the hollowness and shams of society. For Legrandin is a master of snobbery and, as such, is duplicitous with others and perhaps with himself. It hardly is hyperbole to say that he prefigures most of the social practices characteristic of the society the boy will know upon leaving childhood. Legrandin is first encountered, or rather avoids an encounter, when after Mass, in the company of a lady (who is a lady), he refuses to acknowledge the narrator's father's greeting. This singular event is the first of a series in which the narrator discovers that Legrandin, a bourgeois engineer, has been taking lessons in aping the behavior of the aristocracy into which his sister has married.

The boy becomes aware of this on one occasion when he observes the physical movements with which Legrandin mimics aristocratic body posture. Attempting to resemble the stereotype of a noble being, he makes a deep bow to show his aristocratic sense of courtesy. However, as his rear sticks up, he offers to observers (as the older narrator recalls) a sort of "undulation of pure matter," "a carnal fluency devoid of spiritual significance," which is the expression of an "obsequious alacrity of the basest sort" (*SW*, 174). Later the boy sees another, different Legrandin from the one the family usually sees at Mass. This singular event takes place when he has dinner with Legrandin and watches the man go through near contortions to avoid admitting he does not "personally" know the aristocratic Guermantes. In contrast to the verbal antics with which the snob puts up a front (as well as a rear), it is with the body language that he uses to avoid the acknowledgment of his social deficiency that he actually shows himself, as the older narrator observes, to have "instantaneously been stabbed and prostrated like a St Sebastian of snobbery" (*SW*, 180).

The boy's education in what lies outside of paradise begins when he learns what self-duplicity is: Legrandin inveighs against snobs, and perhaps he does not consciously recognize that he is one. The evaluation of the boy's beginning education in the ways of the world is necessarily filtered through the older narrator's observations, based upon his years of experience, which allow him to say in resumé about Legrandin, "it is only with the passions of others that we are ever really familiar, and what we come to discover about our own can only be learned from them" (*SW*, 181). This moralist maxim that La Rochefoucauld could have penned is the result of the narrator's years of attempting to know himself, to know if he has a vocation or if he is condemned to be an unhappy socialite with a tendency toward snobbism. The type of doubt about self-perception expressed by the maxim casts light upon the emptiness or void that I have ascribed to the present instance of narration. In the present moment the narrating self finds, or believes in any case, that it cannot grasp itself and that it must appeal to knowledge it has of others in order to see itself. By the nature of things, these others always already exist in the past—except when knowledge about them is distilled into a maxim or a law. The project of self-knowledge means that the narrator must reach into the past in order to find something with which to fill up the blankness of the present. Education as self-knowledge may appear in this light to be an illusion, or minimally, as the novel demonstrates, an unending project. But knowledge of others is sometimes possible, as Proust demonstrates by concluding this series of events centered on snobbism with the comic scene in which the boy's father tortures Legrandin by trying to trick him into admitting he has a sister in Normandy, near Balbec, who might help the family if they vacation there. Legrandin cannot bear the thought that his bourgeois friends might mix, to his discredit, with his sister's aristocratic milieu, so he engages in comic contortions to circumvent the entire topic. Apparently he is not totally devoid of self-consciousness.

The comedy based on Legrandin's pretensions and delusions comes to an end when the narrator begins to describe the walks he used to take as a boy. The walks are designed to clinch the argument that Combray existed as paradise. However, the walks are marked by singular events that portend the future. Regularly each walk begins at the family house and then goes in one of two opposite directions that radiate from the village's center. One walk goes toward Swann's estate, the other toward the domain of the Guermantes, but because the two ways lead in opposing directions, each walk demands that one leave by a different door from the house, one for the path leading toward Méséglise-la-Vineuse and Swann's property and the other along the Vivonne River toward the Guermantes way. The first offers a view of the plain, the second of a river, each redolent of different myths, such as the cities of the plain or the ever-flowing spring of creation. And the singular events occurring once on each pathway foreshadow different future possibilities for the narrator.

As John Houston suggests in an early, important study of these two ways, they are opposed as two almost atemporal spatial configurations that open up on the narrator's future—not least of which because Méséglise or Swann's way is the direction for bad weather walks. Given this negative association, it is fitting that it is along Swann's way that the young narrator discovers the torments of eroticism. The way to the Guermantes is longer, and hence for fair weather. Appropriately enough it is associated with art, myth, and history.[3] After Houston other critics have often interpreted the two ways in narrowly allegorical terms, as if each narrated a form of pilgrim's progress. However let us resist the seductions of allegory to concentrate here on a few concrete details showing how events interrelate. Admittedly Proust does have an allegorical bent, and it is clear that

Swann's way leads to the first revelation of Sodom and Gomorrah, whereas the path leading to the Guermantes estate is associated with the possibility of writing and creation. However neither association is absent from the other direction, and both paths confirm in their recurrence the intimations of the paradise the boy knew in Combray as well as foreshadow the fall to come. Set against intimations of loss, in springtime the walks end with images redolent of the resurrection in the "rue du Saint-Esprit"—street of the Holy Ghost—where the boy sees a reflection of the setting sun and a "band of crimson beyond the timbers of the Calvary, which was mirrored further on in the pond" (*SW,* 186). The walks end with this revelation, at least in springtime. However Proust puts this image at the beginning of the narration of the walks, as if to make sure that the reader understands the near-theological overtones that characterize the story of the boy's recurrent ramblings in his lost paradise.

Going toward Swann's property, the boy immediately sees signs of paradise in the lilacs, a plant from the East whose flowers offer the vision of "young houris, who retained in this French garden the pure and vivid colouring of a Persian miniature" (*SW,* 190). Islam is not excluded from paradisiacal scenes. However despite the innocence one might expect from houris, moral problems are lurking in the landscape in this direction: since Swann's marriage the boy's family avoids all contact with his wife so that they do not stop at his estate but go beyond it. In spring the boy then finds himself in the company of the hawthorns that invest nature with a religious aura. Continuing in this direction, he comes across a hedge that "resembled a series of chapels, whose walls were no longer visible under the mountains of flowers that were heaped upon their altars; while beneath them the sun cast a chequered light upon the ground as though it had just passed through a stained-glass window" (*SW,* 193–94). Interrogating the flowers, the boy finds they withhold their meaning until the grandfather points out a pink hawthorn, and then festive nature leaps forward with its religious significance: "It was Nature herself who had spontaneously expressed it, with the simplicity of a woman from a village shop labouring in the decoration of a street altar for some procession" (*SW,* 197). The hawthorns become, through metaphorical associations, "a young girl in festal attire" who is smiling in her "fresh pink garments, deliciously demure and Catholic" (*SW,* 197).

Despite the associative web linking Edenic flowering, the church, and a young girl, the first hint of a future fall appears in the form of a little girl with fair, reddish hair, emerging from the hedge on Swann's estate, in an alley "bordered with jasmine, pansies, and verbenas" (*SW,* 197). The girl provides a jarring note in this floral symphony, for she seems indifferent and disdainful and, as the narrator watches her, she seems to make an obscene gesture at him. The narrator, we later learn, misinterpreted this gesture—another sign that he has not known how to interpret signs. The obscene gesture of scorn, however, can be transformed by his desire into a cause for love after he hears the girl's name, Gilberte, called out by an older woman who is present with an unidentified man (though the grandfather says it was Charlus, the homosexual baron who, ironically, the town thinks is sleeping with Swann's wife). An obscene gesture is certainly a false note in Eden. And the narrator's future love for Gilberte will not be a gateway to heaven.

Contrasting even more starkly with the bliss of the garden is the knowledge of evil another event reveals one day. Evil is introduced into the garden, as one recalls from the Bible, when the father's will is disobeyed. And in a repetition in modern terms of the biblical drama, the boy witnesses that the father is not only disobeyed but also absolutely scorned in the sadism that he discovers when, peeping into a window, he observes a profanation ritual performed by a pair of lesbian lovers. This astonishing event presages the endless discoveries the narrator later makes in *Sodom and Gomorrah* and afterward. To establish the context for this discovery, the narrator relates a flashback about a father in the village, Vinteuil, the novel's emblematic musical composer, saying that after a certain year his daughter was always seen accompanied by an older girl, one with a bad reputation (*SW*, 206). The people of the village gossip crudely about what must be going on behind the musician's back (not known as a composer, Vinteuil is considered to be just a piano teacher). Vinteuil seems oblivious to this talk. Indeed he openly deplores Swann's marriage in the name of conventions that reprove what is going on in his own house, Montjouvain. The irony characterizing Vinteuil's life establishes the context for the boy's discovery on a walk, at some time after the composer's death, that his daughter's flouting her father's will not only occurred during his lifetime, but that the denigration of his values continues even after he has been buried.

The boy becomes a voyeur when, hidden, he observes the inside of the house where the two lovers, with a photograph of the absent father placed out in view, perform a ritual profanation of the father's image. The boy watches them chase each other about and uses an analogy drawn from zoology to describe how the two women were "scrambling over the furniture, their wide sleeves fluttering like wings, clucking and squealing like a pair of amorous fowls" (*SW*, 228). Proust uses comparisons drawn from zoology and botany to create his version of a naturalistic discourse about human behavior, especially for sexual rituals. A zoologist who has not understood Proust's irony may observe that no chicken ever needs a photograph of the father to endow its mating ritual with the ultimate thrill of transgression. But irony aside, it is transgression that excites the daughter and her lover: their sexuality requires a moral dimension to violate. This need culminates in the ultimate profanation when the daughter's lover accepts the challenge to spit on the image of the father. The older narrator draws upon his later experience to reflect upon the meaning of what he saw as a boy. As a boy he could not understand that he was observing a theatrical performance of evil and that "it would have been hard to find it exhibited to such a degree of perfection outside of a convinced sadist" (*SW*, 230). The older narrator is convinced that his long life has taught him that the theatrical desire for melodramatic effect generally motivates sadism, which is brought on by a desire to commit evil while denying voluntary participation in it. He says that sadists like Mlle Vinteuil are in general so sentimental and actually virtuous that they can only find pleasure in eroticism by escaping into the "inhuman world of pleasure" through a kind of artistry that releases them from responsibility (*SW*, 231). In short her sadism springs from her being an "artist in evil" (*SW*, 231). This notion will be greatly developed in the staging performed by the Baron de Charlus in *Time Regained*. In "Combray" Swann's way leads the boy to his first discovery of evil as performance, enacted as a type of theatrical creativity that affirms evil even as it denies it. Mlle Vinteuil is at once dutiful daughter and transgressor, vicious and virtuous, sentimental and depraved. The Proustian principle of ambivalence finds no richer application than in this description of performing transgressive perversions.

The other family walk takes the boy toward the Guermantes domain, along a path by the Vivonne River, with the presentation of a different floral Eden. According to the rhythm of the season, the boy encounters early daffodils and primroses, then here and there "the blue flame of a violet," and finally buttercups in profusion (*SW*, 235–36). According to the narrator, buttercups, like the lilacs of Swann's way, have come from the Orient and here offer a "poetic scintillation from the golden East" (*SW*, 327). The botanically savvy reader may feel that Proust is inventing his flowers' origins in order to create more symmetries between the two ways. By situating the origins of both lilacs and buttercups in the East, he can associate both Swann's and the Guermantes ways with the Orient—the putative location of Eden, after all. In fact the buttercup to which Proust refers is a quite common plant native to Europe.[4] His creative botany is well taken, however: with it the child finds intimations of paradise in both directions, most especially as he walks along the river, in the water lilies he views. The painter Claude Monet is more relevant than Proust's favored botanist, Gaston Bonnier, for understanding the creation of the garden here, for the child enters a wonderland in which the water lilies are likened to rocket-flowers washed clean and then to garden pansies that "had settled like butterflies and were fluttering their blue and burnished wings over the transparent depths of this water garden—this celestial garden, too" (*SW*, 239). Here the terrestrial garden of Eden is redone as a celestial vision, much as in an impressionist painting in which images are doubled in reflections on the river's surface. In Proust's self-reflections flowers are metaphors for other flowers that are metaphors for butterflies. The harmony of all beings seems total in this vision of universal correspondences in which earth and sky mirror each other in another metaphor in which, to use I. A. Richard's terms, tenor and vehicle are abolished. This is a notable aspect of Proust's metaphors; they often express equivalencies, and not simply a comparison in which one pole of the comparison is subordinated to the other. The correspondences of all things in nature demands this unity based on equivalence.

Comic foreshadowing of the fall comes quickly in the narration of the walk toward the Guermantes way. The boy projects onto the Guermantes a mythic status, rooted in the history of the region and associated with the gardens and flowers found at their estate. He dreams of the Duchess of Guermantes and has fantasies about the help she might give him to become a writer. In these fantasies he dreams that she talks to him about his poems and gives him important subjects to which he then could "impart a philosophical significance of infinite value" (*SW*, 243). By association he remembers a real event when he was once allowed to go to a marriage in the church at which the duchess was present. During the ceremony the boy looks for her among those attending and, locating her, stares in fascination at the embodiment of his dreams of aristocracy. Staring intently, he sees that the fabled history of the Guermantes is reflected in a woman who has "a large nose, piercing blue eyes, a billowy scarf of mauve silk, glossy and new and bright, and a little pimple at the corner of her nose" (*SW*, 245). And that is all she is—for the moment. To which it must be added that a pimple in paradise is as jarring a note as is Gilberte's putative obscene gesture, though considerably more comic.

The narrator engages in self-directed humor as he describes the capacity he had as a boy to overcome his own vision, or as he puts it, perhaps through some "instinct of self-preservation," he concentrated all his thoughts upon her face so that through this act of will he could find her beautiful (*SW*, 249). As he construes it, he willed to preserve what was best in his own self so that objective reality cannot overrule what is most precious to him in his own subjective world. Madame de Guermantes emerges triumphant in this moment of willed fantasy: she is beautiful. And the young narrator can continue to believe that, as she comes out of the church, she is surrounded by a crowd whose "inferiority proclaimed her own supremacy too loudly for her not to feel sincerely benevolent towards them" (*SW*, 250). This mild hyperbole shows Proust ironically mocking his own narrator—or is it the older narrator mocking his younger self?—for the narrator can really have no idea what the duchess feels about the people about her. This is projection on his part, for it is clear that the narrator as a young man was determined to believe in her superiority in order to preserve the poetic plenitude that the idea of the aristocracy imparts to him. Loss of this poetry is, later, part of the loss of paradise; it is something like the loss of utopia seen in Proust's earlier works. Quite simply the loss is part of the fall from grace that the narrator undergoes as he becomes an adult.

I use the term *poetry* to convey the idea, moreover, that for the boy, as for the older narrator, the existence of the Guermantes seems to underlie his desire to be a writer. Their existence vouchsafes him, as a boy, a sense that he has a vocation. When they cease being guarantors of utopia, the narrator finds that his vocation has ceased to have meaning. This association of the writer's calling with the path toward the Guermantes way is underscored when the routine of the walks is broken one day by another unique event. Once, having walked much further than usual, beyond the "normal limits" of the walk, the family group is given a ride home by a local doctor. On the occasion of this ride, the narrator gives a sample of his first writing and therewith his use of metaphor to describe his experience. In this youthful writing, the narrator, sitting in a moving carriage, describes three church steeples seen in the distance. They are twin steeples in Martinville and a third at Vieuxvicq that comes to join the first two on the horizon as the vehicle moves forward, constantly changing the angle of vision the narrator has. The choice of three bodies is not fortuitous. The description of the three churches' balletlike movement is Proust's demonstration of the relativity of motion. With it he sets at the outset of his novel an emblem of the relativity that characterizes relations throughout his world: all determinations of fact depend upon the frame of reference.

In 1907 in an essay published in *Le Figaro* (collected in *Pastiches et mélanges*), Proust first described this relativity of motion. In "Journées en automobile" ("Days in an Automobile"), he describes being delighted with the sensation of riding in an automobile: when the moving vehicle is taken as an immobile framework, a cathedral seems to rush toward it. The experience of a cathedral rushing toward an automobile is slowed down in "Combray." In "Combray" the young narrator describes the "motion" of these three steeples as they change their position relative to the horse-drawn carriage in which he finds himself: they seem to move on the horizon. The carriage's slowness allows him then to write down his impressions as they occur so that the relativity of motion becomes the occasion for the boy's first creative writing.

The quotation of this youthful writing in the narrative text allows the older narrator to show literally the discovery of the unique truth of the past that metaphor can bring about—for the text and its metaphors are actually part of a past that the narrator has not thought about until the epiphanic recall of Combray. Calling the steeples "three birds perched upon the plain," the youthful narrator describes how they change position as their movement reflects the relative spatial position of the moving observer. The boy is astonished when the carriage suddenly is at the base of the two Martinville steeples. The boy's astonishment springs from the way the Proustian metaphor, abolishing tenor and vehicle, literalizes the scientific viewpoint according to which nothing can be said to have absolute movement: either the carriage or the steeples can be said to move. When the twin steeples stop moving, it is as if the carriage had run into them. The group then leaves Martinville, and as their carriage moves on, the boy sees the third steeple rejoin the other two, to wave "once again their sun-bathed pinnacles in token of farewell" (*SW*, 256). As the narrator's position changes, the steeples "move" metaphorically again, "timidly seeking their way, and, after some awkward, stumbling movements of their noble silhouettes, drawing close to one another, gliding one behind another," and they eventually vanish into the night (*SW*, 256). With these motions the three bodies have danced out their relations in a ballet that metaphorically describes the unique truth of that unique moment for a youthful narrator who is suddenly very happy. With this act of writing describing his impressions of the three steeples, the narrator anticipates his later ideas about writing: to wit that writing should translate the seizure of impressions before they are reduced to perceptual categories. In this case the movement of the steeples is born of immediate perception—before the boy or the narrator can readjust percept to the fact that conventional perception designates the wagon to be in movement, not the normally staid church steeples.

The memories prompted by a cup of lime tea and a taste of the madeleine come to an end with the narrator's breaking off the narrative about Combray in order to recall more recent past moments. He remembers having often recalled various moments from the past—including a love affair of the Swann who used to visit his family in Combray and who once caused him great anxiety. But before beginning Swann's tale, he remembers frequently lying awake in the dark, until the appearance of the light of day would undo the mental construct, representing the room he was in, that he had made for himself in the dark. In another moment of self-directed humor, he recalls seeing the dawn light arriving, and then he suddenly sees furniture and a fireplace rushing to reestablish themselves where they belong and not where his mind had pictured them in the dark (*SW*, 263–64). The point of this humor is at least twofold, I think. First, with humor it puts in question the narrator's hypothesis at the outset where he suggested that the "immobility of the things that surround us is forced upon them by our conviction that they are themselves and not anything else, by the immobility of our conception of them" (*SW*, 5). But as a window rushes to get back to where it apparently belongs, the narrator sees that there is an order of reality that has nothing to do with his conception of things established once dream has freed his mind from its moorings. Second, and relatedly, this comic view of the narrator's nocturnal perception puts in question philosophical idealism, of the post-Kantian sort, that affirms that in knowledge the mind's categories impose order on the universe. The mind's placing furniture in the wrong place in the dark hardly seems to be an ordering of reality. Proust affirms with self-directed irony at the outset of the novel that there is an order of the real, however much difficulty a mind locked in its subjectivity may have in finding it. And as "Combray" demonstrates at this point, a dominant theme of the novel is precisely the often comic interface—the misfit—between the order of the real, often unknowable, and the subjective self believing, often erroneously, that it can deal with that order. (Samuel Beckett was one of Proust's best readers, not only in his volume on Proust but in his way of translating Proust's vision of the misfit of self and reality into the solipsistic comedies of his great novels.)

Proust affirms, on the one hand, the power of subjectivity and, on the other, the indifference of reality to subjectivity. These principles are demonstrated at length by the boy's education and growing up. The reader who grasped these points in "Combray" may well be taken aback, however, when the narrator then affirms that he knows what happened to Swann, with a "precision of detail which is often easier to obtain for the lives of people who have been dead for centuries than for those of our most intimate friends" (*SW*, 262). This precision is not something that can be true of historical figures, but it is true of fictional characters in realist fiction. With his claim to knowledge about Swann, the narrator really affirms, as I suggested earlier, a belief in the kind of omniscient narrator that Balzac and Flaubert had made the staple of realist fiction. Their narrators have little doubt about the correspondence between their statements and the reality of the world they illustrate. In *Swann's Way*, after the fluctuations of subjectivity in "Combray," Proust gives a demonstration of the power of realist narration to lay bare the reality of the world.

In narrating *Swann's Way*, moreover, the narrator is telling something about a past that preceded his own past, but one that is a part of the narrator's history. The narrator's history, like Swann's, intersects a fictional public history, a public history that is larger than any individual's story. What seems to motivate Proust in part is that it is impossible to narrate the intersection of history and subjectivity except in fiction and by subordinating history to fiction. If, for example, a third-person omniscient narrator writes that "Swann thought so and so," this is fictively true. But if the same narrator writes that "Napoleon thought so and so," the narrator is writing a fiction with the pretense to history (as opposed to statements such as "Napoleon may have thought," "seemed to have thought," "could have thought," etc.—all probabilistic statements that make up the contingent truths of nonfictional history). *Swann's Way* is not only the story of an unhappy love affair, but in its fictional objectivity, it is also the beginning of the presentation of the historical narration that Proust uses as the backdrop for his narrator's development. *Swann's Way* is where history begins to intersect with subjectivity in Proust's novel.

I have pointed out that there is no precise chronology in the narrator's recall of the past; but through allusion and reference, the narrator creates nonetheless a great historical collage setting forth the history in which the narrator develops. The collage is clearly put together to illustrate at least one dominant historical theme: the absorption of the aristocracy by the increasingly dominant bourgeoisie. This is the unending spectacle of which the narrator is witness when not a participant therein. It is a process in which Swann is an exemplary player. From one perspective it appears that the rich Jewish stockbroker's son rises in society when he is received by the aristocracy; but with a relativistic reversal of that perspective, it seems that the rich bourgeoisie has begun to absorb the aristocracy. The social history inscribed in the novel turns on a long demonstration of this relativistic process.

A few comments on the historical development can help not only to situate Swann but also to understand the novel's portrayal of the disappearance of a putatively real aristocracy. The historical context Proust presupposes, as he shows in representing Swann's and the narrator's consciousness of it, may not be a familiar one to a contemporary reader. For example the class distinctions the narrator takes for granted are not part of the American experience. And even readers with some knowledge of French history may wonder how, after the French Revolution chopped off a good many noble heads, the aristocracy could continue to play the important role in French society Proust attributes to it. The reader should be aware that it is an error to assume the aristocracy was decimated by the

Revolution or that it permanently lost its importance after 1789. After Napoleon's fall the return of the aristocracy was part of the restoration of the monarchy. Returning to power as a self-contained class that had resisted Napoleon's attempt to enlarge it, the old, pre-Revolutionary aristocracy continued to play an important role in French society and government through the various regimes that ruled in nineteenth-century France, including the bourgeois monarchy of Louis-Philippe and the new empire of Napoleon III. This aristocracy was an especially important political force at the beginning of the Third Republic, established after France's defeat by Prussia in 1870. Playing on fears of radicalism unleashed by the Parisian Commune, royalists and aristocrats nearly managed a restoration of the monarchy in the early years of the Republic (as I noted in the introduction, Proust's friend Daniel Halévy called it the "Republic of Dukes"). The early years of the Third Republic, and hence of Proust's childhood, saw a near restoration in which aristocrats held most high public offices while waiting for the chance to establish something more to their liking than the presidential republic—even if the president was looked upon as a kind of surrogate king.

There were in fact two aristocracies in France, the old, now closed aristocracy existing before 1790 (closed in effect because it was legally abolished in that year) and a new aristocracy created by Napoleon for his empire. It is largely the "true" aristocracy of pre-1790 origins that is the object of young Proust's utopian yearnings. In the novel the scorn the old aristocracy has for the newly titled nobles provides much comic commentary, especially when the Baron de Charlus gives his opinions. It is largely the old aristocracy that sets the tone for what is really high society and decides, for example, who can join the elite Jockey Club of which Swann is perhaps the only Jewish member. From the beginning of the novel, the narrator's attention is focused on a relatively small segment of both aristocratic and bourgeois classes. There is hardly a reference, for example, to prelates and lawyers, though both groups played key roles in the Third Republic. In some ways Swann's world seems almost medieval, resembling the world of the castle and the burg, in which inhabitants of each confront each other as they vie for power and influence.

Seen from this historical perspective, it is not surprising that Proust's characters look upon love and marriage as almost unrelated matters. Marriage is contracted with an eye to furthering family and property interests, especially for aristocrats in need of money (later the narrator's friend, the aristocrat Saint-Loup, will consider a rich marriage simply so that he can continue to spend lavishly on his mistress). However even a bourgeois such as Swann separates the ideas of love and marriage in his own mind, and his marriage to Odette finally seems almost emblematic of the separation of the two: he marries her only after his love for her is dead. One inevitably recalls the world of the medieval troubadours, for whom passionate love could exist only outside of marriage. For love does not necessarily involve erotic attraction. The separation of eroticism and love (with both apparently unrelated to marriage) is striking when Swann first meets Odette. He looks carefully at her, at her features, and in discerning what is appealing about them, notes that she is not his type (*SW*, 276). Here he makes his evaluation clearly in terms of erotic desirability—the most common type of "love" if we hark back to what Stendhal had to say about the four types of love.

Stendhal had impressed Proust when he was writing *Jean Santeuil*. Stendhal's influence still hovers over *Swann's Way*. In describing Swann's love, Proust carefully delineates the stages in its development, which, if not totally illustrative of the theories of *De l'amour*, show nonetheless that Proust believed that love could be studied according to something resembling laws of development. In a mixed series of reactions, Swann is struck with admiration of Odette and begins to project upon her idealizations that recall Stendhal's ideas about crystallization as well as his ideas about the role of music in creating passion. First Swann finds in the emotional appeal of Vinteuil's F-sharp sonata an allure that he transfers to Odette when he encounters the sonata and the woman together in the salon of the very bourgeois Mme Verdurin. Swann had heard the sonata earlier, at which time it had "opened and expanded his soul, as the fragrance of certain roses, wafted upon the moist air of evening, has the power of dilating one's nostrils" (*SW*, 294). If this be eroticism, it is of a most ethereal sort, for Odette's presence does then allow Swann to imagine he finds in the sonata "a world of inexpressible delights, of whose existence, before hearing it, he had never dreamed, into which he felt that nothing else could initiate him; and he had been filled with love for it, as with a new and strange desire" (*SW*, 296). Since Swann has had innumerable affairs with women up to this point, the new and strange desire he feels resembles more the fantasies of romantic passion than the predictable pleasures of bodily contact that Swann has enjoyed countless times.

If the sonata offers—or perhaps creates—something like the moment of "admiration," the moment filled with wonder that Stendhal sees at the beginning of love, it is a painting that completes the crystallization by which Swann, rapidly falling in love, projects upon the beloved the ideal traits that he desires to possess. The aesthete Swann has the history of world art at his disposition for his choice of models of ideal traits. He takes as his prime choice an image from Alessandro Botticelli when he decides that Odette resembles a Florentine painting, in this case Zipporah, Jethro's daughter, found in one of Botticelli's Sistine frescoes (*SW,* 315). Not incidentally he is now guilty of the idolatry of art for which Proust had castigated Ruskin. This occurs when the aesthete uses the beauty of the artwork to justify an affirmation that something—namely Odette—is more than beautiful. Borrowing from the artwork, projecting it onto Odette, Swann succeeds in transforming her beauty: "He no longer based his estimate of the merit of Odette's face on the doubtful quality of her cheeks and the purely fleshly softness which he supposed would greet his lips there should he ever hazard a kiss, but regarded it rather as a skein of beautiful delicate lines which his eyes unraveled" (*SW,* 316). In this act of projection and transformation, Swann is able "to introduce the image of Odette into a world of dreams and fancies which, until then, she had been debarred from entering, and where she assumed a new and nobler form" (*SW,* 317). Perhaps it is difficult to say if his love is more the product of his projecting an image from Botticelli onto Odette to make her more attractive or of his desire to find living presence for a work of art that is the real object of his passion. In any case by associating the two he mentally metamorphoses Odette into something more valuable and precious than what rich hedonistic aesthetes usually seek in an expensive courtesan.

After this crystallization the narrator describes the ensuing torments of love. This is perhaps Proust's unique contribution to a history of the theories of love. Proust, as perhaps no other writer before him, shows that the heightening of amorous passion depends upon jealousy. Jealousy is in effect a heightening of the anguish felt at the absence of the beloved, which originates in the lover's impossible desire to possess the beloved. The narrator himself first experienced this kind of anguish with the absence of his mother—when Swann himself was responsible for the traumatic moment that seemingly underlies the recurrent patterns of love in the narrator's life. But the narrator's anguish is not quite the same as Swann's. As one of the best recent critics of Proust, Joshua Landry, has argued about love in his work, if Proust looks for laws of sameness, he also looks for differences. Swann is thus not quite a double of the narrator, even if he precedes the narrator in his adventures in unhappiness.[5] It appears that Swann has known no great unhappiness before he concocts an idealized Odette who then, in turn, gives him more than adequate cause for jealousy, which is to say, anguish about absence and the impossibility of possession, the two dominant features that characterize Proustian passion when it takes over a character's life.

To some readers jealousy's power over Swann and, later, over the narrator may seem hyperbolic, but I would argue that, in this regard, Proust is not eccentric in his description of love, even if he is unique in his focus. As I suggested earlier, he caps a long tradition of moralists for whom passionate love is considered to be a pathological condition causing madness. The origins of this medico-moralist tradition lie in Plato and Cicero, and then the church fathers who, in repeating Plato, Cicero, and the Greek medical tradition, considered passion to be a form of disease manifesting itself as madness. This medical-moral view of passion had hardly disappeared by the end of the nineteenth century (and one can argue that Freud renewed it for the twentieth century). Thus as against the troubadours, for whom passion is akin to religious salvation, Proust inscribes his lover's passion in the medical tradition for which love is a disease. Like all diseases passion follows a predetermined course, so that the law of its development is not unlike the laws that preside over the unfolding of any other malady.[6]

Jealousy begins one night when Swann returns to Odette's house after he had left her at midnight. He thinks he sees light in her window—though it is the wrong window—but this error causes him to experience doubt about her fidelity. (Proust demonstrated in *Pleasures and Days* that recognition after the fact that an error has caused an emotion does nothing to lessen the emotion.) This doubt is sufficient to set off the genesis of jealousy in Swann. He frequently observes that he cannot explain to himself every moment in Odette's day. One afternoon, when he calls unexpectedly on her, she does not answer the door, though he hears noises within (*SW*, 394). Odette's later explanation as to why she did not open the door appears to contain some truth but also some falsehood. Facing this uncertainty, Swann is also forced to face the fact that he cannot possess every aspect of Odette's being. Like a doctor analyzing himself, Swann is lucid in his prognosis:

> Of course it occurred to him from time to time that Odette's daily activities were not in themselves passionately interesting, and that such relations as she might have with other men did not exhale naturally, universally and for every rational being a spirit of morbid gloom capable of infecting with fever or of inciting to suicide. He realized at such moments that that interest, that gloom, existed in him alone, like a disease, and that once he was cured of this disease, the actions of Odette, the kisses that she might have bestowed, would become once again as innocuous as those of countless other women. (*SW*, 396)

These lines set out the medical metaphor, if metaphor it is, for love, in which Swann foresees what the course of his illness will be. Diagnosis allows prognosis. But this does not mean that he, or any other doctor, can do anything about the disease's development. Prognosis does not bring about a cure.

The narrator appears to take his distance from this viewpoint when he says critically that Swann had adopted "a positivist, almost a medical philosophy" (397) from the men with whom he associated. Nonetheless the narrator himself continues to use medical metaphors in his portrayal of Swann's suffering. The now omniscient narrator is capable of analyzing Swann's inner life and observing that lucid Swann does not really "realize how much he suffered; since it was only gradually, day by day, that Odette had cooled towards him" (*SW,* 457). Likening the suffering to a "deep, secret wound, which tormented him day and night," the narrator portrays a Swann who engages in evasive actions and thoughts to avoid confronting the cause of his disease—the fact that he is a patsy in his relationship with Odette (*SW,* 457). But Swann's recognition does come, in the form of a crisis if not an epiphany, during the soirée given at the home of the Marquise de Saint-Euverte. After listening to the familiar phrase from Vinteuil's sonata, he recalls what he had possessed at the beginning of his relationship with Odette and contrasts it with what he knows he has at that moment: "From that evening onwards, Swann understood that the feeling which Odette had once had for him would never revive, that his hopes of happiness would not be realized now" (*SW,* 502). Yet Swann's love stays alive, following a downward spiral, thus reaching what can be likened to new circles in hell, as new revelations are made to him about Odette's proclivities—for instance that she has worked in brothels or that she likes women as well as men. These revelations are accompanied by the prognosis that upon reaching a certain point of degradation, Swann can undergo a cure. This seems to be the case. Near the end of his suffering, Swann tries to convince himself that he should cling to his love as something precious; at the same time, as the narrator says, Swann knew a diminution of his love, to which corresponded a simultaneous diminution in his desire to remain in love (*SW,* 536–37). His desire diminishes like a fever. There is little volunteerism in being in love (just as one cannot consciously desire to have or not to have a cold). And with the cessation of love comes the cessation of jealousy—for one apparently conditions the other so that neither can be said to come first—at least in Swann's case. No longer in love, Swann can learn at last with indifference that Odette has slept with his rival, the vulgar Comte de Forcheville.

The count's relation with Odette presages the decline of the aristocracy, completed at the end of the novel when he not only marries Odette but also adopts Swann's daughter, Gilberte. These considerations bring us back to the historical perspective. Swann's love affair unfolds in the historical context of the first decades of the Third Republic, a republic struggling not to become a monarchy. Swann's love for Odette takes on an added dimension when placed in the context of the pressures and movements of social classes that set the stage for how his love unfolds. Odette is of poor extraction, a vulgar but apparently attractive woman of great elegance, who has done whatever necessary to become a wealthy courtesan—and then, as it turns out in *Swann's Way,* the wife of a very wealthy bourgeois. By contrast Swann is a prominent man who gives advice to the wealthy and wellborn and sets standards for them in art and style. Swann in this sense is representative of the wealthy bourgeoisie that is assimilating even as it replaces the aristocracy. The values of his class are becoming the common values of the once dominant class. This fact hardly constitutes an endorsement of bourgeois values on the part of the narrator. This is clear in his portrait of Swann. Though the master of social elegance and bourgeois values, Swann finds that his life is "barren" (*SW,* 336) since he is incapable of finding a path in life beyond the rather empty fulfillment of the social rituals that make up his life. Life in society, be it aristocratic, be it bourgeois, comes to have no meaning for Swann.

With regard specifically to the rising bourgeoisie, one is struck by how unflattering is Proust's portrayal of it, at least in its manifestations in social life. The portrayal begins in *Swann's Way* when Swann meets Odette in the salon of Madame Verdurin, a rich and somewhat bohemian social impresario who, at the novel's end, will complete the merger of classes when she marries into the aristocracy and assumes a dominant role there. In *Swann's Way* the Verdurin circle is characterized as being artsy, which largely means shallow and pretentious, and given over to the self-promotion that assures their rise in society. Proust's portrayal of the Verdurin circle verges on satire at moments. In general virtually all characters in society are comic. Because of his infatuation with Odette, Swann himself becomes a comic figure especially insofar as he is willingly oblivious to the obvious vulgarity around him. For example at times Mme Verdurin is a caricature of an aesthete. She is too sensitive to listen to music without getting a headache, which allows her to engage in comically convoluted complaints and lamentations about her superior receptivity to art. Other members of her clan are equally comic. For example the doctor Cottard, though reputedly a great clinical specialist, is a social Neanderthal with his love of pointless wordplay used to cover up the fact that he rarely understands what is going on around him. At their soirées the Verdurins insist upon a "palsy" democratic egalitarianism, to set them and their friends off from the "boring" aristocrats whom they claim not to want even to know. Swann incurs opprobrium, in fact, when he lets it slip that he counts aristocrats among his friends. Thus even if Swann were able to participate in the circle's crude jokes—which he is not—this fact alone would suffice for him to be finally excluded from the group.

Swann's association with this clan because of Odette threatens to undermine his own sense of taste and values. He is drawn down by Odette, who in her lust for social ascension has adopted the shallow values, vulgar mannerisms, and absurd style of what she takes to be the "smart set"— such as the pointless use of Anglicisms on every possible occasion. Odette does in fact ascend in society, and in so doing she undergoes a thorough transformation. Ovid probably describes no more radical metamorphosis. It is Swann's decline, however, that is obvious at the outset of his passion, which is set off by Odette's vulgarity. His critical sharpness is blunted as he rationalizes everything that caters to his love. For example when confronting Odette's inevitable bad taste and confused ideas about social relations, his power of rationalization causes him to adopt a rootless relativism. With what appears to be self-delusion, he can justify to himself that he has not made any attempt to modify Odette's "conception of fashionable life; feeling that his own came no nearer to the truth"; and since he decides his viewpoint was just as fatuous and trivial as any other, "he saw no point in imparting it to his mistress" (*SW*, 345). Proust's pessimistic point is, I think, that the rise of lower classes is bringing on the demise of aristocratic values—once Swann's values. Thus the ascent of the bourgeoisie entails the decline of values rather than the assimilation of higher standards, of which Odette's last husband, the aristocrat Forcheville, is perhaps the prime example.

Swann's love cuts him free from the moorings of his own upper-class values, which is made most explicit when, deeply suffering from his love, he goes to listen to music at the home of the Marquise de Saint-Euverte. This event foreshadows the novel's portrayal of the final demise of the aristocracy, a destruction prefigured in *Swann's Way* in the contrast of the social life at the Verdurin circle and the soirée organized by the marquise. Both are places at which the comedy of social life is played out. However in the depiction of the marquise's soirée, the satire of aristocratic ineptitude is perhaps even more trenchant than the comedy of bourgeois vulgarity.

The narrator stresses that, immersed in his love, Swann arrives in a detached mood at the Marquise de Saint-Euverte's soirée. This detachment transforms him, in the first part of the evening, into a double for the narrator: he becomes a satirical observer. His distanced vision transforms what he sees into strange sights, sometimes recalling famous artworks, at other times suggesting near monsters. Upon entering Swann goes by a "pack" of footmen, one of them recalling a Renaissance executioner, while another resembles the decorative warrior in an Andrea Mantegna painting, who looks "lost in thought" while people around him are rushing about slaughtering one another (*SW*, 460). His satirical detachment continues as Swann advances up the stairs, his ironical observation bringing out the arbitrariness of social relations in which the rich maintain an army of men standing idly and pointlessly around. Swann reaches the concert room, where an "usher loaded with chains" now "bowed low before him as though tendering to him the keys of a conquered city" (*SW*, 463). The culminating moment in this grotesquerie comes with the description of the aristocratic men Swann sees, each standing about with a monocle firmly implanted in one eye (and among them is found a society novelist who is using his optical instrument for observing, as Proust wryly puts it in a moment of self-reflexive comedy). Swann observes the General de Froberville: his monocle is "stuck between his eyelids like a shell-splinter in his vulgar, scarred and overbearing face, in the middle of a forehead which it dominated like the single eye of the Cyclops" (*SW*, 464). This is only one of several monocles that identify their bearers as members of the social elite while suggesting at the same time that they belong to some strange primitive tribe in which the men systematically deform their faces. The aristocratic women seem, on the other hand, to be mainly engaged in slighting other women, especially those who are anxious to associate with them. A prime object of slight is the Marquise de Gallardon, who is absorbed in her favorite subject of meditation, namely her kinship with the illustrious Guermantes family, which is a source of glory and also of shame for her, because "the most brilliant ornaments of that house" remain aloof, "perhaps because she was boring, or because she was disagreeable, or because she came from an inferior branch of the family, or very possibly for no reason at all" (*SW*, 467).

Such are the activities that constitute the foundations of the social elite. To be sure it is an elite in which, in noted contrast with the Verdurin circle, Swann is quite at home. The description of the soirée underscores his belonging when he engages in trivial banter with the epitome of nobility, the Princesse of Laumes (another name for Mme de Guermantes, or Oriane if one is on a first-name basis with her). Swann loses his acute vision at this moment, though the narrator does not, and the dismantling of aristocratic pretensions continues with the demonstration that indeed they are as trivial as the Mme Verdurin, who is destined to succeed them at the pinnacle of society.

A symmetry between the two social circles is created by the presence of music in both, notably Vinteuil's sonata. The varied functions of music in Proust's work is remarkable. If the sonata marked the beginning of Swann's love in the Verdurins' salon, at the later aristocratic soirée it serves to isolate him from these "people whose stupidity and absurdities struck him all the more painfully since, being ignorant of his love . . . they made it appear to him in the aspect of a subjective state which existed for himself alone, whose reality there was nothing external to confirm" (*SW*, 489–90). The music confirms the solipsistic state of the lover who hopes to find in the sonata some exterior confirmation of the reality of his suffering. Turning in upon himself in solipsism, he recalls a man whom Odette once did love, who is, namely, himself: "He was jealous, now, of that other self whom she had loved," which is to say of himself as well as all the other men who may have enjoyed her (*SW*, 493).

Swann's solipsism points up the contrast the narrator knows throughout the novel: on the one hand the narrator confronts the social world and its absurd rituals, games, and vanities, and on the other he wonders what is his own self while trying to negotiate the social web these rituals create. Social psychology and individual ontology exist in a kind of dialectical antagonism. Swann's painful reflection on himself reflects the basic ontological questioning that subtends the novel until the conclusion: What reality can he attribute to his own mind, self, and emotions? Anticipating the narrator's later meditations, Swann listens to the music and wonders what is the nature of this sonata that is so closely bound up with his emotions. Reflecting on the "little phrase" that had had such a role in his emotional life, he wonders if it only existed latently in his mind "on the same footing as certain other notions without material equivalent, such as our notions of light, of sound, of perspective, of physical pleasure" (*SW*, 497). He wonders what ontological status he can ascribe to these notions if they exist only in the mind, perhaps to be obliterated in death—death conceived by Swann as a return to nothingness. He confronts his existence with a sense of possible nothingness, intuited in the middle of his isolation in a crowd. Like a philosopher from a Baroque play, he wonders if "it is not-being that is the true state, and all our dream of life is inexistent; but if so, we feel that these phrases of music, these conceptions which exist in relation to our dream, must be nothing either" (*SW*, 498). From which Swann concludes that perhaps art is a mitigating form of quasi-salvation, or as he muses, "We shall perish, but we have as hostages these divine captives who will follow and share our fate" so that "death in their company is somehow less bitter, less inglorious, perhaps even less probable" (*SW*, 498). With these questions and the emotions attendant upon them, Swann broaches the questions about art that the narrator will pursue until he finds, perhaps, the path of his own vocation as artist. But as Swann's failure to find a vocation shows, questions remain only questions.

Swann's wistful meditation on how unlikely is any permanent form of existence marks the beginning of the end of his love. After his meditation on music, the quickly ensuing succession of degrading revelations about Odette's sexual adventures conclude the tale of his love. Like Proust's earlier version of Sherlock Holmes, Jean Santeuil, and like the narrator after Albertine's death, Swann undertakes detective work, at least as long as he is possessed by the illusion that knowledge about Odette might be a surrogate way of possessing her. Reaching the depths, he makes inquiries about her in brothels. With Dante in mind, we can say that Swann is near the bottom of the rings circling down in Hell, to the lowest where those guilty of betrayal are lodged. In describing Swann at this point, however, the narrator again uses medicine for his conceptual framework. Like an all-knowing doctor, he observes that Swann's "organism" now wants to get well. Swann's newfound resistance to disease means that the "new sufferings" that invade his soul encounter a "natural foundation, older, more placid, and silently industrious, like the cells of an injured organ which at once set to work to repair the damaged tissues" (*SW*, 517–18). Hence convalescence begins to set in. And near the end of his convalescence, only a fortuitous dream of Forcheville appearing in the guise of a Napoleon III bent on pursuing Odette can awaken Swann's now nearly quiescent state of jealousy (*SW*, 539–40). As the medical metaphor would have it, at the end Swann is finally cured. The ensuing marriage with Odette is apparently of little interest to the narrator, for all we really learn is that it happened.

Swann's Way ends with the observation with which it began: Swann sees once again that Odette is not his type. This circularity confirms his recovery as well as the futility of his knowledge. His recognition underscores that the laws presiding over his psychological development certainly allow for contradiction and paradox—at least if falling in love with somebody who is not attractive to you is a paradox. If one holds that Swann is a double in some sense for the narrator, then one may ask whether his love presages the narrator's falling in love with women who are not his type. For example is this true of the narrator's precocious first love for Swann's daughter, Gilberte, the little girl first seen making ambiguous gestures in "Combray"? I defer this question to the next chapter, since the narration of the narrator's first love occupies a large part of *Within a Budding Grove*. It is true that in the third section of *Swann's Way*, "Place-Names: The Name," Proust begins the tale of this precocious love as well as a meditation on the power of proper names. This narration is continued directly in *Within a Budding Grove*. His arrangement and distribution of the narration merits some commentary.

It appears that Proust concluded *Swann's Way* at the point where it concludes today because of the publisher's insistence that he break up the narration. The publisher did not want *Swann's Way* to be too imposing a tome. Thus only the beginning of the story about the narrator's love for Gilberte is in it, and the continuation is in the next volume. Today's conclusion was apparently appended to give the single volume, *Swann's Way*, a logical stopping point and a semblance of unity. If this is all true, it means that Proust capitalized on practical necessity to create a key moment in the novel. For it is at the very end of *Swann's Way* that the narrator recalls the recent past and makes his judgment on the present moment that I eluded to above. At this point the narrator recalls a recent past that lies years in the future from the viewpoint of the world portrayed *Swann's Way*. More precisely *Swann's Way* ends with the memory of the youthful narrator's infatuation with Gilberte's mother, Odette de Crécy, now Madame Swann, who appears in the apotheosis of her glory as the most elegant woman in Paris. Her metamorphosis has been completed. The old narrator recalls those days when admirers gathered to watch her as she walked in the Bois de Boulogne, the woodland park on the western side of Paris. He remembers when as a boy he would stand in the street to look at her in admiration as she passed by, dazzling all present, including gentlemen who remember when they knew her as Odette de Crécy. Proust uses amusing narrative sleight of hand so that the young narrator does *not* hear one of the bystanders say that he slept with Odette on the day that President Mac-Mahon resigned (*SW,* 597). With this allusion to history (that the narrator does not hear), Proust teases the reader with the possibility of a historical collage, created by the fact that Odette was making her way up in the world when the monarchist MacMahon was obliged to step down from the presidency in 1879—a resignation that meant that the republicans had some reason to hope that the Third Republic would last. However the next remark that the younger narrator does not hear suggests that things have not changed that much in the Republic, at least as far as affairs of honor go. The bystander's friend tells him it would not be advisable for him to recall that day to Odette Swann, since she is now wife of a friend of the Prince of Wales. In any case from the young narrator's viewpoint, Odette is now a goddess.

To this childhood memory, the narrator appends in conclusion his memory of the very recent past conceived as a Götterdämmerung. The narrator's recent past is a lived experience for which Richard Wagner created a musical analogy: for the older narrator experienced a sense of the "twilight of the gods" when on a recent November day, he went to the Bois, and instead of the deities of his youth, with their extravagantly beautiful clothes and elegant carriages, he found anonymous people in dull modern dress driving characterless automobiles. This recollection of a recent event contrasting with the recollection of the distant past is another type of memory in Proust. It is elegiac memory, a memory that finds the past inevitably fuller than the present. But there is humor involved in his remembrance of the "happy days" of his unquestioning youth, when he would hasten "eagerly to the spots where masterpieces of female elegance would be incarnate for a few moments beneath the unconscious, accommodating boughs" (*SW*, 602). Now he goes to the Bois only to discover what he calls a meaningless parade of ill-dressed creatures who pass before him in a "desultory, haphazard, meaningless fashion" (*SW*, 603). Though tempered with humor, his discovery nonetheless shows his disenchantment, which is to say, the modernist discovery that the world has no transcendental dimension, it knows only the arbitrary changes represented by meaningless fashion and modes. So as the narrator says, he finds himself deprived of belief; he is left with merely a "fetishistic attachment to the old things which it did once animate, as if it was in them and not in ourselves that the divine spark [*le divin*] resided, and as if our present incredulity had a contingent cause—the death of the gods" (*SW*, 603). On going to the Bois, he finds that the past haunts the present moment, like specters wandering through the Virgilian groves, whose presence he finds, metaphorically, in the woods about him. But the Bois is now a deconsecrated forest that can do nothing to restore in their fullness the images stored in memory (*SW*, 606). Madame Swann did not reappear in all her shimmering beauty on that recent day. And to conclude, the narrator says that he understood, then, that it was useless to seek in reality those pictures stored in memory, for images and time are bound together such that "houses, roads, avenues are as fugitive, alas, as the years" (*SW*, 606). With this elegiac thought ends *Swann's Way* and begins the narration destined to triumph, one sometimes believes, over the fugitive nature of time.

Chapter 5

Within a Budding Grove and *The Guermantes Way*

Intimations of the Fall

Proust may have been under pressure from his publisher to break off *Swann's Way* with fewer pages than he initially intended. If so I suggested in the previous chapter that Proust took advantage of necessity to conclude *Swann's Way* by refocusing the narration on the narrator and, with this change of focus, to grant his narrator a backward glance confirming the death of the gods. This backward glance is a strong moment in the novel, situating the aging narrator once again as the commanding presence in the work. The Götterdämmerung he narrates could be taken as a resumé of his education in the rest of the novel. The death of the gods underlies the next unity of the novel I wish to discuss. That unity is created by the fact that Proust develops *In Search of Lost Time* as a bildungsroman. That *Bildung*, or education in the broadest sense, begins in the final section of *Swann's Way* and ties together the narrated experience of *Within a Budding Grove* and *The Guermantes Way*. In effect the narrator's first education continues throughout these volumes until, at the beginning of *Sodom and Gomorrah*, he moves into a new phase of his learning. Losing his naïveté, he sees what the world is about as he watches Charlus seduce Jupien. The young man then understands that the aristocrat's homosexuality explains much of his seemingly bizarre behavior in *Within a Budding Grove* and *The Guermantes Way*. Up to that moment of pointed awakening, the narrator's younger self is an innocent learner, at times somewhat obtuse and naive, though sometimes a sharp observer whose ironic understanding of society increasingly resembles that of the older narrator: his gods collapse in rapid order. However it is only upon viewing the baron's behavior that the young man suddenly understands that, without knowing it, he has been a denizen of one of the cities of the plain. This discovery was foreshadowed, of course, in "Combray" during one of his walks in the direction of Méséglise, which offered him first intimations of the fall. But he graduates to something like an adult understanding of the world only with the revelation the baron offers him.

Let us now discuss the narrator's education, beginning in the final section of *Swann's Way,* and pursue it through two volumes of youthful growth, before his education culminates in a full recognition of the fall in *Sodom and Gomorrah.* It is an education of the heart as well as the mind in which immature love plays a prominent role. Two experiences of infatuation are most important for the narrator, first with Gilberte and then with the Duchess of Guermantes. The narrator's first affair of the heart actually begins in the last section of *Swann's Way,* in "Place-Names: The Name," a rather strange title that seems to suggest a context in which the narrator is educated in life and love.

"Place-Names: The Name" finds an echo in the title of the final section of *Within a Budding Grove,* to wit "Place-Names: The Place." The two titles underscore the role language plays in the narrator's education. They emphasize in particular the illusions and deceptions that place-names worked upon his young imagination. The title is a bit restrictive, however, since the boy's imagination is as much taken with the names of people as with the names of places, though it is of course true that aristocratic names are often names of places as well as of families. What is essential to the boy's education is that he finally manages to understand that, among all forms of language, proper names most often work a spell upon him and bewitch his mind with poetical illusions. Sonorous and evocative to his imagination, proper names elicit his inner fantasies and cause him to project his desires upon them and, through them, upon the world. Thus one aspect of the young narrator's education is what he learns when he finds that his fantasies run aground on his actual experience. For it is a recurrent event for him that names of people and places are deflated. Quite simply education is the process of deflating what first appears to the boy portentous with promises of revelation and transcendence.

Once one is aware of the ambiguous relation that Proust had with the poet Mallarmé, one may note that, in dealing with proper names, he seems to adopt the poet's idea that language falls into two categories: first ordinary words for ordinary and hence trivial discourse; and, second and by contrast, what Mallarmé called the poetic *parole essentielle* or essential word that brings about revelation. Though Proust was in thrall to the idea of poetic revelation—for what is one form of involuntary memory but a type of revelation?—in the novel's portrayal of education he offers a long demonstration that the boy's belief in privileged language foists off on him mainly delusion and deception, the result of which is a disabused state of mind and then finally disenchantment. Proust's young narrator is not quite a follower of Mallarmé—nor indeed is the Proust who wrote an essay against symbolist obscurity and parodies him in the character of Bloch—but the narrator as young man is a victim of the belief that exceptional language may reveal something bordering on the transcendental. It is another question whether, at the end of the novel, the narrator does not finally endorse another version of transcendental language.

Mallarmé aside, the young narrator also illustrates an intelligent boy's will to believe. His is a normal child's enchantment with magic and ceremonies that transform reality; and one could also argue that it is a historical accident that his exaggerated desire illustrates, undoubtedly with critical irony, a late nineteenth-century view of poetic language. From either viewpoint, with or against Mallarmé, one can ask if Proust is making a generalization about the power of language, especially its power to deceive, or if the narrator's enchantment with names is a form of delusion that affects only him. The question as to the status of truth in Proust's fiction is raised as soon as one asks what is the nature of the education that the narrator receives. Since it is to be doubted that most readers experience a sensation of color upon hearing the nasal vowel in the name Guermantes, it can be argued that the narrator's education is largely centered upon his own psychological makeup.[1] However, it can also be argued that Proust's exposition of the narrator's education is comically persuasive, in fact, for the way it portrays the narrator's *Bildung* as a specific case rooted in the late nineteenth-century's aesthetics at the same time it suggests a law of human development: a recurrent thirst for transcendence and gods whose existence is belied by daily reality. This double focus turning on the general and the specific is frequent throughout the novel, and especially at the novel's conclusion, in *Time Regained,* when the reader must decide if the narrator's vocation is the outgrowth of Everyman's progress or the single case of one writer having probably found his vocation. For the moment let us look at the young narrator as an individual case of *Bildung,* of growth and development, in which he must learn to sort out the names of places and people that bewitch his imagination.

Swann's Way ends with the narrator's evocation of the names of places and persons, of the town of Balbec about which the boy dreams, and Gilberte, the name of Swann's daughter he hears one day while walking toward Méséglise. Balbec, the name of a (fictional) Norman seacoast town, conjures up for the boy wild, unbridled nature—such as the shore and the sea whose storms roar in *Jean Santeuil.* After Swann talks about the church found in Balbec, the name also conjures up for him distorted visions of

Gothic architecture. The narrator is all in all in this regard a rather normal child who dreams of travel and distant places and is endlessly fascinated by the train schedules that lay out the names of stops he might pass through were he ever to travel north to the sea. Casting a wider net than northern France, he is also absorbed by the names of towns in Italy, such as Venice, Florence, and Parma, cities having Stendhalian associations of "sweetness and the reflected hue of violets" as well as being famous for the wonders of their architecture (*SW*, 552). These associations conjuring up blissful regions beyond reality condemn, by contrast, all that makes up his banal everyday routine—not unlike what Proust first portrayed with the youth in his essay on the painter Chardin. Disgusted by daily life, the narrator declares he could hardly bear to go out to play on the Champs-Élysées, obligatorily accompanied by the less than noble family maid, Françoise. The situation changes one day when a girl bearing the magic name of Gilberte comes to play. The very name endows the girl with a magical aura so that she in turn transforms the local terrain into a poetic realm. From his distant viewpoint, the disabused older narrator is aware of the capricious nature of the boy's fantasies, as he makes ironically clear with his disgruntled, ironic remark about the day he encountered Gilberte on the Champs-Élysées: "This day which I had so dreaded was, as it happened, one of the few on which I was not unduly wretched" (*SW*, 567).

Other names appear, each suggesting a region metaphysically beyond the dismal quotidian. The boy goes to look at theater posters and fixates on the name of the great actress Berma, perhaps excited all the more since the family doctor refuses to allow the sickly lad to go to the theater because of the undue excitement he might experience. The name of Bergotte, the writer mentioned by Swann, enters into this web of associations. The boy is enchanted by the world the writer has created (and the older narrator will remain so in this case). In the web of enchantment spun out by names, most comically, even Swann's name is transformed by the contagion of associations. Great comic effect derives from the way the older narrator appraises the ideas to which Swann's name became connected in the boy's mind. Associations so transform the name that it was, as the narrator says, no longer embedded "in the system of which it was formerly comprised" (*SW*, 578). Swann becomes a different person for the boy, who can then admire the man's social connections about which the boy was initially indifferent—though he so particularizes the magic of Swann's life that the narrator sardonically observes that, for the boy, it was as if "no one else had ever known the House of Orleans" (*SW*, 578). As his childish infatuation with the name grows, whatever is associated with it is desirable: he can even wish that he were growing bald like Swann (*SW*, 588).

Proust's presentation, with irony and hyperbole, of the power of names to enchant the boy is fundamentally comic. The names work to produce in the boy forms of belief and behavior that deviate from all sensible norms—such as his pulling on his nose in the hope that he can resemble Swann even in his tics (*SW,* 588). Sometimes bordering on good-humored farce, the commentary on the boy's deviation from the norm is a development of the humanistic vision of comic deviation that Proust began to sketch out in *Jean Santeuil.* However the power of certain names to induce love is less comic, since with the dramatization of the power of names Proust conveys a view of love that is less a matter of comic deviance than an expression of pessimism about the possibility of successful love—as already demonstrated in the characterization of Swann and his delusions. Just as Swann loved a woman who was not his type because he projected onto her an aesthetic model, drawn from painting and then music, so the young boy seems to love Gilberte because of the web of associations into which she enters, much of it born of verbal suggestions. Bergotte's writing is central in this regard. It is true that the narrator says that he first loved Gilberte, from Combray onward, "on account of all the unknown elements in her life in which I longed to be immersed, reincarnated, discarding my own as a thing of no account" (*SW,* 582). But he also claims that he first loved Gilberte because of Bergotte, only then to find that in Paris it was for her sake that he loved the writer (*SW,* 582). In the interlinking network of associations generating love, there is probably no relation of cause and effect, only overlapping and reinforcing waves of emotion, all born of an inchoate desire to transcend what simply is. These are the grounds for the boy's love, a childhood infatuation that ultimately differs little from adult fantasies. And to return to the question I asked earlier as to whether Gilberte is the narrator's type or not, the question is not really germane. Only a skirt chaser such as Swann or an inveterate adulterer such as the Duke of Guermantes worries about what his type is.

Proust concludes *Swann's Way* with the depiction of the boy's growing fascination with Odette, whom he views as the most elegant woman in Paris. This coda about the vulgar *cocotte* become lady of fashion is another marker charting the way toward the transformation of French society. It is also a marker in the boy's education, for who can deny that Odette shows him what elegance is? In any case by the end of *Swann's Way,* most of the major themes for the education to come have been sketched out: love and sex, art and literature, travel and social roles are among the key topics the boy learns to deal with as he sorts out erroneous beliefs and true revelations and makes errors and corrections and still further errors. This process begins at the end of *Swann's Way* with his infatuation with

Gilberte, continues in *Within a Budding Grove*, and, after his first lesson in the inevitable failure of love, eventuates in his passion for the Duchess of Guermantes. It owes its existence as much to the poetry of her name as to her putative elegance. In the creation of the narrator's love, place-names certainly have their place, though after these two periods of infatuation both Swann's way and the Guermantes way have been exhausted. The dramas of "Combray" are finished.

The two ways are not immediately conjoined in the narrator's experience, however. After the end of his infatuation with Gilberte, the narrator finally makes a sojourn on the sea coast where he encounters a place-name, Balbec, that had dominated his youthful imagination. Here he begins an initiation into society. In this initiation he begins to meet flesh-and-blood aristocrats whose names are appended to them like banners waving from the walls of a medieval castle. After this beginning initiation, it is in *The Guermantes Way* that the boy completes his initiation into the world of aristocratic names. He can physically enter their inner sanctum. After being received by the aristocratic world, being received finally into the world of a poetical place-name—the world of the Guermantes—the narrator is squarely disillusioned with the vulgarity of the aristocracy he once dreamed of as inhabiting a privileged, magical realm. The castle walls crumble, as it were. He is especially disillusioned with the doltish duchess, whom he had believed to be a kind of transcendental fairy inhabiting a magical world. If we recall Proust's youthful dreams of a social utopia at the time of *Pleasures and Days*, then Jean Santeuil's remorse at wasting his time in social pursuits, we can see that there is a kind of logical development to the disenchantment that Proust charts out in his progress as a writer. It comes to its logical development at the end of *The Guermantes Way* with an acrid portrayal of the anti-utopia that, to his chagrin, the young narrator is obliged to recognize as the world of the elite.

In brief *Within a Budding Grove* and *The Guermantes Way* offer a unified development in their portrayal of the narrator's education in love and place-names, in childhood infatuation and in adolescent delusion first centered on Gilberte; then on Balbec and the adolescent girls Albertine, Andrée, and their friends; and finally on the Duchess of Guermantes and the aristocratic milieu of the Guermantes. In this development Proust also brings in many other events and characters illustrating the multifaceted nature of the narrator's education, from sex—usually detached from love—and friendship to family life, art, and travel. The central themes of love and place, psychological development and interaction with society, tie events together as the narration progresses more or less chronologically; and one can assert, with some confidence, that the young man comes to maturity roughly at the beginning of the twentieth century. His education is thus part of a historical collage containing many allusions to the political and social development of Europe.

One key historical event serves as a touchstone for anchoring the collage in historical reality. This is the Dreyfus affair, which plays a central role in *Jean Santeuil*. The affair is not directly portrayed in *In Search of Lost Time*. Rather virtually every character in *The Guermantes Way* has an opinion about the affair, which is hardly surprising. It was probably the most important event in French political life at the end of the century. Through these allusions to Dreyfus, Proust places the narrator's education in a moment having historical specificity without tying the events to any exact chronology. The characters have opinions about Dreyfus, about politics and class identities, but they change their opinions so that there is no fixed ideological message in the novel other than that conveyed by the freedom with which Proust deals with a topic that was close to his heart. To be sure there is no doubt about the political climate in which the young narrator comes to maturity, nor is there any doubt that part of his education concerns the way politics intersect with the social order.

Having sketched an outline of the unity underlying *Within a Budding Grove* and *The Guermantes Way*, let us continue to discuss some specific aspects of the narrator's education. Proust opens *Within a Budding Grove* with a scene set in the narrator's home. The narrator's increasing maturity is measured in this opening scene, incrementally perhaps, when he begins to make social contacts. One example of this occurs during the dinner given by his family at which is present an ambassador named Norpois. At first the ambassador seems to be an entirely benign human being. He offers to aid the boy to get to know the Swann household—at the time a sacred precinct for the boy—and even takes the boy's side in the question of his future vocation. He thinks that the boy should pursue his desire to be a writer. Encouraging in effect the boy's self-esteem, the ambassador is an important adult who thinks being a writer is a worthy profession. But the older narrator then reverses the perspective on the ambassador by pointing out that Norpois's idea of writing is, from the narrator's viewpoint, that of a total philistine, as is reflected in Norpois's dismissive judgment of Bergotte. The diplomat haughtily criticizes Bergotte as a mere "flute-player" guilty of manneristic dilettantism (*BG*, 61). With this typical double perspective on a character, Proust allows the expression of positive ideas by characters who are also negatively portrayed, but without their positive side being put into question. This is part of the narrator's education in ambiguity, which perhaps began when he learned in "Combray" that his father's rules were as arbitrary as his father's application of them. In this opening scene, the reader learns that Norpois can pretend to be a friend to the boy's father and yet not support him when the father needs the ambassador's help to be elected to the Academy. True to his trade, Norpois is fundamentally duplicitous. However he is also intelligent. He accurately knows that "the map of Europe has undergone radical alterations and is on the eve, perhaps, of undergoing others more drastic still" (*BG*, 61). Norpois is a helpful philistine, hypocritical and deceitful but not a fool. His accurate perception of contemporary political reality accompanies his condemnation of Bergotte, which shows that Norpois is at home in some realms of discourse but not in others. He is well aware of the development of the German Reich, but like most of Proust's characters, he is unable to understand what eludes conventional perception—notably the innovative side of Bergotte's literary vision and, by implication, the history of artistic insight.

Norpois seems to be an important figure to the boy at this moment. The young narrator's desire to become a manipulator of words—here another aspect of his enchantment with place-names—receives from the diplomat an adult imprimatur. The boy is furthered in his desire with an apparent understanding based upon a real misunderstanding—an ambiguity the narrator recurrently underscores as generally characteristic of all communication. All of this misunderstanding is comically compounded by the fact that the diplomat inadvertently entrances the boy when he utters the magic names of Gilberte and Swann. The boy does all he can to hear these names repeated. The older narrator points up the comic ambivalence permeating the scene when he ironically observes that in this conversation Norpois naturally assumed that the boy was speaking about Swann in the same way he would speak about any other member of a family of intelligent stockbrokers, for "it was the moment in which a sane man who is talking to a lunatic has not yet perceived that he is a lunatic" (*BG*, 66). The narrator recalls that he almost revealed his lunacy, or perhaps did so, by nearly grabbing the ambassador's wrinkled hands and kissing them out of gratitude for the fact that he was going to speak to Mme Swann on the boy's behalf—with which gesture the boy may have sabotaged the realization of his desires. All in all *Within a Budding Grove* opens with a comically delightful yet probing exposition of the great distance separating the older narrator from his younger self.

After the opening scene, the narrator's education in first love takes place on the Champs-Élysées, the avenue bordered by a park area where children play games and gather for camaraderie. Proust sets up a fairly precise time frame for the duration of the education of the narrator's young heart by noting that after the boy had encountered Gilberte, the new year arrived, but he received no letter from her. However after some absence, she and the boy begin to play once again on the Champs-Elysées. When he falls ill, he receives a letter inviting him to Gilberte's home—despite the negative impression the boy believes he has made on Swann. The boy's infatuation continues for some months during which he is well received and becomes a regular visitor to the Swann household and a friend of Odette. But his relations with Gilberte end after a scene of spite, which implies that she is perhaps bored with him. The narrator muses that she no longer wanted a relation with him for any number of plausible reasons, quite possibly because she has another boyfriend, as the narrator may have witnessed one day upon seeing her with another young man. In any case facing Gilberte's lack of enthusiasm for him, the narrator imposes upon himself the obligation not to see her again, primarily to prove to her that he is worthy of her love: his forgoing her company is to be taken as proof that he is capable of dignity and restraint.

The young narrator seems to have taken to heart Goethe's strictures about *Entbehren*, the voluntary renunciation that allows one to hope to possess. The boy imagines to himself that once he proves to Gilberte that he has no inclination to see her, "she would discover once again an inclination" to see him (*BG*, 225). Thus the love affair continues in the absence of the lovers, through the next new year and into the spring, when a truly lasting memory is made upon the narrator, that of the elegant Madame Swann with her parasol, "as though in the colored shade of a wisteria bower" (*BG*, 298). His love has actually lasted some months, but the dirge for the impossibility of love lasts much longer. And this education of the heart, first involving the pain love brings with its seemingly inevitable failure, is then crowned with the memory of Odette and flowers, "since the longevity of our memories of poetical sensations is much greater than that of our memories of what the heart has suffered" (*BG*, 297). In short the boy has received lessons in the power of beauty as much as in the caprices of Cupid.

Actual events involving the narrator and Gilberte are thus few, for the narrator gives much attention to the social world in which Odette, having profited from her marriage, climbs ever higher. When the young narrator first frequents her salon in Paris, she has not yet reached the point where she can be admitted into puritan bourgeois milieus or the most exclusive aristocratic circles. She receives the likes of Madame Verdurin and Cottard as well as artists and writers such as Bergotte. Her advancement makes it obvious that the social kaleidoscope, as Proust calls it, is turning (*BG*, 122). Although the boy's ostensible purpose in frequenting this milieu is to be with Gilberte, or at least where she has been, it is here that the narrator continues his social education as well as his initiation in art and music, notably with Odette's rendition of Vinteuil's sonata. Consequently he continues to frequent Madame Swann and her circle even after he has ceased to see her daughter. It appears, moreover, that the ongoing experience of Gilberte's absence is as important for his sentimental education as is her presence. When she is physically present on the Champs-Élysées, he can wrestle with her, which offers a first, inadvertent sexual contact. But his emotional attempts at love depend little upon Gilberte's being with him, for his love is a product of his imagination. Moreover his first education in love turns on the revelation that, contrary to the boy's expectations, names do not enclose magic citadels. The narrator recalls, with self-critical irony, that it was with tremors of reverence and joy that he went to Swann's house and entered this "enchanted domain," which, unpredictably, had opened to him. As if in enchantment, this entrance took him then into the realm in which Swann and his wife led "their supernatural existence" (*BG*, 111). The narrator's adult perspective on himself ironically underscores the hyperbolic nature of his own childish expectations.

Accompanying this deflationary irony are blunt observations about Gilberte. She is a rebellious child who "never let slip an opportunity of displaying her own indifference to anything that gave her parents cause for vanity" (*BG*, 115). The narrator's success with Gilberte's parents seems to assure his failure with her, as the narrator implies upon seeing her betraying signs of impatience after her father invited the narrator "almost against her will" (*BG*, 214). It is plausible that Swann wants to receive the boy as a kind of psychological compensation for the fact that the narrator's very respectable parents refuse to see Odette. Moreover Swann has placed his hope for a future justification of his life in his daughter's love for him that will, he hopes, exist even after he is dead (*BG*, 192–93). That Gilberte will deny him remains to be seen in *Time Regained*. Swann's desire here simply underscores his fall after his marriage to a woman who, by conventional bourgeois standards, can be no cause for pride. Nor are the people Swann now receives by and large a cause for pride, and the boy himself is surprised by the banal nature of the characters he encounters in what he thought was to be a supernatural realm, such as Mme Bontemps, "so common, so ill-natured" that he wonders how Swann can put up with her (*BG*, 117). (However in this case the vulgar woman is, by a calculated twist of fate, destined to witness the narrator's later education in misery, since she is the aunt of Albertine, with whom the narrator later has the misfortune to fall in love.) As his subsequent infatuation with the Duchess of Guermantes next shows, the narrator only slowly loses his delusions fostered by the magic of names.

In his portrayal of love, Proust depicts the narrator in Odette's salon progressing in a negative education. He is in love with an absence that never leaves his mind. Gilberte's absence, however, is still endowed with the intimations of paradise we saw in Combray, for the narrator remembers her "embowered always in a hedge of pink hawthorn, in the little lane" that he took in "going the Méséglise way" (*BG*, 150). This memory permeated with suggestions of paradise is undoubtedly at the origins of his love, but it cannot overcome the entropy that inevitably develops once the narrator stops actually seeing Gilberte. Having banked upon feigned indifference to win Gilberte back, he finds that his pretense becomes real as time passes, and the energy of first love is slowly dissipated in a downward spiral of loss, culminating in a genuine lack of concern for her. Conjuring up his "imagined happiness," he finds that all his imagination can do little to prolong it. Rather at best it can only enable him to endure the destruction of his "real happiness" (*BG*, 226). This slow decline continues through the next new year, the repetition of which marks for the narrator the "slow and painful suicide of that self which loved Gilberte" (*BG*, 255). And so is first revealed the ephemeral nature of the very self that, in love, posits itself as a source of permanent affections.

With this ongoing loss of his old self, the narrator arrives at that most painful moment for the Proustian lover when, as already experienced by characters in *Pleasures and Days* and in *Jean Santeuil*, though still in love he can foresee the moment when he will cease to be. This moment occurs when the rupture between the lover's old loving self and his emerging indifferent self can be clearly envisaged. With the recognition of the discontinuity characterizing his own self, the narrator must also confront the unfounded nature of love. The lover experiences the groundlessness of love as a painful taunt obliging him to recognize his incapacity not only to honor his commitment to love but also to pretend to exist as a unified being. For Proust this state of rupture is the experience of the "intermittencies of the heart"—as reads the title of a section of *Sodom and Gomorrah*. The lack of continuity characterizing the self is in itself a source of anguish, which explains why the narrator struggles at length to retain some attachment to the past. Without continuity between past and present, he finds his suffering deprived, in advance, of meaning, even if it occurs in the present moment of love—or as the narrator puts it, the present moment of suffering (*BG*, 255). The recognition of discontinuity means that even the present moment is mined from within, since even in the remaining moments of passion, the lover knowingly foresees his future indifference toward the beloved. This lucidity undermines the ground for belief in love or even the

ennobling value of suffering—the value of which Proust very much wanted
to believe in, for he found little else that might be a sign of human dignity.

After the narrator's love for Gilberte, with its roots in memories of
Méséglise, and before his subsequent passion for Madame de Guermantes,
whose origins are found in the historical reminiscence and poeticized past
found on the Guermantes way, lie the boy's preparatory encounters for a
different passion, developed at length in later volumes. These encounters
take place in Balbec, in the second part of *Within a Budding Grove*, when
the narrator meets Albertine and the other adolescent beauties who consort and play together. The girls' importance is underscored by the literal
title of the second volume of *In Search of Lost Time:* in French it reads "In
the Shadow of Girls in Blossom." The implied botanical metaphor signifies
rather ironically how the narrator views his meeting the girl-flowers: he
is drawn to them like a bee to sweet nectar. Proust's ironic use of biology
points up an ongoing aspect of the narrator's education, for as he meets
André, Albertine, and their friends, the blossoming girls act on the narrator
by drawing him in one direction and then another. Whatever be the poetic
states the boy may project upon them, biology is never excluded as a prime
mover in Proust's universe. His characters are indeed randy animals, however much they may be entranced by poetically suggestive names.

The boy's first view of the group takes place under what he calls the
sign of his desire for Beauty, with the capitalization pointing up that the
young narrator is still in thrall to abstractions (*BG,* 503). He may claim
that he has learned by this time that love is the projection onto the beloved
of a state of his soul (*BG,* 563). This does not, however, stop him from
projecting onto the young women his desire to see in them mythological
creatures. Having first thought of them as possibly members of the lower
class, he discovers that, with the exception of Albertine, they are from the
very wealthiest echelon of the bourgeoisie, which incites him to see them as
statuaries—as "these Dianas and these nymphs" (*BG,* 579). Though these
sketches of youthful beauty are prefatory to a love to come, they also strike
an elegiac note about the purity of youth in its "radiant morning time," at
that biological moment offering the phenomenon of blossoming that time
will soon erase: "Their faces were for the most part blurred with this efful-
gence of a dawn from which their actual features had not yet emerged. One
saw only a charming glow of colour beneath which what in a few years'
time would be a profile was not yet discernible" (*BG,* 662). The young narrator is drawn to Albertine for her beauty but also, as he notes, for the attraction offered by the "risk of an impossibility" created by the uncertainty
of the vacation situation (*BG,* 561). Moreover if the conversations and

games he enjoys with the girls are admittedly of little interest in themselves, they offer the charm of not being based on the hypocrisy that is the basis for most social intercourse in which one must pretend that, by exchanging lies, one is not "irremediably alone" (*BG*, 665). In short the final weeks of vacation time at Balbec are a kind of idyll in which the young narrator plays at being a faun amidst a group of athletically inclined nymphs.

The young narrator is now caught up in the process of learning about multiple selves and their discontinuities, his own and others'. His meeting with Albertine is central to this aspect of his education, and perhaps the key event for the development of the young narrator's self as a lover is the kiss he does not receive from her in her hotel room on the one night she spends in the Grand Hotel—perversely, it seems, the nonkiss is more important than when, later during his second stay at Balbec, she apparently goes to bed with him without the narrator so much as making a comment on their first sexual encounter. Far more impressive is her refusal when she is in her hotel room and the boy advances upon her. He advances and Albertine displays a turning motion "like those Michelangelo figures which are being swept away in a stationary and vertiginous whirlwind," so that the boy is rebuffed when he leaps forward like an animal to taste the "strange pink fruit" concealed in the flowering girl (*BG*, 701). The girl reveals herself to be neither a work of art nor a plant. Brusquely refusing his advances—and protectively ringing for room service—Albertine creates at the end of the first vacation in Balbec the image of savage virtue in the narrator's mind.

The vacation season comes to an end with the narrator's mind tantalized by the different images of Albertine that the different selves within himself can perceive—one of which is in love with her. But he finds that the passage of time is accompanied by a deflation of the images he had created for the group: "Thus had there faded and vanished all the lovely oceanic mythology which I had composed in those first days." He ponders what lesson is to be drawn from the recognition that the supernatural creatures had nonetheless introduced, without his being aware of it, "a miraculous element into the most commonplace dealings" (*BG*, 723). It appears at this point that the young narrator at any moment may begin to believe himself to be Hercules or Telemachus: the lesson is perhaps that, when the nymphs appear, the artistic mind, like that of Peter Paul Rubens, has the power to make goddesses out of ordinary women (*BG*, 724).

My earlier comments about Stendhal's influence on Proust's vision of love are germane to the surprise and wonder the young narrator feels about Albertine. They also pertain to the poeticized historical associations the narrator projects on Madame de Guermantes. These associations are the basis for the crystallization, or projection of the ideal upon the beloved, that sets off the genesis of the extravagant and puerile love the narrator experiences for Madame de Guermantes, depicted in the first part of *The Guermantes Way*. An early reviewer of the first part of this volume, the perceptive Paul Souday, suggested the connection with Stendhal in 1921 when he wrote with some sarcasm that, obsessed with genealogies, the young narrator "crystallizes furiously on this name and on this noble title, which seem to him can only belong to a supernatural being, a woman of legend, or a fairy of the lake."[2] Souday went on to say that after the narrator's family has moved into a wing of the Hotel de Guermantes in Paris, the narrator is disappointed to discover that the duchess is only a human being. However his disappointment with her human status is quickly overcome, and the crystallization begins anew when the youth learns that, in spite of the fact that she lives on the Right Bank, she occupies the highest place of rank in the milieu of the Faubourg Saint-Germain—since the Left Bank Faubourg Saint-Germain is still the place where most of the nobility of the Old Regime lives.

In his review Souday was also right to find the name of a fairy at work in the narrator's image of the duchess. The name of the fairy Melusine is associated with the narrator's love for her, since the fairy's legend, like an intertextual double, subtends the narrator's associations of Madame de Guermantes with poeticized myth. The narrator underscores this negatively, at the beginning of *The Guermantes Way*, by pointing out the danger of trying to live a fairy tale: "The fairy languishes if we come in contact with the real person to whom her name corresponds, for the name then begins to reflect that person, who contains nothing of the fairy; the fairy may revive if we absent ourselves from the person, but if we remain in the person's presence the fairy ultimately dies and with her the name, as happened to the family of Lusignan which was fated to become extinct on the day when the fairy Melusine should disappear" (*GW*, 4).

The allusion to Melusine remains obscure until the end of *The Guermantes Way*. Then the reader sees that, using his typical strategy of deploying his revelatory allusions at intervals, Proust indirectly alludes to the fairy theme. This occurs when the Prince of Guermantes, vainly blabbering about his ancestors, informs the narrator that the house of Guermantes descends in direct lineage from the house of Lusignan, the noble French family that ruled Cyprus and that, with the fall of the Latin kingdom of Jerusalem, became extinct (*GW*, 786). (I am not sure how the Guermantes can descend directly from an extinct family; nor for that matter is the narrator very clear on his genealogy. But the point here is not historical genealogy but myth.) From the Prince's allusion, it appears that the myth of the fairy is tied up with the Lusignan family, hence with the Guermantes, and has a direct analogy with the narrator's idealization of the duchess—and the demise of that love—since love in fairy tales makes precise demands in order to exist.

The analogy with Madame de Guermantes draws upon the following legend. The founder of the house of Lusignan, the Count of Poitou, supposedly married the fairy Melusine without knowing that, because of her cursed past, her nether parts were obliged every Saturday to assume the shape of a serpent (or a mermaid in other versions). The count promised not to peep at his wife on Saturdays, but not keeping his word, he looked at her, upon which Melusine turned into a dragon. The lesson is obvious for an incipient Proustian psychologist, if not for the young narrator: upon too close a familiarity with the beloved, her scaly skin becomes all too apparent. One recalls that to maintain his elated trance in "Combray" after the young narrator had looked too intently upon the duchess, he had had to imagine away a pimple on her face—but all the imagination in the world may not be able to do away with the metaphorical equivalent of scales on the lower torso. In Proust's version this myth offers the foundations for comedy, if not for lasting love. The myth is the doublet for the comedy Proust develops in his story of the young narrator's successive enchantments and disappointments with Madame de Guermantes: he discovers again that looking too closely at what is really there never promotes the crystallization love demands.

With regard to names, in the boy's earliest memories of Combray, the sound of "Guermantes" provides material for crystallization. Even the older narrator is still at times subject to the enchantment generated by historical names. Despite his education in the nature of names, at the outset of *The Guermantes Way*, he admits that even now in the indefinite present moment of narration, the name can evoke in him for a moment the poetic emotion it produced on the day of the marriage in Combray, when the boy eliminated the blemish on the duchess's face by projecting upon it a color, namely, "that mauve—so soft and smooth but almost too bright, too new—with which the billowy scarf of the young Duchess glowed, and, like two inaccessible, ever-flowering periwinkles, her eyes, sunlit with an azure smile" (*GW*, 5). Much as in the case of his idealization of Gilberte in Méséglise, in the narrator's imaginative memory, flowers are associated with the duchess, those intimations of paradise, such that the narrator can, upon hearing her name, "breathe the air of the Combray of that year, of that day, mingled with a fragrance of hawthorn blossom blown by the wind from the corner of the square, harbinger of rain, which now sent the sun packing, now let it spread itself over the red woollen carpet of the sacristy, clothing it in a bright geranium pink and in that, so to speak, Wagnerian sweetness and solemnity in joy that give such nobility to a festive occasion" (*GW,* 5). Though narrated from the present, and indeed about the present moment of narration, this series of images opening *The Guermantes Way* encapsulates the circular power of the memories used in the idealizing projection. This circularity is shown in the flowers' association with nobility, then the quality of nobility is projected back onto the flowers, and all is contained within the sacred precinct of the sacristy in a moment of revelation, for the boy and, now, for the narrator remembering the boy.

In the time before the sudden loss of the narrator's love for the duchess, the story of his love for her is a tale of ongoing crystallization, or successive crystallizations, and of the narrator's struggle to maintain his idealized vision of this noblewoman. He must struggle against all that he sees suggesting that she is the contrary of the ideal, for the scales do not disappear easily. Perhaps the greatest danger is that her name might lose its power. The deflation of the word *Guermantes* is first broached at the beginning of *The Guermantes Way* when the narrator learns from his friend Saint-Loup, a nephew of Madame de Guermantes, various details about the Guermantes family, all of which suggest that their historical roots go down less deeply into history than the narrator wants to imagine. The "castle" that bears their name has been in the family only since the seventeenth century, and the Boucher tapestries therein were acquired in the nineteenth century by a family member with execrable taste; it appears he preferred the mediocre sporting pictures that he himself had painted (*GW,* 8–9). Nonetheless the narrator recalls that, countering these facts, he could not imagine, in the entertainments given by the duchess, "the guests as possessing bodies, moustaches, boots, as making any utterance that was commonplace, or even original in a human and rational way" (*GW,* 8–9). In a sense *The Guermantes Way* unfolds as a demonstration that the aristocrats have bodies, moustaches, and boots; and moreover that they rarely speak anything except trivial commonplaces. Clearly the mystique of the "palace" the Guermantes inhabit suffers when the narrator and his family move into a wing of the Guermantes Hotel, one of those "old town houses" in which little shops and workrooms flank the main courtyard. The narrator is not sure whether the presence of these shops and ateliers is due to the "rising tide of democracy" or if they are a "legacy from a more primitive time" (*GW,* 10). In any case the presence of a porter who keeps chickens there suggests, as does the letting of apartments, that times may well have changed since this abode was built for the first nobles who inhabited it.

The danger that mere reality may impinge upon the boy's idealizing is set aside, as we noted earlier, when he learns that the banal woman whom he watches from his window reigns somehow supreme in his imagined world of aristocrats. She may manifest "in her dresses the same anxiety to follow the fashion" that many other Parisian women show (*GW,* 29). However this trivial note does not touch upon the secret found in her house—called "the glowing amber envelope" that encapsulates the secret way of life that "her name enclosed in reality, objectively, for other people," though not for the narrator (*GW,* 30). All of which is to say that the narrator creates another crystallization after he hears a father's friend say "that the Guermantes set was in a class of its own in the Faubourg-Saint-Germain" (*GW,* 30). So long as he has no contact with this milieu, the narrator can imagine whatever he wants, though in this crystallization the negative idealization consists precisely in denying his imagination any precise content.

At this point the older narrator finds that religion provides a good analogy for his younger self's belief that the banally real can somehow contain the transcendental: "The presence of the body of Jesus Christ in the host seemed to me no more obscure a mystery than this leading house in the Faubourg being situated on the right bank of the river and so near that from my bedroom in the morning I could hear its carpets being beaten" (*GW,* 30). His irony is part of the pattern of narration and commentary in which both observed and observer are part of the world of comic deviation; but his comparison with religious mystery also describes the kind of quest that the boy undertakes in his imagination, nourished by the historical legends of medieval mysteries from which modern banality has been resolutely expunged.

It is a historical truism that romantic historicism restored the Middle Ages to a central place in the nineteenth-century imagination: it was conceived as a time whose imagined sense of purity and honor often served to make, by contrast, a critique of the baseness of nineteenth-century bourgeois culture. This critique is not foreign to the young narrator's sensitivity, and a medieval sense of social roles permeates his labile imagination. But his imagination is fundamentally comic. He engages in fantasy about the duchess in which he imagines himself a knight errant, or at times a troubadour, who wishes that God would send a calamity down upon her so that he might save her. For this felicitous calamity, he spends "hours on end imagining the circumstances, rehearsing the sentences" with which he would welcome the duchess beneath his roof (*GW,* 83). He also imagines her helping him with his writing. However less medieval and more topically modern is the way in which in almost voyeuristic fashion he spends a great deal of time spying upon her, which indicates that Proust was not unaware that adolescent fantasies can lead to serious deviant behavior. Spying on Madame de Guermantes is not the accidental or opportunistic voyeurism that allows the narrator as a boy to view Vinteuil's daughter with her lesbian lover and, later in the novel, permits him to witness the baron's seduction of Jupien. The adolescent narrator resembles a stalker with whom, understandably, the duchess initially wants no dealings. And when the stalker declares ponderously that he was genuinely in love with Madame de Guermantes, one may feel that Proust is indulging in a kind of black humor.

The boy gets to view the aristocracy at close quarters relatively early in *The Guermantes Way* when he goes to the opera to watch, for the second time, a performance by the actress Berma. The older narrator's viewpoint dominates in this episode in which the remarkable imagery used to describe the aristocrats in attendance mimics the fantastic worldview that the boy has. At the same time, the description is fundamentally satirical. For the aristocrats resemble mythical sea dwellers; and in their theatrical boxes, their evening apparel makes them appear to be "white deities." They undergo metamorphosis as the evening unfolds and change into something akin to Nereids and bearded Tritons. The metamorphosis is motivated in part by the comic connotations of the French term for a theatrical box, which is *baignoire*, meaning both "theatrical box" and "bathtub." So that the narrator looks at the Princess of Guermantes in semidarkness as if she were in water, on a sofa become a coral reef, "beside a large vitreous expanse which was probably a mirror and suggested a section, perpendicular, opaque and liquid, cut by a ray of sunlight in the dazzling crystal of the sea" (*GW*, 45). This metamorphosis results in a grotesque atmosphere in which he views her attire as something mythological: "At once plume and corolla, like certain subaqueous growth, a great white flower, downy as the wing of a bird, hung down from the Princess's forehead along one of her cheeks, the curve of which it followed with coquettish, amorous, vibrant suppleness, as if half enclosing it like a pink egg in the softness of a halcyon's nest" (*GW*, 45). There is a constant impulse in Proust to convert the members of this strange tribe, the old French nobility, into some kind of biological phenomena differing from normal humanity, though hardly for the better (*GW*, 45). The association of the princess's adornment with a mythical bird is satirical at the same time that it shows the enchantment that the attire works on the boy's imagination when he stares into the boxes, looking for those ideal qualities associated with the name Guermantes.

While viewing marine deities, the boy sees that the beloved Duchess of Guermantes arrives—late—to be well received by the "amphibian monsters" who are gathered about the leading deity, the Princess of Guermantes (*GW*, 61–62). The young man is enchanted, sensing "the mystery of that silent gaze" that he cannot yet decipher, though at the moment he believes that therein is "the essence of the unknown life" that he greatly desires to know (*GW*, 62). This is perhaps the high point of his enchantment with the duchess, especially since he thinks that she actually acknowledges his presence. In this "momentary apotheosis," he is happy to think that he is lost, as he says, among "the nameless, collective madrepores of the audience in the stalls"; he is happy that he has been dissolved in their midst: "At the moment in which, by virtue of the laws of refraction, the blurred shape of the protozoon devoid of any individual existence which was myself must have come to be reflected in the impassive current of those two blue eyes, I saw a ray illumine them: the Duchess, goddess turned woman, and appearing in that moment a thousand times more lovely, raised towards me the white-gloved hand which had been resting on the balustrade of the box and waved it in token of friendship" (*GW*, 68–69). He is mistaken, but with this imagined encouragement, the boy is in his self-abasement on the way to becoming the near psychopath described above.

In the conflict between idealization and deflation in the boy's world, the latter is the destined victor, though the novel demonstrates that much time is required. The narrator pursues his infatuation with the duchess in various ways, for example, going to spend time with his friend Saint-Loup at his military post in hopes of persuading him to use his influence to get the duchess to receive the narrator, with no success. Deflation begins to take the upper hand only when the narrator really meets the duchess and observes her—shades of Melusine. He goes to a reception given by Madame de Villeparisis, to which the duchess also comes. This social occasion is a major event for the young narrator (and it occupies roughly the last half of the first part of *The Guermantes Way*). The impression he makes upon the duchess first seems predictive of their future relations—though this impression is erroneous. The narrator is standing next to a historian to whom she is presented at the same time she is introduced to him. Attempting to impress her, he makes a deep bow, with nugatory results: "After breathing a little sigh she contented herself with manifesting the nullity of the impression that had been made on her by the sight of the historian and myself by performing certain movements of her nostrils with a precision that testified to the absolute inertia of her unoccupied attention" (*GW*, 267). The reader may wonder whether the narrator is observing a human or a sniffing animal. In any case it is clear from the utterly physical nature of the encounter that idealization will soon have little to work upon in the narrator's mind. At the moment, however, he admits that he was hardly able to see the physical being that was before him. With great self-directed irony, he recalls that he was not able to see in her the "sun-splashed coolness of the woods of Guermantes" that her name called forth; in fact not only are there no Guermantes trees inscribed on her face, but there was also nothing there "suggestive of vegetation" (*GW*, 273). But as the older narrator recognizes, his youthful attention was so ardent that it "volatilized at once" whatever he might have been able to take in about her (*GW*, 274). Only the future can correct the constant misperceptions that make up normal social intercourse, not to mention the idealizing distortions springing from the need for enchantment.

In brief this reception given by Madame de Villeparisis is an initiation ritual for the boy, who, now virtually received into the Guermantes fold, finds, perhaps unfairly, that the goddess is a boor. She considers it a matter of breeding to speak only of "the food that they were eating or the games of cards to which they would afterwards sit down" (*GW*, 278). Of course the youth's crystallization and projection of the ideal upon her have been so beyond all measure that the duchess can only disappoint when he finally hears her speak: "I thought . . . that, when she spoke, her conversation, profound, mysterious, would have the strangeness of a medieval tapestry or a Gothic window. But in order that I should not be disappointed by the words I should hear uttered by a person who called herself Mme de Guermantes, even if I had not been in love with her, it would not have sufficed that those words should be shrewd, beautiful and profound, they would have had to reflect that amaranthine colour of the closing syllable of her name, that colour which on first seeing her I had been disappointed not to find in her person and had fancied as taking refuge in her mind" (*GW*, 280).

Only a heroine of a symbolist drama, speaking with an oracular voice and producing synesthesia as her words flow forth, could possibly satisfy the young narrator. Proust's ironies here aim not only at the narrator's younger self and his version of love, but also at an entire cultural moment in which the symbolist dandy, inhabiting the aesthetic realm of a medieval castle, had become, briefly at least, a cultural ideal.

Falling out of love follows various paths in Proust. It takes the shape of a self-imposed denial in the case of the narrator and Gilberte. In the demise of Swann's love for Odette, attrition may well seem the dominant force, though we have seen that Proust uses a series of medical metaphors to show that Swann's case of love follows a predetermined course, like any other disease. The end of love appears somewhat different in the case of the narrator and the Duchess of Guermantes: falling out of love is not unlike having an abscess pierced. This is not quite the metaphor the narrator actually uses, though it appears to be his intent. The boy is abruptly cured of this love by his mother when she lays her hands upon his forehead and tells him he is considered ridiculous for his infatuation with the duchess. The scene describing the cure is narrated as a flashback late in *The Guermantes Way*, after the narrator has already related his grandmother's death and his first involvement with Albertine. The description of the cure occurs in the context of his observation that he is now able to enter Madame de Villeparisis's drawing room and observe the duchess without being disturbed. The reason for this, the narrator casually notes, is that his mother had laid her hands upon his head and told him he was a laughingstock (*GW*, 507). One may doubt the instantaneous nature of the cure, for the narrator has already looked at the duchess most closely and seen her scales. However Proust follows up on the narrator's almost casual recall of his mother's act to propose two more quasi-medical metaphors to describe the cure, the first comparing it to the work of a hypnotist who opens a person's eyes and shows the deluded patient where he or she actually is and the second comparing the cure to the work done by a doctor who "cures you of an imaginary disease in which you have been wallowing" by waking the patient from a protracted dream (*GW*, 508). The register of medical psychology is added to the earlier medical metaphors dealing with the pathology known as love. Thus it appears that the cures for the malady are various, though the medical metaphors consistently imply, as in Swann's case, that if for Proust love is a purely subjective condition, it is also a psychopathology.

Falling out of love entails the end of the enchantments that the name Guermantes works upon the narrator's imagination. But other names still offer material for poeticizing projections in both *Within a Budding Grove* and *The Guermantes Way*. For a significant example, consider that, during his first stay at the seashore in Balbec, the youthful vacationer needs only to encounter an obscure noble family, the Stermaria from Brittany, for his imagination to run away with him in a flurry of fantasy about what he might do in their Breton castle were he to meet the daughter of the family. He dreams up a romantic relation in which they would roam together on an island that "enclosed the everyday life of Mlle de Stermaria and was reflected in the memory of her eyes": "For it seemed to me that I should have truly possessed her only there, when I had traversed those regions which enveloped her in so many memories—a veil which my desire longed to tear aside" (*BG*, 365–66).

Desire seems at times dependent upon a place-name to give fodder to the boy's fantasies. Medieval motifs again play a role in this imaginative flight, for a castle in Brittany perforce conjures up a region where Tristan might have encountered Iseult (or Isolde, if we attribute this association to Wagner's use of medieval legends). Yet what the boy desires remains rather obscure. The narrator seems to want to possess even the girl's memories; but it is clear that he hardly possesses his own, and the desire to possess the girl's resembles a hyperbolic fantasy born of the romantic desire to transcend dismal normal reality. This desire for absolute possession, however hyperbolic, touches upon a question brought up earlier: how can one possess the inner life of another person? Names may temporarily give the illusion of the possession of which the boy dreams, but his education rather insistently points out to him the fundamental postulate of human relations in Proust: that unless one is an omniscient narrator, possession is at best an illusion. In the case in point, the dream of possession boils down to the boy's fantasies about a Brittany seascape.

Most of the education the boy receives with regard to place-names in *Within a Budding Grove* is inflected toward comedy. For example at the outset of part 2, "Place-Names: The Place," the boy finally arrives at the place that has been enchanting him with multiple associations—namely the village of Balbec. Arriving there to see the church, however, he is shocked by what reality obliges him to see. Nothing corresponds to what his imagination has concocted before he arrives by train in Balbec. His arrival is the subject of self-directed comedy in which the older narrator portrays his younger self as something of a dolt. Notably the narrator has not bothered to find out that the church he is about to see is located in a village, called simply Balbec, that is several miles from the village called Balbec-Beach, the place on the seashore where his hotel is actually located. Moreover it seems that he has scarcely looked at the pictures of the church that his imagination had already transformed into a "Persian church" that would directly confront the froth of breaking waves (*BG*, 303). Rather than the "dying foam of the uplifted waves" splashing the church, he finds a banal village scene; for the church stands on a "square which was the junction of two tramway routes, opposite a café which bore, in letters of gold, the legend 'Billiards'" (*BG*, 322). In this Utrillo-like setting, there are no ship masts in sight to carry his Baudelairean imagination away on a nautical journey out onto the abyss. Disarmed by reality, as it were, he is incapable of looking accurately at what the church really has: an impressive array of works of Gothic sculpture, even if found in the banal setting of an ordinary village.

The description of the youthful narrator's vision gone astray is part of Proust's use of comedy to critique the boy's failure to apprehend the concrete particular—that which really is. As in *Against Sainte-Beuve,* his critique aims at abstraction, whether an intellectual construct or an imaginative projection. The first scene in Balbec centers on the way the young narrator had transformed in his imagination, even before seeing it the church statuary into something with no concrete existence. With trenchant irony the narrator notes that the church's sculpted virgin was actually there, in its real location, but with no relation to his abstract imaginings about it. But the statue was "subjected to the tyranny of the Particular to such a point that, if I had chosen to scribble my name upon that stone, it was she, the illustrious Virgin whom until then I had endowed with a general existence and an intangible beauty, the Virgin of Balbec, the unique (which meant, alas, the only one), who, on her body coated with the same soot as defiled the neighbouring houses, would have displayed—powerless to rid herself of them—to all the admiring strangers come there to gaze upon her, the marks of my piece of chalk and the letters of my name" (*BG*, 324). Real stones of real statues reflect real dirt, as Marianne Moore might have written. Unlike Proust theorizing about beauty in *Against Sainte-Beuve,* or the older narrator looking for the meaning of art, the young narrator at Balbec has not yet learned that beauty is always a concrete manifestation of a unique particular—that it is what you point to "right there"—though the older narrator's marvelous irony about the imagined result of his defacing the Virgin shows that he has become a Proustian aesthetician. Even the soot on the stone, this stone present here and now, as the poet Yves Bonnefoy might have it, is part of the contingent beauty of the real.[3]

In *The Guermantes Way* there is a reprise of this comic discovery that places such as the Hotel Guermantes are real in their individuality, with shops in the courtyard and servants in the staircases. However in "Place-Names: The Place," the second half of *Within a Budding Grove,* it is noteworthy that actually few place-names play a role. Balbec, the place and name, plays the most important role in this regard. After the comic deflation of the boy's expectations about the village, the church, and the sea, the narrator describes his move into his hotel with his grandmother. The rest of *Within a Budding Grove* narrates his vacation at Balbec, lasting an indeterminate number of weeks, in which the narrator makes the acquaintance of various people with mainly aristocratic names. Taking the narrator out of the routine of his Parisian existence, this section significantly advances his education in society and art, largely through these acquaintances. He meets vacationing aristocrats who, among other things, illustrate attitudes toward literature and intellectual life. The second part then introduces the band of young girls who give the entire volume its original title, one that suggests a lesson in eroticism as well as botany. At the center of this second part stands the narrator's encounter with Proust's painter, Elstir, a name that becomes emblematic for artistic vision. Thus by the end of *Within a Budding Grove,* the narrator has progressed notably in his education in society, literature, and art as well as the unending topics of love and sex.

With regard to names and the often comic love they inspire, there is a notable hiatus between the two parts making up *Within a Budding Grove.*

In the first half, we have seen that the young narrator underwent an education in the nature of subjectivity and the discontinuity of the self, traversing the subjective states that unfold as the boy progresses toward the end of his love of Gilberte. After this long decline of love for an absent object, the narrator states that some two years pass before he leaves for Balbec. Then he prefaces his stay in Balbec with a kind of manifesto about the work of memory in keeping emotions alive. Emotions like love, he says, have no special power over memories, since memories of love are governed by what Proust calls the general laws of habit, so that with the weakening of habit the beloved begins to fade into oblivion. The narrator thus leaves for Balbec with his memories of Gilberte nearly extinguished, which shows that they are subject to the law that "in the broad daylight of our habitual memory the images of the past gradually pale and fade out of sight, nothing remains of them" (*BG,* 300). At this point, then, progress toward nothingness seems to be the general law of psychic life. It is not yet clear to the narrator what might be the significance of some chance encounter that conjures up a past self from the oblivion in which, as "Combray" shows, the past remains living as if in some unconscious realm that can only be magically opened as though by grace. Though "Combray" has shown a self conjured up from oblivion, its significance remains to be discovered largely in *Time Regained.* The narrator only concludes about what he had learned at the time of Balbec.

In his stay at Balbec, love is put on hold, as it were, while the narrator comes into contact with those aristocrats whose names dazzled him as a boy. They are especially important for his immediate and indeed later education. Madame de Villeparisis, a friend of the boy's grandmother, is a key figure in this regard, for she is the aunt of Madame de Guermantes and presents the narrator to members of the duchess's family, such as Saint-Loup, her nephew, and to the Baron de Charlus (or M. de Charlus, as Moncrieff usually translates it). The deflation of aristocratic ways begins with the first aristocrat to whom Madame de Villeparisis introduces the narrator, in a scene that serves as a comic preface to the narrator's dealings with nobility for the rest of the novel. This occurs when the boy and his grandmother happen to meet Madame de Villeparisis and her friend the Princess de Luxembourg. The wall between classes is described, and never with better irony, in the narrator's observation that he could foresee that the princess, in "her anxiety not to appear to be enthroned in a higher sphere than ours," might put out her hand and stroke them "like two lovable beasts" who had poked their heads out at her through the bars of their cage in the zoo (*BG,* 379). The narrator calls this encounter with the princess his first meeting with royalty. (Apparently an earlier meeting with

Princess Mathilde did not count since, as the narrator observes, she was not at all royal in her ways and, I add, is a member of the Napoleonic nobility.) The meeting with the princess sets the stage for the narrator's forthcoming initiation into the comedy of vanity and snobbery that constitutes the essence of his social education.

During this time as later, the narrator is constantly aware of the fact that he is not making progress in his way toward a vocation, the moment when he will be a writer. He remembers the moment in "Combray" when as a boy he first set down in writing his metaphors about the three steeples (a memory not so forgotten that it could not be recalled by the young man as well as the older narrator). It is significant that this recollection takes place once in the company of Madame de Villeparisis, the aristocrat who is in effect helping the narrator become a socialite and thus furthering his career in procrastination. Riding with her on a drive in her carriage, the narrator views three trees, near Hudimesnil. The trees remind him of the three steeples he described in writing. That experience brought him great joy. This time, however, he experiences, after an initial moment of joy, a sense of loss because the trees remind him that he has not kept covenant with that unique moment when he had written about the steeples and when his vocation as writer seemed to have been revealed to him. In grief about his own incapacity, he then feels as wretched as if he had lost a friend or "broken faith with the dead or repudiated a god" (*BG,* 408). In this moment he also understands what he must do if he is going to begin "to lead a true life" (*BG,* 405). He must overcome the procrastination that is, unfortunately, a dominant leitmotif in his life to come. Riding in the carriage of an aristocrat, he knows he must cease believing that his success in society can play some role in his finding his vocation. He must, in short, overcome the fascination that their names continue to work on him.

The conflict the narrator knows is ironically illustrated by his description of Madame de Villeparisis's opinions on literature. Drawing upon his unpublished thoughts about Sainte-Beuve, Proust endows her, not surprisingly, with an Old Regime belief in the role of society in determining literary values. After seeing the three trees near Hudimesnil, he recalls that he used to quote to Madame de Villeparisis from his favored writers, Chateaubriand, Alfred de Vigny, and Victor Hugo. Alas these major romantics are writers for whom she has little regard. Like Sainte-Beuve she evaluates writers on the basis of their personalities and social selves, about which she knows a great deal since these same writers were received in her home during her youth. She has scorn for Chateaubriand, who, in her father's presence, boasted of resigning from a papal conclave; and she finds no nobility at all in Vigny, a poet who portrayed himself as an aristocratic stoic.

(Proust's quoting Vigny for an epigraph to *Sodom and Gomorrah* underscores his disagreement with Madame de Villeparisis.) Like the narrator's mother in *Against Sainte-Beuve,* Madame de Villeparisis also dislikes Balzac and in general dismisses the French romantics in favor of writers whose names are for the most part unknown today.

The older narrator judges Madame de Villeparisis in this regard with a nuanced judgment that reflects Proust's own reservations, if not about Balzac and Vigny, then especially about the second generation of French romantic writers such as Baudelaire and Arthur Rimbaud. These reservations are presupposed for understanding why the narrator says that his adored grandmother sang the praises of Madame de Villeparisis and her artistic taste. The older narrator recognizes that his grandmother was aware that as a boy he had a "morbid tendency to melancholy and solitude" (*GW,* 418). It is to protect him from his own tendencies that his grandmother assigns the highest value to the qualities of balance and judgment, characteristic not only of Madame de Villeparisis but of "a society similar to the one in which our ancestors saw the minds of a Doudan, a M. de Rémusat flourish, not to mention a Beausergeant, a Joubert, a Sévigné, a type of mind that invests life with more happiness, with greater dignity than the converse refinements which had led a Baudelaire, a Poe, a Verlaine, a Rimbaud to sufferings, to a disrepute" (*BG,* 418). Clearly the grandmother fears the narrator himself may come to know suffering and disrepute if he pursues the experiments of Baudelaire or Rimbaud, experiments not only with poetry but with drugs, sexuality, and other ways of extending their experience. Hence her desire that he take Madame de Villeparisis as a role model. By contrasting writers of lesser reputation with famous poets already part of the modernist canon when Proust was writing, the narrator makes a distinction between the writer who finds his or her fulfillment within the social norms of a well-defined society and the modernist writer who, in experimentation and revolt, pursues a course that may well end in madness or disease—and sometimes poetic vision. Baudelaire probably had more influence on Proust than any single other writer, but he was also well aware of the dangers of madness and pathology inherent to Baudelaire's exploitation of the self that refuses received social norms.

I wish to make a slight, but purposeful, digression, with regard to Proust's treatment of Madame de Villeparisis and of Sainte-Beuve, and of aristocratic society in general, in order to answer what I take to be perhaps the most serious, and interesting, negative criticism of Proust that I have read. I refer to a published lecture given by Marc Fumaroli, *Littérature et conversation: La Querelle Sainte-Beuve-Proust.* A distinguished literary historian and member of the Collège de France, Fumaroli argues that

Proust's treatment of Madame de Villeparisis and of Sainte-Beuve is emblematic of the modernist failure to understand that, for the classical mind of the ancien régime, the forms of civil and polite conversation found in the various salons were the highest form of literary expression. Comparing Sainte-Beuve to the antirevolutionary philosopher Edmund Burke, Fumaroli proposes that Sainte-Beuve wanted to continue that literary tradition by connecting the nineteenth-century salon with an ideal version of the seventeenth-century salon of Madame de Rambouillet. Her salon was one in which, arguably, conversation was the highest art form. Fumaroli criticizes Proust for caricaturing salon life in the novel and even claims that he drew upon Sainte-Beuve's literary portraits to parody conversation found in them. In fine Proust is wrong to criticize the salon as a corrupted form of socializing. With his misrepresentation, says Fumaroli, Proust promoted the modernist view that literature should not be conceived as dialogue. Rather in the wake of Rousseau and Baudelaire, Proust conceived of literature as something "monological, sublime, marginal, which takes the reader not as an interlocutor, but as an astonished and silent witness."[4] From this perspective the great influence of Proust's work has ultimately led to the modernist text conceived by his epigones as écriture, or writing as a "work of solipsistic and autarkic mourning" (17). I suppose that one should take Roland Barthes as an example of one of the unnamed epigones.

Fumaroli is a brilliant critic of the pitfalls of modernity, in both art and literature, though his vision of the civility of a culture once based on dialogic exchange strikes me as a straw man to argue against those aspects of modernity he dislikes. In any case I return to the passage in which the grandmother is laudatory of Madame de Villeparisis in order to point out in it that Proust's narrator is quite aware of the dangers of "monologic" solipsism. Whether the social comedy he portrays, in Madame de Villeparisis's salon as in all others, shows a lack of understanding of Sainte-Beuve is another issue, but I would think that even a few pages of Saint-Simon, La Rochefoucauld, or La Bruyère, to name several of Proust's favored classical writers, show that not all classical writers thought that the social exchange found in aristocratic salons was the highest art form found in the society of Louis XIV. (Perhaps Fumaroli might reply that the work of these writers—respectively memoires, maxims, and portraits—all represent refinements of conversation, with which I would disagree.) Moreover if Proust is at times almost bitter in his social comedy and his satirical portrayal of the futility of the aristocracy, it is because he once entertained the same utopian vision of social intercourse as a supreme art form for which Fumaroli claims historical existence.

To use his own comparison against him, I suggest that Fumaroli's claim that conversation was the pinnacle of literary art does indeed recall Burke's panegyrics about the glories of a Whig aristocracy, which is to say, it is a nostalgia for an imaginary heroic past—of a truly noble aristocracy—that little today suggests ever really existed . . . whenever "today" might be. There is nostalgia, too, underlying Proust's portrayal of salon conversations, and his comic representation of it presupposes either a loss or a failure to realize some ideal: this is part of what is meant by the comic deviation from an (ideal) norm. It also seems misguided to suggest, as Fumaroli does, that Proust needed Sainte-Beuve's description of social norms for the substance of his portrayal of aristocrats and social climbers who are perpetual victims of the fall into trivia: Proust's vision of the fall is archetypical. It is the fall into degraded logos that, as a near-mythical event, has always already taken place, to paraphrase what philosopher Jacques Derrida could have said. Utopia is always somewhere else. Learning that the fall is everywhere, unrelentingly, is certainly a central aspect of the narrator's education after the paradise of "Combray." For Proust himself that education was already underway with *Pleasures and Days*.

Succinctly, then, Madame de Villeparisis does, in her opinions expressed in her lively conversation, embody what Proust saw as the weakness of Sainte-Beuve's belief that a writer's biography trumps his or her literary work. Madame de Villeparisis also places the narrator in contact with other members of the nobility who represent other viewpoints, for instance, the aristocratic Saint-Loup, one of Proust's versions of a would-be intellectual, who along with would-be symbolist Bloch is perhaps most representative of intellectual attitudes then current in modernist milieus. Saint-Loup is at times the narrator's best friend and a paradoxical representative of the highest aristocracy, at once noble in conduct, arguably ridiculous in his love life with his actress mistress, capable of crass materialism, and aloof in his claiming not even to subscribe to aristocratic values. If Madame de Villeparisis looks backward to that intellectual life centered upon her family milieu, the "young Marquis de Saint-Loup-en-Bray" looks to the future, for he reads Nietzsche and undoubtedly has opinions about what the new intellectual must become in order to overcome the nihilism that Nietzsche saw as Europe's future. Proust may also have had in mind Ivan Turgenev's depiction of the conflict between generations as found in the influential novel *Fathers and Sons*. Proust's portrayal of the marquis also centers on the generation gap: Saint-Loup has only contempt for his dead father. In fact he is seriously limited intellectually by his intolerance of what his father would have represented were he alive. The father was open-minded, but not Saint-Loup, who "was one of those people who believe that merit is attached only to certain forms of art and of life" and is contemptuous of a father "who yawned at Wagner and raved over Offenbach" (*BG*, 427). The older narrator is judgmental about Saint-Loup in this regard, especially in observing that the young aristocrat "was not intelligent enough to understand that intellectual worth has nothing to do with adhesion to any one aesthetic formula" (*BG*, 427). The narrator suggests that Saint-Loup rather simplistically thought that his father was the victim of the limits of his times, which seems, ironically, the case with Saint-Loup.

Perhaps despite himself Saint-Loup is an aristocrat, which means he has a name that conjures up the beautiful people about whom Proust dreamed in his youth, as when he wrote his poem on the noblemen whose portraits by Van Dyck embody their glory in *Pleasures and Days*. The name bespeaks the blood lineage that apparently determines him to be the most elegant of young men. One wonders what projection is involved when the narrator first sees Saint-Loup, who is "tall, slim, bare-necked, his head held proudly erect, a young man with penetrating eyes whose skin was as fair and his hair as golden as if they had absorbed all the rays of the sun" (*BG*, 420). Here he appears to be as much a descendant of one of Van Dyck's palatine princes as an inheritor of the house of Lusignan: "The distinctive quality of his hair, his eyes, his skin, his bearing" would have "marked him out in a crowd like a precious vein of opal, azure-shot and luminous, embedded in a mass of coarser substance" (*BG*, 420). Proust's belief in genetics is perhaps less important for this portrait than is his at times unquenched utopian desire that there really should be superior beings. However genetics notwithstanding, the aristocratic intellectual is not on the cutting edge of intellectual life, at least in the narrator's opinion, and Saint-Loup's subsequent conduct shows that if he is a generous as well as elegant friend, he is also dissolute and irresponsible, with a hot temper that causes him to be prone to violence. In a sense Saint-Loup is a kind of limit case in nobility, illustrating to the narrator what an aristocrat can be and what he can learn from such a being, which is finally not very much. This in itself, however, is an important step forward in his knowledge of society.

In his education the narrator thus comes to understand that a clear contrast exists between an older view of literature and society, as illustrated by Madame de Villeparisis, and a more modern view typified by Saint-Loup and a generation that read the symbolists, listened to Wagner, and as we learn from a casual allusion by Saint-Loup, learned about science from Poincaré. Contrasting with both the new and the old is another aristocrat encountered here, namely, Saint-Loup's uncle, the Baron de Charlus, the towering figure of a nearly mad homosexual aristocrat who is, as once was said, supremely cultivated. In this character the very notion of "Guermantes" explodes in a dazzling display of often comic contractions. For in this extraordinary character, Proust synthesizes a worldview, if such a colorless term be allowed, that respects tradition, understands the modern, and transcends both in extravagance and mad pretense. On the one hand, Charlus regards the classical tragedian Racine as a pinnacle of literature but hardly the only one, since, on the other hand, he is also a passionate reader of Balzac's chronicle of the rise of the bourgeoisie; and the baron also collects the works of his contemporary Bergotte. His versatility is evident to the narrator even before he knows who the baron is, for upon first seeing him, the young narrator takes "him at one moment for a thief and at another for a lunatic" (*BG*, 454). Both epithets are appropriate, for the baron's behavior is suggestive of both a charlatan and a grand madman. For the reader familiar with Balzac, in fact, he bears a resemblance to the novelist's most famous thief, Vautrin, Balzac's homosexual pedagogue in crime. I suggest this parallel not to point out Proust's admiration for Balzac but to suggest that Proust drew upon him—and not just on Proust's extravagant friend, the Count Robert de Montesquiou—in creating perhaps his most interesting character. In other words in the baron Proust has updated as it were a bourgeois criminal by transforming him into an aristocratic lecher whose behavior mocks the idea of medieval grandeur—while affirming a grandeur beyond legend. I admit that one inevitably thinks of Boldini's extravagant painting of the flamboyant Montesquiou, now in the Musée d'Orsay, whenever one thinks of the baron. But here I propose that much can be learned by a comparison with Balzac's great criminal.

Some background: Vautrin is the homosexual criminal who, in Balzac's novel *Father Goriot,* dreams of escaping to the American South and establishing himself as a planter aristocrat surrounded by slaves. The criminal will to power provides an ironic foil to the baron with his aristocratic pretensions, monarchist beliefs, and acceptance of medieval Christianity. But there are also direct resemblances to Balzac's protean thief. Like Vautrin, who has at least four names in various novels and appears in various guises and disguises, the baron has several names and, indeed, modes of appearance. He is first seen in "Combray" as an unnamed friend of Swann's about whom the uninformed village gossip holds that he sleeps with Swann's wife, Odette. Then in *Within a Budding Grove,* he is introduced as "Palamède," though known as "Mémé" to his friends. He is usually the Baron de Charlus or M. de Charlus, though he is also a Guermantes and could use the title of Prince of Laumes or even of Sicily. The confusion of names is such that the narrator does not initially understand that the baron is the brother of the Duke of Guermantes. In short like Vautrin he is a

protean character—aesthete, Christian, compulsive seducer, arrogant lunatic—that the narrator must come to understand if he is to understand that
the nobility is not to be subsumed under one simple label. This is of course
another aspect of Proust's comedy with, and the narrator's education in,
the limits of names.

Concerning directly the narrator's education is the fact that the baron
wants to take him under his wing and educate him. Thus one sees that
Vautrin's resemblance with the baron is not only that they are chameleons,
but also that both are would-be pedagogues. Combining the hubris of an
all-knowing educator with criminal genius and pederast lechery, Vautrin
wants to take charge of the handsome young aristocrats he encounters:
first Eugene de Rastignac in *Father Goriot,* then Lucien de Rubempré in
Lost Illusions and its sequel, *Scenes from a Courtesan's Life.* In the case of
both young men, the educator Vautrin promises to make them rich, which
not incidentally resembles a Faustian pact. In the case of Rubempré, the
Faustian results are his suicide, so that there is a closer parallel between
Proust's young narrator and the young noble Rastignac, especially in their
desire to conquer society as well as in their refusal to sign the pact that
would compromise their respective souls. To be sure in Proust the social
strata involved are the reverse of those found in Balzac: Balzac's grand ped-
agogical pervert wants to raise up the sons of the fallen nobility, whereas
Proust's baron is a noble homosexual wanting to bring up to his level the
handsome young bourgeois the reader assumes the narrator to be. In any
case like Rastignac, Proust's young narrator does not follow up on Charlus's offer to direct the development of his soul, though he does learn much
from the baron. But no Faustian hero, the narrator by and large continues
his *Bildung* alone.

Charlus escapes from the intellectual limitations that seem to go with
the name Guermantes, and his superior intelligence accentuates his attrac-
tiveness. It is because of his intelligence that the narrator's grandmother
is willing to forgive the baron his "aristocratic prejudice" (*BG,* 459). But
intelligence notwithstanding, the baron is virtually the only aristocrat who
openly flaunts with no reserve his presumed superiority. His grandiose
arrogance almost seems convincing. Saint-Loup, in describing his Guermantes relatives, thinks that none of them have the "thoroughbred air, that
look of being noblemen to their finger-tips" characterizing his uncle, the
baron (*BG,* 465). However this opinion is actually deflationary, at least
initially, for the narrator cannot see the baron's superiority. Thereupon he
is disappointed; he feels that another of his illusions has been shattered,
since the look of being an aristocrat is simply that: it is what the Baron de
Charlus looks like and nothing more. No abstract essence surrounds him

like a halo. But there is a second movement in the boy's learning to see. For as he continues to look, he sees something else present in the baron. Despite that fact the baron tries "to seal hermetically the expression on his face to which a light coating of powder lent a faintly theatrical aspect," the narrator sees that "the eyes were like two crevices, two loop-holes which alone he had failed to block, and through which, according to one's position in relation to him, one suddenly felt oneself in the path of some hidden weapon which seemed to bode no good" (*BG,* 465). Almost alone among the characters he meets in Balbec, the baron finally resists deflation and seems to possess an interior life that goes beyond the mere social roles that define the comedy in which virtually all the other characters are engaged. The notable exceptions, in *Within a Budding Grove,* are Elstir and Bergotte, artists whose creativity and inner vision allow them to escape the narrow limits imposed by social convention and habit.

After being introduced to Charlus, the narrator has three significant encounters with him in the course of *Within a Budding Grove* and *The Guermantes Way,* each encounter marking, as it were, important moments in the narrator's ongoing *Bildung.* The first meeting occurs during the stay at Balbec, in the second part of *Within a Budding Grove,* when the baron comes to the boy's hotel room to bring him a book by Bergotte. The second takes place at the end of the first part of *The Guermantes Way* when the baron escorts him out of the reception at Madame de Villeparisis's. And the boy meets the baron again at the end of *The Guermantes Way* when, after his first reception with the Guermantes, he goes to the baron's home for an extraordinary comic encounter in which the baron flaunts his pride as he pursues his lunatic way of seducing. However the young narrator shows that he, too, is not without temper: in a rage he smashes the baron's hat to show that he, too, has pride.

The encounters with the baron deflect the comedy from the boy's absurd fantasies generated by names and focus it on a comedy based on the deviance from rational norms the baron manifests with an arrogance rare in life or literature. This is clear in the scene in the boy's hotel room in which the baron brings him a book. It is followed by the baron's demanding the return of the book, which is then followed by his making, with studied caprice, a gift to the boy of the same book, now with a luxurious binding. This game playing with the gift sets the stage for the baron's manifestations of volatile behavior and hardly veiled erotic desires when offering a Faustian pact to the young narrator. This offer comes as a culminating moment prolonging the narrator's *rite de passage* at the Villeparisis reception. After the reception the baron offers to take the narrator in charge, to educate him, and to elevate him to high position in society. The baron's pretension says a great deal about his self-image, not to say fantasy, with regard to his situation in society and in politics. He says he wants to initiate the narrator into a career in diplomacy based upon the baron's superior knowledge of the world and his well-placed contacts. None of this exposition is very clear, and in much of it Charlus appears to engage in a kind of flight of fantasy, but what is clear enough is that the baron sees himself as a central figure in a perhaps inchoate, perhaps developing movement to restore monarchy and hence the aristocracy in France and Europe. For an interpretation of the way Proust charts the demise of the aristocratic classes, it is worth pondering what the baron thinks he represents in the society of the early Third Republic.

I noted earlier that one cannot dismiss the aristocracy of the late nineteen century as a marginal group of parasites. Clearly they still had power upon the fall of Napoleon III. In fact after the French defeat at the hands of Otto von Bismarck in 1870, the nobility could hope realistically to bring about a restoration, and in the early years of the Third Republic, they were undoubtedly close to achieving that goal. By the last years of the nineteenth century—approximately at the time of the narrator's encounter with the baron—Charlus could almost plausibly be dreaming of reviving the recent past. This explains why, while supposedly worrying if the young narrator is "worth" the trouble the baron might take for him, Charlus is carried away expounding a self-serving vision of himself as the one who might have already brought about the restoration, if only the pretender "the Comte de Chambord had had at his side a man as thoroughly conversant with the undercurrents of European politics" as he—or so he considers himself, and also so thinks the emperor of Austria, also according to the baron (*GW*, 389).

The Comte de Chambord is generally considered to have been the last Bourbon hope to restore the monarchy. Naturally enough in his speech to the narrator, the baron does not mention that Chambord is generally considered a reactionary romantic dreamer who sabotaged his own restoration when he refused to become king if he could not replace the tricolor French flag with the white banner bearing the lilies of the house of Bourbon. The baron is pontificating at a moment after the pretender's death in 1883, when there thus appeared to be little real chance of a restoration—though conflicts produced by the Dreyfus affair kept some hopes alive. It is in this ideologically charged context that the baron makes his diatribe. Ultimately in this scene the baron is part Vautrin, the realist seducer, and part Don Quixote, dreaming of the restoration of a past imbued with noble values, which perhaps never existed and is now really gone forever. A perverted pedagogue, he nonetheless wants to confer the benefit of his knowledge "on a soul that is still virgin and capable of being fired by virtue" (*GW*, 395). And he is a brilliant maniac who can say that he does not consider the Dreyfus affair to be worthy of interest. The reason for this startling opinion is that he does not think that Jews could ever be French; therefore a Jew cannot be guilty of treason to the French state (*GW*, 390). The baron seems still to be living in an ancien régime, if not *the* ancien régime, one perhaps as imaginary as the boy's Middle Ages. Proust does a marvelous narrative pirouette to conclude this scene when, to point up the extent of the baron's comic pretensions, the narrator shows that none of the baron's aristocratic posturing stops him from visibly cruising a drunk young cab driver. This occurs as he takes leave of the narrator, after having described the nobility of the education he might offer the young man, if only the lad were to allow him to direct the course of his life.

For this education the baron demands, for reasons that the reader may guess, that the young man give up all social life until he has achieved the grandeur the baron promises him. Not too surprisingly the young narrator then seeks no more contact with the baron and even neglects to write him to say what he thinks about the baron's proposal. It is with symbolic timing that the baron invites him to come to his home precisely when the young man has "arrived," as it were. He has been well received at the soirée given by the Duke and Duchess of Guermantes. In the scene that ensues after the soirée, the baron rages that he has been slighted by the boy, while he also rants contradictorily that the boy is too miserably low to be able to offend a personage of such exalted rank as himself. The insulted young man finally explodes in anger at the baron's behavior and in a fit of temper destroys the baron's hat. And it all comes to an inconclusive end with, first, the baron banishing the young narrator from his presence forever and, then, accompanying him home. In this exchange of tantrums, Proust creates one of his great comic scenes in which the aristocrat shows at once his extraordinary ego, his intelligence, and his willingness to do anything when urged on by erotic desire. Comic, too, is the fact that the boy is still not sufficiently educated to understand what is going on, as he shows when he wonders why the baron keeps several strong male servants posted at the door of his living room, ready to intervene in case of need—apparently there are limits to what physical violence even the masochistic baron can enjoy. But the baron is not a bully; he is a sensitive soul who is perhaps genuinely offended that the narrator has not been sensitive enough to figure out that the book binding of the volume of Bergotte the baron gave him represented the "lintel of myosotis over the door of Balbec church"—

myosotis, a flower of the borage family, is more popularly known, in English as in French, as the forget-me-not (*GW,* 761). The young Proustian narrator is not as subtle as Proust or his baron.

After experiencing these scenes of titanic and comic arrogance, the narrator has made a major step forward in understanding what the upper classes are about, but he is still remarkably naive. He is still partially enchanted with names, with a world that does not exist, though he intuits at times that utopia does not exist. At the end of *The Guermantes Way,* the narrator looks back on these moments and makes the following evaluation: "We are attracted by any life which represents for us something unknown and strange, by a last illusion still unshattered. Many of the things that M. de Charlus had told me had given a vigorous spur to my imagination and, making it forget how much reality had disappointed it at Mme de Guermantes's (people's names are in this respect like the names of places), had swung it towards Oriane's cousin. Moreover, M. de Charlus misled me for some time as to the imaginary worth and variety of society people only because he was himself misled" (*GW,* 778).

His comments, with their retrospective character, emphasize that the narrator has at this point nearly reached the limits of possible naïveté. He has almost finished his education in names, hence in the nature of his impulse toward poetic projection. In retrospect one also sees that his education is now ready to take a plunge more directly downward, as if to illustrate fully the biblical allegory of the Fall. Knowledge is the end of innocence, for as the biblical allegory has it, knowledge constitutes the Fall itself.

This reading seems confirmed by the way Proust ends *The Guermantes Way* with a conclusive demonstration of the limits of aristocratic virtue. The narrator sees what an utter egomaniac, one without the virtues of intellect and culture, is the baron's brother, the Duke of Guermantes. This meeting comes about when the narrator, doubting the good luck he has in furthering his social life, goes to see the duke to ask if an invitation the young man has received from the Princess of Guermantes is genuine. (I recall that a comparable scene is a prelude to the narrator's discovery of homosexuality in one manuscript in *Against Sainte-Beuve.*) The duke receives him at the moment he is preparing to go out to a dress ball. The narrator can thus witness the duke's extraordinary insensitivity: he makes great effort to avoid knowing if a cousin is dying, since that knowledge might interfere with his pleasure that evening. The lesson this scene offers is immediately followed by a repetition of this shallow egotism—Proust himself is nothing if not a pedagogue convinced of the value of repetition—when Swann comes to see the duke and duchess. Swann is now quite ill and probably dying. In his weakened state, he nonetheless resists being pressured by the maniacal duke into certifying as a genuine Velázquez a dubious painting that the duke has recently acquired. In turn the duke refuses to take seriously the fact that Swann might be dying. Even the charming duchess is caught up in the egomaniac's dilemma about having to take seriously suffering that might be an impediment to pleasure. Or as the older narrator says with incisive irony: "Placed for the first time in her life between two duties as incompatible as getting into her carriage to go out to dinner and showing compassion for a man who was about to die, she could find nothing in the code of conventions that indicated the right line to follow" (*GW*, 816). Therefore like the duke she chooses not to believe something that would interfere with her evening; she pretends not to believe, as the narrator says, and puts off talking to Swann about his illness. Thus *The Guermantes Way* ends with the narrator having witnessed several less than admirable sides of the Guermantes: their despicable egotism and grand lunacy. He has come a long way from the moments in which poetry was encoded for him in the very sonorities of the noble name.

With regard to his education in society in general, the narrator's biggest step forward comes in *The Guermantes Way* at the Guermantes dinner party, where he makes his debut among the old aristocracy. This occurs after the narrator has begun his initiation into aristocratic ways in Balbec and after, having discovered the pleasures of the "girls in flower" on the beach, he has returned to Paris to live in his parents' new abode in the Guermantes townhouse, where he has freely projected his puerile fantasies upon the duchess. Before entering society in a grand manner, he has gone to the reception of the somewhat déclassé Madame de Villeparisis, which prepares him for the apotheosis of his then being received by the elite of the Faubourg Saint-Germain. These events are punctuated by his encounters with major characters, such as the Baron of Charlus or the painter Elstir, and by other, less important recurrent characters, all of whom contribute, to a greater or lesser extent, to his education. I offer this brief resumé to underscore that the Guermantes dinner party is staged so as to come at a seminal point in the narrator's *Bildung*. It is staged to grant him a final grand experience of the deflation of aristocratic pretensions and vanity.

The dinner party responds to a long and deeply held desire that the young narrator first conceived in inchoate form in Combray. The desire took on greater immediacy and precision after his family moved into the Guermantes hotel, for here he could look upon their quarters. Picturing to himself who was received there, he "imagined the guests as seated like the Apostles in the Sainte-Chapelle" (*GW*, 31). But there are no halos about the heads of the characters he finally meets in the inner sanctum of the aristocracy. They are shallow and trivially banal, as their sense of wit illustrates with their repetition of a silly play on the words *Caesar* and *teaser,* as the translation has it, in reference to Charlus as a teaser (*GW,* 636). (The bourgeois Cottard is not alone in shallow wit.) The party encompassing such lame verbal banter is a very long narrative piece, mixing dialogue and flashbacks, as if Proust wanted to make sure that the vacuity of the conversation is proved by its endless repetition. However the party begins significantly with a contrasting scene, when, immediately upon arrival, the narrator asks the duke to be left alone to look at his collection of Elstir's paintings. Alone to meditate, he thinks of the lessons that he learned earlier from Elstir's art and from conversation with the artist at Balbec. The meditation here on the fullness of artistic vision entertains negative symmetry with the end of the dinner party: one then learns that Madame de Guermantes hates Elstir's paintings—even if Elstir has done a good portrait of her—but with naive egotism she thinks they must have some value if, after all, they are in her house (*GW,* 685). The narrator's viewing art in silence is also set in notable contrast with the subsequent noise of the guests' largely meaningless conversations, as when Madame de Guermantes reveals herself to be a remarkably poor judge of painting. From the older narrator's perspective, she is incapable of understanding the experience of art, which is proven by the fact that the stylish duchess thinks art can be profitably viewed quickly, as, say, from a moving vehicle. The narrator concludes that her bizarre idea stems from her very "misconception of the way in which artistic impressions are formed in our minds," which is, she must think, something like a "recording machine which takes snapshots" (*GW,* 718). A mechanically copied image is not a work of art, for reasons that Proust's view of art makes clear: the artistic image must be the expression of the artist's inner vision.

The educational experience at the Guermantes party is at once a lesson in the self-deceit these aristocrats practice among themselves and in the way they are by and large of a single piece in their artistic judgments, snobbery, and political views. One of their favored pseudoparadoxes, if not forms of hypocrisy, is that, except for Charlus, the "Guermantes, while living among the cream of the aristocracy, affected to set no store by nobility" (*GW,* 600). This affectation is largely cant. The narrator stresses that the Duke of Guermantes, in mouthing platitudes to the effect that aristocracy does not count, is making facile statements for public consumption. They are easily said by a man who is a deputy and is ready to play a role in the government in the republic run by dukes. Although the duke seems to espouse a democratic viewpoint, the narrator finds the duke "did not believe it for a moment" (*GW,* 651). True, the duke as deputy appears at times more open and receptive to his constituents than do bourgeois deputies, but this is actually because he has contempt for democracy and "despised political position" so that he did not even bother to put forward the "starchiness of high office which makes others unapproachable" (*GW*, 651). His contempt means that "his pride protected against every assault not only his manners, which were of an ostentatious familiarity, but also such true simplicity as he might actually possess" (*GW*, 651). His lack of belief in democracy is not surprising, since it appears that the duke is ultimately obsessed with his genealogy and, except when pursuing a new mistress, thinks about little else.

The narrator's education in sexual matters is not the same as an education in love, and both are only tangentially related to learning about marriage. At the dinner party, the narrator comments on what he has learned about the sorrowful state of Madame de Guermantes that has been brought about by her marriage. In marrying a fellow aristocrat who is her intellectual inferior but her financial superior, she has condemned herself to the role of an observer watching the sexual conquests her husband periodically makes. Certainly she shares some of his shallow egotism, for she "languished whenever people spoke of the beauty of any woman other than herself" (*GW*, 634). Her beauty notwithstanding, she does not attract her husband, "who had never loved her," so that he spends his time "pursuing a single type of feminine beauty" in mistresses "whom he constantly replaced" (*GW*, 646). He does respect his wife for her services as a clever, well-read showpiece who is good at entertaining and "upheld for their salon its position as the premier in the Faubourg Saint-Germain" (*GW*, 646). This is one of the most damning judgments the narrator makes about the characters, for it shows this woman to be a kind of modish puppet who allows herself to be used by the egomaniacal duke for his social purposes. It is a profound lesson; it is one that plays no practical role in the narrator's own life, however attuned he might be to the moral nuances of the duchess's situation.

Madame de Guermantes accepts her role, putting up a good front with her wordplay and her love of paradoxical opinions that assure that she is the talk of the Faubourg. With his gift for wordplay, Swann has found a role to play with her. Swann has been complementary to the duchess precisely in the display of the snobbish banter that allows her to accept her role as the duke's chattel by proclaiming her verbal superiority to her dismal state. At this point the narrator is categorical in his judgment of Swann, which is another form of damnation: "Certainly men of wit, such as Swann for instance, regarded themselves as superior to men of merit, whom they despised, but that was because what the Duchess valued above everything else was not intelligence but—a superior form of intelligence, according to her, rarer, more exquisite, raising it up to a verbal variety of talent—wit" (*GW,* 631). However the dinner party, with its demonstration of aristocratic intelligence taking the form of foolish wit amusing to dolts, is something like a last judgment at which the Swann and the duchess are irrevocably condemned—however clever they may really be.

Yet the narrator is not willing to condemn entirely these frivolous and empty pleasure seekers. Despite and perhaps because of his newly educated vision of society, he finds in some of them something of which they themselves are unaware: namely the remnants of the historical past that the aristocratic names once elicited in the form of romantic fantasies from his poetic mind. Words still play a role in this regard, though it is not to generate fantasies. Sealed off from modern ideas—unlike her nephew Saint-Loup, whose "mind is troubled by the ideas of Kant and the yearning of Baudelaire"—Madame de Guermantes uses a language that is the "exquisite French of Henry IV," a language of the sixteenth century that in its purity shows that both her "intelligence and sensibility had remained closed against innovation" (*GW,* 689). The young narrator now realizes that the duchess is incapable of understanding what he had earlier sought in her, namely that charm of her historic name, which offered in "the tiny quantity of it," "a rustic survival from Guermantes" (*GW,* 689). But this recognition of what the duchess genuinely does embody from the past does little to offset the narrator's disappointment. He even recognizes that his misunderstanding of her was inevitable, since it arose between a "dreamer" and an imaginary "superior woman" (*GW,* 690). The fault lies as much with himself as the duchess, and the misunderstanding will continue to be inevitable so long as "he has not resigned himself to the inevitable disappointments he is destined to find in people, as in theatre, in travel and indeed in love" (*GW,* 690). Here is the seminal moment in his education, pointing to ongoing disenchantment, so long as the narrator has not found his vocation.

Concomitant to his education gained by frequenting society is the boy's ongoing education in art. Art, in the broadest sense of the term, is the one force that can fortify his mind against the erroneous expectations he has. Quite simply art can work against the disenchantment resulting from his education in society, for there is nothing in society that can satisfy his mind. One should never lose sight of the fact—even if the narrator seems to do so at times—that his education is that of a potential writer: from the beginning the novel is the story of a vocation taking shape, and that vocation is based on the understanding of art. Some, perhaps much, of the socializing that the narrator does is undertaken so as to bring him into contact with what he believes to be the sources of art. For it is in the salons and aristocratic milieu that music is performed and painting is on display, and it is there he hoped to find what he once perceived to be the poetic resources of French culture itself, in the aristocracy whose names promised poetic revelation about the past. By the end of *The Guermantes Way*, the latter idea has been discredited, but the narrator has set himself upon a path as socialite that he does not have the force of will to leave. Wallowing in luxury, as it were, he finds that he has little willpower. Habit seems to take over his life. His major disappointment is increasingly himself.

At this point it seems almost inevitable to think of the portrait of the young writer given by Proust's near contemporary, James Joyce, in his *Portrait of the Artist as a Young Man,* published a year after *Swann's Way.* Joyce gives a portrait of working-class Irish culture and shows the destruction it could work on the writer and his integrity, the result of which is that the future artist must flee this milieu and, in rebellion and in solitude, seek the redemption that his art provides. Having recognized the probability of self-destruction in the milieu he frequents, by contrast with Joyce, Proust's narrator continues nonetheless to pursue the meaningless, if comic, social rites of which he becomes a master. Proust's future artist will seek solitude only later, if he is successful in following his vocation. He lacks the will-power of Joyce's Stephen Dedalus, though both endorse the idea that art can be realized only in the solitude in which the artist rejects the demands of a smothering environment.

However, unlike Joyce's artist, Proust's youthful narrator does find art omnipresent in his upper-class milieu. An education in art and an education in society are, in Proust's novel, intertwined and mutually reinforcing, at times through mutual repulsion. There is a pattern the narrator follows in his education in art as well as in society: he has a priori ideas and fantasies, tests them, is disappointed, has more experiences, and then reshapes his previous impressions on the basis of new impressions and experiences. Consider in this regard theater, a hybrid art that brings society, literature, and visual spectacle into contact. The young narrator was long denied the privilege of entering a theater. Thus the boy used theatrical advertising posters, as seen along the Champs-Élysées, in order to concoct an idea as to what might happen on a stage. Because the diplomat Norpois advises the narrator's father that the boy should be allowed to see Berma in her interpretation of *Phèdre*, he finally sees a performance by the great actress. It disappoints him (*BG*, 20–21). He cannot find in her acting what it is that would constitute her "genius." He looks for Berma to superimpose upon

the well-known text some additional "work," but, alas, it does not appear
that her talent has added anything to the words the young narrator already
knows (BG, 26).

Only later in The Guermantes Way, when he appears to be initially
more interested in the Guermantes family's loge in the theater than in the
performance taking place, does the narrator discover that the great actress's art is *there* in what he sees and hears concretely on the stage and not
in the revelation of an essence imposed from above. At the second performance, he does not confront her acting with some "pre-existent, abstract
and false idea of dramatic genius," so that he is open to the "individual
impression" that the actress makes upon him (GW, 56). And he sees that
what she does is exactly "what was meant by nobility, by intelligence of
diction" (GW, 56). Proust sounds somewhat like Ludwig Wittgenstein, the
Viennese philosopher who requested that we not define but that we look
at what is happening when we want to know what we mean. We may use
terms such as "broad, poetical, powerful interpretation," as Proust says, to
speak of a particular performance, though that is, he adds, a bit like giving mythological names to planets of the solar system that in themselves
have "nothing mythological about them" (GW, 57). The narrator finally
concludes that we feel and perceive in one world but think and give names
to things in another; and that if we may establish a certain correspondence
between the two worlds, we cannot bridge the gap. This seems to be rather
consistently Proust's view of the self and its relation to the world.

After recognizing his propensity to project words and ideas upon the
world, the narrator concludes that he had done the same thing to Gilberte.
We may add that we have seen that he does the same when he begins looking at the "girls in blossom" under the auspices of Beauty. His education
in art is at a turning point when he comes to see that with ideas such as
"beauty" and "pathos," "in a pinch" one can have the illusion of recognizing them "in the banality of a conventional face or talent" (GW, 57). But the
challenge of a performance of a work of art is indeed to recognize that there
is a challenge and, furthermore, to recognize that, when there is no "intellectual equivalent" offered by an original artist or performance, the mind
must "disengage the unknown element" with no reliance on preformed
ideas (GW, 57). It is in this challenge, made by an originality not known
in advance, that art offers to educate vision with respect to people and life.

A dubious reader may well ask whether music can offer an education
in vision. One answer is sketched out later in the novel when the narrator
puts forth the hypothesis that music does grant access to a world superior
to our own. In Within a Budding Grove, Proust concentrates on how the
young narrator assimilates music, as exemplified by Vinteuil's sonata,

heard when he goes to visit Madame Swann. The older narrator evaluates his experience of the music from the boy's viewpoint and from his mature standpoint. The young narrator did not understand the sonata, though he enjoyed Odette's performance (*BG,* 144). This is inevitable, since, for the real understanding of music, the older narrator says that memory is necessary so that the mind can participate, through anticipation, in the complexity of the experience; and this can happen only after repeated hearings. The older narrator knows from experience that in works that are "truly rare," one does not grasp upon the first audition what is most valuable in them— the "unknown element," as it were—and so the young narrator made the mistake in Odette's salon of believing that the sonata "held nothing further in store" for him: "When the least obvious beauties of Vinteuil's sonata were revealed to me, already, borne by the force of habit beyond the grasp of my sensibility, those that I had from the first distinguished and preferred in it were beginning to escape, to elude me. Since I was able to enjoy everything that this sonata had to give me only in a succession of hearings, I never possessed it in its entirety: it was like life itself" (*BG,* 141). Unlike life, however, the great work of art eludes the force of habit, the law governing the reduction of perception in daily life. Perhaps it is a test of great art that it retains its capacity for revelation even after the first and repeated contacts. Indeed many contacts are necessary even to begin to grasp what a major artwork can convey. This necessity contrasts greatly with the nature of the contacts one has with people, for in society one tires quickly of the facile beauties that one immediately perceives. Social life must inevitably be a bore. However in Proust's world one also goes into society to hear sonatas. There could be no education in art found in total solitude.

In both *Within the Budding Grove* and *The Guermantes Way,* the narrator underscores the social matrix in which his younger self encounters art. For example the artist Elstir is initially part of the world of initiation the young narrator undergoes at Balbec. The mature artist does need his solitude and thus lives largely apart from the summer crowd. In fact the narrator first meets him in a chance encounter in a restaurant on the coast. (He is accompanied by Saint-Loup, and the two here resemble the couple meeting by chance the writer on the coast in *Jean Santeuil.*) Nonetheless frequenting Elstir and seeing his work is part of social activity. The same can be said about the narrator's initiation into literature. Both Swann and Charlus introduce him to the work of Bergotte, who is then encountered as a participant in Odette's salon. Vinteuil led a rather isolated life, though his music is now an integral part of high society entertainment. From this perspective the "lesson" the narrator garners from the presence of art is that society seems to be set dialectically in opposition to the redemption that art might seem to promise. As the only artist portrayed who participates in social rituals, Bergotte, in his person and social speech, offers the lesson of an artistic self divided by the opposing pull of influences. Bergotte tries to hide his quest for social success: "He was only half-successful; one could hear, alternating with the speech of the true Bergotte, that of the other, self-ish and ambitious Bergotte who talked only of his powerful, rich or noble friends in order to enhance himself, he who in his books, when he was re-ally himself, had so well portrayed the charm, pure as a mountain spring, of the poor" (*BG*, 180).

If Bergotte is a model for the narrator, it is obviously as a writer and not a socialite, for as a socialite Bergotte is rather much a vain failure. Of course Vinteuil is not a model either, for it does not appear that in his life as the village music teacher he found much satisfaction. If the opposition of art and society can be resolved for the narrator, perhaps it would be by imitating Elstir, who seems to balance solitude and social contact in ways that do not harm his art. Thus it may appear that with the three artists, Proust sets out three quite different possible models for the life of the artist in society. What the narrator will select at the end of the novel remains an open question, though he explicitly envisages a kind of monastic renuncia-tion, which is not quite the model any of the three propose.

Elstir's life and work offer a great lesson in art and in the generosity of the artist during the time the narrator spends in Balbec. He goes to the artist's studio and can view at close hand works that are making Elstir justifiably famous. The narrator sees that in his paintings Elstir does not let himself be taken in by the habitual abstractions used in looking at the world: "I was able to discern from these that the charm of each of them lay in a sort of metamorphosis of the objects represented, analogous to what in poetry we call metaphor, and that, if God the Father had created things by naming them, it was by taking away their names or giving them other names that Elstir created them anew" (*BG*, 566).

The narrator views the artist as a kind of demiurge renewing the percep-tion of the world, bringing his viewer back to the moment of origins—the moment that is a key to Proust's desire for resurrection. Origins are always that moment of first being, such that the narrator says that Elstir's work brings the viewer back to the "rare moments in which we see nature as she is, poetically," which is to say, created anew (*BG*, 566–67). These are the moments undistorted by knowledge and abstraction, in which "our first sight" is restored (*BG*, 570). This is not a mystical moment, since it obeys the laws of optics that Elstir brings into play. Rather it is a moment of pris-tine perception in which one might say that Elstir's metaphors restore the plenitude of being. Later in the novel, one can argue that narrator's mature understanding of Vinteuil's music provides another lesson in understanding this plenitude.

The experience of plenitude is one pole and, indeed, goal of the narrator's education. The pole diametrically opposed to plenitude is the experience of absolute absence that the death of the narrator's grandmother inflicts upon him. The death is another seminal moment for the young narrator. Some critics argue that the earlier traumatic experience of the mother's absence, narrated as a recurrent memory in *Swann's Way*, finds an adult parallel in the anguish the narrator knows with the trauma of accepting his grandmother's death. The critics see the grandmother as a surrogate for the mother—the narrator's or Proust's. There is perhaps some truth in this, though it is equally plausible to see the grandmother's death as a normal part of what it means to mature. Accepting death in the family is part of an education in becoming an adult. After all at this stage in the young narrator's life, grandparents die, and usually not parents. Moreover her death is all the more traumatic in that the grandmother has been the narrator's frequent companion and source of emotional support. (And in a family with multigenerational ties, the grandmother is often as important for a grandchild as is the mother.) The experience of her death is one of the most remarkable moments in *In Search of Lost Time* and seems to subtend the narrator's meditations on nothingness: the prime example of nothingness is found in the grandmother's death.

True, the narrator's full knowledge of this absence does not occur until he has moved on to the revelations of *Sodom and Gomorrah*. Perhaps this is because the knowledge of death is so fundamental a part of the fall that Proust reserves the emotional shock for that part of the novel in which the narrator realizes the full scope of the fall into time. At the moment of her death, he is still gathering intimations of the fall. The narrator's assimilation of the grandmother's death, of its meaning or the impossibility thereof, presents, moreover, a remarkable instance of the manner in which the narrator offers an example, draws a lesson from it, and then changes that lesson later, showing that his first impressions were not accurate or were inadequate to what the experience would bring: it is only later during his second stay in Balbec that he feels the fullness of the loss of his grandmother. And it is only later that he realizes that he is too frail to bear up long under the weight of that loss, the memory of which oblivion must carry away if he is to survive.

The young narrator has a first intuition of what the meaning of his grandmother's death might be even before she dies. The intuition occurs in *The Guermantes Way* when he goes to the town of Doncières to visit his friend Saint-Loup at his military base. He goes there in hope of getting his friend to use his influence on his aunt, the Duchess of Guermantes, so that she will receive the would-be lover. Toward the end of the stay, the narrator uses a telephone—a new and uncanny experience—to talk to his grandmother. Despite the presence of the sound of grandmother's voice, talking on the telephone gives the narrator a foretaste of what her death will entail. Because of the sweetness of her distant voice, he becomes aware of her fragility, and this fragility in turn makes the narrator aware of their isolation. For the first time, he realizes she is separated from him (*GW*, 176). Moreover her voice has a phantom quality that he imagines will come back to visit him in the future, in memory, when she is actually dead (*GW*, 177). With this imagined voice accompanying the real voice, he recalls earlier anguish: not the anguish of Combray, but that associated with the grandmother once when, as a small boy, he was separated from her and lost in a crowd. The recalled experience of this past anguish makes him feel that she is already nearly lost in a ghostly world (*GW*, 178). Upset by this memory, he decides to return home immediately, despite his grandmother's having freed him of any obligation toward her. Perhaps one might call this Proust's version of involuntary traumatic memory—with a proleptic emphasis.

The photograph, another invention of modernity, is used metaphorically to describe the narrator's perception of his grandmother and how his perception of her anticipates her demise. Having returned home, he enters the drawing room where she is sitting. She does not sense his presence, and he views her directly with no communication or consciousness of mutual presence enfolding them. For a moment he looks upon her, as the narrator says, as if he were viewing a photograph, which is to say, the moment is devoid of the existential reciprocity of exchanged looks. She is viewed by the boy as are viewed those beings who are "out of the animated system, the perpetual motion of our incessant love for them" (*GW*, 184). Moreover for a moment she benefits from none of the ideas or habits that inform his normal perception of her—especially of the tenderness that hides the work of time. She stands revealed in her immediate contingency, and therein her inevitable death is no longer camouflaged: "I, for whom my grandmother was still myself, I who had never seen her save in my own soul, always in the same place in the past, through the transparency of contiguous and overlapping memories, suddenly, in our drawing-room which formed part of a new world, that of Time . . . I saw, sitting on the sofa beneath the lamp, red-faced, heavy and vulgar, sick, day-dreaming, letting her slightly crazed eyes wander over a book, an overburdened old woman whom I did not know" (*GW*, 185).

Such is the snapshot in which time reveals its pure work. It is another signal moment in the narrator's education. In a sense little can be added to this vision in the rest of the novel, except at its end, in *Time Regained*, when time's ravages are about to demolish not just an individual but an entire generation. But anguish is not associated later with this work of time. For by then nothingness, prefigured here in the revelation of the grandmother's flesh, is part of the great comedy of a masked ball performed by the nearly dead.

The narration of the grandmother's actual death is less grim than these two moments when the narrator anticipates it. In narrating the grandmother's stroke and her rapid decline, the older narrator concentrates more on the attendant doctors than on death. With black humor the narrator makes an ironic critique of the medical profession, especially in the character of the "nerve specialist" Dr. du Boulbon, who thinks the grandmother is simply neurotic. But it is her body, not her mind, that kills her—the body about which the older narrator sharply observes that while you may succeed in eliciting sympathy from a brigand intent upon robbing you in the road, asking for pity from your own body is like discoursing in front of an octopus (*GW*, 404). With regard to medicine itself, it seems it is at once a deception and a science that can describe laws ruling reality, which is a fact we know once we know those laws. Proust's ambivalence about medicine reflects modernity's own ambiguity insofar as we distrust science but know that we have no other source of knowledge. Neither Proust nor the modern reader can really doubt that the laws of physiology unfolding in time proceed to destroy the woman whom the narrator had not imagined separate from himself before these anguish-filled moments. Yet Proust's is a strangely lyrical materialism: in the end the grandmother's body is transformed, since death removes from her face what the years had deposited there in the course of the destruction they had worked. The narrator sees on her face in death something like a smile hovering on her lips, and the smile allows him to liken death to a medieval sculptor who has laid the grandmother down on her funeral couch in the form of a young girl (*GW*, 471). Proust's love of the Middle Ages, obviously shared by his narrator, comes at a seemingly incongruous moment; yet it is somehow appropriate. The narrator's comparison alludes to the faint smiles of Gothic statuary in which the destructive power of time seems to be opposed by a will to perdure, in stone, of a culture that placed the resurrection of the body at the heart of its beliefs. And so the grandmother, in her absence, remains a faint smiling presence that may mute, for the time being, the anguish that the narrator has learned is the ultimate due of all who love.

Chapter 6

Sodom and Gomorrah, The Captive, and *The Fugitive*

Intimations of Hell

Proust considered using the common title *Sodom and Gomorrah* for the three parts of the novel now known in the revised Moncrieff translation as *Sodom and Gomorrah, The Captive,* and *The Fugitive* (the last two were first published in French as *La Prisonnière* and *Albertine disparue*). As Antoine Compagon has observed, in 1918 Proust considered the entire "Albertine novel" to be illustrative of what he then designated as *Sodom and Gomorrah I* and *II*.[1] A suggested unity of theme is given by the title's biblical reference: in the Old Testament, Sodom and Gomorrah are the cities on the plain whose inhabitants God punishes with destruction for perversions they refuse to relinquish (or so goes the usual interpretation of their woes). However Proust did not keep a common title for the three parts, perhaps because the title *Sodom and Gomorrah* might imply too strongly the idea that Proust's narrator, like a modern Isaiah, is denouncing those who live there by calling upon them to "give ear unto the law of our God" (Isaiah 1:10). For if the narrator takes his place in the lineage of Hebrew prophets, it is rather more as a comic ingénue ironically portraying his own ineptitude than as a moralist denouncing the sins of his contemporaries, especially in the last two parts. This is not to say that the biblical perspective on human history does not correspond to Proust's view of society. In a sense it does, and it certainly corresponds to the damnation that conventional society once held out for those who transgressed its conventional morality. Oscar Wilde can be called to witness in this regard. Moreover the narrator's sudden discovery of the "cities of the plain" follows quite plausibly, in biblical terms, the portrayal of the paradise the boy knew in Combray and then his initiatory wandering in the desert of Guermantes high society. After the narration of his unsuccessful loves and dismal discoveries about society in *Within a Budding Grove* and *The Guermantes Way,* his discovery of Sodom probably comes as a surprise only to the young narrator. For the reader it is the logical culmination of the boy's education in the fall, an education taking the shape of a prolonged initiation accompanied by an inevitable, if at first slow, loss of innocence.

The narrator's *Bildung* takes a sharp turn with his discovery of the universality of sin, conceived of first as the loss of the ideal and only later as the commission of forbidden acts. The young narrator becomes cognizant of this loss as, after "Combray," he begins to understand how thoroughgoing is the lack of the plenitude that once seemingly invested his earthly garden. In *Sodom and Gomorrah,* this understanding of loss culminates in his full consciousness, well after the fact, of his grandmother's death. This lesson about death is reinforced subsequently by Albertine's sudden accidental death. However the discovery of the depravation resembling that described in the Bible occurs suddenly, with the revelation of forbidden acts at the outset of these three tomes dealing with those—with Dante in mind—we can call the damned. The narrator finally realizes that the Baron de Charlus is a frenetically active homosexual. In an act greatly resembling the boy's earlier voyeuristic discovery of lesbianism in "Combray," he accidentally sees and hears Charlus pursuing Jupien the tailor in the Guermantes courtyard. The scales fall from his eyes, to use a New Testament allusion that Proust undoubtedly had in mind.

This revelation is sudden, and it only the beginning of disclosures illustrating the universality of the fall and the presence of perversion. For the rest of the novel, the narrator repeatedly discovers the omnipresence of sexual deviance accompanying the universality of hypocrisy and deceit. This universality is an almost necessary postulate to justify the narrator's own nearly paranoid form of jealousy. Convinced of the universality of Sodom and Gomorrah, he can never be sure who is doing what to whom, nor can he trust anybody to tell him the truth about it. Thus he discovers that the fall into which he has been initiated is an ongoing process. It is coterminous with all human beings. It is also often quite comic, for, as I have said on several occasions, in Proust the permanent deviation from the norm characterizing human conduct is a mark of the comic—most of the time.

We have seen that Proust worked out an early version of the fall in *Pleasures and Days.* There it took the form of a comedy deriving from Pascalian premises about human misery. Much the same kind of comedy also characterizes *Sodom and Gomorrah* and shapes the narrator's self-portrayal in *The Captive* and *The Fugitive,* where it is his often comic fate to become, through love, a member of the damned. The fall he thus knows first concerns his deception and disenchantment with society. Only subsequently does hell then become a more personal matter. It is created by a state of jealous suffering brought about, in part, because he knows he is too weak and despicable to be able to hold onto his suffering: his love of Albertine must eventually come to an end because of the lover's own imperfection. This is a constant theme in Proust, found in both published and unpublished works. In *In Search of Lost Time*, the universal fall characterizes both the lover and the beloved in hell, for what often generates the suffering is his belief that his beloved is participating in the joys of the fall: sexual perversion.

These comments on Sodom and Gomorrah highlight most pointedly the question as to why a nonbeliever like Proust framed his bildungsroman as a social comedy using a biblical allegory. It would be useful now to preface a discussion of the next three parts of the novel with some commentary on the question of this allegory. Indeed it may seem that Proust's comparison of Parisian life with life in Sodom and Gomorrah is not necessarily the most appropriate image of Parisian society before World War I, however much people enjoyed, probably then as now, pursuing their sexual proclivities, and however much pain they may have inflicted on others in doing so. Confronting the suffering inevitably found in human relations, Proust showed that he had the kind of metaphysical mind that dreams of the transcendence of reality, with its aborted misfit to human desire. There is no question but that his sensibility in this regard was shaped by his knowledge of the Bible, its moral codes, and the Western tradition of Christian art. However his knowledge and sensibility must also be placed in the context of the general modernist desire to find a transcendent form of artistic being as a response to the nihilism that seemed on the point of engulfing European culture. In the early twentieth century, Proust was hardly alone in his desire for transcendence: many other modernists had a comparable desire to find some kind of revelation that would lift them above the muck— as Beckett might have put it a bit later. They shared a common goal in reaction to this nihilism. Paradoxically, perhaps, religion's loss of credibility may explain why Proust turned to the Bible and Christian myth for the structure of his novel. Though no longer the uncontested foundation of Western culture, the Bible nonetheless offers a universal allegory whose scope is broadly accessible. Biblical myth is almost part of the structure of mind, at least the European mind in question here, a mind that, like Proust's, sought to find structure to give it stability and permanence.

The search for some type of transcendental allegory was not just a limited literary phenomenon in the early twentieth century. To enlarge upon this point concerning Proust's modernism and his relation to biblical myth,

I want to make a comparison, though not a strictly literary analogy, for an explanation pointing up that other thinkers were engaged in a comparable quest. To be sure a literary analogy might be offered by comparisons of Proust's recourse to allegory and myth with, say, Robert Musil's search for a nonreligious mystical utopia, Joyce's concoction of various mythical schemas for overcoming time and history, Franz Kafka's yearning for an impossible revelation of the Word, Virginia Woolf's desire to find eternity in the present moment, or Jean Cocteau's whimsical creation of poetic myths that turn the poet into a priest. The list could be greatly extended. But rather than compare Proust's exploitation of myth with these literary uses of religious myth, I propose a different analogy in order to demonstrate how widespread was the conscious use of myth in early twentieth-century culture. Namely the use of myth to explain the permanent nature of the self is also a characteristic of the work of Proust's near contemporary, the inventor of psychoanalysis, Sigmund Freud. Remarkably like Proust in many respects, Freud constructed mythic allegories drawing on the Bible as well as the Greek myths of Oedipus and Electra to explain the normal abnormal development we all undergo as we lead our usually unhappy lives.

Both Proust and Freud construct allegories to portray the stages of human development, with both starting with the individual's fall from an allegorical paradise. Much like the Proust of "Combray," Freud posits that our lives begin with dreams of paradise on the mother's breast, in a bliss of union, which comes to a rapid end when the Father, much like an archangel with a castrating sword, chases us from the garden of delights found in hoped-for eternal possession of the Mother. A caveat here: Freud's allegory has scientific pretensions, which means it makes claims to universal validity. Proust's allegorical use of the Bible makes no such explicit claims. Minimally his enterprise is to illustrate the universal truth of the individual case, which, if this is not a contradictory undertaking, means that his claim is to offer the truth of an individual, namely of his narrator, and not necessarily even of himself, the author, or of you, the reader who is invited to witness an individual development, in part illuminated by an allegory based upon a foundational myth for European culture, namely the Bible. Proust's work aims at translating the extraordinary complexity of one case, his narrator's, a case, like that of every concrete individual, that is far too complex to be grasped by scientific generalization. This can only be done, if at all, by art, according to the narrator in his various theorizing moments. Having said this, I note nonetheless that both Proust and Freud share this modernist desire to use myth and allegory in the service of some kind of permanent knowledge, starting with knowledge of the self. Freud was probably not as lucid about the nature of his desire as was Proust, for he seems to have believed that the allegory he used to explain neurosis resembled a scientific law, whereas, as we shall later see, Proust understood the scientific epistemology of his time to postulate that individual human reality is too complex to be reduced to mechanical laws.[2] His allegory takes on its significance when regarded as an alternative to the universal claims of a scientific model.

Freud, a Jew, took myth from the Old Testament, as did Judeo-Christian Proust, though Proust also wants to complete it with a New Testament vision of resurrection. For both writers humanity began existence in paradise, but because of human weakness and the Father's interdiction of knowledge, man and woman are forever chased from the garden once they know what sin is. And once they know what sin is, they want to luxuri-ate in it—at least in thought and dream. According to the Bible, they did so openly in the cities of the plain, which in turn called forth the wrath of God upon them. For the Judeo-Christian tradition, this is a parable of universal significance: the Father's will cannot be flaunted with impunity. Freud makes this central to his meta-psychology: the Father's law with its ongoing judgment is encoded in human conscience and, renamed the *Uber-Ich* or superego, is the source of universal guilt neurosis generated by the thoughts one cannot control. There is a different sense of guilt in Proust. If the narrator feels condemned for his uselessness by the moral code he has inherited from his parents, he does not seem personally to know the neurotic guilt feelings of the Freudian sort. Nonetheless knowledge of sin in the biblical sense is omnipresent in Proust's novel, the most pervasive example of which is given by the narrator's sense that sexual perversion is sin. Given what Proust had written before about the neutrality of sexual desire, this attitude may seem contradictory, at least with his early writing, published and unpublished. But the narrator is not Proust. Proust's narra-tor reflects his social milieu. He seems at times to feel strongly that deviant sexual desire is to be censured, though when older, he also takes a natural-istic viewpoint about sexual behavior. From both perspectives sex is part of the Proustian comedy, and if deviance from a norm is a precondition for the comic, this includes all forms of deviance.

For Freud guilt is inevitable, since our conduct and especially our de-sires can never square with the imperatives of the Father's law: we want to sleep with our parents, often according to some bisexual distribution of de-sire, and repressed incest is universal. Proust's narrator is also guilty of not living up to his parents' expectations, though because of different moral imperatives: the Father's law is that the narrator must lead a convention-ally successful life and hence resemble him. Of course as in Freud, in Proust bisexuality is clearly inscribed in the novel's agenda, almost in the form of a universal law. It is a recurrent manifestation of desire that the moral law reproves, however, even if scientific understanding does not—at least the moral law generally accepted, if scarcely practiced, in the France of 1900. With regard to the universality of depravity, it should be noted that the child narrator's desire for his mother's kiss, portrayed in "Combray," does not seem especially Oedipal—which is to say, incestuous—however much it bespeaks the narrator's need for a reassuring love that eliminates anguish from his world. Freudian critics, wanting to make Proust one of their own, point to the bedroom scene in which this desire takes place, though this is a bit of a misreading. The bedroom is the locus for the narrator's desire of basic ontological security. Sex seems notably absent from the child's desire of his mother.

However that may be, it seems indisputable that by designating a potentially long series of works as *Sodom and Gomorrah I, II, III,* and so on, Proust envisaged an intertextual allegory deriving its meaning from its portrayal of the violation of the Father's law. This general title also suggests the kind of repetitive mechanisms that are at work in the three parts published as *Sodom and Gomorrah, The Captive,* and *The Fugitive.* In these volumes sin, like the comedy generated by the perpetual fall, is nothing if not repetitive. It can be argued that for Proust, as for his relative by marriage, the philosopher Henri Bergson, the essence of comedy is mechanical repetition. One then wonders if, in contrast to the comedy of the fall, salvation would be a unique event of which the narrator can only dream while meditating in distress on his repetitive failure to accomplish anything his parents would call an achievement.

My drawing parallels between Proust's and Freud's use of allegory is intended to offer a context at once rhetorical and historical. One can further enlarge the historical context by recalling how "comedy" is used by another of Proust's Christian references, one favored by modernists from Joyce through Beckett, Dante's *Divine Comedy,* whose vision of hell seems never to have been too far from Proust's mind. *Commedia* refers, for Italian medieval rhetoric, to a genre between the tragic and the elegiac, and as such it seems to describe well Proust's work, since Proust, if he touches upon both the tragic and the elegiac, writes mainly with this sense of comedy in mind. Moreover Dante's *Inferno* also demonstrates that the wages of sin are eternal repetition and that, at times, hell is indeed a dark comedy. The narrator's portrayal of the machinations of the Parisian aristocrats thus finds analogues among the Florentine damned, repeating forever their sins in the circles of hell. The narrator himself presents an analogy with one of Dante's damned: he is condemned to repeat the suffering caused by the mechanism of jealousy that can never be quieted because there is no knowledge that can ever satiate it. His punishment would be potentially infinite if his self were to last forever—but the recurrent death of the social self is the only aspect of the self that seems to repeat.

Recall that the redemption found in Dante's paradise is to be gained at the end of the poet's journey, if the poet is steadfast enough. Proust's poet-narrator, as we shall see, also faces the question of whether his will is sturdy enough to carry him forward to the redemption foreseen. The route to redemption must be traced out to the narrator by memory, for only memory can tie together that which must be redeemed of a human life. But as Dante points out, memory is problematic. For Dante, the poet of memory, finds, much like Proust, that he confronts at least two kinds of recall: first the memory that "does not err" when the poet draws upon it to recount the *Inferno* (canto 2, verse 6); and second the memory that needs divine help when it approaches "the blessed realm inscribed" within his mind by the vision of heaven in the *Paradiso* (canto 1, verse 24). It appears that Proust's narrator also needs the gift of grace, in the form of involuntary memory, to narrate paradise, as first demonstrated by "Combray," and that he will undoubtedly need more if he is to succeed in writing his novel. Clearly he is on more certain grounds when his memory "does not err" as it deals, often omnisciently, with the hell found in such places as the Guermantes salon or the soirées at the Verdurins.

Let us conclude this discussion of biblical and Christian references in Proust by turning to the beginning of *Sodom and Gomorrah,* where, in addition to the title itself, Proust himself adds another key for interpreting the biblical framework for his comedy. In an epigraph he quotes from Vigny's poem "La colère de Samson" ("Samson's Anger"). The quotation implies that Samson is an ironic double for Proust's young narrator, for the biblical Samson is famously betrayed by a woman. In Vigny's poem itself, one can read that the warrior specifically bemoans his fate of being trapped in the "eternal struggle" that pits man's goodness against woman's guile (ll. 35–37). And in the monologue from which Proust quotes the two lines composing the epigraph, Samson laments that man is a victim of the need for love and caresses that he acquires when his mother first takes him into her arms, which thus leaves the male forever dreaming of "the warmth of the breast"—"la chaleur du sein" (l. 44). A victim apparently of the fate described by both Freudian allegory and Old Testament history, Vigny's Samson finds himself at a juncture in time in which the nurturing woman herself has become man's enemy, the result of which will be that, as Samson puts it in the line Proust quotes, "La femme aura Gomorrhe et l'Homme aura Sodome" (Woman will have Gomorrah and Man will have

Sodom). With this line predicting the future of the sexes after the fall, the reader is invited to enter a textual world in which inversion, as Proust calls it, is far more frequent than good bourgeois society wishes to recognize. With Vigny's lines perversion seems to be declared universal under the patriarchy of the Third Republic, in which the archetypical conflict between Samson and Delilah gives rise to a plethora of bisexual possibilities. Freud would undoubtedly have approved.

My reference to the French Third Republic should remind us that there is also a realist dimension necessary for contextualizing these three parts of the novel. For as we shall see, an essential moment in the transformation of French society is portrayed in *Sodom and Gomorrah.* And in *The Captive* and *The Fugitive,* the narrator's dealings with Albertine are not only framed through analogy with biblical myth but also in terms of the real possibilities of sexual relationships in France in the period before World War I. The context for these relationships is a thoroughly patriarchal society in which women had virtually no legal rights: not to vote and not even to own property if married. Contrasting with Anglo-American society, only a few gains were made by women during this period. Women in France could become teachers, doctors, and finally lawyers—but not judges. (It never occurs to Albertine, for instance, to think about going back to school.) By and large, however, in real terms women were excluded from professional life and from politics. To be sure there was a great variety of groups seeking women's rights in the Third Republic, but they were largely outside the mainstream of the social life Proust portrays.[3] The issue of feminism is not broached in Proust, which is not surprising, since those groups pushing for women's rights are largely absent from the novel's social world centered on the Faubourg Saint-Germain. These missing groups would include socialists, Protestants, and philanthropic reformers often taking their lead from Anglo-Saxon puritans. In short feminist concerns are not part of the novel. The portrayal of men's victimization of women, and vice versa, is part of a social reality in which the narrator, rather like Vigny's Samson, spends much time in anguished fantasy, wondering if he has been betrayed. Albertine's life is a secondary question for him. That he poses no questions about what she might become in life shows how extremely limited are the options that a woman like Albertine has in her dealings with men; and given these limits, it is not surprising that Albertine, not unlike Odette, allows herself to be kept.

Let us now turn to the beginning of the revelations starting at the outset of *Sodom and Gomorrah.* Proust begins his comedy set in Sodom with the encounter of the Baron de Charlus with Jupien. It is narrated in some of the most contradictory and humorous pages in Proust. The humor suggests that Proust, if not his young narrator, was quite aware that the ascription of sin to the baron, or to any other physiologically driven pleasure seeker, is at odds with a scientific description of the wellsprings of human behavior. But neither Proust nor, a fortiori, his narrator could overlook the biblical view that has long been the basis for European beliefs about deviant sexual desire. So the narrator recognizes metaphorically that, on the one hand, deviant desire is part of nature; and on the other, it is an abomination castigated by the gods and religious taboos. Proust's narrator draws on both sides of a contradictory attitude in his description of Charlus's randy behavior. His narrator naturalizes it with comic biological description and, at the same time, seemingly decries it while lamenting the conditions in which homosexuals are obliged to live.

Proust prefaces the narrator's observations of the scene of sodomy with humorous commentary showing that the narrator is still quite immature at the moment of this scene. The narrator ascribes to his younger self the thought that he should not be afraid to sneak across the courtyard to view the unfolding seduction scene, since he is after all no less brave than the Boers who expose themselves to British fire when they run cross open spaces. This military image of himself is even more inflated when the narrator recalls he just had several duels on account of the Dreyfus affair (SG, 11). Invocation of the art of dueling seems to reassure the younger narrator, as it did Proust, that he has enough normal masculinity to face the following sight: the baron admiring Jupien's bum while vaunting, to Jupien's total lack of comprehension, the nobility of his own parts (SG, 13–15).

The comic description of the mating ritual is followed by a short essay on the state of homosexuals in France. With obvious echoes of what Proust had written in *Against Sainte-Beuve,* the narrator describes the sodomites as a "race upon which a curse is laid and which must live in falsehood and perjury because it knows that its desire, that which constitutes life's dearest pleasure, is held to be punishable, shameful, an inadmissible thing; which must deny its God" since, as Christians, they will be obliged to lie at the bar of justice when they appear before Christ and to lie to their mothers even "when they close her dying eyes" (SG, 20). Espousing in effect the traditional Christian point of view, the narrator describes the fall the homosexual undergoes when he is forced to live a lie.

This biblical condemnation contrasts greatly with the way the narrator then describes Charlus's conduct, for he often uses ironic terms that naturalize the baron's conduct as a product of nature. Speaking as a wry biologist, the narrator says that the homosexual who has taken a wife will nonetheless find "some way of attaching himself to a man, as the convolvulus throws out its tendrils wherever it finds a pick or a rake up which to climb" (*SG,* 29). In other words as in the case of a very common weedy wildflower, the gay man is drawn to and inevitably finds what nature decides for him to seek. The narrator's queer botany becomes frankly comic when he offers other naturalizing comparisons. He concocts a capricious taxonomy for gay men in which, for example, one sees that nature has, for the needs of the aging, created a species of frail young man who awaits the advances of a "robust and paunch quinquagenerian" while remaining indifferent to other young men (*SG,* 39). This seemingly abnormal behavior is illuminated by a comparable law of nature that decrees that "the hermaphrodite flowers of the short-styled *primula veris* remain sterile so long as they are fertilized only by other *primula veris* of short style also, whereas they welcome with joy the pollen of the *primula veris* with the long style." The double entendre may not be evident to those who have not looked at a flower known as the cowslip with a botanist's eyeglass, but even those who have peered through one may not have seen expressions of joy about the size of the flower's sexual organs. Here Proust's descriptions are double-edged ironic swords, at once close to a parody of pretensions to knowledge while, at the same time, they suggest that homosexuals, and by extension, all human beings, are biological beings constrained by the laws of nature. If this latter viewpoint were really believed, Proust implies, the sodomite would not be a primary example of depravity after the fall. But the historical fact is that the Bible has named the sodomite as an abomination in the sight of God. Botany and the Old Testament are not easily reconciled.

Nonetheless the lesson Proust appears to draw from this naturalism is that nature cannot overcome culture: the homosexual is driven by society into isolation, lying, and deceit largely because nature has played a dirty trick on him. For example if the homosexual male finds a man who desires him, then the homosexual cannot really desire in return that man because the latter perforce is not really a man. Thus the dilemma of the gay male is that his desires impose a contradiction upon him. Proust foreshadows the homosexual writer Jean Genet, who also found that homosexuals belong psychologically to the same league as thieves. Perhaps Genet would have found that Proust's insistence on his own masculinity put him into that category of the *surhomme* (or "superman") that Genet, with at least as much humor as Proust, found to be a solution to the contradiction.

The narrator emphasizes that the encounter of Charlus and Jupien is due to chance. Their finding each other resembles the kind of chance event that the narrator observes when he watches a flower waiting in isolation in the courtyard for the fortuitous encounter with a bee that brings about fertilization—this is precisely what he was observing when his attention was caught by Jupien and the baron's strange activity. The narrator draws the conclusion that aleatory processes are an intrinsic part of nature. Thus the encounter of the baron and Jupien is part of a general pattern illustrating Proust's belief that chance presides over most of what happens. Like the narrator's own experience, it is characterized as a largely aleatory result of a discontinuous flow of events—much like his just happening to taste the lime tea and madeleine pastry. Given the role of chance the narrator finds at work everywhere, it is not surprising that he attributes to chance the same omnipresence that Charles Darwin ascribed to it in the development of nature's blind path along evolution. Or so the narrator says with explicit reference to Darwin in describing Charlus's and Jupien's gestures. At first he says he could not understand them, perhaps because they resembled the seductive gestures that Darwin describes in telling how certain composite flowers "erect the florets of their capitula so as to be seen from a greater distance" (SG, 41). The telltale erection is part of a flower's strategy for overcoming chance. This comic Darwinism seems to say that all of nature is engaged in seeking ways to minimize chance and augment the possibility that one can realize one's desires. Proust's hedonistic Darwinism has little to do with Herbert Spencer's crude contemporary doctrine of the survival of the fittest. It does imply, however, that a naturalistic perspective can be taken on all behavior.

After the revelation of Sodom in his own back courtyard, another chance encounter reveals Gomorrah on the dance floor. This fateful event also takes place under the aegis of modern science. It occurs in *Sodom and Gomorrah* after the narrator has returned for his second stay at the seacoast at Balbec. Possessed now by a desire for happiness, as he puts it, he has begun a relation with one of the flowering girls he met there earlier, Albertine. The narrator goes with her to a dance at which she begins to waltz with her friend Andrée. The two girls' physical closeness first strikes the narrator as innocent dancing. But by chance at this moment Doctor Cottard crosses the narrator's path. Pompous and patriarchal, he decides to demonstrate to the narrator his scientific mastery of all things human. Thus the doctor tells the young man the "insufficiently known" fact that women derive most of their sexual excitement from their breasts (SG, 264). He demonstrates this law, to the narrator's dismay, by pointing to Albertine and Andrée. As they dance their embrace does indeed bring their breasts into constant contact. And so is planted in the narrator's mind the knowledge of Gomorrah. He is not at first convinced, but as he says, this image illustrating a supposedly scientific fact will act upon him "as happens with those forms of poison which begin to act only after a certain time"(SG, 266). Chance has foisted off upon him a "medical fact," promulgated by a successful if witless man of science engaging in a shallow bit of egomania. But the narrator cannot dismiss it, no matter how much he may try.

Cottard may be an ass, but his chance comment is a pivotal moment in the narrator's education, especially in doubt and suspicion. In this way the chance happening becomes a determining fact in the narrator's development, for from this moment he will become increasingly obsessed with the pleasure that Albertine may (or may not) find in the world of Gomorrah. In this way knowledge, even dubious scientific knowledge, turns out to be in the service of the fall. Or more precisely the narrator finds that knowledge perhaps is the fall: according to the Bible, only after man and woman have knowledge do they know what sin is and what death is. The narrator's paradox is that, after garnering his first bit of knowledge about Gomorrah from the doctor, he wants to get more knowledge about Albertine in order somehow to still his anguish—which supposedly springs from his knowledge in the first place. And so jealousy is generated by the jealousy he already knows, especially in *The Captive,* in which the belief that knowledge might grant power over, and possession of, Albertine is amply shown to be a self-generating illusion.

Let us return to *Sodom and Gomorrah* with regard to knowledge. Knowledge of the fall comes as a result of an education unfolding with symmetrical revelations. Part 1 of *Sodom and Gomorrah* opens the book with the revelation of the hidden world of Sodom, the world of male homosexuality exemplified by the baron and Jupien. It ends, in chapter 4 of part 2, with the strong implication that by frequenting Albertine and her friends, the narrator has now entered the world of Gomorrah. This is stressed at the very end of *Sodom and Gomorrah* when, knowing how much the narrator cares for Vinteuil's music, Albertine tells him that she is a good friend of Mlle Vinteuil and of Mlle Vinteuil's friend, whom the boy had spied upon in "Combray." The narrator is shocked. Albertine has inadvertently disclosed that she is close to a person the narrator characterizes as a "practicing and professional Sapphist" (*SG,* 703). (This terminology may suggest that the boy has yet to mature.) Moreover the importance of his witnessing the scene of lesbian sadism in "Combray" now appears in retrospect something like the first unknowing knowledge of the forbidden fruit. The consequences of forbidden knowledge are indeed long lasting, for through eternal repetition knowledge generates the everlasting fall. At the end of *Sodom and Gomorrah,* the narrator is aware that his painful knowledge has brought him to a new moment in his development. He must manically try to discover what Albertine is up to if she is the friend of a "professional Sapphist."

At the end of *Sodom and Gomorrah,* the narrator feels guilty, for like a new Adam, he associates the knowledge of the fall with the knowledge of death. And briefly but pointedly he associates it with his grandmother's death that had occurred some time before. Knowledge brings guilt, and consequently he feels guilt for her death. This guilty knowledge of her death perdures as "an image" alive in the depths of his inner world, where the image exercises a "noxious power," as he describes it in the following remarkable passage:

> I should have supposed that in the course of time it had lost it
> [noxious power]; [it was] preserved alive in the depths of my being
> . . . as a punishment, as a retribution (who knows) for my having
> allowed my grandmother to die; perhaps rising up suddenly from
> the dark depths in which it seemed forever buried, and striking like
> an Avenger, in order to inaugurate for me a new and terrible and
> only too well-merited existence, perhaps also to make dazzlingly
> clear to my eyes the fatal consequences which evil actions eternally
> engender, not only for those who have committed them but for
> those who have done no more, or thought that they were doing
> no more, than look on at a curious and entertaining spectacle,
> as I, alas, had done on that afternoon long ago at Montjouvain,
> concealed behind a bush where (as when I complacently listened
> to the account of Swann's love affairs) I had perilously allowed
> to open up within me the fatal and inevitably painful road of
> Knowledge. (*SG*, 702)

The narrator also makes a comparison between his conserving of the image of his grandmother's death and the gods' preserving Orestes so that he may return to Greece to avenge the murder of Agamemnon. Like Dante, Proust joins classical and Christian analogies for divine and secular reference. In this passage it is the biblical side of the analogy that points up the remarkable coincidence between the narrator's self-interpretation and the biblical allegory in which he, like all humanity, is embarked. He expresses guilt for his grandmother's death, though this is guilt about something for which he is obviously not responsible. Clearly guilt derives from its association with knowledge or, more specifically, with knowledge of the evil that he saw in the past and which will continue to engender evil in the present. This is a central meaning of the fall, visited upon all who continue to have that knowledge first garnered in the earthly garden, rather literally so in the case of Proust's young narrator in "Combray" when he had his first experience of Gomorrah. Even his listening by chance to tales about Swann's misery now seems to play a role in his life, since these aleatory events combine to create a kind of Christian destiny that contrives the young narrator's continuing fall—for original sin is nothing if not repetition in time ad infinitum.

The narrative space between the revelations of Sodom and of Gomorrah in *Sodom and Gomorrah* is filled with a portrait of social life of the upper classes in the Third Republic: descriptions of meetings in salons, at soirées, and the like. The narrative also traces out the narrator's education in love as he begins his relationship with Albertine. Proust's chapter headings are perhaps intended to underscore the relative importance of the narrated experience. The revelation of Sodom gets a "part" all to itself and occupies the relatively short part 1. Part 2, divided into four chapters, is much longer. In part 2 two social events dominate the narration: in chapter 1 the evening the narrator spends at the home of the Princess of Guermantes; and in chapter 2 the entertainment he attends given by Madame Verdurin at the summer place she has rented for the season at the seashore near Balbec, La Raspelière. There is an opposition between these two milieus, the opposition of antagonistic social classes. On the one hand, the Guermantes and their entourage are the last pure aristocrats, or so they claim. They are on the defensive, and they try to maintain their dominance in society by avoiding contact with whatever might dilute their purity. (Swann and the narrator are obvious exceptions to this defensive rule, though Swann's wife and daughter are not.) On the other hand, the Verdurins and their "clan" are representative of the rising bourgeoisie, here largely associated with the arts and professions. In the novel and undoubtedly in reality, the Verdurins of this world eventually absorb and replace the Old Regime aristocrats. In *Sodom and Gomorrah,* this transition is becoming clear.

In this regard I stress again that Proust is a chronicler of social change, and in his representation of society virtually every character is assigned a rather exact standing or status quotient defined by their position in the social hierarchy. However the modes of representation of individual characters range from the elegiac to the comic, or perhaps tragicomic in the case of Baron de Charlus. Comedy clearly dominates, however, and is largely generated by the deflation of aristocratic pretensions and the revelation of bourgeois hypocrisies. At times the comedy is broad, merging on satire, or grandiosely Shakespearean when Charlus achieves absurd sublimity in pressing his claims to superiority. Once the reader grasps that Proust is at once sympathetic to his doomed aristocrats—did he not once dream of an aristocratic utopia?—and also portrays them as vacuous egomaniacs, then it is obvious that he has created a comedy of class and manners closer to that found in the works of Dickens, Eliot, or Tolstoy than to that of Balzac or Flaubert. In short Proust is a master of social comedy.

Besides the narrator himself, the common presence found in the two salons is Charlus, the supreme egomaniac, who while discoursing on his ancestors is often actively cruising for handsome pickups with little concern for their class origins. From the narrator's viewpoint, after the opening revelation about the baron's sexual tastes, Sodom now appears to be ubiquitous, as he sees at the soirée given by the Princess of Guermantes. He observes the baron talking with fellow sodomites there and sees that Charlus takes lubricious interest in the young sons of the "latest mistress" of the Duke of Guermantes (*SG*, 116). Afterward he observes that the pursuit of lechery takes the baron into the Verdurins' milieu, where he appears as the patron of Morel, a young musician whose star is rising. If Proust leaves in doubt what exactly the baron gets from Morel in return for his generosity, it is patent that the baron is willing to overlook the rabble found in a bourgeois salon for the sake of pleasure and perhaps even love.

The social analysis in *Sodom and Gomorrah* is at times complex. For example Morel is the son of a servant who once worked for the narrator's family. He has, to say the least, some conflicts about encountering the narrator in a society in which he has pretensions of coming from a higher class. Pretense often becomes reality in Proust, however, and ambivalence reigns throughout the social order, for the characters constantly undergo metamorphosis. This is true of Odette and Morel and undoubtedly of the narrator himself. Moreover Proust seems to conceive of the fate of classes on the order of the fate of the individual. History exists as the individual's fall writ large so as to encompass entire social classes, as well as groups such as Jews and sodomites. However there are counterentropic trends that raise up individuals and even groups. For example though scorned by the Faubourg Saint-Germain in *Sodom and Gomorrah*, Odette has already risen to a spot of special eminence where her salon has become among the most brilliant in Paris, in part because she has captured the leading writer of the time, Bergotte. Like the other authentic artists in Proust, Bergotte seems to escape from the contingencies of history and rise above the fall insofar as he is a writer and not a socialite. And there is no doubt that the Verdurins, through the aggressive single-mindedness of Madame Verdurin, are on the rise. Symbolically in *Sodom and Gomorrah*, they displace an aristocratic family, the Cambremers, by renting for the season the aristocrats' home by the sea. The lack of, and hence need for, money is not a negligible part of the ongoing fall of aristocratic families. In short to trace Proust's historical sociology, one must trace the development of each major character, for finally history is a summation of individual trajectories.

The Dreyfus case complicates social relations, and Proust breaks up expected patterns by showing that, by chance, the reactionary aristocrat may unexpectedly be a supporter of Dreyfus. For example Swann tells the narrator that the Prince of Guermantes told him that he had become a supporter of Dreyfus in spite of the prince's love of the army. In addition the Princess of Guermantes also becomes a Dreyfusard without the prince knowing it. Revealingly it turns out that both are reading the newspaper *Aurore,* in which Zola published his letter, "J'accuse," accusing the army of injustice and anti-Semitism. In other words both prince and princess have overcome their aristocratic prejudice and ideology to embrace the truth. By contrast Jewish Swann appears ambiguous in his attitude toward Dreyfus, for he is not willing to sign a petition in favor of Dreyfus that a Jewish writer, the narrator's friend Bloch, is circulating. Proust complicates social issues at this point to show that interest in the truth can cut across class interests, which he undoubtedly knew from his own active participation in the Dreyfus affair (and which, as we have seen, Proust portrays in remarkable fashion in *Jean Santeuil*).

The narrator's education continues as he frequents the two milieus in question, though other events also inflect the development of his *Bildung.* In chapter 1 of part 2, he returns to Balbec for the second time and goes to the same hotel he had stayed in with his grandmother during his first visit. Between chapters 1 and 2, Proust inserts an unnumbered title, "The Intermittences of the Heart," using this title to set off the section in which his grandmother's living presence at Balbec is restored to him by an involuntary memory (*SG,* 211). This memory might be called elegiac, for the grandmother's full presence to memory overwhelms the narrator by her seemingly real absence. In this moment the narrator has more proof of the Pascalian misery of the human heart. He recognizes that he cannot remain concentrated on any emotion for any duration of time. For it is months after his grandmother's death, and it is only because he is by chance again in Balbec that he finally can realize that she is really dead. Involuntary memory brings him up against the nothingness of death and the capriciousness of his own moods since she had died: "I had often spoken about her since then, and thought of her also, but behind my words and thoughts, those of an ungrateful, selfish, cruel young man, there had never been anything that resembled my grandmother, because, in my frivolity, my love of pleasure, my familiarity with the spectacle of her ill health, I retained within me only in a potential state the memory of what she had been" (*SG,* 211). Finally he knows real pain, perhaps not least of all the pain of recognizing in oneself a creature of the fall. But there is also a promise in this recall, for it might someday offer some little truth to which he can have recourse, a truth that has not been traced by his intelligence nor deflected by his pusillanimity, as he puts it in a judgment of himself that also points to a possible way leading to a vocation dealing in painful truth (*SG*, 215).

Chapter 2 of *Sodom and Gomorrah* begins with the narrator's return to life, with the desire for happiness noted above, and with this renewed buoyancy, he rises above his depression and begins to pursue Albertine. She now comes to his hotel room, and they apparently make love, though this is said, more or less, only later, in a passing remark at the end of *Sodom and Gomorrah*. Chapter 3 continues to trace the development of the narrator's relationship with Albertine as he motors around the countryside with her—and becomes increasingly jealous. The third chapter also offers a portrait of varied sexual practices in Sodom, though the main thread of narrative development is established by the narrator's capricious sentimental life. He is at once obsessed with Albertine and bored with her, all of which brings him to the reasonable conclusion, at the end of chapter 3, that it would be folly for him to marry the girl.

The brief chapter 4 ends *Sodom and Gomorrah* with the revelation of Gomorrah that causes the narrator to change his mind about staying with Albertine. This is his learning, through utter chance, of Albertine's friendship with Mlle Vinteuil and her friend. Utter chance thus seems to decide his destiny, since in despair about how he might deal with her and forgetting his earlier decision to break off with her, the narrator asks Albertine to come live with him in Paris. Probably no moment in the novel better illustrates the intermittences of the human heart and the fortuitous events upon which they depend. For after the chance revelation about Vinteuil's daughter, the narrator is determined to possess Albertine, though in some manner less casual that the manner in which he first "possessed" her, as he says, on the night the elevator boy brought her up to his room in Balbec (*SG*, 717). By delaying the narrator's admission of having had sexual relations with Albertine, Proust underscores the narrator's mitigated interest in eroticism. This deferral also underscores that the term *possession* is really a psychological matter for the narrator, for in his desire for possession at the end of Sod*om and Gomorrah* he is now bent on something more like ownership of her soul.

Albertine accepts his proposition, motivated perhaps as much by the narrator's money as by any passion for him, though this is never clear. More or less middle class in outlook, she is nonetheless a woman without fortune in a world in which, as I suggested above, being a kept woman, if one cannot be a wife, is not an implausible option. With regard to the narrator's education, one may feel that his making a prisoner of Albertine leads to the end of his *Bildung*, for his cohabitation with her introduces a period of stasis in which he repeats fruitless attempts to control her. The comic side is certainly not lacking in the inept way the narrator tries to be on top of the situation. At times it is close to farce. One might argue that it is only after Albertine's death that the narrator again advances in his education in life. Especially in *The Captive* the narrator repeats a lesson that he seemingly cannot easily learn; to wit he can no more possess another being than he can foresee the consequences of his acts. In seeking to become Albertine's master, he becomes her slave, which he finally realizes toward the end of *The Captive* when he returns home one night and looks up at the light in the window of the room in which captive Albertine is waiting: "It was true that I endowed those luminous streaks which I could see from below, and which to anyone else would have seemed quite superficial, with the utmost plenitude, solidity, and volume, because of all the significance that I placed behind them, in a treasure unsuspected by the rest of the world which I had hidden there and from which those horizontal rays emanated, but a treasure in exchange for which I had forfeited my freedom, my solitude, my thought" (*C*, 444–45). Accompanying this stasis is the fact that, though still recalling he once had pretentions of becoming a writer, he flounders now in total procrastination. He can accomplish nothing except keeping up the ineffectual attempt to dominate Albertine—which mainly means keeping her away from other women, a thought that obsesses him as he unendingly speculates about what she actually does.

We have seen that procrastination characterizes the narrator before *The Captive*, but in *The Captive* it becomes what one might call an existential malady. The narrator joins a legion of modern antiheroes for whom a vacuous existence ensues from their incapacity to make decisions in some consecutive and consequential way. Swann is a precursor, offering a model of the narrator's failure to find a meaningful vocation, though other models abound both in history and literature. For example Proust's narrator comes to bear a great likeness to the nineteenth-century Russian master of living without willpower, Oblomov, created by the Russian novelist Ivan Goncharov in the 1859 novel named for him. It seems accurate to say that in *The Captive* Proust's narrator has caught that postromantic neurosis that Goncharov called Oblomovitis, a genteel form of nihilism that affects the nerves and paralyzes the will, resulting in obsessive repetitions of doing nothing. Procrastination underlies the narrator's lament about doing nothing earlier in the novel, and it continues through *The Fugitive*, reaching a culminating moment in the scene in Venice when the narrator does not want to leave the city but knows that his mother is leaving and does not know what he is going to do. So he listens to somebody singing "'O Sole Mio" in order not to decide. This act of doing nothing other than listening to a song may seem like a clever synecdoche for the entire novel:

from this perspective all that happens until the end of *The Fugitive* appears fortuitously to distend time so that the narrator never has to make a real decision.

With the arrival of springtime in *The Captive*, after several months of living with Albertine, the narrator rationalizes his neurotic incapacities in terms that show him to be quite conscious of being the dilettante nihilist that his education has finally produced: "I had promised Albertine that, if I did not go out with her, I would settle down to work. But in the morning, just as if, taking advantage of our being asleep, the house had miraculously flown, I awoke in different weather beneath another clime. We do not begin to work as soon as we disembark in a strange country to the contradictions of which we have to adapt ourselves. And each day was for me a different country" (*C*, 100).

The weather and the seasons play a role in *The Captive*, for it is as if the cycle of seasons moves the lethargic hero in its wake. *The Captive* begins with a spring day arriving by mistake in winter, after which the spring does come, and the cycle of seasons continues until the following spring when Albertine, perhaps herself actively stimulated by the renewal of nature, flees her captor. Thus she disappears from her prison at the end of *The Captive* and leaves the hapless narrator pondering in anguish how he might get her back.

In resumé the drama of procrastination accompanies the narrator's ineffectual and often farcical demonstrations of a will to power over the woman he sometimes thinks he loves. The drama is framed by the passage of time in the cycle of the seasons. Within this framework the central experience narrated in the first part of *The Captive* is largely concentrated in one exemplary twenty-four hour period in the characters' life, during which the narrator struggles to keep Albertine from having chance encounters. *The Captive* opens, however, with the narration of repetitive events characteristic of the narrator's life in Paris, such as his dealing with his irascible maid, Françoise, his visits to the Duchess of Guermantes to ask for advice about fashion, and his unending jealousy caused by everything that Albertine wishes to do. Then the narration is focused, in something like a burlesque of Racinian intensity, on a sequence of events that unfold in roughly the twenty-four hours after the narrator learns that Albertine wants to go to a soirée at the Verdurins. Her desire is made all the more suspicious by the fact that she tries to dissuade the narrator from accompanying her. The narrator manages, however, to convince her not to go to the soirée but rather to attend a theatrical performance in the afternoon. The next day, after Albertine has left the apartment to go to the theater, he learns from the newspaper that Léa, an actress with lesbian propensities, is performing in the play. In a state of dismay, he decides he must find a way to get Albertine back from the theater. To this end he sends Françoise to retrieve her with a contrived message about his needing her. This strategy works, and the narrator is able to go out in the evening, without telling Albertine where he is going. He goes, in fact, to the same soirée she had wanted to attend in the first place. There he learns to his chagrin that Mlle Vinteuil and her lesbian friend had been expected for the performance of Vinteuil's music, featuring Morel, the latter event arranged by Charlus.

After this near-farcical series of events, the narrator quarrels with Albertine; and in response to her anger, he feigns to want separation from her. Days of repetition then unfold as he plans strategies for leaving her and keeping her. In all this the narrator keeps up his quest for knowledge about his beloved, though he never really has any clear idea about what he should think about her. By contrast with the only hypothetical knowledge the narrator has about Albertine, true knowledge about what is happening is granted to narrator and reader in the case of the debacle that occurs for Charlus. When the baron is kicked out of the Verdurins' salon, the narrator relates exactly how the bourgeois couple have succeeded in poisoning his relationship with Morel. The nature of knowledge granted about the characters notwithstanding, the reader can see that the heterosexual couple of narrator and Albertine, linked to Gomorrah through his fantasies about her, find a mirror image in the novel's second half in the homosexual couple linked to Sodom. In the unhappy affair that Charlus pursues with Morel, the power eros exercises over the aging baron parallels the amorous charm that Albertine possesses when the narrator suffers in wondering incessantly about where, and what, she is. And in both cases the lover, the narrator and the baron, ends up losing the beloved, Albertine and Morel. In this way the parallel portrayals of pursuer and pursued broached in scenes set in Balbec in *Sodom and Gomorrah* continue here in Paris in *The Captive,* with lessons in unhappiness for all the characters concerned, be they gay or straight.

Parallel to the idea of the mock epic, we might invent for Proust the notion of the mock tragic and speak of the pseudotragic falls of the narrator and the baron. The baron's fall is parallel to the narrator's in that both are unsuccessful in the quest for love, which is to say, to possess or dominate another's life. However the baron comes perhaps closer to being a truly tragic figure: not only is he expelled from the society in which he wanted to install his beloved musician, but one can read his expulsion as the sign of the coming fall of his entire social class. I stress again in this regard that the baron's fall is illuminated by the kind of omniscient narration that the narrator cannot undertake for his own life. It appears that neither when young nor when old does the narrator ever really learn much of anything reliable about Albertine, except that she seemingly lies fairly frequently. But we see with certainty that Madame Verdurin has contrived to embitter Morel against the baron by telling him outright lies, even though the narrator is not present to hear them. As in Dante the other's hell is recalled with unerring memory.

Limited to his own subjective view in the case of Albertine but not in the case of other characters, the narrator is never privy to what happens to her when she is not with him. In this way his relationship with her unfolds much like an existential demonstration of the Cretan liar's paradox: all Cretans lie, so that if one of them says that she is lying, she must be telling the truth, which is then perforce a lie. Proust's demonstration of the semantic dynamics motivating the narrator's jealousy is perhaps not so paradoxically logical as is the logician's traditional demonstration that self-referential statements can lead to unresolvable self-contradiction. Rather the narrator's situation is existentially a fact of subjectivity, grounded in the first-person narration in which he faces Albertine as a kind of opaque presence about whom he learns only more and more possible facts that often contradict themselves. Albertine may admit that she is lying, as, say, when she tells him she did not really spend three days in Balbec as she had earlier told him. Instead of going to Balbec, she says that she actually hung around being bored so that the chauffeur could have a fling. But with this rather vulgar revelation, the narrator cannot be sure if Albertine is covering one lie by inventing another or using two lies to cover up another, untold lie by omission.

This revelation of Albertine's prevarications comes toward the end of the long story of the narrator's jealousy. This slow developmental story is part of an educational process, though one caught in a cycle of repetition reflecting the narrator's obsessive neurosis—so that it is an education that does not educate in any practical sense. The story's end and beginning are clear, however. The end finally comes in *The Fugitive* with the onset of the narrator's indifference toward Albertine, whereas his obsession's birth is pointedly marked in *Sodom and Gomorrah* at the dinner party of the Princess of Guermantes. Swann here comments that he personally has never been inquisitive except when in love and when jealous—states in Swann that are synonymous, which the reader knows well through the narrator's earlier omniscient narration. Swann asks the young narrator, with what we might call proleptic irony, if he is jealous, to which the benighted young man answers that he does not know what jealousy is since he has never experienced it. The narrator's education in jealousy does not wait long to begin, since on the very night during which he speaks so assuredly to Swann, he knows anguish when Albertine fails to show up on time for the date she has with him after the princess's reception. The narrator does not know what she is doing. Her absence sets off the genesis of the emotion the narrator says he has not known before: the jealousy born of not knowing how the other may be behaving. We suppose along with him that Albertine, at his coaxing, has gone that evening to see a performance of *Phèdre.* The reader notes, if the narrator does not, that the young man has sent her to a tragedy in which the Greek heroine allows her beloved to be destroyed, out of jealousy, when she understands that he loves somebody else. Psychology replaced the gods in Racine's version of the Greek tragedy, and so it seems that this Jansenist version of Greek tragedy offers a pertinent parallel for Proust's version of the fall from grace known as jealousy: it is born in the fifth and final act, when Phèdre discovers that her beloved is indeed capable of loving a woman, just not her.

Jealousy is a form of suffering that springs from the limits of the lover's subjectivity. These limits disallow the possibility of certainty and hence any idea of possession based on the seizure of the other that knowledge could supposedly grant. Quite simply the narrator can never really ascertain if Albertine and Andrée are lovers or not. From his really quite pathological perspective, the limits to love are aspects of the limits of the power of the knowledge he has. These limits stand out when the lover tries to pin down the beloved, put a label on her, as it were, and put her in a collector's cage. Confronting the impossibility of possessing her through some absolute knowledge of her, the narrator concludes at the end of *The Captive* that Albertine was several persons in one (C, 453). In a sense this is true of every character in the novel insofar as every character's perspective on the other characters reveals each to be different according to the different perspectives the characters have upon them. But Albertine's multiplicity, born of the lover's incapacity to know with certainty what she is, is viewed from mainly one perspective—the unchanging perspective of the jealous lover incapable of dealing with a possible multiplicity he wants to eliminate to assure his conquest.

Despair about the limits of possessive knowledge is, for Proust, a form of pathology. In a sense the jealous lover is sick, and accordingly the narrator describes himself, as he does Swann, with metaphors of disease. Following the emotional perturbation brought about at the end of *Sodom and Gomorrah* by the revelation of Albertine's friendship with a lesbian, Proust opens *The Captive* with a description of the narrator's diseased state. The narrator has brought Albertine to Paris and installed her in his apartment, against his absent mother's wishes and without telling his friends. He then proposes a self-diagnosis, saying that "jealousy is one of those intermittent maladies the cause of which is capricious, arbitrary, always identical in the same patient, sometimes entirely different in another" (C, 28). Jealousy is a disease that apparently defies the regular classifications of medical taxonomy, though it nonetheless has a real, if singular, existence (which some doctors claim to be the case with many diseases). In effect the narrator can explain himself only be emphasizing his absurd peculiarity. Jealousy has made him a jail keeper who cannot justify himself to others through rational discourse. Medical images offer the only mediating discourse.

Earlier I argued that by presenting love as a pathology, Proust and his narrator join in effect a long tradition of thinkers who condemn passionate love as a form of mental aberration. This tradition goes from the time of the Greeks through Cicero and the Roman and Christian Stoics, with a reprise by classical medical and psychological discourse of the premodern era. The French classical moralists whom Proust knew well were often antistoic in their views, and they also viewed passion as a demonstration of the weakness of human willpower. From this perspective, moreover, Proust may appear to want to emulate or perhaps outdo Pascal when his narrator calls jealousy one of the "intermittent maladies." The fact that the disease is intermittent seems to serve the narrator as proof of his intrinsic misery—the misery that Pascal saw as a paradoxical mark of humanity's fall from grace. For the narrator proof of humanity's intrinsic misery is the weakness that passion attests to, and a second and even greater proof is that his soul is too weak to remain constant even in its depravation and pathological sorrow. In brief the hyperbole of Pascalian pessimism underwrites Proust's view that his narrator is too feeble even to sustain his only intermittently insane passion for any great length of time. It is a hyperbole that at times is not without comic effect.

The Captive is characterized by several narrative symmetries. For example after the opening diagnosis of jealousy, the narrator concludes *The Captive* with another demonstration of the pathology analyzed at the volume's outset. The conclusion centers on a bravura scene in which the couple confront each other. Albertine is angry because she undoubtedly understands that the duplicitous narrator, motivated by suspicion, has gone to the Verdurins without telling her, after persuading her not to go; and he is again in jealous shock and pain after discovering Vinteuil's daughter was supposed to be present for the performance of her father's music that evening. What is perhaps most important in this scene preceding Albertine's flight from her prison is that the narrator recalls what, when he was a boy, he had believed love to be: "What I had dreamed of, as a child, as being the sweetest thing in love, what had seemed to me to be the very essence of love, was to pour out freely, to the one I loved, my tenderness, my gratitude for her kindness, my longing for an everlasting life together" (C, 464). The child's dream of love as utopia has run afoul of his manic hypotheses about what sordid things Albertine may be doing, which means that his own pathology has undermined his capacity for tenderness. And his ongoing fall is again measured by the distance between the ideal the narrator once held and the reality of the present moment.

Parallel to the narrator's jealous fantasies are the delusions, mental charades, and degradation characterizing Charlus. Upon seeing a handsome young man, for example, the aging baron thinks himself still to be also handsome and young and, seemingly incapable of seeing the truth, betrays his wishful desire with "risible affectations of virility" (C, 464). The baron offers the narrator an image of his own delusions in the sense that no person in love can see the image that he or she projects to the world. By way of significant contrast, the narrator remarks that only art allows us to see what we might be, whereas our conduct in love borders constantly on madness. At this point it appears that the antithesis of art and love—or mental aberration—might explain the narrator's failure to find a vocation. As long as he is in love, or so it is implied, he cannot extirpate himself from his own delusions, from the pathology of jealousy, in order to turn his gaze toward the truth to be garnered from such memories as his grandmother's death. In short he cannot become a writer.

With its exploration of pathologies, *The Captive* winds down toward its conclusion: Albertine's flight. In the course of the narration, the narrator becomes more or less aware of his own psychodynamics. He realizes that in part he has desired Albertine because others desire her. He makes a lucid generalization about the nature of his desire, saying that "it might well occur to us, were we better able to analyse our loves, to see that women often attract us only because of the counterpoise of all the men with whom we have to compete for them, although we suffer agonies from having thus to compete; this counterpoise removed, the charm of the woman declines" (C, 557). Of course, though the narrator does not mention her, Odette offers the prime example of women who have "strayed," for whom some men have a predilection. The same may be said about Albertine, for whom the narrator's love seems to exist much because of the imagined competition he fantasizes about (C, 557). With this idea in mind, I recall that some years ago the critic René Girard started a wave of discussion about the so-called triangulation of desire in Proust. By this one can understand that characters in Proust desire another only when they see the other desired by a third party—desired in the other's look, in *le regard d'autrui,* to recall the existentialist terminology of Jean-Paul Sartre.[4] All desire is mediated by another's desire, an idea that is partly confirmed by the narrator's view about competition, though only partly, since it seems that he desires what he imagines others to desire, whether they really do or not. Desire is an imaginative game of inner mirrors from this perspective, in which the narrator, perhaps like Swann or Charlus, finds his desire mediated by the image he projects for his own use. From this viewpoint love is an imaginative construct that has little to do with what others might actually hold to be the case. Finally love is a kind of dialectical pathology in which the lover—the narrator or Swann or the baron—pursues his imagined delights by trying to deny the inconvenient facts that the world imposes upon him.

What is amenable to generalization in Proust is the fact that opposing desires create conflict, of which the relation between the narrator and Albertine is a continuous example. But perhaps the sharpest single dramatic moment in the novel is created by the agon between Charlus and Madame Verdurin. With an instinct for the kill characteristic of all conquerors, she mercilessly expels the hapless baron from her salon while getting Morel to repudiate him. Her victory is emblematic of course of the demise of the aristocratic classes and the concomitant rise of the bourgeoisie, of which Madame Verdurin is an exemplary member. It also presents the kind of psychological conflict in which characters mechanically and hence comically try to act out their fundamental desires. Forgetting her hypersensibility, Madame Verdurin seems sadistically ruthless in her desire to castigate the baron and separate him from his prodigy. Setting each other in relief, the Baron de Charlus and Madame Verdurin appear to be comic egomaniacs. Her sadism is in fact matched by the unheedful arrogance with which he conducts himself in her salon. With no concern for Madame Verdurin's feelings, utterly without empathy for her desires, Charlus ignores her wishes about the composition of the soirée that she, not he, is hosting. He imposes a guest list upon her and subsequently acts as if he were the host. The aristocratic guests whom he has invited to hear his protégé perform reinforce this snubbing by showing obvious disdain for Madame Verdurin, treating her as if she were something like a doorkeeper. And the baron triumphs at the end of Morel's performance by acting as if he were responsible for it.

Confronting the baron and his disdain for her, Madame Verdurin is cocksure in her desires, especially in her overwhelming desire for social prestige. Sympathy is not part of her character, and one might argue that her egomania transcends any determination of character by class. In fact she exactly resembles the Guermantes in this regard, as is seen when early in the evening she shows that she is indifferent to the death of a faithful member of the clan, the dowdy Princess Sherbatoff. A display of undue regret on her part might interfere with the success of her soirée. Her indifference shows her to be an unfeeling double of the Guermantes, who in *Sodom and Gomorrah* refuse to allow the death of a cousin to interfere with their going to a ball (the duke dismisses his death as exaggeration!) (*SG,* 169). Proust presents his bourgeois hostess from a deadpan frontal perspective, both here and earlier in *Swann's Way,* so that it is difficult to decide whether she is a hypocrite feigning, or a lunatic really suffering, the headaches and pains she claims to have because of her supposedly excess sensibility to the music she cannot refrain from listening to. It is clear she does not have, however, excess sensibility with regard to people if it should interfere with her desires.

It is important to understand that from the novel's historical perspective, for all her foibles, egomaniacal aggressiveness, and underhandedness, Madame Verdurin maintains a brilliant salon, having great importance for the arts during the Third Republic. Proust presents her as a maniacal dragon whose role in saving Vinteuil's music is nothing less than if she were contributing to saving from oblivion the work of a musician on a par with Gabriel Fauré or Maurice Ravel. Moreover, not unlike Gertrude Stein's collecting early works by Pablo Picasso and Henri Matisse, she usually knows better than the aristocrats what is the future in art, which in itself suggests that she will replace them, as they understand nothing about modern art. If she is egotistic and pathetically possessive, driven by her self-image, she can also be capriciously generous. Like all Proustian characters, she is multiple, as the narrator stresses at the end of the same evening during which she shatters Charlus's dreams about Morel: with her husband she decides to give a stipend, without the beneficiary knowing it, to Saniette, the impoverished archivist who has been a faithful member of the "clan" in spite of the Verdurins' treating him as if he were an idiot.

If Proust were totally systematic with this latter kind of characterization, one might speak of a dialectic in which character traits automatically seem to engender their opposite in any strongly delineated character such as Swann, Odette, the Duchess of Guermantes, Charlus, and Madame Verdurin. There is some truth in this idea. For instance Swann is the most elegant and intelligent man of his milieu and a vacuous dilettante who is made a fool of by Odette, herself an empty, trite prostitute who becomes the most fashionable woman of the day. The Duchess of Guermantes is the most elegant woman the narrator has ever seen and at times a near idiot when it comes to understanding art. Charlus stands out in his egomania and yet has a certain noble grandeur, like King Lear, as the narrator says in *Time Regained.* Capable of sensitive understanding of classical and modern literature, the baron does not see what a fool he makes of himself in public with his queenly displays of virility. In this play of oppositions centered on each character, it is hard not to speak of a kind of Pascalian dialectic showing how opposite traits demonstrate at times the grandeur, but usually the misery, of fallen humanity (and Pascal thought that recognition of our utter misery was proof of our lost grandeur). I temper this suggestion about opposites by noting that Proust is too subtle to engage only in sharp allegorical dialectics. His characterization plays fully with the conflicts generated by each character within himself as well as in interaction with others. When Morel triumphs as a musician, it seems that he may be on the pathway to greatness (or not), but this does not undo the fact that he is a rude bumpkin, an unprincipled social climber who, without hesitation, works harm on all around him—as is especially clear in *Time Regained* when he makes vicious public attacks on the baron. Finally one may conclude that the very variety of traits embodied by each character blunts the sharp dialectic of oppositions. Each character is a constellation of traits that may well be in opposition, but not always: the maid Françoise can be a sadist in her kitchen, inflicting suffering on a poor girl who is there to help her, but Françoise cries easily about the pain caused by distant calamities. However, her basic loyalty to the narrator's family suffers no opposition.

Proust ends *The Captive* with the rupture that in retrospect may appear inevitable: Albertine flees without warning the narrator even as he is trying to figure out how to leave her so he can finally go to Venice. I say "in retrospect" because the nature of the narrative has left all possibilities open up to this point, including an eventual unhappy marriage à la Swann. And the narration remains open even after her flight, for *The Fugitive* continues the narration of the distraught young man's attempts to get back the woman he wants to leave. These attempts point up once again that he is hardly in control of his own capricious desires, not surprisingly since his suffering is the main force generating his love. A cure of the amorous pathology demands the cessation of suffering; in effect it demands the elimination of what keeps it alive. This may appear to be something of a tautology. Be that as it may, the narrator's love exists as an existential projection toward the future in which the ultimate possession of Albertine would mean that she could no longer cause him anguish and jealousy. With the elimination of suffering, as he is well aware, he would cease to love her, or as the narrator puts it with self-reproach: "Suffering, the prolongation of a spiritual shock that has come from without, keeps aspiring to change its forms; one hopes to be able to dispel it by making plans, by seeking information; one wants it to pass through its countless metamorphoses, for this requires less courage than keeping our suffering intact" (*F*, 578).

The idea that suffering demands courage to keep it intact is the other side of the lover's dilemma: love exists for the narrator only insofar as he keeps his suffering alive. But the dilemma for which he feels guilt is that he is too weak, too fallen, too miserable to envisage this possibility—a dilemma that occupied Proust from as early as *Pleasures and Days*—so that the impossibility of lasting love, which is to say suffering, is a constant source of additional suffering. Nonetheless the desire to get on with suffering so as to get rid of it establishes the narrator's itinerary for the first part of *The Fugitive*. For example he sets about trying to cope with the objects around him in his apartment; he wants to be able to touch and see with impunity those physical embodiments of anguish Albertine has left behind her, in the many objects that testify to her having lived there. In this manner he may quiet the different selves that memory throws up at him with each chance encounter with an object that recalls a past supposedly less laden with grief.

His anguish is shot through with moments of lucidity in which he realizes that he really wants to be alone. He writes a long letter asking Albertine to come back, though he knows that he really wants to elicit a refusal so that he can, as it were, throw all the blame on her. Thus he hopes to find solace in a negative reply—though he also knows that he ought to foresee that a negative reply, setting off a renewal of suffering, would revive his love "to its fullest intensity" (*F,* 616). It is at this moment that he sees in the newspaper an announcement of a performance of *Phèdre* with Berma. The announcement calls forth an entire chain of past events tied up with a play that, as we have seen, has already had a kind of premonitory role in the novel. It also recalls that the role of art for Proust's characters is often that of an intermediary or relay or even a support mechanism for their emotions, as when Swann is able to love Odette by transforming her into a Botticelli. In a reverse movement in *The Fugitive,* the narrator imagines himself the tragic heroine who sees her destruction written in the eyes of the beloved who refuses her. It is the case that in Racine's play the queen Phèdre sees that her stepson, Hippolyte, supposedly indifferent to women, can love a woman, for he in fact loves Aricie, so that Phèdre jealously commands her maid to slander Hippolyte to his father, Phèdre's husband. Thésée then kills his own son, and Phèdre kills herself out of guilt and anguish. Her jealousy is her undoing. The narrator's admonitory mental staging of a play is, as he says, a "sort of prophecy of the amorous episodes" in his own life (*F,* 620). It has no effect on him, however, for he continues to pursue strategies to get Albertine to come back. The narrator's power of analysis does little to support his willpower, though it all contributes to a moment of high comedy illustrating his patent contradictions.

Proust's view of contingency might appear to be opposed to the idea of universal tragic fate, though this is not entirely the case. If nothing is fated in the narrator's world—and this seems clearly to be the case—nonetheless he can aspire to be a victim, at least in his imagination. A more serious objection to Proust's view of contingency might appear to be that, if chance freely rules in the universe, how is it that the fall appears to be universal? This might appear to be a contradiction Proust inherited from the Christian tradition. One might also reply by arguing that no single act is determined in Proust's world, even if they all add up with near-statistical certainty to a continuous demonstration of the characters' fall from grace and ideal. (This is analogous to the reasoning introduced by the then recently invented theory of thermodynamics, with which Proust would have been familiar.) Contingency is much at work in *The Fugitive*, for it is pure chance that brings out Albertine's death when she falls from a horse. Thus it is chance that revives the narrator's love because of the unexpected renewal of his suffering occasioned by this event. And Albertine's death again offers the narrator the ultimate knowledge that comes from the fall, that the forbidden knowledge concealed in the garden was the knowledge of death. To be sure the narrator's experience of Albertine's death is preceded by his knowledge of his grandmother's death, occurring well after she actually died, but Albertine's death occurs out of cycle, it is not part of the natural rhythms of life, it is a pure demonstration of the absurd.

Albertine's death also offers another variant demonstration that the knowledge of death is a knowledge born of feeling, and feelings do not obey the laws of normal chronology. Recall that in Balbec the narrator belatedly feels the void created by his grandmother's absence, when he feels a wild desire to fling himself into her arms "more than a year after her burial, because of the anachronism which so often prevents the calendar of facts from corresponding to the calendar of feelings." From this experience he learns, "For with the perturbations of memory are linked the intermittencies of the heart" (*SG*, 211). He discovers that the self is a fragile construct, easily dislocated by both memory and feeling, and they in turn may wreak havoc on each other as they ravage the hapless self. The psychodynamics of suffering generated by Albertine's death again throws into relief the Pascalian side of Proust's vision of the misery of the self. Her death demonstrates that a unique kind of hell exists when the living cannot hold on to their grief in the face of the unacceptable scandal of death. Hell—suffering because one is suffering or, alternatively, suffering because one foresees no longer suffering—is a product of the intermittent self, its transient passions, and its contemptible weakness.[5]

The Fugitive illustrates the intermittencies of the narrator's feelings and especially his grief by first narrating Albertine's death and his renewed suffering as a fact. Then near the end of *The Fugitive,* a mistaken reading of a telegram causes him to believe that Albertine is alive and is desirous of renewing her relationship with him. His reaction to this erroneous reading offers a more elaborate demonstration of the weakness of the self first disclosed in his incapacity to hold on to his grief about his grandmother: quite simply he finds that the self that loved Albertine is dead and that her return would hardly be welcome. And so much for the months during which she occupied all his waking thoughts. To be sure upon first learning of Albertine's death, the narrator strives to keep his love alive, perversely perhaps, by keeping his jealousy alive. *The Fugitive* becomes even more frankly comic as it portrays him, in his grief, engaging in a continuing quest for knowledge about what the living Albertine "really" did when she was with other people. For example the narrator turned detective sends the Balbec hotel manager to garner information about what Albertine might have been doing in the bathing establishment there—and of course he does not know in the end whether or not he can believe the rather damning result of the manager's inquiries. The necessarily inconclusive quest for knowledge is the essence of jealousy, and it has no need of a living object to keep jealousy alive. In fact the narrator's quest to elicit more and more testimony could go on forever in principle, though the power of, and the need for, oblivion bring it to an end.

The older narrator judges his younger self with a severity that points up again that he cannot come to a final judgment about his own sentiments, much less those of others:

> My grief was related not to what Albertine had been to me, but to
> what my heart, anxious to participate in the most general emotions
> of love, had gradually persuaded me that she was; then I became
> aware that the life that had bored me so (or so I thought) had been
> on the contrary delightful; the briefest moments spent in talking
> to her about even the most trivial things were now augmented,
> blended with a pleasure which at the time—it is true—had not been
> perceived by me, but which was already the cause of my having
> sought those moments so persistently to the exclusion of any others.
> (*F,* 665–66)

The older narrator judges himself as a younger man for his involvement with a woman who was largely a creation of his own desires. That is indeed the central trait characterizing Proust's vision of love: it is a subjective state marked by all the inconsequence caused by the fall. This suggests not only why the narrator (and reader) ultimately knows nothing about the so-called love object, but also why the narrator (and reader) has no problem in knowing everything about the loves of all the other characters. Omniscient narration, a product of the Dantesque memory that does not err, is about third parties, never about the second person of direct discourse that faces the speaker when he speaks. Facing Albertine, the narrator is facing an opacity on which he projects what he may. Finally at the end of *The Fugitive,* the narrator's indifference to Albertine is another lesson about the fall from the paradise once promised by parental love and then by the myth of erotic love. Pursuing lost paradise, he wanted to be in love and so he was.

The narrator tries to describe, more or less systematically, the path he takes in becoming indifferent toward his love in *The Fugitive.* He says that there are three stages on the way. This description may appear to be another oblique homage to Stendhal, who theorized the stages on the way to love but not the stages on the way out of it. In any case the stages the narrator adumbrates are at best approximate. First he begins to look at other girls (though it appears that he had never really stopped looking) and renews his friendship with Swann's daughter Gilberte, a personage rising on the social scene; second he has conversations with Andrée, the girl who may or may not have been Albertine's sometime erotic partner; and third and perhaps most important, he goes to Venice, finally undertaking the journey that he once thought would require him to leave Albertine. The power of oblivion is amply demonstrated in Venice, for it is there that the narrator realizes that he takes no joy in the fact that Albertine might be alive. His belief that a telegram from Gilberte is from Albertine lasts long enough for him to understand that not only love is dead, but also the self that was in love. Undoubtedly for Proust, this is the final stage in falling out of love.

After finding renewed erotic interest in others, and facing his putative rival by confronting Andrée, he can face the distress of recognizing that he is unable to maintain his love. But this discovery is accompanied by something more distressing: he again finds that he cannot hold on to the self that was in love, or as the narrator puts it: "One is no more distressed at having become another person, after a lapse of years and in the natural sequence of time, than one is at any given moment by the fact of being, one after another, the incompatible persons, malicious, sensitive, refined, caddish, disinterested, ambitious which one can be, in turn, every day of one's life" (*F,* 870). Proust makes such strong claims about the discontinuity of the self that several critics have wanted to see in the narrator's views the demonstration of a near Buddhist belief in the unsubstantial self.[6] Perhaps, though by this point it should be clear that the narrator's view of his possible multiple selves is primarily a sign of human frivolity springing from the fall. To be sure the fall is something of a metaphor in this context, though the Pascalian sense of human misery is not.

In *Time Regained* the narrator returns to Paris after some years in a sanatorium and finds, at a morning reception, the ravages of time engraved in the faces and in the bodies of many of the socialites whom he knew earlier in life. A foreshadowing of this vision of time written in the flesh occurs in Venice at the end of *The Fugitive,* when the narrator, his mother, and her old friend Mme Sazerat run across the aged Marquise de Villeparisis and her lover, the former ambassador M. de Norpois, who once seemed to be a friend to the narrator as a boy. The old couple is dining together. The narrator becomes a voyeur in a minor key to observe them and record the conversation of this still affectionate but now debilitated pair who had more or less concealed their relationship for years. The final point about the ravages of time is made, with black humor, when Mme de Sazerat asks the narrator to point out to her the marquise, a woman who, once as "beautiful as an angel, wicked as a demon," had seduced and ruined Mme de Sazerat's father (*F,* 859). But the daughter, in looking for this aristocrat who supposedly conducted herself like the basest prostitute, sees no famous beauty; as Mme de Sazerat tells the narrator upon looking in the direction to which he points, "there's only an old gentleman and a little hunchbacked, red-faced, hideous woman" (*F,* 859). Devil and angel, beauty and hunchback, all are contained as possibilities in one human being, subject to the irrevocable laws of time.

The foreshadowing scene with the marquise and the ambassador may well give the impression that Proust seems to have been almost overwhelmed by the temptation of dialectical reversals at the end of *The Fugitive.* Venice is the promise of paradise and the last stopping place of those condemned by time, where a woman once both angel and devil is now a hideous demonstration of the laws of time. Such reversals abound in other events in *The Fugitive.* Social change is highlighted, for example, in the ongoing process of the aristocracy's demise. The son of the aristocratic Cambremer family has married Mlle d'Oloron, a newly minted member of the nobility, thanks to Charlus, who has made an aristocrat out of the niece of the tailor Jupien—the same Jupien whose antics with the baron initiated the narrator into the universality of Sodom. The narrator's friend Saint-Loup, the aristocrat who had a passionate affair with the actress Rachel, is revealed as gay. Not only does the aristocrat come out of the closet, but he also marries Gilberte, in another marriage uniting opposing classes. With this marriage, moreover, Swann's daughter completes her ascension, as it were, ceasing to be the daughter of a famous *cocotte*, with an inherited fortune from the Jewish side of her family, and becoming an adopted aristocrat, then a married aristocrat and, in a final reversal, an unhappy wife whose noble husband is deceiving her with other men, most notably Morel, whom the baron pursued. (The narrator sadly notes that this change has tarnished his friendship with Saint-Loup.)

Some critics, enthusiastic about most aspects of Proust's novel, become reticent when facing the reversals he offers with increasing frequency as the novel develops, especially with regard to the labile sexuality some of the characters display. The philosophically inclined psychologist might retort that it is at least arguable that the postulate of bisexuality derives almost logically from the near-dialectical view of human character Proust adopts, especially in the later part of the novel. Of course not all critics are hostile to Proust on this score. For instance some years ago, in an answer to critics hostile toward his portrayal of the universality of depravity, the critic J. E. Rivers used the then famous Kinsey report to buttress Proust's view of bisexuality and homosexual experimentation. With this report's statistics in hand, one can simply retort that, as Proust well knew, nearly everybody does it.[7] However, whatever be the truth of this retort, the empirical evidence provided by sociological inquiry is not really the issue in Proust's case.

Whether 5 or 60 percent of humanity are involved occasionally or permanently in the practices of Sodom and Gomorrah is not really germane. Proust's point is broader. Because of the fall—and perhaps causing it—the human self is malleable, in an indefinite number of ways, and sexuality is only one of the forces that shape it. For Proust it is almost as if the dialectic of human development decrees that, if most people are heterosexual, then most can become homosexual. All is a question of time and chance, though it may require a lifetime of leisure to discover that the self is never a permanent acquisition. Saint-Loup also seems to be a case in point when he stops being entirely straight. But many other types of reversals are possible, too. The one-time avant-garde poet and rebel Bloch becomes a socialite; and Legrandin, we learn, stops being a snob at the end of life. One can see that the reversals that characterize Proust's characters cover a wide spectrum, ranging from devils to angels with much in between, and all permutations seem plausible once one accepts the impermanence of the manifest self. This demonstration is one of the reasons for the length of the novel: only in time, much time, do all the permutations reveal themselves.

From a novel using the allegory of the garden and the Fall, one might reasonably expect redemption to be an issue, though the subject has had little relevance in the novel until now. However the theme of redemption and resurrection will occupy us for much of the remainder of this study. Critical interpretations are wildly different with regard to what Proust meant by these themes. To avoid ambiguity, if that is possible, let me say that however much metaphors of, and allegorical allusions to, redemption and resurrection may tempt Proust, I do not think that one can affirm that Proust ever thought that redemption in a conventionally religious sense was the subject of his novel. In fact there is a tension in the novel between the power of the biblical allegory Proust uses and the vision of the bleak universe of modernity that predominates in the novel. To be sure the tension derives from a sometimes sotto voce hope about redemption, in some form or other if not in a strictly religious sense. The narrator's tentative hope is sometimes expressed in the form of questions and hypotheses. Sharing these questions and hypotheses, the reader is carried on by the expectations that the allegory arouses, for who can deny the power of the redemptory promises that hawthorns and sonatas seem to offer, despite a narrative voice that increasingly seems mired in hell even before death. Of course the reader also understands that such a narrator inevitably dreams of transcending his misery.

Nonetheless it is difficult to entertain the idea that some kind of redemption is the telos of a novel as little committed to transcendence as *In Search of Lost Time.* How, one wonders, can the fragmented and intermittent self that the narrator ascribes to himself, as well as to his characters, find any redemption if the self exists only as a fleeting moment buoyed along by the transient sensations in which it finds an ephemeral identity? The narrator is quite aware of this difficulty. He confronts it, for example, in an amusing scene that he recalls after the evening spent at the Verdurins' salon at La Raspelière in *Sodom and Gomorrah.* His philosophical musing after this evening is worth some commentary. Finding himself alone at night, the narrator recalls a conversation in which a "Norwegian philosopher" present at the soirée spoke about historically real philosophers such as Boutroux, Proust's professor at the Sorbonne, and Bergson, probably the best-known philosopher of the moment. The Norwegian philosopher claims to reproduce curious remarks Bergson supposedly said to Boutroux about memory. He said that "soporifics taken from time to time in moderate doses have no effect upon that solid memory of our everyday life which is so firmly established within us," although other drugs may trouble other, more unstable forms of memory—such as a memory of Greek texts (*SG,* 521). This distinction of solid and unstable forms of memory, attributed to Bergson, leads the narrator to meditate on his own memory.

Feeling very sleepy, the narrator begins a meditation on sleep as he recalls the philosopher's comments. He notes that in his own case, oblivion does not strike literary texts or his capacity to recall philosophical systems. Rather his forgetting wipes out the concrete lived detail of "the actual reality of the ordinary things that surround" him—when he forgets things, then oblivion threatens the individual stuff composing one's life (SG, 521). It is this daily reality that must be redeemed if redemption is to have any meaning—since as the narrator says ironically in a sharp critique of Bergson, he has no problem waking up and remembering lines of Baudelaire or the philosophical system of Porphyry or Plotinus.

The narrator's meditation on types of memory becomes an exploratory essay on existential ontology: the narrator affirms in effect that individual human being is coextensive with memory, at least up to the moment where it intersects the present. Without the memory of the details of one's life, there is no individual human being in any real sense. His meditation ends with an even more pointed irony against Bergson, as quoted by the Norwegian philosopher, when the narrator wonders what would be a memory that one could not remember (SG, 522). What can it mean to talk about past or future life, on this or that side of the grave? For without memory there is no substance to life, hence to a human being: "If I can have in me and around me so many memories which I do not remember, this oblivion (a de facto oblivion, at least, since I have not the faculty of seeing anything) may extend over a life which I have lived in the body of another man, even on another planet. A common oblivion obliterates everything. But what, in that case, is the meaning of the immortality of the soul the reality of which the Norwegian philosopher affirmed? The being that I shall be after death has no more reason to remember the man I have been since my birth than the latter to remember what I was before it" (SG, 522–23).

This passage shows again that Proust's narrator is closer to his near contemporary Wittgenstein than to Bergson, especially here in his thought experiment about what it might mean to have a self that one could not remember. He resembles Wittgenstein in the latter's attempt to imagine what it would be to experience oneself in another's body. Proust asks what could be a self that one could not remember: would it be any different from being somebody else? The import of this is to bring up the question of what the claim of that self on existence would be if each moment of its existence did not have the same weight as every other moment. And each moment of that self's existence can only be known, weighed, and evaluated if it is remembered. Without a madeleine and a cup of lime tea to restore it in its fullness, it appears the self verges on nonbeing at every moment.

Moreover his self-questioning takes on an added dimension late at night when, musing on the philosophers, the narrator rings for the valet and realizes that, though he first thought he had already rung for him, actually he had only dreamed that he had rung for him, such that "this dream had the clarity of consciousness" (*SG,* 523). The question as to how one differentiates the dreaming self from the waking self is a fundamental one for any thinker who wants to argue for the reality of a substantial self, as the great rationalist René Descartes demonstrated in trying to make the thinking self the basis for certain knowledge. The narrator's moment of dreaming obliges him to wonder what criteria allow a self to know itself to be real, especially if the froth of dreams can foist upon it an exact illusion of reality. Proust stops his thought experiment here, for it suffices that he has shown that his young narrator understands what is at stake were he to speak of a self having an existence linking the past and the shadow of the present moment when dream can seem as real as waking consciousness.

Underlying the narrator's meditation is the recognition that redemption in any meaningful sense demands the restitution of memory and the things of memory, the everyday stuff that makes up consciousness and is constitutive of real individual identity. Facing the challenge of dream, one recalls that Proust opens *In Search of Lost Time* with a kind of phenomenology of dream affirming the autonomy of the dreamer with regard to the order of the world he or she perceives. One can argue that Proust's position has been modified by this point in *Sodom and Gomorrah* with the reversal implicit in this passage about the narrator's mistaking dream for reality: the dream may well order what the dreamer takes to be the self. Can that be called a self? To be sure this possibility is hardly excluded at the novel's beginning, when, after declaring that the sleeping self could grasp the world's order, the narrator finds that the order of chairs and windows in his chamber does not necessarily obey the order he projects on them in the dark. As the furniture scrambles at dawn to get back to where reality assigns each piece, the narrator discovers what Descartes did not: the dreaming self can be the source of self-directed comedy.

In any case redemption, if redemption there is to be, depends in some sense on the existence of a self to be redeemed, though what this might entail is hardly spelled out in the three tomes charting the reaches of *Sodom and Gomorrah.* The beginnings of an answer to the question are, however, sketched out by the narrator, for it is clear that he believes art is one of the means by which questions about redemption can be raised, if not answered. Juxtaposed with the narrator's portrait of the ongoing fall into time are his views on art—music, painting, literature. This is especially true of *The Captive*. I add parenthetically that Proust was apparently writing much of this volume while dying; and thus it is not at all surprising that he relates this discussion of the nature of art and its ontology to what he sees as the precondition for any kind of redemption, namely, the affirmation of a lasting self that might reasonably hope to find a domain in which redemption takes place. At times this domain is what the narrator calls the real, undoubtedly in homage to the Western tradition, from Plato onward, of casting doubt on the reality of the world in which we actually find ourselves—in the narrator's case, the fallen world of Sodom and Gomorrah.

Throughout the novel art is often, perhaps usually, construed by the characters to have functions ancillary to what the narrator sees as its ultimate function of revealing something beyond the fallen world. This misunderstanding, or willful misuse, of art is especially evident in *Sodom and Gomorrah,* in which artworks are evoked like so many tags to show that characters have an often comic, misguided understanding of art. Two examples can suffice to make the point. Brichot, the garrulous professor, makes a typically long disquisition, in the pretentious language of a moronic pedant, to tell Charlus that Balzac is not an interesting writer, since, as Brichot says, "the copious improviser whose alarming lucubrations you appear to me singularly to overrate has always struck me as being an insufficiently meticulous scribe" (*SG,* 612). The baron's acerbic but accurate retort is that the professor says this inflated nonsense because he knows nothing about life. The baron's comment is undoubtedly true, but lost in a salon in which art is evoked for the purposes of self-display and aggrandizement of ego (which in this example then allows Doctor Cottard the display of one more of his idiotic play on words, which shows in fact that he has not understood Brichot's pointlessly quoting Rabelais). A second example, showing the subordination of art to egotism, is provided by Madame Verdurin. At times she seems to have some understanding of art, except when her overriding vanity is at stake. The point is made comically clear when she coyly declares that Elstir was a good painter as long as he was coming to her salon, but today, she says, "I don't know whether you call it painting, all those outlandish great compositions, those hideous contraptions he exhibits now that he has given up coming to me" (*SG,* 459).

In *Sodom and Gomorrah,* art seems to be an adornment of the fallen world, and the idolatry of art is a form of modish egomania. Moreover art is threatened by the same disenchantment that the narrator feels when he says that the world is losing its poetic aura. Traveling about the seacoast, for example, he finds that it has lost its charm: "It was not merely the place-names of this district that had lost their initial mystery, but the places themselves" (*SG,* 693). The social world itself is one source of his disenchantment, but so is the very language in which he once found, he thought, a source of poetic transcendence. Not surprising, perhaps, the savant Brichot's etymologies have played a role in this disenchantment, for, traveling on a train along the coast, the narrator adds with an ironic twist that "the names, already half-stripped of a mystery which etymology had replaced by reasoning, had now come down a state further still" (*SG*, 693–94). In brief one can draw upon Proust's contemporary, the German sociologist Max Weber, to say that the narrator's feelings are the result of a disenchantment that one can take as emblematic of a fallen world. His is the world of materialist modernity that Weber well described.

Disenchantment is the background for understanding the narrator's meditations on art that follow in *The Captive.* These meditations are intercalated, as it were, into the scenes in which the narrator is acting as jail keeper for Albertine. They are a part of Proust's at times comic demonstration that solitude is necessary for all essential thought, though the narrator in his obsessive mania has contrived to deprive himself of that solitude. When in solitude, however, he finds that the art of the three artists he admires—Elstir, Bergotte, Vinteuil—allows him, as he says, to "unconsciously summon up" from within himself the dreams that Albertine had inspired in him "long ago" before he knew her and "that had been quenched by the routine of everyday life" (*C*, 65–66). In a sense the narrator uses art, for art allows him, as he puts it, to be "suddenly and for an instant capable of passionate feelings for this wearisome girl" (*C*, 66). But this use of art, analogous to Swann's use of Botticelli to transform Odette, is not the central theme in *The Captive,* however much Albertine may be a dubious beneficiary of the sparks of enchantment that art occasionally introduces into the narrator's life. The central question in *The Captive,* as it is for the rest of the novel, is whether art allows in some sense a transcendence of the fall. It is broached principally in the narrator's reflections on music, especially on Vinteuil and Wagner, but also in thoughts on literature and painting, notably on the occasion of Bergotte's death, taking place when the writer is viewing Vermeer's painting *View of Delft* (*C*, 244).

These reflections on art spring from the narrator's wondering how it is that a work of art brings him to "descend into" himself and enter into contact with his own inner being at the same time it offers something beyond his own individuality (*C*, 206). Meditating on the effect of music, he finds that Vinteuil's sonata takes him back to the days of Combray when, in walking along the Guermantes way, he had longed to be an artist before disenchantment had, it seems, caused him to abandon his ambition. This was before he then lost hope that life itself might console him for the loss of art. This meditation takes the form of an elaborate question. The narrator asks himself whether there is in art "a more profound reality" in which one's true personality finds an expression that is not afforded by the activities of normal life (C, 204–5). His interrogative meditation culminates in thoughts about great writers of the nineteenth century, such as the novelist Balzac, the poet Hugo, and the historian Michelet. The narrator finds that these writers are characterized by work that was first considered incomplete, "which is the characteristic of all the great works of the nineteenth century, that century whose greatest writers somehow botched their books, but watching themselves work as though they were at once workman and judge, derived from this self-contemplation a new form of beauty, exterior and superior to the work itself, imposing on it a retroactive unity, a grandeur which it does not possess" (C, 207). These thoughts first strike one as strange but can take on a forceful coherence when one views them as a kind of self-description of the work Proust is writing (or that the narrator perhaps may write). In offering a description of how these writers achieved the closure of their works, the narrator shows that the works can be perceived as artistic in Proust's sense: through "self-description" or self-reflection, they achieve the unity and integrity necessary for the perception of the individual world constitutive of an artwork. This unity is the unified vision of the artistic self expressed therein, which exists somehow exterior to the work. Whether this is an accurate description of Balzac or Hugo is an open question. It is arguably a description of *In Search of Lost Time*.

The notion of "work" that Proust uses to describe the artwork is in this context almost synonymous with the concept "world" or "universe." Hence it is important to understand Proust's meaning of the notion of "world" with regard to the artwork. In the most general sense we can understand that "world" means an ensemble of elements delimited by closure, and which can be perceived as a closed set (whether they are actually perceived or not) so that the elements exist within some kind of unified field. A world is a delineated and hence unified set of elements perceived within a closure—such as is signified by the unity the narrator speaks of with regard to Balzac, Hugo, and Michelet. Accordingly Proust would allow that I can speak of my world or, hypothetically, your world and, historically, Marcel Proust's personal world, for we assume that each of us perceives a closure that is probably unique to our own perception—though in the case of my world and your world, nobody else can perceive it. This is the subjective world of which the narrator frequently speaks. However if we speak of Balzac's novelistic world or Hugo's poetic universe, not to mention Proust's novelistic world, we speak of a closure containing elements that we can all perceive as a closed set, and according to Proust's narrator, this is not only because these writers wrote works of art but also because they reflected back on them so as to assure that their works could be perceived in their integrity as one world. (This also means we can speak of a world according to somebody else, such as Balzac's world according to Proust, or Proust's novelistic world according to Allen Thiher or anybody else who writes about Proust.) The fact that my world cannot be perceived by you seems to Proust's narrator to be part of our fallen nature. However the fact that we both can perceive Balzac's world is more than a simple recognition that we both can read a novel. The literary text in this sense represents a triumph over subjectivity in that the closed ensemble of elements perceived as a world is open to universal conspectus. Proust begins here with questions about whether this world perceived as larger than mere subjectivity might offer some hope of transcendence.

A critic may observe that perception is not writing, and that Proust is using an unquestioned metaphor, equating vision to writing, to relate subjectivity to writing. The same critic may react with even greater hostility when she finds that Proust speaks of Wagner's world or Vinteuil's world, a world constituted by pure sounds to which it seems difficult to attribute anything clearly semantic or any perceptual dimension other than pure audition. However let us return to the most general meaning of *world* and note that with regard to the notions of work and world, neither logic nor experience requires Proust to explain the nature of the constitutive elements found in the closure delimiting the world of the work. In fact there is no requirement to say what is required for the delineations that create unity. We know a world when we perceive one, whatever the elements constituting it. Consider that by analogy one has no problem speaking of a mathematical world, say the world described by Euclidean geometry or the different worlds described by the different non-Euclidean geometries (and elsewhere I have argued that Proust was quite aware of the significance one can attribute to the end of the hegemony of Euclidean geometry: new geometries showed the possibility of many different mathematical worlds and, by implication, the kinds of worlds whose existence we may postulate). Music in some way presents a more ambiguous problem than mathematics, for when the musician picks up the sheet music of a musical composition, he or she sees immediately a set of instructions for performance expressing a series of mathematical relations deriving (usually) from the diachronic scale. But when the music is performed, as the narrator's meditations amply show, the object of perception is not a group of mathematical relations as such. Rather one perceives unfolding relations in sound. If one perceives these relations as a closed set of unified elements, then in Proust's nonmetaphorical sense, one perceives a world. This is an argument, I believe, subtending the narrator's discussion of music, its revelation of another subjectivity, and the possibility that this world may transcend the fallen world in which the narrator finds himself most of the time.

While playing a transcription of Wagner for the piano, the narrator wonders if it is only skill that gives to "great artists the illusory aspect of a fundamental irreducible originality"; he wonders if the originality is only "apparently the reflexion of a more than human reality" (C, 209). If only "industrious toil" is involved in the creation of the artwork, then art is "no more real than life," and the narrator can feel somewhat relieved for having wasted his life in procrastination (C, 209). But a question is posed, here by Wagner, then by Vinteuil, which asks if the "more than human reality" that the artwork seemingly presents is not in some sense superior to the reality of the fallen world. Can simply the tricks of "industrious toil" explain the workings of a work of art?

Proust circles back, orchestrating his themes à la Wagner, to the leitmotif of transcendence through art when the narrator considers Bergotte's death immediately after the writer viewed, at a special exposition in Paris, Vermeer's *View of Delft* (usually in the Hague). The encounter of dying writer and dead painter has been the occasion for much critical discussion, for it is not immediately obvious what Bergotte might mean by saying upon viewing Vermeer that he should have written as Vermeer painted, even going so far in his self-criticism as to wish that he had gone over his last books with a "few layers of color" so as to make his language "precious in itself," like the "little patch of yellow wall" that he sees in Vermeer's painting (C, 244). Perhaps Bergotte's self-criticism is to be taken to mean that he recognizes, with regret, that later in life he did not organize in language the elements of his world with the intensity or the coherence with which Vermeer organized his world in colors. Be that as it may, Proust's narrator thinks that Bergotte sacrificed his last works to furthering his social life and personal interests, bringing up again the leitmotif of the antagonism between the artistic and the social self. Somehow his quest for social success led to Bergotte's failure to continue to emphasize in his work that language is "precious in itself."

But what is of greater interest in Bergotte's demise is that perhaps at no point in the entire novel does Proust so explicitly broach the question of immortality as in the case of the writer's death. Meditating on the fact that Bergotte collapsed at the moment of viewing a great work of art, the narrator asks:

Dead for ever? Who can say? Certainly experiments in spiritualism offer us no more proof than the dogmas of religion that the soul survives death. All that one can say is that everything is arranged in this life as though we entered it carrying a burden of obligations contracted in a former life; there is no reason inherent in the conditions of life on this earth that make us consider ourselves obliged to do good, to be kind and thoughtful, even to be polite, nor for an atheist artist to consider himself obliged to begin over again a score of times a piece of work the admiration aroused by which will matter little to his worm-eaten body, like the patch of yellow wall painted with so much skill and refinement by an artist destined to be for ever unknown and barely identified under the name of Vermeer. (C, 245)

Proust's narrator wonders, as in the prose poem "Marine" of *Pleasures and Days,* if some Platonic preexistence of the soul might explain why we sense that we are not at home in the universe. Our thirst for the ideal testifies to some other existence, as does the fact, according to the narrator, that there is nothing intrinsic to the fallen world that asks for art and ethics, humanity's highest achievements. The belief in the lack of foundations for aesthetics and ethics is something like the narrator's basic axiom for much of the novel. However, thinking of Bergotte's death, he wonders if from Vermeer's or Bergotte's examples he might infer that the fallen soul could be impregnated at its origins with a sense of moral and aesthetic obligations that explain the drive to produce both ethics and art in a world whose fallen nature is a matter of perceived fact—it is the perceived substance of Proust's novelistic world, we might now say. However lest his Platonic hypothesis seem too ponderous, the narrator reverts to the semiserious ironic mode to conclude about Bergotte that on the night he was buried, the bookstores' windows were lit, and his books, "arranged three by three, kept vigil like angels with outspread wings and seemed, for him who was no more, the symbol of his resurrection" (C, 246). The allusion to the classical mode of literary survival after death, through fame and reputation, is ironically contrasted with a metaphor comparing Bergotte's books to those angels of Christian belief—leaving the reader to puzzle out what might be the meaning of an image of resurrection that seems more parody than promise.

Questions about the world of the artwork's superior reality and resurrection and associated questions about the narrator's relation to art and his vocation come together again in the passages relating his discovery of a new work by Vinteuil. Upon listening to it during an evening at the Verdurins, he compares it to the sonata by Vinteuil that he has frequently heard. The narrator's descriptive terms may seem a little problematic, as perhaps do any attempts to use language to describe music. The sonata opens, he says, "upon a lily-white pastoral dawn," whereas the new work begins with a storm and then "it was into a rose-red daybreak that this unknown universe was drawn from the silence" (C, 333). The once well-received idea that musical sound evokes colors or *Tonfarben* undoubtedly lies behind Proust's use of colors to describe the elements here. However the idea of *Tonfarben* would seem to be at odds with the narrator's belief that each type of art is individual, and it is unlikely he means to imply, for example, that C flat is codified as green or red or something of the sort. Surely musical sounds, or sounds perceived as music, are part of a unique universe, not a universal color code. So the reader has to concede Proust his use of colors as part of a not quite successful attempt to describe in words a musical world, something that the narrator later admits is not possible. One may describe the notes on the page by repeating them, but no words are commensurable with the individual elements and their relations making up a musical world, be it of Ravel or Vinteuil. This is already the sense of the narrator's statement when, having listened more, he stops trying to describe colors and dramatic situations: "I began to realize that if, in the body of this septet, different elements presented themselves one after another to combine at the close, so also Vinteuil's sonata and, as I later discovered, his other works as well, had been no more than timid essays, exquisite but very slight, beside the triumphal and consummate master-piece now being revealed to me" (C, 335). A world is revealed in the septet, and with it the narrator understands that Vinteuil's compositions are all components of one world, some more impressive than others, but parts of one individual artistic world nonetheless. Vinteuil's compositions make up an opus, expressing the "vision" of the individual artist or writer, though in this case it is a vision without sight.

The recognition of the unitary nature of Vinteuil's world is accompanied by the narrator's question as to whether art is nothing more than some kind of continuance of "life," which is to say, "as unreal as life itself" (C, 339). The musician's septet impresses the narrator that this is not the case, though for the moment all he can affirm is that, in spite of science's reliance upon universals to define truth—which is to say that the truth takes the form of universally valid propositions—the music shows that "the individual did exist" (C, 340). Vinteuil's example then shows the narrator that this individuality is so distinctive that, "free from analytical forms of reasoning as if it were being carried out in the world of angels," it cannot be translated into human speech (C, 341). Proust's meditating on the artist's world comes to an interrogative conclusion asking if "those elements"—"all the residuum of reality which we are obliged to keep to ourselves," all that which we cannot say or share, all "that ineffable something"—if all these are "brought out by art, the art of a Vinteuil like that of an Elstir, which exteriorizes in the colours of the spectrum the intimate composition of those worlds which we call individuals and which, but for art, we should never know?" (*C*, 343). This is a complex rhetorical question marking the narrator's progress, first in understanding the ontology of art and second in his questioning what might be the relation of art to the unreality he lives in. The narrator does not stint in the use of religious imagery when he describes his immediate situation after listening to the septet, for he finds that he is like an angel who has just fallen from the inebriating bliss of paradise and wonders if music, in some prelapsarian moment, might not have been the means of communication between souls (*C*, 344). His impression of falling from paradise is made all the more plausible by the fact, of course, that he "awakes" from listening to the septet to find himself at the Verdurin reception, from which Charlus will be driven out in humiliation. The entire episode repeats as a short mise en abyme (inner representation) the general development of *In Search of Lost Time*.

Proust brings the leitmotif of art and metaphysics to the fore in the latter part of *The Captive* with a restatement of the theme: the restatement takes the form of two hypotheses that emerge from the narrator's meditation on art when, this time, he tries to explain his ideas about aesthetics to Albertine (it must be said that Albertine rather fades from view at this moment). On the one hand, Vinteuil's music obliges him to entertain the hypothesis that art is "real" and is more than "the merely nerve-tingling joy of a fine day or an opiate night" (*C*, 504). To which the narrator adds, "It is inconceivable that a piece of sculpture or a piece of music which gives us an emotion that we feel to be more exalted, more pure, more true, does not correspond to some definite spiritual reality, or life would be meaningless" (*C*, 504). Whatever might be its import for the meaning of life, the narrator cannot avoid facing the materialist hypothesis about art. This proposes that ultimately there is nothing but states of matter, so that there is no reason to believe that the vagueness of certain states of the soul, such as the narrator experienced with music or upon tasting the madeleine soaked in lime tea, is any sign of "their profundity rather than of our not having yet learned to analyze them" (*C*, 513). All experiences are simply sensations. With the first hypothesis about art, the narrator thus wants not only to defend the belief in art's transcendence but also to deny what nineteenth-century aesthetes had thrown up as a challenge to bourgeois moralizing about art: that art is merely a pleasurable way of arranging nerve impulses, which can be done with hashish as well as with virtue, as Baudelaire put it with deliberate provocation. With the materialist hypothesis, the narrator accepts something like the material basis for the aesthete's position or the reductionism of the positivist, although from a scientific viewpoint, he also recognizes that it may well be the case that mental states induced by art are too complex to be analyzed. But this difficulty does not mean that in principle mental states induced by art are not amenable to some type of materialist explanation involving causality. Here the narrator leaves the two hypotheses open, one entertaining the idea of transcendence, the other admitting that art is just another aspect of the same material world that science explains and that, until now, the narrator has found to be devoid of transcendent interest.

In fine the theme of resurrection and transcendence in these three parts of the novel is related to the narrator's ongoing discomfiture with existence, and it cannot be said that at any point he manages to come up with more than a momentary triumph over this discomfiture. However at the end of *The Fugitive*, Proust concludes the experience of Sodom and Gomorrah with the narrator's trip to Venice. Here he experiences not only the scene of the old lovers' demise in time but also the annunciation the city seems to offer. In this regard the sojourn in Venice contrasts sharply with the experience of Sodom and Gomorrah narrated up until then. Venice is a kind of promised land for the narrator. It is not a city on the plain. If the narrator calls his trip there part of the third stage of his growing indifference to Albertine, it is because it is there that he reaches something like the nadir in his recognition of his self's lack of substantiality—and perhaps therefore the final point in the fall and the knowledge thereof that has been the essence of his education.

But his recognition of his self's nothingness does not negate the fact that Venice also contains signs or hints of a possible, if not actual, end of the fall: for upon arriving there, the narrator, notably accompanied by his mother, finds himself at moments transported back to what may be likened to another prelapsarian time of grace, or as he says, "I received there impressions analogous to those which I had felt so often in the past at Combray, but transposed into a wholly different and far richer key" (*F,* 844). He sees that the angel on the campanile of St. Mark's glitters in the sunlight, with its outstretched arms, as though proffering the promise of "a joy more certain than any that it could ever in the past have been bidden to announce to men of good will" (*F,* 844). The annunciating angel seems to promise the end of the fall, but it is only a promise, one that the stay in Venice itself does not fulfill. But it does fulfill the promise of something's being different, almost a different order of being, as first imagined by the child in Combray. In Venice, Proust's narrator becomes, at times, the enchanted stroller that he was in Combray, where mystery and adventure, possibly erotic, seemed to loom at every corner. Enchantment is perhaps not a state that can long last for an adult, but it does suggest a possible escape from the fall. So not only does the stay in Venice point positively back to Combray and the promise of paradise, it also looks forward to those revelations yet to come. For these we turn now to *Time Regained.*[8]

Chapter 7

Time Regained

Intimations of the Resurrection

For the conclusion of Moncrieff's translation of *In Search of Lost Time,* Andreas Mayor decided to use *Time Regained* as the title of the last volume. With this translation of *Le temps retrouvé*—literally "Time Found Again" and earlier translated as *The Past Recaptured*—Mayor evokes another canonical English writer, as Moncrieff did with Shakespeare in his original choice for the novel's title, *Remembrance of Things Past,* taken from the bard's thirtieth sonnet. Mayor's *Time Regained* is inevitably redolent of Milton's epic *Paradise Regained,* the sequel to *Paradise Lost.* The Miltonic title actually suggests an optimistic reading of the final volume, and a pessimistic reader may prefer the rather pedestrian *Finding Time Again* coined by Ian Patterson for the more recent British translation. In addition to different titles, there are stylistic differences between the two translations, as well as a difference as to where exactly *Time Regained* should begin. The revised Moncrieff translation finished by Mayor follows the 1954 Pléiade edition of the novel, whereas the later translation uses the later Pléiade edition. Roughly speaking, Mayor's translation (cited in this chapter) ends *The Fugitive* in the middle of the narrator's stay at Tansonville with Gilberte, whereas the later translation moves the beginning of *Finding Time Again* forward several pages, correcting what Patterson sees as an error on the part of Pierre Clarac and André Ferré in 1954 when they moved the starting point of *Le Temps retrouvé* some seven pages back from what the original edition had proposed. (Bernard Brun also begins his useful 1986 Flammarion edition at a slightly later point.)

The conclusion of *The Fugitive* and the beginning of *Time Regained* present a more or less continuous narration. After returning from Venice in *The Fugitive,* the narrator goes to Tansonville, where he visits Swann's daughter, Gilberte. They discuss their past and people they know in common. In a real sense, the narrator's return to Combray completes a circle in the novel's development—a circular return to the place of childhood foreshadowed in his stay in Venice by the brief trip he makes to Padua to see the works of Giotto that Swann had shown him when the narrator was a child in Combray. In returning to Combray itself, he comes back to the childhood paradise that opens the novel. He returns, however, only to confront a meaningless present. He finds that nothing is left of the scenes of paradise once known along the two paths that led away from the boy's house, Swann's way and the Guermantes way. Having reached adulthood, the narrator has now followed these paths toward the knowledge prefigured along each way. He has come to know eros and art, Sodom and Gomorrah and Vinteuil's sonata, disappointing passion and the promise of creation. After this education, on returning to Combray and the paradise from which he started out, he finds that his disenchantment is total.

This disenchantment is figured at the beginning of *Time Regained* in the chiastic rhetoric the narrator uses. In effect he finds himself in Combray when Combray has the least interest for him: "I should have no occasion to dwell upon this visit which I paid to the neighborhood of Combray at perhaps the moment in my life when I thought least about Combray, had it not, precisely for that reason, brought me what was at least a provisional confirmation of certain ideas which I had first conceived along the Guermantes way, and also of other ideas which I had conceived on the Méséglise way" (*TR*, 1).

Essential here is not only that Combray has become a dead memory but also that, on being physically present there, the narrator cannot find the living past that the lime tea had previously evoked for him—of which "Combray" is the record at the novel's beginning. He finds only memories taking the shape of ideas. In ideas he finds only intellectual abstraction and hence desiccation. In the present moment he can only conjure up the past as a series of abstract and meaningless memories. Hence he finds little that can interest him now at Combray. Indeed the once magical stream of his childhood, the Vivonne, appears now to be a narrow and ugly little river along which he dejectedly walks on a pedestrian towpath (*TR*, 2).

The two ways he has trod in his *Bildung* have led to this nadir. In a state of inner emptiness, all the narrator can do is look back, with disinterest and some distaste, upon the past and meditate on the reversals and deceptions it has unfolded. Some of this recall is comically ironic. For instance he learns that Gilberte was actually attracted to him, during those moments in Combray when, as a boy, he had not dared to speak to her when he saw her in her father's garden. The dialectics of perception in Proust often entails that the opposite of the narrator's first impression later turns out to be true, not that he or the other characters can ever be sure of the truth of the corrected impression revealed by time in its unfolding. The inevitability of error is illustrated now by Gilberte's confiding to the narrator that she knows her husband, Saint-Loup, is deceiving her, though she in turn is deceived about the nature of the deception. In times past Saint-Loup did frequent many women—he was passionately in love with the now famous actress Rachel—so that Gilberte draws erroneous conclusions about her husband from what she knows of his past. But in fact, as the narrator apparently unerringly knows in this case, Saint-Loup is, like his uncle the Baron de Charlus, enamored of Morel, the violinist whom the baron had patronized. In short deception and error are recurrent features of social life and personal relations in the fallen world the narrator has come to know all too well. And immediate perception is no guarantee of anything.

At this nadir the narrator reflects on what he might find were he able to overcome his disappointment with the world and especially with himself. Central to this meditation is the image of the steeple of the Combray church. It is visible through the window of the narrator's room at Tansonville. Finding no symbolic value in this image of hope, once conceived as the center of the town and his own life, and indeed of paradise on earth, he looks upon the church steeple merely as a "discordant tone" interjected into the midst of the luminous verdure about him there (*TR*, 10). (It is with this moment of discord that later editions of *Le Temps retrouvé* generally begin.) Set in counterpoint to the narrator's disenchantment, however, this image imbued with religious values suggests a possible reversal of vision that might be a prelude to the narrator's eventual discovery of his vocation and a renewal of his life. But more time must past before disenchantment can be overcome. In short at the opening of *Time Regained*, the narrator's education has come to an end where it began, in Combray, in his near-nihilistic vision of a world gone flat.

If the vision of Combray at the end of *The Fugitive* and the beginning of *Time Regained* is the nadir of the narrator's education, it hardly marks the end of new revelations about humanity's capacity for undergoing the fall. But the new revelations found in *Time Regained* begin to liberate the narrator from his disenchantment. To this end Proust discards in *Time Regained* a strictly realistic vision of time's slow decline and changes his narrative mode. In fact I am going to argue that he uses narration that revels in decadence and destruction. In a sense old revelations of the fall are hyperbolically extended and heightened as the narrator discovers that depravation and the fall are even more ubiquitous and grandiose that he could imagine. Epic depravation is exemplified by the baron's flagellation in a male brothel; whereas the fall into time eventuates in the reception at the Guermantes, where the characters become puppets in a masque of aging grotesques. In short the narration, after the narrator's stay at Tansonville, offers a nearly systematic strategy of hyperbolic negation, which in effect turns his world upside down. It is against this backdrop of a celebration of destruction that the narrator hits upon the revelations that may allow him to undertake the resurrection and redemption of the fallen world.

Let us now see how inversion and reversal—overturning and destruction—characterize nearly all the remaining narration dealing with the narrator's experience of society and others during and after World War I. My argument here is that the baron's descent into the night of abjection during the war and that the Guermantes reception featuring the living dead are inversions with which Proust creates a carnivalesque comedy in *Time Regained*. In parody and derision, this type of comedy differs from the comic but more realistic narration that has preceded it. I will discuss further what I mean by carnivalesque presently—literary scholars will recognize here an allusion to the work of the Russian theorist Mikhail Bakhtin. But first I want to describe what happens in this volume: the narrator's discovery of his possible vocation takes place precisely amid a narration portraying a symbolic destruction of his world. It is in a context of decline and fall that he seems to discover his calling as a harbinger of resurrection.

By returning his narrator to Tansonville and Combray at the beginning of *Time Regained,* Proust prepares the reader for a change in perspective. Here it is clear that the bildungsroman has come to an end. It is also clear that if the narrator is not to sink into total nihilism, he must encounter some truth that can elevate him above the abyss to which the fall has brought him. Change is necessary. The change in his perspective begins in fact at the beginning of *Time Regained* with a unique event in the novel's narrative modes. Proust has his narrator read a fictive "real" text that is supposed to represent a high point of literary art: he reads a passage from Edmond de Goncourt's journal. But his reading makes the narrator realize that he no longer has any stomach for the type of realist narration that many in his milieu have held up to him as the ideal for an aspiring writer. The fictive quotation from Goncourt occurs when the narrator, at the lowest point of his fall from grace at the end of the stay at Tansonville, reads from what he says is the "newly published volume of the Journal of the Goncourts" (*TR,* 26). Proust uses his gift for pastiche to write a fictional text, attributed to a real author, in which are found descriptions of the same social milieu that, some years after Goncourt had supposedly frequented it, the narrator himself has subsequently come to know in Balbec and Paris. (It is to be assumed that Proust is inventing a quotation purporting to be from the continuation of the journal that Edmond de Goncourt continued alone for twenty years after his brother, Jules, died in 1870.) In the long pastiche read by the narrator (and hence the reader), the fictive Goncourt narrates that he was invited to dinner by none other than Verdurin—who we learn is the author of a book on the great painter Whistler, though in the clan nobody seems to suspect that Verdurin is a writer of great sensibility (dixit Goncourt). Goncourt is enchanted with the Verdurins and offers in great detail "realist" descriptions of their furnishings and dishes. For example they have "Yung-chen plates with nasturtium-coloured borders and purple-blue irises" (*TR*, 30). This description of the Verdurins and their milieu offers precisely the kind of detail that one has *not* read in what the narrator has said of them up to this point; nor has the reader learned from Proust's narrator that Madame Verdurin is a "charming woman, whose speech betrays her positive adoration of local colouring" (*TR*, 32). In short the reader learns a great deal about the Verdurins and their milieu from a realist point of view, which is to say, a great deal that is both silly and mainly false, not to mention rather pointless.

Proust is skewering Goncourt here in an indictment of the kind of realism that Goncourt and many other nineteenth-century writers endorsed, both as a literary form and as a philosophical doctrine. The satirical pastiche of Goncourt is, moreover, introduced at this precise moment to incite the narrator to meditate on his continued failure to begin his vocation. Contemplating the journal, he ponders what would be the point of producing literature if the only goal of writing were to produce the kind of banal tedium found in the fictive Goncourt journal, the naïveté and falsity of which has been implicitly demonstrated by the preceding volumes of Proust's own novel. The narrator, however, leaves the door open for a future change of heart, since he decides that he will "ignore the objections against literature raised" by the pages of Goncourt that he reads (*TR*, 39).

The decision to ignore Goncourt hardly results in his discovery of his vocation, though it opens the door to it. Moreover the pages of pastiche function remarkably well as a kind of demonstration and justification by counterexample of the narration Proust himself is about to embark upon in *Time Regained*. In the rest of *Time Regained*, he eschews narrow realism in his descriptions of Paris during the war. In short with the pastiche of Goncourt, he sets out an apology by negation for the extraordinary nonrealist scenes forthcoming in *Time Regained*. Realism of the Goncourt sort is not merely naive with its focus on the infinite details of surface reality, but Proust also holds it up as an example of meaningless triviality and prevarication. Up to this point, he has shown that he has no use for these surface details if they are not part of a social comedy that portrays social mendacity for what it is. In the rest of the novel, he shows that truth in fiction can also be a matter of powerful dislocation of real details.

Yet it is not entirely accurate to imply that there is no realism in Proust's *Time Regained* with its portrayal of Paris during the war. In fact this is the only section of the novel in which the narrator uses some precise historical dates to relate his own life to the unfolding of public history. Because of illness the narrator says he is obliged to leave Paris to go to a sanatorium at some undefined moment, but then he says he comes back briefly precisely in 1914, at the outset of the war, declared in August; and he returns again in 1916, at a time when Paris is under threat of nightly bombardments. Proust thus sets up a realist scaffolding for the narration about the unreality of contemporary history and the hyperbole of the human fall whose comedy he takes to its ultimate conclusion. Proust uses a semirealist ploy to send his narrator away from Paris, for the narrator says his health at this time obliged him to seek a cure for an illness away from the city. He offers no details about the time spent away, nor does he say anything about the nature of the disease, though he states he was not cured. So much for Goncourt-like details. The effect of this narrative sleight of hand is a foreshortening of time in which years, though precisely located in public chronology given by the war, speed by for the narrator, who is largely absent from Paris for many years. The absence in effect produces a gap in the time span of the narration that nothing fills but that grants him a greater temporal perspective from which to view characters, society, and, ultimately, history. It sets up the perspective for the "telescope" he invokes as the optical instrument of choice for viewing the long-term unfolding of the social cosmos and the life of individuals in it.

There is something like a crescendo effect in the accumulation of inversions (and indeed inversions of inversions) and reversals as Proust describes the topsy-turvy world created and destroyed by the basic laws of time—of which the war is a form of acceleration. This inversion of the world is part of what one calls a carnivalesque perspective: from this perspective Proust creates through hyperbole a near parody of the basic laws presiding over death and birth, destruction and resurrection. In this context the reversals and inversions that the narrator encounters upon returning to society make of him an even more distant observer than he has been as an often naive participant in a bildungsroman. A few examples: consider for instance the meaning of the narrative disjuncture that occurs when he first describes his return to Paris. He begins with his second return to Paris in 1916 and not the earlier, shorter stay in 1914. This disjuncture allows him to observe at different times Gilberte and her husband, Saint-Loup, and to compare what is supposedly true at one moment with what is offered as truth at another. It also allows the narrator a distanced perspective from which to focus on the new society that the war years have created: the war has accelerated the turning over of the old social order and has installed Madame Verdurin and even the lowly Madame Bontemps at the apex of the social elite. Becoming a historian of overturning and inversion, the narrator exploits his time away to give himself the distance necessary to grasp the sudden transformation of Parisian society. In fact from his distanced perspective, he sees it as comparable to what occurred under the Directory after the French Revolution. He refers to the period when, six years after the taking of the Bastille, France became a republic governed by a committee—and Paris became the scene of extravagant fashions and an unbridled quest of pleasure while French armies were victorious in defense of the Republic. A new social order had reached the top, one soon to be toppled by Napoleon's seizing power. History is a description of successive inversions, or so the distanced narrator suggests with his comparison of the Parisian social scene of 1916 with that created in the wake of the Revolution of 1789.

A pointedly illustrative example of this topsy-turvy world is offered by an individual such as M. Bontemps. Once a noted proponent of Dreyfus who had been abominated by right-wing nationalists, he is now a fervent nationalist whose act in sponsoring legislation for three-year military service has given him the reputation of a super patriot. The "anti-patriotism, irreligion, and anarchy" of the Dreyfusards have been forgotten as the politically left-wing becomes the right and the bottom becomes the top in public consciousness (*TR,* 53). The reversal is such that Bontemps, a man of equity who once supported Dreyfus's demand for justice, is now a believer in bloody vengeance, proclaiming that justice will be done only when the German Kaiser is placed up against a wall and shot (*TR,* 55).

The narrator then recalls his first visit to Paris after going to the sanatorium, which occurred early in the war in 1914, but this only after first sketching out how society has been transformed by 1916. This narrative strategy allows him to narrate another series of contrasts stressing reversals that have occurred as the war has unfolded. Notably he says he received a letter in 1914 in which Gilberte tells him that she is returning to Tansonville to flee Paris as it may soon be occupied by the Germans. She assumed, or so she says in the first letter, that she would be safe there; however she arrived to find that the Germans were overrunning the district around Combray (*TR,* 89). In 1916, however, the narrator notes sardonically that he receives another letter from Gilberte in which she boasts of her courage in leaving the safety of Paris to face the dangers found at Tansonville. Recognizing the sagacity of her friends who had discouraged her going to her estate, she goes on to claim that she could not leave her beloved Tansonville to be defended against the Germans by her bailiff. Thus she says she went there to defend the house from the German army. This contrast of the motivation offered by the two different letters from two different times is an egregious example of the kind of reversals that Proust charts in a festive display of inconstancy, and an especially good one to demonstrate the egomaniacal power of rationalization.

Moreover the final effect of Gilberte's letter is to turn the narrator's picture of the world upside down, for she claims that Combray, the unknown region of the narrator's youth, the site of his obscure personal paradise, has now become a world-historical place: "Probably, like me, you did not imagine that obscure Roussainville and boring Méséglise, where our letters used to be brought from and where the doctor was once fetched when you were ill, would ever become famous places. Well, my dear friend, they have become forever a part of history, with the same claim to glory as Austerlitz or Valmy. The battle of Méséglise lasted for more than eight months; the Germans lost in it more than six hundred thousand men, they destroyed Méséglise, but they did not capture it" (*TR*, 95).

Proust's evenhanded irony is at work in this transformation of paradise into hell, for Gilberte points out, with pride, that the French also contributed to the destruction by blowing up a bridge he once knew well. The reversal is completed later when he learns, from a conversation with the Baron de Charlus, that the church at Combray has been leveled—by which side it is not clear. In short the paradise of Combray has become world famous even as it is blasted into nothingness thanks to the march of history and its destructive processes. Moreover the example of the church produces a notable inversion of an inversion, for the obscure church achieves worldwide fame now because of its nonexistence.

The narrator's return to his memories of 1914 reintroduces Saint-Loup, whose sexual inversion does not preclude his exhibiting manly heroism and soldierly virtues—or what the narrator calls a "certain conventional idea of virility" that, borrowed from the average male's self-image, the homosexual projects as his ideal (*TR*, 78). Proust's play with the concept of inversion takes its full resonance in the ironies about Saint-Loup's conventional masculinity. Other forms of inversion are also centered on Saint-Loup, for example, in his claims to know what is going on in the war. Pointedly his superior knowledge of warfare does not make him a reliable source of information about it, for in 1914 he argues, bookishly, that the war will be short. Needless to say that argument has been turned on its head by 1916.

Later in *Time Regained*, perhaps the most interesting reversal centering on Saint-Loup is that he is able to aestheticize the war, to transform the spectacle of death and destruction into something resembling an operatic performance. In effect Proust transforms war scenes into a nocturnal spectacle as he reverses the polarities of night and day. This occurs in 1916 when Saint-Loup comes to the narrator's room in Paris and begins to describe his reaction to the nocturnal vision of war in the Parisian sky, which, the narrator admits, "had in fact looked marvelously beautiful from our balcony when the silence of the night was broken by a display that was more than a display because it was real" (*TR*, 98). Saint-Loup completes this reversal of conventional expectations with a comparison of the war scene to an opera. With no little irony, he draws upon the German repertoire and compares the airplanes and their pilots to Wagner's Valkyries. The narrator observes that the simile is not misleading, for in the play of the searchlights on the dark sky, "each pilot, as he soared thus above the town, itself now transported into the sky, resembled indeed a Valkyrie" (*TR*, 100). (This aestheticizing of destruction is something rather foreign to English literature about the Great War, though the reader may turn to the poetry of frontline soldier Guillaume Apollinaire to find in French comparable praise of the "marvels of the war.") In fine the revelation of the beauty in destruction depicted in *Time Regained* turns over all normal expectations and prepares the reader for other inversions.

Night replaces day in the novel when the world is totally inverted. This inversion is motivated realistically by the war, but the narrator then undertakes a descent into night, which is also a topos that has a long history outside the realist tradition. It is to this topos that Proust explicitly appeals after the nocturnal aestheticizing of the war, first in the narrator's encounter with Saint-Loup, then during the walk with Charlus taking place in 1916. Day again becomes night, and the poles of the world of the novel are inverted. In effect the conventional world is again turned upside down, and it is for this reason that I have called Proust's narration, with its reversal of conventional polarities, a carnivalesque celebration. The Russian literary theorist Bakhtin can be credited with the development of the concept of the carnivalesque in literature. In modern literature he saw carnivalesque reversal best exemplified in Dostoyevsky's fiction, especially in those moments when Dostoyevsky brings together assemblies of characters and allows them, at pivotal moments in the narration, to enact the destruction of their own beliefs and even their sanity through scandal, hysterics, and wildly agonistic encounters. Bakhtin argued that this inversion or turning over of conventional values, norms, and expectations is the essence of the carnivalesque, which is found in a long tradition running from the classics of antiquity such as Lucian's *Menippus, or a Journey to the Kingdom of the Dead* and Petronius's *Satyricon* through the Renaissance in the works of Rabelais and Cervantes and culminating in Dostoyevsky. Bakhtin argued that the goal of this type of satirical and burlesque narration is actually to bring about the renewal of cultural life through the criticism and destruction of old cultural forms. Carnival turns things over in order to raise them up: resurrection and renewal are its end products.[1]

It is of course noteworthy that Proust himself documents his debt to Dostoyevsky, for example with the lecture on Dostoyevsky the narrator gives Albertine in *The Captive* when he explains to her "the new kind of beauty that Dostoievsky brought to the world" (*C*, 509). But Dostoyevsky's influence on Proust is a secondary issue.[2] What is of interest in *Time Regained* is the way Proust undertakes a carnivalesque destruction of conventional notions and perception, of cultural forms and icons—in short of the world the narrator has come to know.

Perhaps the greatest carnivalesque episode in *Time Regained* is centered on Baron de Charlus, during which the baron achieves the status of one of the great carnivalesque characters of world literature. The episode begins with the narrator's walk with the baron. Their walk takes place during the war in 1916, at the end of day, though the narration itself flits back and forth in time as the narrator recalls events the baron tells him about the past, and he even goes forward in time to relate that, after Charlus's death, he later learned that the distraught baron once threatened to kill Morel. In terms of duration, the walk itself moves forward continuously as a descent into night, to culminate, after the narrator and the baron have separated, in the extravagant scenes in which Charlus is flagellated in the male brothel.

The walk begins quite precisely when, after his second return to Paris from the sanatorium, the narrator sets out to go to the home of Madame Verdurin. In the street he encounters a man who appears to be cruising two Zouaves. With comic predictability the lascivious admirer of the soldiers turns out to be Charlus (*TR*, 107). Sketching out for the reader what has become of the baron in the preceding years, the narrator says that Madame Verdurin has succeeded with her venom in discrediting him almost entirely. His sexual proclivities are widely known in all circles now, and in addition he is considered an unpatriotic defeatist because of his pro-German sympathies. The baron's views have also been publicized by his former protégé Morel, for the musician uses his position in a press office to vilify the baron. The fact that the baron is a courageously outspoken critic of the war has led to his becoming a pariah.

He is a fallen hero as well as a comic invert. If there is a tragic dimension to Charlus—and the narrator later compares him to King Lear—it lies perhaps in his raging defiance of society, especially as embodied in Madame Verdurin and her upwardly mobile clan, after he has been exiled from it. The comparison with tragedy is justified by the images of Charlus presented now in his towering decrepitude and then again, supposedly years later after the war, when the narrator encounters him immediately before attending the reception at the Princess of Guermantes (whose title now belongs to the remarried Madame Verdurin). The baron remains through *Time Regained* a grand outcast, the symbol of the carnivalesque inverted world—with an even more extravagant play on "inverted" than any other character—for he is at once elevated and fallen, and his fall only serves to underscore his elevation.

For Bakhtin it is by inverting the world of convention that art allows the truth to spring forth. This idea is literally illustrated by the baron, especially by his refusal of the lies of official war propaganda passed off as the truth. Much of the baron's pro-German feeling springs from the fact that he cannot stand the lies told by the French propaganda machine—he cannot tolerate the mendacity of the nationalist essays that an opportunist such as Brichot now writes—and so he sets himself against the lying official sources. He points out that he knows the truth by simply reversing whatever they say. As the narrator recognizes, this understanding of truth resembles the reason in madness found in *King Lear*. Or from another perspective the baron shows up lies by comparing competing claims. He shows himself illuminated by lucid reason when, walking in the darkness of night, he declares to the narrator that, depressingly, each combatant country, with its conventional truths, says the same thing: "The reasons for which the industrialists of Germany declare the possession of Belfort indispensable for safeguarding their nation against our ideas of revenge, are the very same reasons as those which Barrès [a French nationalist writer] gives for demanding Mainz as a protection against the recurrent urge to invade which possesses the Boches. Why is it that the recovery of Alsace-Lorraine seemed to France an insufficient motive for embarking on a war, yet a sufficient motive for continuing one, for redeclaring it afresh year after year?" (*TR*, 155). Viewed from below all high-placed official liars look the same; or as the baron astutely notes, without attribution of nationality, one cannot differentiate the words of the German emperor Wilhelm from those of the French president Raymond Poincaré (*TR*, 159).

This illumination produced by reason is a moment of lucidity in the darkness, which is to say, in the darkness generated by a war that only madness could produce in the first place. It is also a moment of reason in the baron's own near-insane arrogance in which he performs, now in self-parody, the enactment of his pretensions to grandeur and superiority. This parody is another aspect of a high carnivalesque reversal. His sense of his aristocratic worth has not been diminished a jot by his fall, so that in his megalomania he can, like Lear, while speaking with total lucidity, parody himself with the most absurd statements. Or as the narrator observes, "So systematic was his frivolity that for him birth, combined with beauty and with other sources of prestige, was the durable thing and the war, like the Dreyfus case, merely a vulgar and fugitive fashion" (*TR*, 141). Thus the baron finds it to be quite appropriate that the grand master of the Order of Malta, a pure German, continues to live in the enemy city of Rome, since aristocrats are above mere national declarations of war. Accordingly the baron believes that if the Duchess of Guermantes were shot for trying to make her own separate peace with Austria, she would be no more dishonored by this "mischance" than was the Austrian Marie Antoinette for having been condemned by the French to the guillotine (*TR*, 141). He can hold that the pro-German czar of the Bulgars is an "out-and-out nancy and a monstrous liar" ("une pure coquine, une vraie affiche") but nonetheless is very intelligent since he likes the baron a great deal (*TR*, 142). The baron is a megalomaniac whose comic deviation from the rational norm allows him in fact, by a reversal of the reversal, to embody a rational norm by which can be measured the deviations of other characters, be they nationalists, opportunistic patriots, or skillful social climbers.

The narrator's promenade with the baron comes to an end when the baron looks at the stars in the night. He acquires another role in this passage, in which he resembles an Old Testament prophet right before descending into the depths of the brothel. It then appears that the baron embodies at once the sodomite and his opposite, the righteous prophet who condemns him. The setting for this series of reversals is a night now illuminated by moonlight that "was like a soft and steady magnesium flare" by whose light a camera might have been recording, "for the last time," the groups of well-known Parisian buildings the narrator and the baron walk by (*TR*, 164). The prophetic baron foresees that Paris may be the next Pompeii, a city about to be buried beneath the lava of some German Vesuvius. With the pleasure of one soon to be vindicated, he predicts that German guns may well bury the living in the cellars in which they take refuge. The baron towers in the night above the present moment as he foresees a catastrophic end for Paris, not like that of a pagan city such as Roman Herculaneum but in a disaster brought forth by the biblical curse that his own life calls upon the city. His oration ends with words that mirror his very Christian sense of the sin embodied in his own sodomy: "If I reflect that tomorrow we may suffer the fate of the cities of Vesuvius, these in their turn sensed that they were threatened with the doom of the accursed cities of the Bible. On the wall of a house in Pompeii has been found the revealing inscription: Sodoma, Gomora" (*TR*, 170). So comes to an end the baron's soliloquy, with his casting an anathema upon the French for their dilettantism, as he becomes a parodic prophet of destruction.

One asks, has the baron in his performance been an aristocratic clown endowed with reason, a buffoon who judges events rationally as the fool does in *King Lear;* or is he simply a garrulous old man who in his arrogance does not really understand the forces of destruction that modernity has unleashed about him? All viewpoints are partially true, with the baron's constant reversals in attitude setting off each perspective against the other. Finally his evocation of the destruction of Sodom and Gomorrah not only conjures up the novel's allegorical development and the education that the narrator had undergone but also points to the baron's own knowledge that he has continually transgressed the Christian law that he deeply believes in. The forthcoming scene in the male brothel amply demonstrates this contradictory self-overturning. There he willingly transgresses the law in the name of the sin and guilt that procure him the pleasure he greatly enjoys atoning for.

The descent into night continues as the narrator, alone after the baron's departure, continues to walk the nocturnal streets of Paris. He finds himself gradually losing himself as if he were in "the hidden quarters of Baghdad" in the *Arabian Nights*, that is, in a poor area that "poverty, dereliction, fear inhabit" (*TR*, 173). It is almost as if the narrator were lost in a dream, for only thus could he lose himself in a city he knows well, though of course he is also in a wartime blackout. In the night, now identified as a literary descendant of Caliph Harun al-Rachid, he finds that the only place that is lit up is a hotel. It turns out that it is a *maison de passe* for homosexuals, which, as the allusion to the *Arabian Nights* suggests, is also a place where are found, in the unfolding of tales of the night, fictions and metamorphoses. At first the narrator does not recognize the nature of this brothel any more than he realizes that the shadowy figure who exits before he enters is probably Saint-Loup (who, it appears, has lost a military medal there). The narrator enters, desirous of drink and shelter, and finds a group of men marked as lower class by their language. The men remark on the war and politics while making what are at first some enigmatic references to chains and beating.

The narrator is taken to a room, has a drink, and then, motivated by curiosity, goes up to the top floor and hears the sound of a beating taking place behind a closed door. He finds a small window through which he can view, without being seen, the spectacle in the room that is the source of the uproar. He hears a voice pleading not to be hit so hard: the voice is that of the Baron de Charlus, who is having himself flagellated while pretending that he is being tortured by a notorious villain. The scene of inverted fantasy is symmetrical to the scene in Combray in which the youthful narrator hides to view the scene of lesbian sadism at Montjouvain. At Montjouvain he discovers sadism as the enjoyment of evil inflicted upon another, though it must occur symbolically in a staged fiction, since Vinteuil is dead and only his photo is present to create the sense of guilt that his daughter and her lover enjoy when they defile him. Hence their pleasure is a fantasy found in imagining the suffering they would cause him if he were to view their frolics. (One may recall such a scene causes the mother's stroke in "A Young Girl's Confession" in *Pleasures and Days*.) The notable difference between "Combray" and the brothel of *Time Regained* is that in his masochism—a word missing from Proust's vocabulary—Charlus wants real physical pain to accompany his self-abasement. And he wants to imagine that "real" thugs carry out the rape and torture—though it appears they are just working-class fellows wanting to earn some easy money. Thus the baron must rely upon his fantasy to imagine that genuine evil is being done to him, though it is also clear that his masochistic imagination requires vigorous stimulation, at least at the baron's age, for him to take pleasure in evil. Furthermore it is another of Proust's ironic reversals that part of Charlus's punishment is that no one genuinely evil enough can be found to profane him with sufficiently hard blows for him to take pleasure in his remorse for his pleasure.

The narrator sees in the torturers men who "in a vague way" were substitutes for Morel, the baron's protégé who has jilted him (*TR*, 185). The psychosexual dynamics of the baron's need for punishment, and the need to enjoy that need, suggest the complexity of his amorous attachment to the violinist. Though the narrator says he has no real idea as to what went on in the relationship between the baron and Morel, he does speculate that this violence may be a surrogate for what Charlus could not have with his protégé. This is a significant case of Proust limiting the narrator's vision so as to suggest dimensions beyond even his capacity for analysis.

What I am calling the carnivalesque dimension in *Time Regained* is quite clearly at work when the narrator subsequently encounters the hotel's manager. It turns out that the hotel is managed by Jupien, the tailor whose lubricious antics with the baron revealed Sodom to the young narrator years earlier. Jupien tells the narrator he now manages the brothel for the baron. He is an intelligent, cynical viewer who is well positioned to view the world from below, from the depths of the netherworld, as it were. With Jupien's lucid conversation with the narrator, Proust completes the narrator's voyage to the end of the night and the overturning of norms and conventions. To the narrator's surprise, Jupien offers an apology for inversions—in all senses of the word, including turning the world on its head. He understands the world in quite carnivalesque terms, for he knows that the fictions he stages in his hotel exist for the purpose of overturning the highest notions of virtue and thereby affirming them. Indeed he praises his hotel and its social function. He says that in it, "contrary to the doctrine of the Carmelites, it is thanks to vice that virtue is able to live" (*TR*, 202). The Carmelites are a Catholic religious order, under special consideration of the Virgin Mary, for whom virtue consists in silent meditative prayer—rather much the contrary of the baron's groaning in pain and pleasure. Illustrating his carnivalesque understanding of vice, Jupien points out to the narrator that the scenes of sadism and masochism he stages are negative affirmations of the Christian order of the world, represented here for Jupien by the aspirations of the Carmelites. By inverting these aspirations and the moral code they represent, he knows that the baron also accepts them. Transgression presupposes the code to be transgressed. Otherwise there would be no frisson given by the pleasure of committing evil. Although one may have some doubts about virtue's need of sadomasochism in order to survive, there is no doubt that in *Time Regained* the mimed destruction of Christian values is a carnivalesque parody through which the highest values are affirmed by their negation—in the baron's masochistic atonement. In Jupien's staging of victimization, the baron's need to suffer at the hands of imaginary thugs affirms his belief in the tenets of decency and conventional morality that condemn him for the pleasurable if ghastly indecency he stages for himself. The baron is throughout the novel a good Christian believer.

Charlus's situation is not unlike that of the lewd carnival reveler who needs the carnival mask to hide his identity, for that need to hide affirms the moral order that the reveler is intent upon violating. It does not lessen the pleasure, however. Indeed it heightens it.

The narrator, however, is aghast at the theater of debasement he has seen and tells Jupien that his hotel is worse than a madhouse, since in the hotel the "mad fancies of the lunatics who inhabit it are played out as actual, visible drama—it is a veritable pandemonium" (*TR*, 206). The narrator understands nonetheless that what he has seen are acts stimulating the imagination, much like literature: for he goes on to say that what he has witnessed, here in the imagined Baghdad night, is not a crime but something like a tale from the *Arabian Nights* "in which a woman who has been turned into a dog willingly submits to being beaten in order to recover her former shape" (*TR*, 206). Beating restores virtue as well as human form. However the narrator's comparison also points out that he has entered a realm of metamorphoses in which the order of the world is at best tentative.

Jupien retorts with his own interpretation of his work, for he suggests a different use of the *Arabian Nights* by telling the narrator that he once saw a copy of *Sesame and Lilies* at the baron's house, a book whose title suggests an idea to him. He proposes that the narrator come to the hotel again for more spectacle. The narrator will know whether Jupien is present at the hotel if a light is shining in a small window, for that will be the "sesame" that opens the "cave" in which he can descend to view the thieves within (*TR*, 206–7). But as the philosophical brothel keeper observes, the lilies referred to in the book's title are to be found elsewhere: the hotel offers only a netherworld in which, as in the *Arabian Nights,* one enters a cave wherein are kept treasures of evil. Where the lilies are is left an open question.

With the overt reference to Ruskin's *Sesame and Lilies,* Proust plays a curious rhetorical game. He steps obliquely into the text with an indirect reference to himself, the author who once translated Ruskin's book. Some of Proust's personal appearances may be due to a lapsus, such as the narrator's use of the name "Marcel," but the reference to the book by Ruskin that he translated hardly seems to be negligence. The translation of Ruskin's *Sesame and Lilies* is attributed in fact to the narrator by the narrator himself, who had given a copy to the baron. Reflecting on the fact that Proust himself translated these Ruskin lectures obliges the reader to do a kind of double reading to grasp his self-directed irony: Proust is at once in the text as an allusive presence and outside it mocking his own literary pretentions. He is perhaps reversing in carnivalesque fashion his own stance toward the novel, taking on the narrator as his comic mask. With this, perhaps he is offering a "sesame" for entering his world while suggesting that the lilies one might yearn for do indeed grow elsewhere—perhaps in Ruskin's religion of art or perhaps at the end of the novel Proust himself is hoping to finish with its vision of resurrection that will positively affirm the world now fallen into total darkness—except for a light in the brothel. Before this world can be redeemed, Proust qua author points out, it seems, that he has taken his narrator into a netherworld of destruction that is symbolized as well by a cave full of thieves as by a hotel for gay masochists plunged into the dark night of an air raid.

However another salient example of authorial intervention occurs midway through of *Time Regained* dealing with the war, with a quite different effect, this time offering an example of lilies, as it were. The narrator qua author offers praise of what he says is the example of generosity on the part of a real couple in the real world who have come to the rescue of a relative who is in need because her husband, a cousin of the maid Françoise, was killed in the war. This a strange intervention, since a purportedly real husband is the cousin of a fictional character. This may suggest Proust had some difficulty in separating his fiction from his life as it was coming to an end. Or it can well be taken as part of a strategy by which he wanted to offset the darkness into which he had cast his fictional novelistic world: with an allusion to real light in the real world. Be that as it may, one intent is clear. After charting the world's capsizing into the depths of the night, with his homage Proust wants to bring it back, momentarily at least, to a world in which heroic virtue really exists, as it undoubtedly did during the war in which many a Frenchman bore testimony to what the narrator calls, referring to the couple's charity, an example of "the greatness of France, her greatness of soul, her greatness after the fashion of Saint-André-des-Champs, a kind of conduct displayed as much by thousands of civilians living in safety far from the front as by the soldiers who fell at the Marne" (*TR*, 224).

The narrator refers here to the church Saint-André-des-Champs, near Combray, that seems to embody for him, in his recollections of Combray, all the virtues of medieval France represented in the very stone of the church's facade. And this vision of, or belief in, the rebirth of medieval virtue is also conveyed immediately afterward in the narration when the narrator describes the death of his friend Saint-Loup on the battlefield. This aristocrat—a Guermantes whom the narrator views at times as the embodiment of the Middle Ages—gives himself unstintingly in death to the men he commands: "Later I had come to understand the many great virtues and something else as well which lay concealed behind his elegant appearance. All this, the good as the bad, he had given without counting the cost, every day, as much on the last day when he advanced to attack a trench, out of generosity and because it was his habit to place at the service of others all that he possessed, as on that evening when he had run along the backs of the seats in the restaurant in order not to disturb me" (*TR*, 227).

Society may be undergoing upheaval, the aristocratic ethos that Saint-Loup incarnated is disappearing in a bourgeois world that counts the cost of everything, but for this moment, Proust suggests, the trends of modernity have been reversed in the heroic death of a nobleman in whom the values of the Middle Ages live on. The world has been temporarily set aright by again being turned over. This affirmation is a unique moment in the narration.

The narrator's discovery of his vocation comes years after his descent into the night during the war. It occurs only shortly before he enters the reception given at the Prince de Guermantes's mansion. In elapsed time the descent and the reception are distant, but in narrative effect they are conjoined to act as a kind of frame for the narrator's discovery that he might be able to resurrect the past. I refer now to the series of revelations taking the form of involuntary memories the narrator has in the courtyard. His thoughts on resurrection are directly juxtaposed with the reception and the sight of its *danse macabre* that shows the ultimate decline and fall of the entire society he has known. The quick series of memories in the courtyard gives rise to the narrator's meditation on what this kind of memory might mean. At this point Proust inserts something like an essay on the novel before continuing the narration of carnivalesque destruction enacted at the reception. I will presently comment on the significance the narrator attributes to these epiphanic memories afforded by sensory experience. They are among the most discussed aspects of the entire novel. This is partly because they seem to offer an interpretation of the novel set in the novel itself; and partly because it is not entirely clear what Proust intends to accomplish by the narrator's meditation of what he has discovered about his vocation. In any case I propose that these revelations of the possibility of resurrection take on their full meaning only when framed by the preceding walk to the end of the night and then the subsequent revelation of the final destruction time has wrought upon the narrator's world. It is this latter vision of the final fall into time, narrated in the spirit of carnivalesque parody, that sets out the necessity of the narrator's meditation on a possible future in which he might redeem this fallen world.

Let us consider the reception taking place some years after the end of the war. Upon his return to postwar Paris, after some indefinite number of years in the sanatorium, the narrator decides to go to a reception given by the Princess of Guermantes, now the remarried Madame Verdurin. He is as disenchanted with life as he was at the beginning of *Time Regained*. His attitude is summed up in his statement that he continues to believe that nature has nothing to tell him. In a state of near anomie with regard to life and art, he thinks he has nothing to lose by wasting his time at a meaningless event such as a Parisian social gathering. Proust undoubtedly conceived the narrator's alienation as a necessary state, as an emptiness waiting to be filled, before he can discover his vocation to bring about some fullness. However one interprets the series of positive revelations he receives in the courtyard, it is clear that they are followed up immediately by the negative revelation that the laws of physiology have been at work transforming, in near parody, the social elite while the narrator has been away. The narrator enters the room in which the reception is held to discover that merciless time has grotesquely transformed his acquaintances assembled there. Metamorphosis in time has turned them into aging marionettes whose forthcoming demise is inscribed comically in their hair, their expressions, and their flesh. Their flesh has taken on the appearance of carnival masks. Thus the effect on the narrator is that after the preceding discovery in the courtyard of his possible vocation, the world is turned upside down again. In this case the inversion is embodied in a physical transformation of the characters. They have undergone metamorphosis in conformity with the laws of human physiology, the mechanical processes of which have contrived to create a carnival scene recalling those at which late eighteenth-century Venetian painters excelled: a masked ball featuring tottering grotesques.

Proust stages the not quite metaphorical masked ball—for the masks are permanent—as a series of surprise encounters that are so many reversals of the narrator's expectations. In a sense these reversals begin even before he arrives at the reception, for he chances upon Baron de Charlus, escorted by the ever-attentive Jupien, as they go along the Champs-Élysées. Tottering under the effect of recent illnesses, the decrepit baron is nonetheless grand in his decline, with a forest of white hair, which the narrator says confers upon him "the Shakespearian majesty of a King Lear"—suggesting perhaps Jupien is to be likened to a faithful Kent (TR, 245). After this sight of magnificent fall from grandeur, and after the revelations he experiences in the courtyard, the narrator goes into the main Guermantes drawing room to find himself in the midst of the reception that Proust once thought of calling le bal des têtes (the masked ball). The narrator's first impression is that all in attendance have put on a disguise, since they wear white wigs. The Prince sets the tone for disguise with his white beard and dragging feet. The narrator then sees that the "young Fezensac" had not used dye for his disguise but had "found some means of covering his features with wrinkles and making his eyebrows sprout with bristles" (TR, 337). A servant calls out the name "Duc de Châtellerault," which seems to refer to "a little elderly man with the silvery moustaches of an ambassador" in whom survives "a tiny fragment" of what the narrator can remember of the young aristocrat he first met at Madame de Villeparisis's tea party (TR, 337). And so it continues until the narrator realizes that the disguises are not flattering because they are not intentional (TR, 340). Finally comes the recognition that he, too, is playing in the charade of metamorphosis when the aging Duchess de Guermantes, with her "salmon-pink body almost concealed by its fins of black lace and throttled by jewels," looked upon by the others as if she were "some archaic sacred fish," greets him with the salutation, "you, my oldest friend" (TR, 346). He is taken aback, because anybody who should be able to claim to be her oldest friend—Swann, M. de Bréauté, M. de Forestelle—is now dead.

As the description of the duchess shows, Proust relies upon metaphors for this comedy of metamorphosis, though one metaphor is dominant:

a performance of marionettes. Mayor's translation uses the term *puppet show,* though this is not literally in the text (*TR,* 342). However *puppet show* captures well the text's intent, for the narrator views the guests as "poupées"—literally dolls—and then calls them "vielliards fantoches," or "old people marionettes" who dance on the strings of time. They are thus dolls or puppets one must identity, as the narrator says, by reading "what was written on several planes at once, planes that lay behind the visible aspect of the puppets and gave them depth and forced one . . . to make a strenuous intellectual effort; one was obliged to study them at the same time with one's eyes and with one's memory" (*TR,* 342). Derisive dolls, puppets, feeble masked revelers, all these images concur to portray the world turned over through derisive carnival images portraying the work of time. These are comic images, not only for the grotesque metamorphoses but also because the narrator views them through the lens of hyperbolic distortion, which cuts both ways. For the narrator seems as naive as his acquaintances are grotesque. With this image Proust's comedy affirms at once the power of the laws of time and their destructive regularity even as the narrator's mock astonishment ironically belittles the observer himself as he reports on time's work. The mock astonishment, however, implies that the narrator must recover his intellectual acuity before he can be taken seriously, even by himself. This acts as a kind of caveat about his reliability that weighs upon the conclusion of the novel.

With an overall view of the narrative development in mind, culminating in the parade of grotesques, one sees the ingenuity of Proust's narrative strategy. He at once affirms historical reality in the portrayal of the war years while refusing traditional realism when he sends his narrator off for an indefinite period of time in an unnamed sanatorium. Thereby the narrator can return and, with justified naïveté, observe with mock astonishment the laws of time finally made visible at work. He is able to see "Time which by habit is made invisible" when, seizing upon bodies, it shines "its magic lantern upon them":

As immaterial now as Golo long ago on the doorknob of my room at Combray, the new, the unrecognizable Argencourt was there before me as the revelation of Time, which by his agency was rendered partially visible, for in the new elements which went to compose his face and his personality one could decipher a number which told one the years of his age, one could recognize the hiero-glyphy of life—of life not as it appears to us, that is to say perma-nent, but as it really is: an atmosphere so swiftly changing that at the end of the day the proud nobleman is portrayed, in caricature, as a dealer in old clothes. (*TR,* 342)

The narrator comes thus to an atemporal view of the laws of time that, in producing the carnivalesque metamorphoses, turn the noble into a bum and the courtly beauty into a hag. These transformations affect more than individuals. If we enlarge upon Proust's view of time, it appears that he wants to demonstrate that social movements and the overturning of classes are part of a constant historical process produced by time—if that is not a mere tautology but perhaps a meaningful tautology. Historical processes are the unending metamorphosis affecting all things human. From this perspective it then appears that vagaries about precise historical referents in Proust's novel indirectly translates an ahistorical view of history: the historical process is, finally, always the same at any moment, since it is relentless metamorphosis. This ahistorical historicism explains why dates and years lose their importance. The novel's lack of chronological precision irritates many readers, and critics have often attempted to pin events to a public chronology they concoct for it. With regard to the period after the war, for example, it requires little historical acuity to note that the narrator makes a reference to an influenza epidemic, which recalls the well-known fact that the Spanish flu ran rampant in 1919. But it makes little sense to read the text by, say, trying to date the Guermantes reception with respect to the epidemic. At this point historical reference is not only beside the point but really against the text's intent. The narrator finds himself present at the masque of aging puppets simply "many years" later—from any point in time one might care to select. His perspective might be likened to the one granted by the time of scientific laws, or with the time of the eternal recurrence implied by the carnival's denial and affirmation. Thus it would make as much sense to ask what year the reception takes place as to ask when the law of gravity works or when autumn occurs. Time affixes a mask to all, at every moment. To be sure Proust offers a comic variant on eternal recurrence by showing that an expert in metamorphosis such as Odette may seem to defy time, though only briefly, for the narrator does a flash-forward to describe her finally succumbing to time's laws a few years later.

Having made this argument about Proust's ahistorical historicism, I would immediately concede that he has also created a remarkably accurate portrayal of the demise of the aristocracy that we readers know did take place, in part because of the war years.

In conclusion to this commentary on the characters' metamorphosis, I note that the narrator integrates into his description a contrasting note of rejuvenation. At first glance Proust seems to introduce a young person to allow his narrator to make an exposition of his views on hereditary. Proust's views of genetics are of minor interest in themselves. His belief in the mechanical acquisition of hereditary traits is of a piece with the genetics of late nineteenth-century medicine. With no causal specificity, medicine explained, almost by definition, the recurrence of traits that characters share with their relatives (and at times Proust rather exaggerates the specificity of these traits). But the notion of genetics as a harbinger of constant recurrence brings the narrator back to nature, and what is important in the novel and especially at the Guermantes reception is that heredity is ultimately in the service of nature—and thereby the idea of resurrection. One sees this affirmation of rejuvenation and resurrection, appropriately in the final moments of the reception, when the narrator meets Gilberte's daughter. The girl is the embodiment of all that has preceded in the novel in that she is the reincarnation of Swann and Odette, Gilberte and Saint-Loup, and even of the narrator himself, as he concludes after judging how much of Guermantes and how much of Swann is present in this sixteen-year-old: "It seemed to me wonderful that at the critical moment nature should have returned, like a great and original sculptor, to give to the granddaughter, as she had given to her mother and her grandmother, that significant and decisive touch of the chisel. I thought her very beautiful: still rich in hopes, full of laughter, formed from those very years which I myself had lost, she was like my own youth" (*TR, 507*).

The sight of this reprise of all that is past is a positive vision, affirming nature, and it is a spur to the narrator to contemplate a quest that would resurrect the time that Mlle de Saint-Loup incarnates in her beauty. She is the image of recurrent resurrection that, as Bakhtin has it, is the ultimate goal of carnival's destruction—or as Proust has it, a redemptory goal for a writer seeking a vocation.

In striking contrast with this vision of resurrection offered by the young woman at the reception is the finale of the great actress of the narrator's youth, Berma. She is humiliated without pity by Rachel, the tart who, after being Saint-Loup's mistress, has become a well-known actress. True, even Rachel is now a wretched old woman who, perhaps raging against time, is merciless in stripping Berma of all recognition, even to the point of causing Berma's child to desert her for the chance to come to the Guermantes reception. This drama of humiliation offers a final image of the drama of social relations. With it Proust mirrors the drama of social change that can be viewed as an ongoing theatrical performance. Comparably one also learns that Madame Verdurin has seen two husbands die in the saddle, but she has continued her performance as social prima donna with her marriage to the aging Prince of Guermantes—marking thus her final triumph over Lear-Charlus now wandering on the Champs-Élysées, a name perhaps now to be recalled in its Greek sense of the Elysian fields. Her final role is to play the Princess of Guermantes. These images stand in contrast to the image of Swann's granddaughter, who perhaps represents an image of nature set against society, so that taken together they sketch out the polarities of the narrator's world as he comes to the moment of decision with regard to his vocation.

In this way Proust's play of affirmation and negation brings the narrator to his final chance to overcome procrastination as he undertakes to fulfill his vocation. His project would be now nothing less than to triumph over the laws of time—by being the writer he has never become. In a sense his task would be to resurrect all that he has previously experienced in the novel that the reader has just read. At the novel's ending, however, it appears that the narrator is not overly optimistic about his chances of overcoming time's laws: he is old now, and he must needs live a good many years if he is to succeed in his project. The skepticism he expresses about his vocation is undoubtedly a reflection of the growing pessimism Proust felt about the chances for resurrection through art. In any case it is an understatement to say that his narrator faces the future with subdued optimism: "No doubt my books too, like my fleshly being, would in the end one day die. But death is a thing that we must resign ourselves to. We accept the thought that in ten years we ourselves, in a hundred years our books, will have ceased to exist. Eternal duration is promised no more to men's works than to men" (*TR*, 524).

One hundred years after publication of the first volume, we can say that at least Proust himself has exceeded his narrator's expectations, though that is not quite the same thing as the narrator's meeting, or not, his own expectations. What can we say about the novel that the narrator hopes to write in the future? Many critics think that the novel Proust wrote is in fact the novel that the narrator will write, or indeed has written, though I do not think there is anything in the narrator's discussion of his vocation, or elsewhere, to indicate that the novel Proust has written is the novel that the narrator plans to write. However there is nothing in Proust's novel that says it is not the novel the narrator would write or, at least, hopes to write. Let us say, minimally, the novel that Proust has in fact written perforce greatly resembles the novel the narrator would like to write, were he to have the time to undertake and complete the resurrection of his own past. But Proust's novel is open-ended with regard to whether the narrator will succeed. The last sentence of *Time Regained* suggests doubts, although the sentence could also be read as a description of the novel the reader has just finished reading: "So, if I were given long enough to accomplish my work, I should not fail, even if the effect were to make them resemble monsters, to describe men as occupying so considerable a place, compared with the restricted place which is reserved for them in space, a place on the contrary prolonged past measure, for simultaneously, like giants plunged into the years, they touch the distant epochs through which they have lived between, which so many days have come to range themselves—in Time" (*TR*, 532).

One can argue that this last sentence describes the novel to which it is the concluding sentence, not least of all for the immediately preceding scenes of the "monsters" living in time presented at the Guermantes reception. The sentence also seems to describe the novel's unfolding through epochs, and thus to apply to those many characters whom the reader has followed throughout the years of, and before, the narrator's life. And so one might say that logically Proust's novel is the novel the narrator would like to write, since it narrates the experience he must resurrect. Or alternatively his novel surely would not differ much from Proust's, though the narrator's novel might have an ending saying that he has finished the novel for which he once discovered his vocation in the courtyard of the Guermantes mansion.

Let us step back from the novel's last sentence to consider a larger context for what the narrator conceives to be his vocation and his future project. Up to the concluding volume, *Time Regained,* the interpretation of *In Search of Lost Time* I have proposed has been that the central project of Proust's novel is to describe an education that unfolds as a prolonged fall from paradise. The fall is to be understood as a central metaphor or allegorical figure characterizing the narrator's development in time. Proust's use of Christian tropes is recurrent, if not constant, throughout the book, and from this perspective it is hardly surprising that the narrator couches his discovery of his vocation largely in Christian terms, to wit, in terms of resurrection. His discovery of his vocation comes as the revelation of what he must do to realize a resurrection. And if one accepts a carnivalesque reading of *Time Regained,* then the theme of resurrection is also emphasized by the need to overcome the inversion of existence itself. However it is notable that in *Time Regained* the narrator also uses other figures to describe the artist's vocation, drawing mainly upon the tradition of romantic poetry as well as contemporary science.

In fact by the time the narrator has worked out his project to be a writer, by the novel's end, much of the metaphorical inspiration provided by the Christian notions of salvation and resurrection have lost their central, overriding function. There is one Christian axiom, however, that is never stated as such but that remains central to an explanation of what the narrator means in *Time Regained* by the notion of aesthetic resurrection: for him one meaning of resurrection is given by the idea of Parousia. Parousia is a New Testament notion, translated into English as the "second coming" of Jesus (in Matthew 24, for example). It is a term replete with all the nuances of Greek metaphysics, for it can mean that with the resurrection comes the plenitude entailed by the recovery of the totality of one's being. In simpler terms the full significance of Parousia is given by medieval representations of the dead climbing out of their tombs with a literalness that is difficult for us to entertain today, since for the medieval religious imagination, the resurrection entailed by the doctrine of Parousia signifies the return of the full presence of the concrete body with all its fleshly appurtenances. Proust's imagination is at times literally medieval with his narrator's demands that the recall and restoration of the past omit *nothing*—not the odor of a single madeleine. The restored "presence" or Parousia brought about by resurrection means that every moment of the past, every detail of a life, every relationship held by a being, must be fully restored in their total, lived plenitude.

Parousia is another trope, unspoken but patently guiding Proust's way in formulating the demands of fiction and his desire to restore the plenitude of the past, or more accurately for Proust, the past as a plenitude. Earlier we saw that, in *The Fugitive,* another Christian, which is to say, neo-Platonic figure was present in the narrator's wondering if he finds in music the possibility of transcendence. He wonders if the music reveals another world characterized by a metaphysical fullness not present in this world. This theme is downplayed in *Time Regained.* Rather here the narrator places greater accent on the romantic idea that literature is a quest for the artist's inner world. It affords contact with the inner world that might offer a form of salvation, for authentic literature brings forth the true self from the hidden inner depths. This view of the self was widely developed in the nineteenth century, especially with the German romantics, then in French poets such as Rimbaud and others, including the later surrealists—and of course Freud. However the romantic idea of self is then displaced by another motif with nineteenth-century origins. Namely the neo-Kantian rationalist in Proust is given voice at the end of the novel when the narrator also conceives his vocation as an artist to be comparable to that of a scientist. For the writer's task is an epistemological quest. This means that the artist offers knowledge, knowledge of the self and hence of a unique world—springing from the artist's total inner world—which is knowledge even if it cannot be formulated in words. I am not sure that these various motifs—Christian, romantic, epistemological, or scientific—are ever coherently tied together in a total portrait of what the narrator proposes to accomplish, but Proust was not overly concerned about the need for systematic coherence. There is an Emersonian side to Proust that in no way scorned inconsistency.

These new motifs come to the fore when the disabused and perhaps despairing narrator enters the courtyard of the Guermantes mansion after his years of absence from the Parisian scene. He has just seen the once regal Baron de Charlus, who is now suffering aphasia and is thus impaired in his use of the language that made him tower above all others. Perhaps it is this sight that sets the narrator to pondering his incapacity to use language except to reproduce "snapshots" of the past—another metaphor for abstract memories. He recalls the error that the writer Bergotte made when he believed that the narrator was not to be pitied for his illness. This is because Bergotte believed that, despite his illness, the narrator nonetheless enjoyed the pleasures of the mind (*TR,* 254). However in Proust's French, Bergotte attributes to the narrator a capacity for the "joys of the *esprit,*" the latter term meaning both mind and spirit; and it turns out his mistake was probably to think the narrator was enjoying the latter, whereas the narrator says that all he has are the sterile joys of the intellect. He must find a way to have contact with his own true "spirit"—or the self that is not addressed by the intellect. This recall of the distinction of mind and spirit parallels Proust's distinction of shallow intellect and deep self, and it sets the stage for the distinctions the narrator begins to make in his meditation on the revelations he receives in the courtyard.

These revelations, though sensorial in origin, speak to the narrator's spirit or deep self. To describe these epiphanic moments, he first uses biblical metaphors. He speaks of them as the "intimation" or "warning" he receives that may save him (*TR,* 254). In French the *avertissement* the narrator receives has clear biblical overtones, for it is the term for the warning that the New Testament lays down for those who neglect their salvation and do not knock at all possible doors to find it. (This was the dilemma that tortured Pascal: in spite of the warning, he did not know where to find the door.) Chance would have it that at this moment, in crossing the courtyard, the narrator apparently knocks at the right door. With a clear allusion to Matthew 7:7, he finds that a door is opened, for he accordingly "stumbles without knowing it on the only door through which one can enter—which one might have sought in vain for a hundred years—and it opens of its own accord" (*TR,* 255). Finding the door to salvation is a matter of chance, a pessimistic idea showing that Proust is reading Christian tropes from a Jansenist perspective. Like many of their Protestant contemporaries, the Jansenists believed that salvation is indeed a matter of preordained grace, which is to say, pure chance from the lost soul's viewpoint.

The rival Jesuit doctrine that the doing of good deeds is sufficient for the acquisition of grace could hardly appeal to Proust's narrator. Indeed he has no willpower; he is a confirmed procrastinator; undoubtedly he needs the unmerited gift of grace if he is to be saved.

The narrator almost literally stumbles through the door he has been seeking when he trips on the "uneven paving-stones in front of the coach-house" (TR, 255). After his foot touches a stone, he experiences a sensation akin to that of being visited by grace, which is to say, he feels the same happiness he felt when viewing the church steeples in Martinville; or upon once tasting the madeleine dipped in lime tea; or in listening to Vinteuil's last works. In the courtyard the simple sensation of touching a stone restores to him, in all its plenitude, his experience in Venice when he stood on uneven stones in the baptistery of St. Mark's—there where, we recall, the annunciating angel seemed to hold out a promise of felicity for him (TR, 256). A comparable moment of felicity occurs twice more in quick succession: first still in the courtyard, when he hears a servant knock a spoon against a plate; and then again in the Prince's library, when he wipes his mouth with a napkin. The sound of the spoon duplicates the recent sound of a railway worker striking a wheel; and the napkin's touch recalls the feel of the towel with which he dried his face upon first arriving at Balbec many years earlier. In the association of napkin and towel, he realizes that he is enjoying not just sensations deriving from the ocean at Balbec; rather, as he says in referring to the colors and sensations of the ocean, he is experiencing a "whole instant of my life on whose summit they rested, an instant which had been no doubt an aspiration towards them and which some feeling of fatigue or sadness had prevented me from enjoying at Balbec but which now, freed from what is necessarily imperfect in external perception, pure and disembodied, caused me to swell with happiness" (TR, 259). The joy of Parousia is inscribed here in the moment of a felicity born simply of the fullness of restored being.

After the three epiphanies—and in this context the word is hardly an exaggeration—the narrator is perhaps ready to undertake a quest for permanent Parousia. He believes the task of a writer to be the resurrection of being, conceived as the total past in its plenitude and purity, a purity that had escaped him when he actually lived the past moment but which characterizes its plenitude when recalled. By resurrecting the total past, he would apparently know some form of salvation. At this point one may well wish to ask why one cannot enjoy the purity and plenitude of experience in the present moment. The impossibility is not self-evident. Hence one can ask why the experience of something in, or from, the past is better than the same experience when lived in the present. Perhaps anticipating such a question, in the quotation above the narrator refers to what he calls the "necessarily imperfect in external perception." This notion implies a psychological explanation of the superiority of the past when it is recalled: the present is always imperfect according to the narrator, because it is perturbed by "external" factors that interfere with one's perceiving the essence of one's experience. Time, through the power of oblivion, suppresses these exterior relations, these superfluous distractions intruding in the present moment, which leaves pure being in itself to be recalled from the past. Something like a theological notion again underpins this idea that in the present moment every aspect of our existence is tied up with extraneous things that "logically" have nothing to do with its essence. From this quasi-theological perspective, grace consists in forgetting so that the past is purified of the inessential and then, through the miracle of involuntary memory, recalled in its purity. Or as the narrator puts it in a revealing metaphor, in the act of pure remembrance, it is as though one were on a mountaintop where one could suddenly breathe new air, "an air which is new precisely because we have breathed it in the past, that purer air which the poets have vainly tried to situate in paradise and which could induce so profound a sensation of renewal only if it had been breathed before, since the true paradises are the paradises that we have lost" (*TR*, 261). After the opening of *Time Regained,* with its dismal scenes set in Combray, the reader can have no doubt that the narrator has lost paradise. And the narrator continues to doubt that he can recover it in the present: the air that must have been breathed once earlier before it can be the pure air of paradise can only exist if it has been lost. And lost it has been.

In spite of the narrator's wavering about the loss of that paradise, *In Search of Lost Time* concludes with his outline of a program for recovering it. The theological, philosophical, and psychological justifications for his program depend on his metaphors for their persuasiveness. I have argued here that biblical allegory is used as the dominant metaphor for the narrator's figurative description of the novel he wants to write. The recollection of the past as resurrection is also a key metaphor, one that is also figured as a "miracle." The "miracle of analogy" is, according to the narrator, that a sensation in the present is (can be likened to) a sensation in the past. The sameness allows the purified fullness of the past to emerge into the present (*TR*, 262–63). Since the embodiment of the past in metaphors depends on language in order to exist in a text (for there are also iconic metaphors), the fullness the narrator seeks demands figurative language for the translation of the plenitude of the past into literature. Language must pull off the miracle of overcoming the transience of all existence and all existing beings. It must do this in a struggle with the power of the present; or as the narrator describes it, the problem for him has been heretofore that "when these resurrections took place, the distant scene engendered around the common sensation had grappled, like a wrestler, with the present scene" and then "always the present scene had come off victorious" (*TR*, 267). The narrator's task will be to continue to grapple, using metaphors in the service of his intellect to bring this sensual recall into the permanent purview of language, and thereby the lure of the present can be vanquished.

As the narrator outlines his program, his reliance on religious imagery is displaced in his subsequent analysis of the epiphanies. On the one hand, he meditates on beauty in psychological terms. He thinks that beauty is only accessible to the imagination, but that what is to be imagined must be absent. However the pure coincidence of past and present sensations can get around this psychological law of the imagination so that the essence of the past experience can emerge in the present. After this psychological explanation, the narrator then has recourse to metaphysics, for he declares that in art what is actually liberated in the coincidence of two sensations, in this "celestial nourishment," is the concealed essence of things that is "real without being actual, ideal without being abstract" (*TR*, 264). The language here is neo-Platonic, though it is Platonism turned on its head. As we saw in the case of Vinteuil's sonata, "real" means that which transcends daily, fallen reality so that "ideal" is then used, perhaps synonymously, to describe what is a contradiction in classical Platonic terms: the ideal is the essence of the unique particular, found in the individual without recourse to abstraction. It is the atemporal essence of a particular thing or moment. When captured by analogy, this essence discloses pure experience: it is, for example, what the narrator has captured in the metaphors of chapel and flowers, those labile metaphors constituting the paradise of Combray.

The ruminating narrator has a fourth epiphany, this one somewhat anticlimactic. The noise of water running in a pipe recalls to him a noise "exactly like those long-drawn-out whistles which sometimes on summer evenings one heard the pleasure-steamers emit as they approached Balbec from the sea" (*TR*, 266). After this further example of separate and singular "resurrections," as the narrator calls them, his meditation hesitates between religious thought and romantic beliefs. He says that although these privileged moments are "fragments of existence withdrawn from Time" that offer a contemplation of eternity, they are nonetheless fugitive and fleeting (*TR*, 268). They resemble moments of mystical contemplation. However in themselves they can offer little to an aspiring novelist, whose essential task is to find a way to construct a work of art. Only the artwork offers access to these essences that spring from the artist's true self.

The narrator's meditation then veers even more sharply away from the religious and metaphysical allegories that he has just used to develop his thought about his revelations. It is at this moment that Proust's Kantian rationalism comes to the narrator's aid when he must think through a positive program for himself. For it is in thinking about what he must do to become an artist that he has recourse to comparisons with philosophy and with science. The narrator realizes that the work of art offers not just feeling but also knowledge about that feeling as it exists in a real world. With this turn in his meditation, the narrator's theory of the novel takes on epistemological complexity. He believes he must justify his work through its claim to knowledge, which means he must justify it in the face of the imperious claims of philosophy and science. To do this he wants in some way to differentiate the work of art from intellectual activity (and all those products of pure intellect for which Proust expressed scorn in *Against Sainte-Beuve*). But he also wants to vindicate a claim that literature offers knowledge. This is the task the narrator sets for himself then after the revelations of essence and the feelings embodied therein.

The first step toward setting up art's proper domain is, the narrator declares, that writers must be faithful to what life has dictated uniquely to them and not lose themselves in general abstractions. For the narrator these abstractions include such worthy causes as the "triumph of justice" or the "moral unity of the nation," as well as abstract philosophical truths of the kind having "a logical, possible truth" (*TR*, 273). Literature cannot be in the service of moral causes or political crusades, nor can it hope to illustrate general scientific truths—even if the narrator himself frequently speaks of laws. To attempt any of these tasks would entail a subordination of the artist's self to something exterior to the self that must be the ground of the artwork's being. For any subordination to an exterior world prevents the artist from expressing an individual vision and hence world, which is the necessary prerequisite for art from Proust's viewpoint. The narrator's position is, succinctly, that an artist's truth is quite simply of a different order of truth than that of ethics or science.

The narrator's position is in some ways close to that of a scientific rationalist. Like a modern epistemologist, he recognizes the contingency of all scientific laws. This means that no scientific law can be the basis for the artwork's knowledge, since a law is not characterized by the necessity that the narrator thinks should be embodied in the work of art. Therefore truths deriving from science or philosophy cannot be a source of vision or creativity. Actually creativity is the wrong word here, for the narrator rejects that idea that the artist freely creates what is found in the artistic work. That freedom would be another aspect of contingency. Rather he argues that the artist is bound by necessity to interpret the signs found in his own inner world. No more than in the case of the Jansenist gift of grace is there freedom involved in the election that characterizes the artist. He is elected by what the world imposes on him. In other words the writer's task is imposed by what the writer has known as an individual:

> For the truths which the intellect apprehends directly in the world
> of full and unimpeded light have something less profound, less
> necessary than those which life communicates to us against our will
> in an impression which is material because it enters us through the
> senses but yet has a spiritual meaning which it is possible for us to
> extract. In fact, both in one case and in the other, whether I was
> concerned with the impressions like the one which I had received
> from the sight of the steeples of Martinville or with reminiscences
> like that of the unevenness of the two steps or the taste of the mad-
> eleine, the task was to interpret the given sensations as signs of so
> many laws and ideas, by trying to think—that is to say, draw forth
> from the shadow—what I had merely felt, by trying to convert it
> into its spiritual equivalent. (*TR*, 273)

The shift in the narrator's thought is notable in this passage, for he now conceives the problem of literature as an epistemological problem involving knowledge of his inner world. Using metaphors that go at least back to Plato, he sees that he must draw the self's contents from the dark out into the light. The contents of authentic self must be projected into the light illuminated by the knowing mind. Knowledge is thus a kind of illumination, and the artist's task is to convert that illumination into something that the mind can interpret—into language adequate to the experience that reality has imposed upon the artist.

From this perspective it is perhaps clear now why the narrator worries about the criteria for truth. Believing that every artist must offer knowledge of the self, the writer becomes an epistemologist, which means that he finds himself working in a domain that scientists have staked out for themselves: namely that of the truth. So the narrator duly takes on the task of delimiting the realm of science—the realm of general, contingent truths—from that of literature, the realm of the artist's individual, necessary truths. This task leads him to the following dictum: What general law is to science, the artist's impressions are to literature. He is categorical: only the impression "however trivial its material may seem to be, however faint its traces, is a criterion for truth"—which is to say, for a necessary artistic truth as opposed to a contingent intellectual truth (*TR*, 275). From the narrator's later perspective, this means that the writer and the scientist work symmetrically as equals in the quest for knowledge: "The impression is for the writer what experiment is for the scientist, with the difference that in the scientist the work of the intelligence precedes the experiment and in the writer it comes after the impression" (*TR*, 276). The mind—or the intellect—reasserts its rights at the end of the artistic process at that moment when the narrator sees the artist confronting the necessity of making his world of impressions known to others.

Before entering the Guermantes reception, the narrator goes to the prince's library. Here his meditation is interrupted. While waiting to be admitted, he runs across a novel by George Sand, *François le Champi*, a book from his childhood—in fact the first novel of his childhood. Paralleling Proust's reactions in the essay "On Reading," the narrator is moved by the material presence of book itself, for this book is an integral part of the past and its sensations and especially of the night in Combray when his mother spent the night reading it to him in violation of the paternal law. The book in its physical presence forms a link between the child and the adult narrator: "If, even in thought, I pick from the bookshelf *François le Champi*, immediately there rises within me a child who takes my place, who alone has the right to spell out the title *François le Champi*, and who reads it as he read it once before, with the same impressions of what the weather was like then in the garden, the same dreams that were then shaping themselves in his mind about the different countries and about life, the same anguish about the next day" (*TR*, 284).

The narrator has interiorized Sand's novel in such a way that it can evoke the temporal strata that surrounded it when it was first read to him. Perhaps this encounter in the library could be called his fifth epiphany, for it offers the revelation that literature itself is a generator of literature when it reveals the fullness of time past attached to it. The recollection of reading allows, moreover, the narrator to adumbrate further the nature of the impressions that it is the task of literature to bring to light. These impressions include the very materiality of a book once encountered, and sensations tied up with the entire world of sensations that once surrounded it—as the narrator has already demonstrated in "Combray" when he recalls, with appropriate irony, those magic moments he knew as a boy when reading in the toilet.

Alone in the prince's library, the narrator returns to his meditation on the relationship between art and reality with the tantalizing thought that "an hour is not merely an hour, it is a vase full of scents and sounds and projects and climates, and what we call reality is a certain connexion between these immediate sensations and the memories which envelop us simultaneously with them . . . a unique connexion which the writer has to rediscover in order to link for ever in his phrase the two sets of phenomena which reality joins together" (*TR*, 289). In this thought the narrator's notion of analogy is given its full development. Literary analogy or metaphor acts as a form of knowledge in recovering the past in all its complexity—a form of Parousia, if you will, but now defined psychologically. And included in that complexity may be the memory of literary texts such as novels leading to other memories and finally, perhaps, to the novel the narrator may pursue in his quest for knowledge of the self.

In pursuing the comparison between literature and science, the narrator affirms some rather sweeping propositions. He totally rejects the idea that a photographic image can engage the past, for it does not link together the past and the present. (Theorists of the ontology of the image may blanch at that idea.) Not only does artistic truth depend upon the connection made between two "sets of phenomena," but he also says that this connection is analogous to "the unique connexion which in the world of science is provided by the law of causality" (*TR*, 290). In comparing the nature of analogy itself with causality, the narrator introduces determinism at the microlevel, it appears, since the connection is what transforms the narrator's chance encounters in his life experience into a necessary relationship. This idea about causality allows one to understand that the writer's task is precisely to convert aleatory encounters with contingent events into the necessary world of the artwork. Indeed the writer, presumably like any other artist, has no choice, since these chance impressions are in fact all that the artist has. Hence the artist must necessarily work with them. For all eternity it will be a necessary truth that the narrator remembers his mother's once spending the night with him reading George Sand, and for him there can be no other truth.

Having sketched out the narrator's views on his future task as a writer, I now wish to conclude this study with some more general thoughts about his conclusions in *Time Regained,* which may shed light upon the novel as a whole. To this end I also want to offer some additional thoughts about Proust's novel in the larger context provided by scientific epistemology in Europe at the end of the nineteenth century (and for the European scientist then, as now, *epistemology* usually means the theory of scientific knowledge). This larger context is often passed over by critics. When this happens they fail to see that Proust's thoughts about art are conditioned by his thoughts about science and science's claim to be the adjudicator of the truth value of all propositions—precisely the sort of attitude he found in his father's medical milieu. To understand fully Proust's literary aesthetics, it is essential to recognize that the goal of his narrator, especially in *Time Regained*, is to define the work of art so that it respects the laws of time and its contingent processes, especially physics and physiology. In a sense science comes first in his thinking since, facing the lack of determinacy in the world described by science, the narrator wonders if all knowledge is contingent. For in his confrontation with the world described by science, and the nihilistic conclusions many have drawn from this description, it clearly appears that a need for certainty lies behind the narrator's desire to find a way to explain how the artist converts contingent impressions into a necessary realm of knowledge. This need for certainty means that he does not and cannot want to be a scientist, since he will be satisfied only if he can find a realm of certain truth. Science does not offer that realm. Epistemology at least since Kant has held that certain truth does not exist in the realm of contingent laws, which seemingly allows the narrator to infer that certainty must therefore exist in a realm where these contingent laws hold no sway. It must be sought in a realm other than that of the objective world, where many different laws can be invoked, plausibly and indifferently, to describe the essentially underdetermined world of historical and physical phenomena.[3]

This domain of contingency, which is to say the objective world, is set against the inner realm of the self of the narrator-observer. This domain is presupposed by the fact that he can look, from his subjective narrative framework, upon the world with the hope of finding a realm that is not subject to contingency. It is not self-evident that he can find this realm. If contingency signifies that his perceptions cannot be inscribed in any deterministic matrix that would explain them by reducing them to a universal scientific model, it also means that the narrator's perceptions are initially chance events. The aleatory reigns over everything. And clearly nothing decrees that the narrator meet Albertine, look at the stones of Venice, or even love his mother. Hence no deterministic model can really account for the perceptions tied up with these events.

Countering this realization is the narrator's theory that the artist can convert random sensations, or perception, into a necessary work of art in which certainty holds sway. The logic of his theory is perhaps unassailable, if one accepts that every individual is the singular repository of a unique world of perceptions. The narrator theorizes that the work of art is a realm of necessity because it is unique to the artist creating it. Because of its uniqueness, it defies contingency: once the artist had had an impression, it is necessarily his or her impression—sealed in a necessity created by the passage of time. Thus every event, every fleeting impression, found in the Combray of "Combray" is a necessary part of the revelation of the narrator's world, for *seen from the present moment* his world can be no other than what it is because that is what it *was*. The singular past is logically the realm of the certain from this perspective. Because it has been, it is certain that it is and can be nothing else.

The other major axiom that underlies the narrator's meditation is the belief that the artist's mind escapes reduction to, or explanation by, the deterministic laws of the universe, as described by classical physics and physiology. This view is quite consonant with then contemporary European epistemology. One can document many sources for this doctrine, ranging from Proust's neo-Kantian teachers and their critique of positivism to examples of the great scientist-epistemologists of the late nineteenth century such as Poincaré, Ernst Mach, and Pierre Duhem. They relegated determinism to a restricted role in epistemic problems, which buttressed a concomitant belief that there are realms sheltered from the iron hand of deterministic laws. To be sure in the novel Proust does not entirely dispense with the theoretical claims for determinism, at least not for the ordinary world of objective phenomena. His narrator offers numerous examples of deterministic laws that rule over the human body and society, including his own body—for genetics and physiology are not negligible themes in *In Search of Lost Time*. But the narrator accepts that determinism has limits. He finds these limits inscribed in his own mind.

In this regard the narrator is in agreement with scientists such as Poincaré, Mach, and Duhem, who postulated that knowledge of objective reality is always relative to the subjective realm. This viewpoint justifies the conception of what can be called the inertial framework of the knowing self, such as the framework created by the subjective perception of Proust's present-tense narrator, who throughout the novel always exists in the present and hence is always existing as a virtual horizon of perception. Representation in the novel is always relative to a subject, in Proust's case to the narrating voice in the present moment of enunciation. Moreover the way that the narrator theorizes the primacy of the subjective realm in the determination of what one knows closely parallels the then contemporary epistemological tenet that the subject has the power to opt for any of an indefinite number of models and laws with which the knower may choose to describe reality. However both the scientists and the narrator agree that what the subject cannot opt for, what the subject must accept as a necessity, is the subject's experiential world of sensation and perception. In essence once the subject has experienced the world, then that is the world experienced. The world is the ultimate determining locus of experience and hence knowledge. Neither Poincaré nor Proust is in any sense an idealist.

I refer primarily to Poincaré because of several parallels between Proust's narrator and this mathematical physicist. Proposing a doctrine of relativity that was a precursor to Einstein's, Poincaré also denied that perception was determined by any geometry intrinsic to the nature of things in space. If we think the world exists in three dimensions, this is an effect of habit—that ultimate law of the mind for both the narrator and Poincaré. This idea that habit determines perception is not the same as the idealist claim that the structure of mind determines perception and knowledge. On the contrary mind itself is determined by habit, which may vary greatly from period to period, culture to culture. This idea became matter for public debate after, for example, Poincaré published an essay in 1895, "Space and Geometry," in which he affirmed that there are no laws intrinsic to the nature of perception. Rather the association of ideas is the result of habit, and habit itself is the result of numerous experiences. If these experiences, if the education the senses received, took place in a different environment, then one would have different habits and sensations would be associated according to different laws. A more radical expression of contingency in an underdetermined world is hard to imagine.

The power habit has in ordering the mind explains why Proust's narrator theorizes at length about habit's determination of perception. Consequently he believes he must liberate his own perception from habit if he is to be an artist who has his own vision and not the conventional vision of received reality. His opening meditation on the world in "Combray," when habit has lost its grip on perception, offers a humorous exposition of this possibility. The plausibility of the claim that perception is underdetermined is also essential for Proust's affirmation that the artist's perception offers a unique truth that escapes from the rule of law. To be sure habit is a psychological law in Proust, and it is perhaps the dominant force ordering a mind that does not reflect upon its perceptions. But habit can be broken. With proper education, as Poincaré mused, one could perhaps become habituated to two dimensions or even to those four dimensions that Proust's narrator finds in the church at Combray, where he perceives the dimension of time embodied in the church's stones. It strikes me that this perception of a fourth dimension in Proust is not unlike what Poincaré points to when he claims that we could use either Euclidean or non-Euclidean geometries to describe or even to perceive the real world. There could be more or fewer dimensions than three.

Devotees of science fiction probably have little difficulty with these ideas about the conventionality of perception, for in science fiction this is frequently the stuff of imagined worlds. With regard to the question of space and geometry, one precursor to Proust is Edwin A. Abbott, whose *Flatland* in 1884 offered a satirical thought experiment about what it would be like to live in a two-dimensional universe. If Proust did not know this work, he certainly did know H. G. Wells, to whom he refers in the novel and, as early as 1902, in his correspondence. Proust was undoubtedly fascinated by the way Wells used the idea that with four dimensions one could realize time travel. Of course Proust's time travel goes in the opposite direction from the anti-utopian future toward which Wells sends his scientist in *The Time Machine* of 1895. From this perspective it is fruitful to think of Proust's narrator as a time traveler who does his exploration by voyaging back into the past, effecting a return to that moment when the narrator perceives the past as an embodied fourth dimension investing things and sensations with the palpable patina of the past.

Proust radically translates the doctrine of the underdeterminism of perception with his narrative structure. His narrator finds escape from habit in his own subjective realm. For the reader who wants to know where that realm of subjectivity is located, I think it must be answered that from the novel's outset, this subjectivity can only be situated outside of the ordinary world of space and time that the narrator recalls. It is in this sense that one can literally entertain the narrator's proposition that, as a sleeping man, he escapes the empirical laws and patterns that habit usually accepts, because, to cite again the famous line, the sleeper "has in a circle round him the chain of the hours, the sequence of the years, the order of the heavenly bodies" (*SW*, 4). Sleep, dream, sensual recall, and finally self-reflexivity can break with habit—though of course this may have little influence on the world. But with this break, the conventional laws governing matter and perception may no longer necessarily hold, any more than do the metric conventions that habit accepts for ordering the regular perception of space and time. But it appears that only by breaking with habitual perception can the narrator perceive his necessary and original world of certain truth. Otherwise the past is simply a collection of memories resembling lifeless photographs.

In Search of Lost Time embodies an elaborate epistemological dualism precisely in order to justify the discovery of this underdeterminism. Proust's epistemic strategy is to use classical scientific models to talk about a largely deterministic world of habitual perceptions exterior to the narrator but a relativist and conventionalist model to talk about the subjective world of the narrator's unique perception. This mix corresponds, interestingly, to Baudelaire's idea that a novel is a mixed genre, containing objective truth as well as self-sufficient poetic correspondences that in Proust's case translate the narrator's subjective experience. In the wake of Baudelaire, but with more epistemological rigor and perhaps less irony, Proust stakes out for his narrator the self-sufficient inner realm in which Baudelaire found poetic autonomy—the realm of beauty produced by correspondences in language.

Perhaps it would be well to make a brief resumé here to clarify my argument up to this point. Proust's narrator says that poetic self-sufficiency derives first from the writer's impressions. Recall that he claims that impressions are the unique material that forms the truth of his world and hence the certain truth of art as found in the novel. These impressions ultimately are not contingent, though they owe their existence to chance because they come about through fortuitous encounters. But once the impressions are given to the narrator, they are his necessary material for certain truths. It is in this sense that one can speak of a necessary and certain world when he recovers the entire first section of the novel, "Combray," through a fortuitous encounter of tastes and odors, due to a bit of pastry that he has dipped into a cup of lime tea. In this chance encounter—or resurrection if one prefers—he overcomes the contingencies of ordinary existence, which is to say, this experience cannot be explained by those conventionally deterministic paradigms of physics and physiology that, unfortunately, condemn us to death—a contingent truth, it must be said, about which one can have little doubt. Moreover the experience born of lime tea seems to be a translation from poetry to fiction of Baudelaire's doctrine of correspondences, but one occurring as an epistemic experience: it comes as the knowledge of—or the resurrection of—the plenitude of the past. The narrator's present sensations coincide with sensations he experienced in the past, and, through the correspondence between the two, the past plenitude is resurrected in the present. All of Combray surges forth as the living paradise of his youth. In this moment Combray is, for the narrator, a form of necessity that escapes contingency. When converted into writing, perhaps it is a necessity for the reader, too.

Proust thus begins his novel with a demonstration of the certain truths about the paradise of Combray that the narrator must recover, if he is to realize his vocation, once he has gone through the years of experience that constitute the novel itself, with its portrayal of characters and society beginning at a time before his childhood and lasting until an indefinite time after World War I. In "Combray" Proust sets out what the narrator must do in his uncertain future. The status of the later parts of the novel is more ambiguous. They seem less inscribed with the sign of necessity. And the history of the novel's composition shows that Proust could have expanded the intermediary sections indefinitely, for they present, in all their contingency, the development of characters and events, fortuituously interlinked in that empirical realm of history that has no intrinsic necessity.

One may speculate that had death not cut short Proust's life, the novel might have been even longer. One can argue that the novel would have been longer with more contingent events that, once experienced, all become the narrator's necessary impressions. And of course the ending Proust planned for *In Search of Lost Time* would have been the same, no matter how long it became, since from the beginning the outline for an ending was given by his epistemic model for the novel. (I accept by and large Proust's claim he had the novel's end in mind along with its beginning, which means that his thoughts on epistemological contingency in *Time Regained* were probably conceived before he wrote the thoughts on the transcendence suggested by Vinteuil's sonata.) No matter what contingent events happen before the end, the revelation of the nature of aesthetic knowledge must come at the end so that the narrator discovers the meaning of artistic experience in the novel itself. This is the discovery granted by the revelations taking place in the Guermantes courtyard, years after the revelation experienced with the lime tea and the madeleine and even more years after the childhood experience of Combray that the tea and madeleine revealed. With this discovery he can turn to these preceding moments of chance events and turn them through writing into the necessary and certain world that, by chance, Proust has already written out for the reader, which is to say, the world of the novel the reader has been reading. This double perspective on the world of the novel—Proust's and the narrator's—means that we can read a double meaning in the title *Time Regained—Le Temps retrouvé*, a title that we may perhaps now consider to be optimistically predicting that time has been, and perhaps will be, recovered.

The narrator's final analysis of his perceptions in *Time Regained* takes place after he had realized years earlier, in his meditation on art and literature in *The Fugitive* and especially *The Captive*, that art is analogous to science in its study of relations. Having arrived at the theory of literature proposed in *Time Regained*, the reader can then look back to see that the narrator's earlier reflections on the nature of art are an essential complement to his later theorizing—for at the end of the novel he speaks little about music and virtually not at all about painting. But earlier his most interesting meditation is prompted as much by the music of Vinteuil as by writers. It is in meditating on music that, trying to find a general reason for the effects caused by the music, he entertains the two hypotheses about art discussed earlier. In light of his epistemological reflections in *Time*

Regained, one can see that for him Vinteuil's sonata is a form of transcendence that escapes intellectual explanation—not unlike the moment of eternity he attributes to literature. The music is, for the younger narrator, the primary example of art that in some sense offers access to a reality lying beyond the limits of ordinary perception and the contingent laws of daily reality. The hypothesis about transcendence might also explain, or so the narrator thinks at the time, the type of pleasure he felt at the outset of the novel upon experiencing the memories of Combray recalled by the cup of lime tea. In *The Captive,* however, he goes no further in this direction. Rather he then reflects upon what science, or really, materialist positivism, might say about art and our perception. Here the challenge offered by science is clear. In this context the narrator speaks of the viewpoint underlying the materialist hypothesis, a hypothesis about the nothingness to which we as material beings are destined by the inexorable laws of physiology and physics that govern our bodies (C, 513). This hypothesis would seemingly reduce art to something like the reproduction of a psychological state, having no more reality than any other such state and presumably no more duration. In this case art has the status of a state of feeling that science has not yet analyzed, though it was and is part of the positivist project to analyze such complex states. Comparing Vinteuil's musical phrase with an inner state analogous to the one the narrator had experienced upon tasting the madeleine and the lime tea, he asks what makes these states different from any other experiential state. He has no ready answer at this point in the novel. Thus he entertains the hypothesis that the fact that Vinteuil's musical phrases resist analysis does not necessarily mean that there is something more real in them than in the experience of ordinary reality—the "material" reality that the positivist mind encounters everywhere.

At this point, however, the narrator questions whether science can in principle ever account for such a complex psychological phenomenon as the state induced by hearing a sonata. In this regard he shows he is acquainted with the nineteenth-century critique of determinism. For he says that the spirit of doubt suggests rather that the states produced by the musical phrases cannot be analyzed precisely because "they put in play too many forces for which we as yet have no account": "Ils mettent en jeu trop de forces dont nous ne nous sommes pas encore rendu compte" (C, 513–14). So without opting for either a transcendental or a materialist interpretation of art but by invoking an analogy with a system of complex forces, Proust's narrator suggests in *The Captive* that the reduction of artistic states to component elements is too complex a problem to be resolved. The order of complexity is too great, the narrator muses, for there to be any deterministic resolutions of the forces that would allow them to be described by some contingent law.

An explanation of the effect of art cannot then in principle be found using a deterministic model. It should not be thought that the narrator is indulging in nitpicking in his self-defense against positive science. The question of complexity has been a public issue in France at least since Pascal divided up knowledge into mathematical and intuitive domains, with human complexity reserved for the latter, since its complexity prevents it from being described mathematically. In Proust's youth public attention in France had recently been drawn to the impossibility of solving what should have been a simple problem of celestial mechanics, the so-called three body problem: the complexity of forces between more than two celestial bodies defies mathematical resolution. (Poincaré first offered a partial solution to the three body problem, though it has not been resolved entirely to this day.) The narrator's thoughts on complexity take the form of scientific reasoning consonant with a French tradition of recognizing the limits of mathematical modeling. I add that, arguably, his thought has not lost its relevance for an era that believes the mind is a computer.

For all the richness of these early meditations on art and science, it is of course only in *Time Regained* that the narrator finally discovers that his task as a novelist is to restore a world by recalling the perceived real that he carries within himself. However at the end of the novel, he is facing the prospect of death after a long period of illness. In this dismal situation, he sees that for the remainder of time that he has yet to live, he must recall and explore the multiple sensations that are too complex to be reduced by analysis. Facing death, he must work to free these sensations from the patterns imposed by conventional perception and grant access to a realm of unique and necessary truth lying outside of the ken of science. His future task is an epistemic endeavor, though different from the discovery of relations that science undertakes, for it is the endeavor of a single knowing subject expressing a unique world.

The narrator envisages a difficult future. Perhaps it must remain a future, which is to say the time of contingency. We do not know what contingent events—namely death and illness—he may experience, since Proust does not allow the narration itself to catch up with the act of narration. The narrator is never joined in time by a narrative act, so that his presence remains suspended outside of time even at the novel's end, or to put it in different terms, the novel's narrated events never coincide with the space of narration. It stretches the reader's imagination to try to conceive that the narrator is an epistemic quester outside the realm circumscribed by conventional time and space and thus outside any deterministic realm of conventional science. Given the epistemological reflection we have seen in the novel, it might appear that Proust quite intentionally refuses to allow the narrative act to be inscribed in space and time. Quite intentionally the novel's recall of the narrator's unique past experience is to be considered a fiction narrated from something like the viewpoint of a nontranscendental transcendence. It is with no taste for paradox that I suggest that this paradoxical situation is perhaps the best way to consider the noncontingent realm that Proust's narrator finds in literature and undoubtedly in painting and music. Thus the novel transcends, through its own fictional ontology, the world in which it is born. As Proust's novel shows, literature is a fictional space that, in never coinciding with the contingently real, offers the enactment of a unique truth as a necessary truth, as necessary as the narrator's subjective fiction that posits a realm of noncontingent truth in a contingent world. And transcendence is one way of considering this relation of artist, artwork, and the world.

The narrator himself refuses to do more than speculate that artistic significance may derive from a realm of transcendence. His speculation is at times persuasive, and, I add, his view of a possible transcendence is perhaps not as paradoxical as I may have implied, if one is willing to grant that the ontology of art allows that in some sense it transcends contingency. This fictional transcendence of time, and hence history, accomplished by art explains much about art. It accounts for the historical fact that the truth of works of art, unlike that of scientific models, is not subject to historical revision. Monet need never revise his vision of Etretat in view of new optical theories, nor can the transcendence experienced in a Bach cantata be meaningfully denied. Or with regard to literature, there will never be a truer version of *Don Quixote* or, to use contemporary jargon, a more pragmatically adequate version of *Madame Bovary*. As Proust might have argued, if there is no progress in art, there is no superseding either.

I have made the claim that the narrator is something of a rationalist, which is shown, I think, by his own procedures for thought and argument. He adopts a scientific viewpoint in the way he entertains alternative hypotheses about the nature of art. He finds that neither metaphysics nor science offers an entirely adequate explanatory model. Like all scientific issues, the question remains open to unending questioning and debate. This attitude of open skepticism toward the claims of theory of course does not constitute a rejection of science—*au contraire*. In fact according to the narrator, scientist and writer are actually united in their complementary quest for truth, one for the truth of unique particular and the other the truth of a general law. The artist, like the scientist, is not constrained in this quest by any objective system of reference, for both can propose any model they find adequate to their purposes. Nonetheless constraints for both exist by the very nature of research—and note that Proust's title for the novel uses a term that means both seeking and research, to wit, *la recherche*. In a complementary way, both artist and scientist seek in effect to make discoveries in a world disclosed by *la recherche*. Once the artist has chosen the area to explore, the artist, like the scientist, then discovers that his world imposes its limits on what the artist can accomplish. Discovery is made by the world as much by the researcher,[4] for it is the world that determines what the researcher may find there.

It is clear from the narrator's meditations, first in *The Fugitive*, then in *Time Regained*, that artistic states depend entirely on the subjective realm of a subject, namely the artist's. Proust's idea is that there is a relation of priority between the subjective and the objective, since it is in the subjective realm that one finds the origins of the objective modeling of experience given by art. Analogously late nineteenth-century epistemology held that subjective choices in science lie behind the choice of a model for scientific knowledge. Or as Poincaré puts it about much scientific work, it is the scientist's choice to use a deterministic model that, through habit, grants him his operational power as a knowing subject—which the narrator also points out with humor at the novel's beginning when he wonders if the immobility of the things around us is forced on them by the perceiving subject's conviction that things are themselves and not anything else. If the subject imposes determinism through choice or by accepting it as a habit, then it is logical that the subject lies outside the realm of simple determinism in the sense of being prior to this realm. Poincaré's conventionalism about scientific models follows from this conclusion because, quite simply, according to Poincaré, it is the subject that determines epistemic conventions—not vice versa.

Nonetheless the limits of research are the limits that the world imposes. This is true for both artist and scientist, whether it is a question of the unique particular or the general law. This is another idea that points to the dichotomous nature of modern epistemology that Proust embodies in his novel. He uses the dichotomy by embodying both sides of the meaning of discovery in his novel, conceived as unique poetic truth and in the form of the scientific laws that can describe objective phenomena. Proust could affirm his novel's totalizing power of discovery with good intellectual conscience because he knew he was exploiting the way modern epistemology itself oscillates between realism and antirealism, and both of these aspects are endorsed by Proust (*real* used here in the non-Platonic contemporary sense). In its antirealism modern epistemology says that phenomena are underdetermined. In its realism it declares that there are limits imposed by objective phenomena that cannot be transgressed. Antirealism allows that there can be as many laws and models, or theories and worlds, as there are scientists and artists. But realism points out that the world imposes a limit, specifically in the form of the invariant relations that characterize the world. However because they are invariant, these relations may be assumed and used by an indefinite number of different models or types of explanation. So not only is there an indefinite number of scientific models to explain relations about the world but comparably an indefinite number of novels that may explain relations in the world.

In conclusion Proust's description of the artist's epistemic task parallels the kind of epistemological critique that made Mach and Poincaré famous (or infamous among traditional scientists). The narrator makes a critique of realism that is analogous to their critique of epistemological naïveté. Poincaré and Mach frequently stressed that science does not describe things in themselves: all one can know are the relations between things. A poet such as the young Paul Valéry accepted this viewpoint, whereas a near contemporary of Proust, the Austrian novelist Musil, struggled with it all his life. Modernist writers were as much troubled by the loss of realism as were the scientists. Nonetheless nearly all modernists accepted that the realism of Goncourt, like the realism of traditional physics grounded in Euclidean geometry, was inadequate. In Proust's view the writer's quest for analogies is analogous to the scientist's search for relations, for as the narrator says, artistic truth begins only when the artist takes two objects and posits a relationship between them. The unique truth of the artist's experience is rendered in effect through the description of relations, which for Proust usually meant the use of metaphor that produces artistic truth by describing from the artist's viewpoint the "relations between things"— or what Poincaré calls "les rapports entre les choses."[5] Poetic practice and scientific research coincide as forms of discovering relations.

That the narrator's reflections on the nature of art in *Time Regained* should be followed by the grotesque carnival at the reception given by the Guermantes points up the great range of Proust's novel, but the contrast also makes an important point about theorizing (or engaging in philosophical speculation, if one prefers). The novel may theorize its own existence, perhaps its own transcendence, but the narrated stuff of the novel is the comedy of social existence culminating in the carnival of unremitting fall. So in the end we return to the religious register, for the carnival ball seemingly presupposes and demands the affirmation of something other than inversion and debasement. The affirmation of life that these grotesqueries demand is both Proust's novel and the novel to which the narrator plans to devote himself with the ascetic zeal of a religious convert who has "died to the world"—as some monks and nuns do. If Proust had not already followed this ascetic path, if he had not completed his novel, we might doubt that the narrator has the strength to follow on the same way. But Proust set the example: the narrator will need only to continue.

Notes

Chapter 1. Life and Career

1. Halévy wrote several historical studies that are of great use for an understanding of social and political context in which Proust was working, notably *La fin des notables* (Paris: Grasset, 1930) and *L'études de la troisième république* (Paris: Grasset, 1937). In this chapter I also rely greatly upon Jean-Yves Tadié's definitive biography of Proust, *Marcel Proust*. Quotes in text are from the first edition.

2. Quoted from the "Marcel Proust ephemera site," www.yorktaylors.free -online.co.uk. Though not entirely accurate, this site offers access in translation to a large selection of Proust's scattered writings and a bibliography thereof.

3. Proust, *Correspondance*, 1: 121–22. Commenting on this letter, Tadié likens Proust to Valéry (*Marcel Proust*, 108). Much information on Proust's school years is to be found in Ferré, *Années de college*.

4. Tadié, *Marcel Proust*, 151–52.

5. Ibid., 159.

6. Ibid., 250–51.

7. I have consulted the edition of Leibnitz's *La Monadologie* edited by Emile Boutroux, "suivie d'une note sur les principes de la mécanique dans Descartes et dans Leibniz, par Henri Poincaré" (Paris: Delagrave, 1930). Boutroux's edition of *La Monadologie* was first published in 1881. He wrote a long eulogy for Poincaré in 1913, republished in the *Nouvelles études d'histoire de la philosophie* (Paris: Alcan, 1927).

8. One of the most influential of Proust's readers, the poet and critic Roger Shattuck, was quite enthusiastic about Proust's strategy of ingratiating himself with the wealthy and aristocratic so that he could carry out "a brilliant escape from his bourgeois background and from the professional career expected" (*Proust's Way*, 7). I recall that Shattuck's father, like Proust's, was a very prominent doctor.

9. I refer to the unpublished "L'irréligion d'état," first published in *Textes retrouvés*, now available in the Pléiade edition of *Contre Sainte-Beuve*, 348–50. Among other things young Proust showed himself to be quite enthusiastic about the exporting of French Catholicism to the colonies.

10. Carter, *Marcel Proust*, 235. This is a rich source of information for many previously unknown details of Proust's life.

11. Tadié, *Marcel Proust*, 352.

12. Proust, *Correspondance générale*, 3: 86. Letter of November 1920, of which I have given a paraphrase in English of the following: "Au moment où je vais publier *Sodome et Gomorrhe*, et où, parce que je parlerai de Sodome, personne n'aura le courage de prendre ma défense, d'avance vous frayez (sans méchanceté, j'en suis sûr) le chemin à tous les méchants, en me traitant de 'féminin.' De féminine à éffeminé, il n'y a qu'un pas. Ceux qui m'ont servi de témoins en duel vous diront si j'ai la mollesse des éffeminés."

13. Proust, *Lettres retrouvées*, 40–41.

14. Proust, *Correspondance générale*, 6:62–63.

15. Proust, *Lettres à Reynaldo Hahn*, 122.

16. Proust, *Correspondance*, 9:155–57.

17. Proust, *Correspondance générale*, 3:72. Interestingly in this letter Proust concedes that the general title of his novel, *A la recherche du temps perdu*, is a bit misleading.

18. Proust, *Correspondance générale*, 6:133.

19. In a letter to Madame Straus, June 1914, in Proust, *Correspondance générale*, 6:167.

20. Cf. Henri Bonnet, *Amours et la sexualité*, 66–68.

21. Letter of September 1915, in Proust, *Correspondance*, 14:218.

22. Letter to Madame Straus, October 11, 1917, in Proust, *Correspondance générale*, 6:179.

23. Tadié, *Marcel Proust*, 816.

Chapter 2. What Proust Published before *In Search of Lost Time*

1. Proust, *L'indifférent et autres textes de jeunesses*, 30.

2. Proust, "Choses normandes," in *Écrits sur l'art*, 64. This is a very convenient anthology with good annotations.

3. Ibid.

4. Proust, "Un dimanche au conservatoire," in *Écrits sur l'art*, 83.

5. Proust, *Les plaisirs et les jours*, 135. The notes and introduction make this edition superior to all others, and all page references to the text here refer to it. Here one can learn that, before publication in *Pleasures and Days*, Proust managed to publish only the poems on painters. With regard to the first edition of the book, I add a note that the Proust scholar J. Theodore Johnson sent to me: "Have you seen the first edition of 'Les Plaisirs et les Jours?' It's a huge and heavy book. Numerous illustrations by Madeleine Lemaire, and her drawn out production of these many images delayed the publication. The music by Hahn for the four painters is published in manuscript form and dated printemps 1894. These manuscript pages separate the poems on the painters and the poems on musicians. These poems on painters were recited several times in public to the music of Hahn, and there is a

recording of these poems recited to Hahn's music on the LP disc 'A la recherche du temps de Proust,' Arion: ARN 37169, Stereo, 1972."

6. Gicquel, "Composition."

7. For Proust's relation to Tolstoy and the literary historical context, see Henry, "*Les plaisirs et les jours.*"

8. Beckett, *Proust*, 13.

9. Proust, "Contre l'obscurité," in *Écrits sur l'art*, 96

10. Proust, *Chroniques*, 22. This edition is used for the quotations here.

11. Translation taken from Proust Ephemera website: www.yorktaylors.free -online.co.uk.

12. Bisson, "Proust and Ruskin," 32.

13. Ibid., 35.

14. For the reader, like Bisson, having trouble keeping these essays and prefaces straight, I recommend Richard Macksey, "'Conclusion' and 'Incitation.'" Macksey also wrote the introduction to the very useful Proust, *On Reading Ruskin*.

15. Proust, "L'irréligion d'état," in *Textes retrouvés*, 90.

16. "La mort des cathedrals" was first published in *Le Figaro*, August 16, 1904. Republished in part in *Pastiches et mélanges*, 198–211.

17. "La Bible d'Amiens," in *Écrits sur l'art*, 179–80.

18. But it is perhaps the Greek image that comes to dominate Proust's career, or so argues Daniel Simon, who makes the following statement about this concluding image of the "Post-Scriptum": "Proust has begun his journey to the center of the labyrinth that comes full circle in the depths of the *Recherche*." Simon, "Translating Ruskin," 162. The labyrinth is also a useful metaphor to describe the process that I call Proust's quest for narrative form.

Chapter 3. What Proust Did Not Publish

1. One can find Proust's previously unpublished essays in a variety of places, in French and in translation, as well as on various sites on the Web. The most substantial selection to be found in one place is offered by the 1971 edition of *Contre Sainte-Beuve*, edited by Pierre Clarac and Yves Sandres.

2. "Chardin et Rembrandt," in *Contre Sainte-Beuve* (1971), 380.

3. Borowitz, "Watteau and Chardin."

4. For example the distinguished Proust scholar Jean Tadié makes this argument in the introduction to his edition of *Jean Santeuil*. This edition is at present the definitive one, and quotations in this chapter from *Jean Santeuil* are my translations from it.

5. Maurice Blanchot, "L'expérience de Proust," 35–37.

6. George Eliot, *Middlemarch* [1874]. The scenes I refer to are to be found at the end of chapter 12 and the end of chapter 16.

7. Bardèche, *Marcel Proust romancier*, 1:68.

8. Gaubert, *Proust et le roman de la différence*, 47.

9. Brée, "Proust et l'affaire Dreyfus," 6.

10. In later editions of *Jean Santeuil*, editors have added a strange text to the beginning of "Beg-Meil," which probably should not be included in it or even be in *Jean Santeuil* at all. I refer to the text called "L'inconnu," a Kafkaesque text by Proust that was added to *Jean Santeuil* after it was published by Philip Kolb and Larkin B. Price in *Textes retrouvés*. The absurd series of events it narrates does not fit with my discussion here, though it is not without interest for showing that Proust could experiment with narrating radical disjunctures among events.

11. Letter to George de Lauris, November 1908, quoted in *Contre Sainte-Beuve*, ed. Bernard de Fallois, 15–16. (I quote and translate from this edition in my discussion of *Contre Sainte-Beuve*.) Bernard Brun, a more recent expert on Proust manuscripts, thinks much the same thing as Fallois and dates the beginning of an essay on Sainte-Beuve from the beginning of 1908. See his *Marcel Proust*, 119.

12. The name of Boaz recalls the importance Victor Hugo has for Proust's poetic imagination. Proust often refers to Hugo's "Booz endormi" ("Boaz Asleep"), in which is found another representation of the tree of Jesse.

13. Proust, "A propos du 'style' de Flaubert," in *Écrits sur l'art*, 318–19. My translation.

Chapter 4. *Swann's Way*

1. Proust, *In Search of Lost Time*, 9. As said at the beginning, all quotations made in the text here and in the following chapters will be from the 2003 Modern Library edition. See the list of abbreviations at the beginning of this study. I add that I do not wish to say that this translation is superior to the more recent one, but it is the translation most readers are likely to have at hand. It has been widely praised by critics.

2. I have not encountered exactly this viewpoint in the critical literature on Proust. In perhaps the most sophisticated analysis of his rhetoric of fiction, Gérard Genette writes that the opening sentence could be written in the simple past but not in the imperfect, since this tense at the outset "n'a pas assez d'autonomie syntaxique pour ouvrir une itération" (doesn't have enough syntactical autonomy to open an iterative sequence)—which, I point out, is exactly what the Moncrieff translation implies with its use of *would* to translate the *passé composé*. See *Figures*, 3:160. I add that Genette pays little attention to the use of the *passé composé*, contenting himself later to observe that the opening sentence cannot be interpreted without consideration for the person who makes the statement and the situation in which he makes it and that "le passé révolu de l'action racontée n'est tel que par rapport au moment où il la raconte" (the past occurrence of the narrated action is only past with regard to the time at which he is telling it [225]). This idea should perhaps have suggested that the past perfect is a key tense for Proust's narrative structure.

3. Houston, "Temporal Patterns."

4. With regard to buttercups, so says Gaston Bonnier about the buttercup called *bouton d'or*, or *Ranunculus acris*, in his classic *Flora complète portative de la*

France, a book that Proust undoubtedly used in his botanizing (still useful today, I add). Moreover lilacs come from southeastern Europe. Monet's paintings of water lilies from Giverny are a source of Proust's inspiration, as are other paintings using river scenes. See, for example, Monet's *Autumn on the Seine, Argenteuil,* now in the High Museum in Atlanta, in which the river functions as a mirror.

5. Landy develops this argument in his *Philosophy as Fiction.* For the argument that Swann is the narrator's precursor, see, for example, the arguments elegantly expressed by Howard Moss in *The Magic Lantern of Marcel Proust.* Most critics agree with Moss that Swann is in many respects the narrator's predecessor or precursor, something like a metaphorical Virgil who goes before his pupil Dante in negotiating Hell.

6. One of Proust's most influential critics, Germaine Brée, was extremely harsh in her judgment of this world in which the rich are "interested in love only as another means to an immediate gratification of a sensory pleasure which has no deep emotional significance" (*Marcel Proust and Deliverance from Time,* 146). Considering eroticism simply a worldly pastime, Brée excoriated the Proustian lover as a sleepwalker, wandering in a phantasmagoria of love. Certainly the Proustian lover is usually locked into his own subjectivity, projecting onto the beloved whatever fits his desires; but if my former thesis adviser were still alive, I would like to argue with her that passionate love in Proust's novel is not an erotic pastime, something like the tennis or hunting that aristocrats enjoy. In fact Swann is so passionately caught up in his love—passion understood as a mental state—that the erotic component seems rather minor.

Chapter 5. *Within a Budding Grove* and *The Guermantes Way*

1. An essay that contributed to my discussion here, and which brings out how Proust struggled with names, is Milly, "Sur quelques noms proustiens."

2. Souday's review appeared in *Le Temps,* November 4, 1920. The quotation here is from the volume in which his reviews on Proust are reprinted: *Marcel Proust,* 31. This review is also reprinted in Proust, *Le côté de Guermantes,* vol. 1, ed. Elyane Dezon-Jones (Paris: Garnier-Flammarion, 1987), 468.

3. I refer to Marianne Moore's well-known poem "Poetry," of which there are several versions. Yves Bonnefoy's poetry in celebration of the presence of the world is to be found in a number of volumes, beginning with *Du mouvement et de l'immobilité de Douve,* which Gallimard has keep constantly in print since 1953. (Now in the Collection Poésie.) He is also well known for his art history and criticism.

4. Fumaroli, *Littérature et conversation,* 10.

Chapter 6. *Sodom and Gomorrah, The Captive,* and *The Fugitive*

1. In his preface to his paperback edition of *Sodome et Gomorrhe* (Paris: Gallimard Folio, 1989), Antoine Compagnon says, "En 1918 Proust entend par *Sodome et Gomorrhe* tout le 'roman d'Albertine,' non seulement les actuels *Sodome et*

Gomorrhe I et II, mais encore *La Prisonnière* et *Albertine disparue,* alors réunis sous le titre *Sodome et Gomorrhe II"* (In 1918 Proust meant by *Sodome et Gomorrhe* the entire novel about Albertine, not just the current *Sodome et Gomorrhe* I and II, but also *La Prisonnière* and *Albertine disparue,* joined together at the time under the title *Sodome et Gomorrhe II* [xxiv]).

2. For a different perspective making a Freudian argument, see, for example, Bowie, *Freud, Proust, and Lacan.* And I read as I correct this manuscript that the indefatigable Jean-Yves Tadié has just published a constructed dialogue between Proust and Freud, *Le lac inconnu.*

3. As the historian James F. McMillan has argued, if there was one thing that the dominant clerical and anticlerical groups were united on, it was opposition to women's demand for more rights—this was true of many liberals in the anticlerical party, because they feared that most women were reactionary, anti-Republican Catholics who would bring down the Republic if allowed to vote as the priests would tell them. See "Clericals, Anticlericals and the Women's Movement in France under the Third Republic," *Historical Journal* 24 (1981): 361–76.

4. See René Girard, *Mensonge romantique,* for the discussion of "le désir triangulaire." Jean-Paul Sartre's definition of desire can be found in a number of his writings, though his central work in this regard is *L'être et le néant* (Paris: Gallimard, 1943).

5. Throughout the novel Proust echoes Pascal's *pensée* about the need for divertissement to mask one's misery: "Les hommes n'ayant pu guérir la mort, la misère, l'ignorance, ils se sont avisés, pour se rendre heureux, de n'y point penser" (Men not being able to cure death, misery, and ignorance, they realized that, in order to achieve happiness, they shouldn't think about them at all [*Les pensées,* no. 168, Brunschievg edition]). The socialites' frivolity and vanity are thus proof of misery, for the great function of these qualities is to mask what produces them. In fine this view is also consonant with Proust's Pascalian vision of the *moi*—the hateful self.

6. Most recently the connection of Proust and Buddhism was argued by the noted theorist Eve Kosofsky Sedgwick. In her posthumously published papers in *The Weather in Proust,* she found in Proust a "psychology of surprise" based on his view of the disjunctive self. This led her to compare Proust and his type of mysticism with the Buddhist doctrine she was mastering in order to face, in peace, her impending death from cancer.

7. See Rivers, *Proust and the Art of Love.*

8. In a history of the city of Venice, Christian Bec turns to Proust at the conclusion to voice a complaint about the famous tourist. The historian is not happy that Proust, in describing Venice, first gives the impression of avoiding clichés and then goes on to fall into the usual platitudes about the mysteries and enchantments of the city. Perhaps true from a purely historical view, this interpretation does not take into account (nor should it) that in his wandering, Proust's narrator is, for a moment, an enchanted traveler, not a realist. Bec, *Histoire de Vénise* (Paris: PUF, 1993), 116.

Chapter 7. *Time Regained*

1. For a fitting commentary on the final reception of the self-parodying social-ites in *Time Regained* as well as the baron's descent into the netherworld of a male brothel, I recommend Bakhtin's description of the typically carnivalesque gathering of characters in Dostoyevsky. For example after describing the satirical dialogues of the dead in a cemetery found in the short story "Bobok," Bahktin goes on to com-ment on the dialogic exchange at social gatherings in the major novels such as *The Idiot* or *The Brothers Karamazov*:

> These scenes, usually taking place in drawing rooms, are of course
> considerably more complex, more motley, more full of carnivalized
> contrasts, abrupt mésalliances and eccentricities, fundamental crown-
> ings and decrownings, but their inner essence is analogous: the "rotten
> cords" of the official and personal lie are snapped (or at least weakened
> for the moment), and human souls are laid bare, either terrible souls
> as in the nether world, or else bright and pure ones. People appear
> for a moment outside the usual conditions of their lives, on the carni-
> val square or in the nether world, and there opens up another—more
> genuine—sense of themselves and of their relationships to one another.
> (Bakhtin, *Problems of Dostoevsky's Poetics,* trans. Caryl Emerson [Min-
> neapolis: University of Minnesota Press, 1984], 145)
>   Resurrection and revelation are both products of the carnival, in
> which truth emerges out of the destructive confrontation of competing
> lies.

2. For example the comparatist Philippe Chardin has written a good study of the matter in his three-part study "Proust lecteur de Dostoevski."

3. Besides the viewpoint of his neo-Kantian professors, Proust undoubtedly knew Poincaré's thoughts on this epistemological point, for instance from the phys-icist's widely read *La science et l'hypothese* of 1902. For a good book on Poincaré's reception among the general public, especially with regard to his philosophy of mathematics, see Linda Henderson, *The Fourth Dimension and Non-Euclidean Geometry* (Princeton: Princeton University Press, 1983).

4. There is also a remarkable overlap between the scientist and the novelist concerning artistic truth and mathematics. Poincaré's epistemology allows the mind in fact to find a type of certainty in itself, one comparable to Proust's description of the artist's certainty. Poincaré recognized that scientific truth is largely a product of reasoning through recurrence. He describes both empirical statements and math-ematical statements as products of induction. Empirical inductions are contingent statements—uncertain because they are about the exterior world, so that "they rest upon a belief in a general order of the Universe, an order that is outside of us" (*La science et l'hypothèse* [Rueil-Malmaison: Editions de la bohème, 1992], 30). But mathematical induction can impose itself as a form of certitude, because faced with the infinite recurrence that characterizes mathematical propositions, the mind

recognizes, in direct intuition, its own power to make such infinite extensions. Or to quote Poincaré again: "Mathematical induction, which is to say, demonstration through recurrence, imposes itself . . . because it is simply an affirmation of a property of mind itself" (31). From this perspective the type of certainty that mathematics offers is a property of the mind, and the fact that the world allows mathematics to describe it is a tribute to the mind.

5. Poincaré, *Science et l'hypothèse,* 11.

Bibliography

Editions of *A la recherche du temps perdu*

A la recherche du temps perdu, 3 vols. Edited by Pierre Clarac and André Ferré. Paris: Pléiade, 1954. Still useful and easy to read.

A la recherche du temps perdu, 10 vols. Edited by Jean Milly et al. Paris: Garnier Flammarion, 1984–87. Well edited, much information.

A la recherche du temps perdu, 4 vols. Edited by Jean-Yves Tadié. Paris: Pléiade, 1987–89. The definitive edition.

A la recherche du temps perdu, 7 vols. Edited by Jeans-Yves Tadié. Paris: Folio, 1988–94. Reproduces the novelistic texts of Tadié's Pléiade edition in paperback. Highly recommended.

A la recherche du temps perdu, 7 vols. Edited by Bernard Brun et al. Paris: Livre de Poche, 1992–93. Done under direction of a specialist in Proust manuscripts (includes different versions of *La Fugitive*).

Translations of *A la recherche du temps perdu*

In Search of Lost Time. 6 vols. Translated by C. K. Scott Moncrieff and Terence Kilmartin. Revised by D. J. Enright. New York: Modern Library, 1992.

In Search of Lost Time. 6 vols. Edited by Christopher Prendergast. London: Lane, 2002. A different translator for each volume.

Other Works by Proust

Les plaisirs et les jours. 1896. Preface by Anatole France. Edited by Thierry Laget. Paris: Folio, 1993.

Pastiches et mélanges. 1919. Paris: Gallimard, 1992.

Chroniques. Preface by Robert Proust. Paris: Gallimard, 1927.

Jean Santeuil. 3 vols. Preface by André Maurois. Edited by Bernard de Fallois. Paris: Gallimard, 1952.

Contre Sainte-Beuve. Suivi de "Nouveaux mélanges." Edited by Bernard de Fallois. Paris: Gallimard, 1954. Continuously in print in a Gallimard Folio edition.

Contre Sainte-Beuve. Précédé de "Pastiches et mélanges" et suivi de Essais et articles. Edited by Pierre Clarac and Yves Sandre. Paris: Pléïade, 1971.

Jean Santeuil. Précédé de "Les plaisirs et les jours." Edited by Pierre Clarac and Yves Sandre. Paris: Pléïade, 1971.

Textes retrouvés. Edited by Philip Kolb and Larkin B. Price. Cahiers Marcel Proust, no. 3. Paris: Gallimard, 1971.

Le carnet de 1908. Edited by Philip Kolb. Cahiers Marcel Proust, no. 8. Paris: Gallimard, 1976.

L'indifférent. Nouvelle. Edited by Philip Kolb. Paris: Gallimard, 1978. Reedited in various editions.

Écrits de jeunesse, 1887–1895. Edited by Anne Borrel. Illiers-Combray: Institut Marcel Proust International, 1991.

Écrits sur l'art. Edited by Jérome Picon. Paris: Flammarion, 1999.

Jean Santeuil. Edited by Jean-Yves Tadié. Paris: Quarto Gallimard, 2001.

L'indifférent et autres textes de jeunesses. Paris: Mille et une nuits, 2006.

Translations by Proust

Ruskin, John. *La Bible d'Amiens.* Paris: Mercure de France, 1904. Reedited by Jean-Michel Argal. Paris: Bartillat, 2007.

———. *Sésame et les lys.* Paris: Mercure de France, 1906. Reedited by Antoine Compagnon. Brussels: Complexes, 1987.

Selected Translations of Proust's Other Works

Marcel Proust. A Selection from His Miscellaneous Writings. Translated by Gerard Hopkins. London: Allan Wingate, 1948.

Pleasures and Regrets. Translated by Louise Varèse. New York: Crown, 1948. Republished in *Pleasures and Days, and Other Writings.* Edited by F. W. Dupee. New York: Fertig, 1978.

By Way of Sainte-Beuve (Contre Sainte-Beuve). Translated by Sylvia Townsend Warner. London: Chatto & Windus, 1958. Republished as *Marcel Proust: On Art and Literature.* New York: Carroll & Graf, 1984.

Jean Santeuil. Translated by Gerard Hopkins. London: Penguin Books, 1985.

Against Sainte-Beuve and Other Essays. Translated by John Sturrock. London: Penguin Books, 1988. Based on the 1971 Pléïade edition.

Pleasures and Days. Translated by Andrew Brown. London: Hesperus Classics, 2004.

On Reading Ruskin: Prefaces to "La Bible d'Amiens" and "Sésame et les lys." Translated and edited by Jean Autret, William Burford, and Phillip J. Wolfe. New Haven: Yale University Press, 1987.

The Complete Short Stories of Marcel Proust. Translated by Joachim Neugroschel. New York: Cooper Square Press, 2001. Seven major texts.

There exists a useful Marcel Proust Ephemera site on the Web: www.yorktaylors.free-online.co.uk. Bibliography of nearly all short texts by Proust with many translations of them into English.

Proust's Correspondence

Correspondance générale de Marcel Proust. 6 vols. Edited by Robert Proust, Paul Brach, and Suzy Mante-Proust. Paris: Plon, 1930–36.

Correspondance de Marcel Proust. Edited by Philip Kolb. 21 vols. Paris: Plon, 1970–93.

Lettres à Reynaldo Hahn. Edited by Philip Kolb. Paris: Gallimard, 1984.

Index general de la correspondance de Marcel Proust. Edited by Kazuyoshi Yoshikawa. Kyoto: Presses de l'Université de Kyoto, 1998.

Numerous editions and reprints of correspondence to various individuals have been published.

Letters Translated into English

Selected Letters. 4 vols. Edited by Philip Kolb. Vol. 1: 1880–1903. Translated by Ralph Manheim. New York: Doubleday, 1983. Vol. 2: 1904–9. Translated by Terence Kilmartin. London: Collins, 1989. Vol. 3: 1910–17. Translated by Terence Kilmartin. London: HarperCollins, 1992. Vol. 4: 1919–22. Translated by Joanna Kilmartin. London: HarperCollins, 2000.

Bibliographies

Ahlstedt, Eva. *La Pudeur en crise: Un aspect de l'accueil d'"A la recherche du temps perdu" de Marcel Proust 1913–1930.* Paris: Touzot, 1985.

Alden, D. W., and R. A. Brooks, eds. *A Critical Bibliography of French Literature: The Twentieth Century.* Enlarged ed. Syracuse: Syracuse University Press, 1952.

Alden, Douglas W. *Marcel Proust and His French Critics.* 1940. New York: Russell, 1973.

Bonnet, Henri. *Marcel Proust de 1907 à 1914.* Paris: Nizet, 1959. Repr. 1971. General bibliography before 1970.

———. *Marcel Proust de 1907 à 1914: Bibliographie complémentaire (II).* Paris: Nizet, 1976. Supplement to Bonnet's first bibliography.

Graham, Victor E. *Bibliographie des études sur Marcel Proust et son œuvre.* Geneva: Droz, 1976.

Pistorius, George. *Marcel Proust und Deutschland: Eine Internationale Bibliographie,* 2nd ed. Heidelberg: Winter, 2002.

Price, Larkin B. *A Checklist of the Proust Holdings at the University of Illinois Library at Urbana-Champaign.* Urbana: University of Illinois, 1975.

Stock, Janet C. *Marcel Proust: A Reference Guide, 1950–1970.* Boston: Hall, 1991.

———. "Marcel Proust: A Selected, Annotated, and Critical Bibliography, 1968–1978." PhD dissertation, University of Michigan, Ann Arbor, 1982.

Taylor, Elisabeth Russell. *Marcel Proust and His Contexts: A Critical Bibliography of English Language Scholarship.* New York: Garland, 1981.

Tadié, Jean-Yves. *Lectures de Proust.* Paris: Colin, 1971. Excerpts of critics.

The following periodicals contain annual bibliographies: *Bulletin Marcel Proust, Cahiers Marcel Proust* (1971–87), *Bulletin d informations proustiennes*. The content of each issue of *Bulletin de la société des amies de Marcel Proust* is online through 2008. For recent work on Proust, the annual bibliography of the PMLA is probably the most accessible and complete resource.

Selected Biographies of Proust

Albaret, Céleste, and Georges Belmont. *Monsieur Proust.* Paris: Laffont, 1973. Translated by Barbara Bray. New York: McGraw-Hill, 1976.

Bardèche, Maurice. *Marcel Proust romancier,* 2 vols. Paris: Les sept couleurs, 1971.

Bonnet, Henri. *Les amours et la sexualité de Marcel Proust.* Paris: Nizet, 1985.

Brun, Bernard. *Marcel Proust.* Paris: Cavalier Bleu, 2007.

Carter, William. *Marcel Proust: A Life.* New Haven: Yale University Press, 2000.

Ferré, André. *Les années de college de Marcel Proust.* Paris: Gallimard, 1959.

Hayman, Ronald. *Proust: A Biography.* London: Heinemann, 1990.

Maurois, André. *A la recherche de Marcel Proust.* Paris: Hachette, 1949.

Painter, George D. *Marcel Proust,* 2 vols. London: Chatto & Windus, 1959–65.

Pierre-Quint, Léon. *Marcel Proust, sa vie, son oeuvre.* 1925. Paris: Le Sagittaire, 1976.

Tadié, Jean-Yves. *Marcel Proust.* Paris: Gallimard, 1996. Translated by Euan Cameron. New York: Viking, 2000. Today's definitive biography.

White, Edmund. *Marcel Proust.* New York: Viking, 1999.

Selected Critical Books on Proust

Autret, Jean. *L'influence de Ruskin sur la vie, les idées et l'oeuvre de Marcel Proust.* Geneva: Droz, 1955.

Bales, Richard, *Proust and the Middle Ages,* Geneva: Droz, 1975.

Bales, Richard, ed. *The Cambridge Companion to Proust.* Cambridge: Cambridge University Press, 2001.

Beckett, Samuel. *Proust.* London: Chatto & Windus, 1931.

Béhar, Serge. *L'univers médical de Proust.* Paris: Gallimard, 1970.

Bersani, Jacques. *Proust et les critiques de notre temps.* Paris: Garnier, 1971.

Bersani, Leo. *Marcel Proust: The Fictions of Life and of Art.* New York: Oxford University Press, 1965.

Bouillanguet, Annick, and Brian G. Rogers, eds. *Dictionnaire Marcel Proust.* Paris: Champion, 2004.

Bowie, Malcolm. *Freud, Proust and Lacan: Theory as Fiction.* Cambridge: Cambridge University Press, 1987.

———. *Proust among the Stars.* New York: Columbia University Press, 1998.

———. *Proust, Jealousy, Knowledge.* London: University of London Press, 1978.

Boyer, Philippe. *Le petit pan de mur jaune: Sur Proust.* Paris: Seuil, 1987.

Brady, Patrick. *Marcel Proust.* Boston: Twayne, 1977.

Brée, Germaine. *Du temps perdu au Temps retrouvé. Introduction à l'oeuvre de Marcel Proust.* Paris: Les Belles lettres, 1950. Translated by C. J. Richards and

A. D. Truit as *Marcel Proust and Deliverance from Time*. New Brunswick: Rutgers University Press, 1955.

———. *The World of Marcel Proust*. Boston: Houghton Mifflin, 1966.

Bret, Jacques. *Marcel Proust, Étude critique*. Geneva: Mont-Blanc, 1946.

Compagnon, Antoine. *Proust entre deux siècles*. Paris: Seuil, 1989. Translated by Richard E. Goodin as *Proust between Two Centuries*. New York: Columbia University Press, 1992.

Curtius, Ernst Robert. *Marcel Proust*. 1919. Frankfurt: Suhrkamp, 1952. Translated by Armand Pierhal as *Marcel Proust*. Paris: Revue nouvelle, 1928. (First version available in *Die literarischen Wegbereiter des neuen Franksreich*. 3rd ed. Potsdam: Kiepenheuer, 1923. Also available online.)

Deleuze, Gilles. *Proust et les signes*. Paris: Presses Universitaires de France, 1964. Translated by Richard Howard as *Proust and Signs*. New York: Braziller, 1972.

Descombes, Vincent. *Proust. Philosophie du roman*. Paris: Minuit, 1987. Translated by Catharine Chance Macksey as *Proust: Philosophy of the Novel*. Stanford: Stanford University Press, 1992.

Dezon-Jones, Elyane, and Inge Crosman Wimmers, eds. *Approaches to Teaching Proust's Fiction and Criticism*. New York: Modern Language Association of America, 2003.

Doubrovsky, Serge. *La place de la madeleine*. Paris: Mercure de France, 1974.

Dubois, Jacques. *Pour Albertine. Proust et le sens du social*. Paris: Seuil, 1997.

Feuillerat, Albert. *Comment Proust a composé son roman*. New Haven: Yale University Press, 1934.

Finn, Michael R. *Proust, the Body and Literary Form*. Cambridge: Cambridge University Press, 1999.

Fraisse, Luc. *L'oeuvre-cathédrale. Proust et l'architecture medieval*. Paris: Corti, 1990.

———. *L'esthétique de Marcel Proust*. Paris: Sedes, 1995.

———. *Le processus de la création chez Marcel Proust. Le fragment experimental*. Paris: Corti, 1988.

Fumaroli, Marc. *Littérature et conversation: La Querelle Sainte-Beuve-Proust*. Cassal Lecture. London: University of London, 1991.

Gaubert, Serge. *Proust et le roman de la différence: L'individu et le monde social de "Jean Santeuil" à "La Recherche."* Lyon: Presses Universitaires de Lyon, 1980.

Genette, Gérard. *Figures*. Vol. 3. Paris: Seuil, 1972. Translated by Jane E. Lewin as *Narrative Discourse: An Essay in Method*. Ithaca, N.Y.: Cornell University Press, 1980.

Genette, Gérard, and Tzvetan Todorov, eds. *Recherche de Proust*. Paris: Seuil, 1980. Essays by Roland Barthes, Leo Bersani, John Porter Houston, Philippe Lejeune, Jean Rousset, and others.

Girard, René. *Mensonge romantique et vérité romanesque*. Paris: Grasset, 1961. Translated by Yvonne Freccero as *Deceit, Desire, and the Novel: Self and Other in Literary Structure*. Baltimore: Johns Hopkins University Press, 1965.

Girard, René, ed. *Proust: A Collection of Critical Essays.* Englewood Cliffs, N.J.: Prentice-Hall, 1965.

Graham, Victor E. *The Imagery of Proust.* New York: Barnes & Noble, 1966.

Henry, Ann. *Marcel Proust. Théories pour une esthétique.* Paris: Klincksieck, 1981.

———. *Proust romancier. Le tombeau égyptien.* Paris: Flammarion, 1983.

Hier, Florence. *La musique dans l'œuvre de Marcel Proust.* New York: Columbia University, 1933. Early thesis that is still useful for overview.

Hindus, Milton. *The Proustian Vision.* New York: Columbia University Press, 1954.

Hodson, Leighton. *Marcel Proust: The Critical Heritage.* New York: Routledge, 1989. Overview with translations of early critical reception.

Houston, John Porter. *The Shape and Style of Proust's Novel.* Detroit: Wayne State University Press, 1982.

Huas, Jeanine. *Les femmes chez Proust.* Paris: Hachette, 1971.

Hughes, Edward J. *Marcel Proust: A Study in the Quality of Awareness.* Cambridge: Cambridge University Press, 1983.

Jauss, Hans Robert. *Zeit und Erinnerug in Marcel Proust's "A la recherche du temps perdu."* 1955. Frankfurt: Suhrkamp, 1986.

Ifri, Pascal. *Proust et son narrataire dans "À la recherche du temps perdu."* Geneva: Droz, 1983.

Karpeles, Eric. *Paintings in Proust.* London: Thames & Hudson, 2008.

Landy, Joshua. *Philosophy as Fiction: Self, Deception, and Knowledge in Proust.* New York: Oxford University Press, 2004.

Large, Duncan. *Nietzsche and Proust: A Comparative Study.* New York: Oxford University Press, 2001.

Luckhurst, Nicola. *Science and Structure in Proust's "A la recherche du temps perdu."* Oxford: Oxford University Press, 2000.

Matoré, Georges, and Irène Mecz. *Musique et structure romanesque dans "La Recherche du temps perdu."* Paris: Klincksieck, 1972.

Milly, Jean. *Les pastiches de Proust.* Paris: Colin, 1971.

———. *La phrase de Proust: Des phrases de Bergotte aux phrases de Vinteuil.* Paris: Larousse, 1975.

———. *Proust et le style.* 1970. Geneva: Slatkine, 1991.

Mortimer, Armine Kotin, and Katherine Kolb, eds. *Proust in Perspective: Visions and Revisions.* Urbana: University of Illinois Press, 2002.

Moss, Howard. *The Magic Lantern of Marcel Proust.* New York: Macmillan, 1962.

Muller, Marcel. *Les voix narratives dans "À la recherche du temps perdu."* Geneva: Droz, 1965.

Picon, Gaëtan. *Lecture de Proust.* Paris: Mercure de France, 1963.

Piroué, Georg. *Proust et la musique du devenir.* Paris: Denoël, 1960.

Poulet, Georges. *L'espace proustien.* Paris: Gallimard, 1963. Translated by Elliot Coleman as *Proustian Space.* Baltimore: Johns Hopkins University Press, 1977.

Price, Larkin B., ed. *Marcel Proust: A Critical Panorama.* Urbana: University of Illinois Press, 1973. A collection of essays by major scholars.

Raimond, Michel. *La crise du roman, des lendemains du naturalisme aux années vingt.* Paris: Corti, 1966.

———. *Proust romancier.* Paris: Sedes, 1984.

———. *Le Signe des temps.* Paris: Sedes, 1976.

Richard, Jean-Pierre. *Proust et le monde sensible.* Paris: Seuil, 1974.

Rivière, Jacques. *Quelques progrès dans l'étude du coeur humain.* 1926. Edited by Thierry Laget. Cahiers Marcel Proust, n.s. 13. Paris: Gallimard, 1985.

Rivers, J. E. *Proust and the Art of Love: The Aesthetics of Sexuality in the Life, Times, and Art of Marcel Proust.* New York: Columbia University Press, 1980.

Rosengarten, Frank. *The Writings of Young Marcel Proust: An Ideological Critique.* New York: Lang, 2001.

Sedgwick, Eve Kosofsky. *The Weather in Proust.* Edited by Jonathan Goldberg. Durham, N.C.: Duke University Press, 2011.

Shattuck, Roger. *Proust's Binoculars.* New York: Random House, 1963.

———. *Proust's Way: A Field Guide to "In Search of Lost Time."* New York: Norton, 2000.

Souday, Paul. *Marcel Proust.* Paris: Kra, 1927.

Strauss, Walter. *Proust and Literature: The Novelist as Critic.* Cambridge, Mass.: Harvard University Press, 1957.

Thody, Philip Malcolm Waller. *Marcel Proust.* New York: St. Martin's, 1988.

Topping, Margaret. *Proust's Gods: Christian and Mythological Figures of Speech in the Works of Marcel Proust.* Oxford: Oxford University Press, 2000.

Sprinker, Michael. *History and Ideology in Proust.* Cambridge: Cambridge University Press, 1994.

Tadié, Jean-Yves. *Le lac inconnu: Entre Proust et Freud.* Paris: Gallimard, 2012.

———. *Proust et le roman.* Paris: Gallimard, 1971.

Wolitz, Seth. *The Proustian Community.* New York: New York University Press, 1971.

Wilson, Edmund. *Axel's Castle: A Study in the Imaginative Literature of 1870–1930.* New York: Scribner, 1931.

Watt, Adam A. *The Cambridge Introduction to Marcel Proust.* Cambridge: Cambridge University Press, 2011.

Selected Articles and Essays on Proust

Barnes, Annie. "Proust et Pascal." *Europe* 502–3 (1971): 193–204.

———. "Proust lecteur de Pascal." *Bulletin de la société des amis de Marcel Proust* 27 (1977): 392–409. Both essays deal with Proust's important relation to the seventeenth-century mathematician and Jansenist apologist of Christianity.

Barthes, Roland. "Proust et les noms." In *Degré zéro de lécriture*, 121–34. Paris: Seuil, 1972. Early application of semiology.

Bisson, L. A. "Proust and Ruskin: Reconsidered in Light of *Lettres à une amie.*" *Modern Language Review* 39 (1944): 28–37. Proust's debt to the English critic.

Benjamin, Walter. "The Image of Proust." In *Illuminations,* translated by Harry Zohn, 201–16. New York: Schocken, 1968. Dense meditation on memory by one of the most influential twentieth-century critics.

Blanchot, Maurice. "L'expérience de Proust." In *Le livre à venir,* 19–37. Paris: Gallimard, 1959.

Borowitz, Helen Osterman. "The Watteau and Chardin of Marcel Proust." *Bulletin of the Cleveland Museum of Art* 69 (1982): 166–88. Proust's debt to two important painters.

Brée, Germaine. "From *Jean Santeuil* to *Time Regained.*" *Bucknell Review* 6, no. 3 (1956): 16–21.

———. "*Jean Santeuil.* An Appraisal." *Esprit créateur* 5 (1965): 14–25.

———. "Proust et l'affaire Dreyfus à la lumière de *Jean Santeuil.*" In *Marcel Proust: A Critical Panorama,* edited by Larkin B. Price, 1–23. Urbana: University of Illinois Press, 1973.

———. "Proust's Dormant Gods." *Yale French Studies* 38 (1967). 183–94. One of Proust's most influential critics, especially for his work and society.

Carassus, Emilien. "L'affaire Dreyfus et l'espace romanesque: De *Jean Santeuil* à la *Recherche du temps perdu.*" *Revue d'histoire littéraire de la France* 71 (1971): 836–53. Politics of turn-of-the-century France and Proust.

Champigny, Robert. "Temps et reconnaissance chez Proust et quelques philosophes." *PMLA* 73 (1958). 129–35. A philosopher who influenced many readings of Proust's vision of time.

Chardin, Philippe. "Proust lecteur de Dostoevski." *Lettres Romanes* 2 (1971): 119–52; 3 (1971): 231–69; 4 (1971): 339–49. Overview of how Proust read several works by Dostoyevsky.

Clark, Priscilla. "Proustian Order and the Aristocracy of Time Past." *French Review* 47, no. 6 (1974): 92–104. Insight into Proust's analysis of social classes.

Cohen, Robert G. "Proust and Mallarmé." *French Studies* 24 (1970): 262–75. Proust's relation to the most important of the French symbolist poets.

Cohn, Dorrit. "Proust's Generic Ambiguity." In *The Distinction of Fiction,* 58–78. Baltimore: Johns Hopkins University Press, 1999. One of our best critics on the rhetorical aspects of fiction.

Dancy, Jonathan. "New Truths in Proust?" *Modern Language Review* 90 (1995): 18–28. Considerations of epistemology.

Eells, Emily. "Nos pères nous l'ont dit: Proust et *La Bible d'Amiens.*" *Bulletin Marcel Proust* 54 (2004): 51–63. Relationship of Proust and Ruskin.

Fieschi, Pascal. "Le temps perdu est retrouvé." In *Proust,* edited by Antoine Adam, 243–73. Paris: Hachette, 1965. Proust, metaphysics, and differences between him and Henri Bergson.

Gatrall, Jefferson J. A. "Contre Bakhtin? The Problems of Poetry in Proust's *A la recherche du temps perdu.*" *Studies in Slavic Cultures* 4 (2003): 81–102. Reading of *Against Sainte-Beuve* in the context of an imagined confrontation between Proust and Bakhtin.

Genette, Gérard. "Proust et le langage indirect." In *Figures II,* 223–94. Paris: Seuil, 1969.

———. "Proust palimpseste." In *Figures I,* 39–67. Paris: Seuil, 1966. Genette is a theorist of rhetoric who is one of Proust's best readers.

Gicquel, Bernard. "La composition des *Plaisirs et les jours.*" *Bulletin des Amis de Marcel Proust* 10 (1960): 249–61.

Gross, David. "Bergson, Proust, and the Reevaluation of Memory." *International Philosophical Quarterly* 25 (1985): 369–80. A philosopher looks at problems of memory in Proust.

Henry, Anne. "*Les Plaisirs et les jours:* Chronologie et metamorphoses." *Cahiers Marcel Proust* 6 (1973): 60–93.

Houston, John Porter. "Temporal Patterns in *A la recherche du temps perdu.*" *French Studies* 16 (1962): 33–44.

Johnson, J. Theodore. "La Lanterne magique: Proust's Metaphorical Toy." *Esprit créateur* 11 (1971): 17–31. A specialist in Proust and painting analyses a key metaphor.

Kolb, Philip. "Historique du premier roman de Proust." *Saggi e ricerche di letteratura francese* 4 (1963): 217–77.

———. "The Making of a Novel." In *Marcel Proust 1871–1922: A Centenary Volume,* edited by Peter Quenell, 25–56. New York: Simon & Schuster, 1971.

———. "Proust et Ruskin. Nouvelles Perspectives." *Cahiers de l'association internationale des études françaises* 12 (1960): 259–73. Kolb was the scholarly trailblazer on questions of genesis of Proust's texts.

Large, Duncan. "Proust on Nietzsche: The Question of Friendship." *Modern Language Review* 88 (1993): 612–24. Essay on the vexed question of Proust's attitude toward friendship.

Macksey, Richard. "'Conclusion' and 'Incitation': Proust à la recherche de Ruskin." *Modern Language Notes* 96 (1981): 1113–19. Help in making sense of how Proust dealt with Ruskin.

Maranini, Lorenza. "*Le côté de Guermantes,* Swann e il narratore proustiano (Dal mito alla demistificazione)." In *Atti del convegno internazionale di studio sullopera di Marcel Proust,* 123–65. Padua: Liviana, 1971. Major study of narrative roles in Proust.

Milly, Jean. "Sur quelques noms proustiens." *Littérature* 14 (1974): 65–82.

O'Brien, Justin. "Albertine the Ambiguous: Notes on Proust's Transposition of the Sexes." *PMLA* 64 (1949): 933–52.

———. "Marcel Proust as Moralist." *Romanic Review* 39 (1948): 50–69.

———. "Proust, Gide, and the Sexes." *PMLA* 65 (1950): 653. Articles that, before gay liberation, set up a debate about sex in Proust. Includes a letter answering Harry Levin's criticism of him.

Simon, Agathe. "Proust, l'instant et le sublime." *Revue d'histoire littéraire de la France* 103 (2003): 861–87. Time and postmodern sublime.

Simon, Daniel. "Translating Ruskin: Marcel Proust's Orient of Devotion." *Comparative Literature Studies* 38 (2001): 142–68. Good on Ruskin's influence on Proust.

Spitzer, Leo. "Zum Stil Marcel Prousts." 1928. In *Stilstudien.* Munich: Hueber, 1961. Translated as "Le style de Proust." In *Etudes de Style,* translated by Alain Coulon, Éliane Kaufholz, and Michel Foucault, 397–473. Paris: Gallimard, 1970. Fundamental study by one of the founders of modern stylistic studies.

Strauss, Walter A. "Proust-Giotto-Dante." *Dante Studies* 96 (1978): 163–85. For the Italian connection.

Suzuki, Michihiko. "Le 'je' proustien." *Bulletin de la Société des amis de Marcel Proust* 9 (1959): 69–82. Sensitive and influential reading of Proust's narrative voice.

Ullmann, Stephen. "The Metaphorical Texture of a Proustian Novel." In *The Image in the Modern French Novel,* 124–238. Cambridge: Cambridge University Press, 1960.

———. "Transposition of Sensations in Proust's Images." *French Studies* 8 (1954): 28–43. Republished in *Style in the French Novel,* 189–209. Cambridge: Cambridge University Press, 1957. Major studies in Proust's style from a critic versed in linguistics.

Vitanen, Reino. "Proust's Metaphors from the Exact and Natural Sciences." *PMLA* 69 (1954): 1038–59. Early study showing how much Proust's work is informed by science.

Waters, Harold A. "The Narrator, not Marcel." *French Review* 33 (1960): 389–92. The narrator is not Proust.

Weber, Jean-Paul. "Bergson and Proust." In *In Search of Marcel Proust, Essays,* edited by Monique Chifdor, 55–77. Claremont, Cal.: Scripps College, 1973. Good appreciation of how Proust is not beholden to Bergson.

Yacobi, Tamar. "Narrative Structure and Fictional Mediation." *Poetics Today* 8 (1987): 335–72. Intelligent study of the rhetorical structure in Proust.

Index

A la recherche du temps perdu. See *In Search of Lost Time*

A l'ombre des jeunes filles en fleurs (*Within a Budding Grove*). See under *In Search of Lost Time*

Abbott, Edwin A., 282

"Accursed Race, An" ("La race maudite"), 105–7. See also *Against Sainte-Beuve*

Action Française, 14–15

"Against Obscurity" ("Contre l'obscurité"), 52–54, 61, 131

Against Sainte-Beuve (*Contre Sainte-Beuve*), 18, 24, 27, 30, 68–69, 93–110, 131, 175. See also Sainte-Beuve, Charles-Augustin

Agostinelli, Alfred, 16, 19–20

Albaret, Céleste, 24

Albertine disparue, 21, 24, 200. See also *In Search of Lost Time—Vol. 6: The Fugitive*

"amour de Swann, Un" ("Swann in Love"). See under *In Search of Lost Time—Vol. 1: Swann's Way*

anti-Platonism. See Platonism

aristocracy, 141–42, 180–81. See also *In Search of Lost Time*

"Article in Le Figaro" ("L'article dans 'Le Figaro'"), 95–96. See also *Against Sainte-Beuve*

Aurore (newspaper), 215

Auteil, 1

"Avant la nuit." *See* "Before the Night"

Bainville, Jacques, 23

Bakhtin, Mikhail, 249, 254–55, 256

Balzac, Honoré de, 12, 27, 97–99, 104–5, 108, 114, 140, 179, 183

Banquet, Le (student journal), 5–6, 7

Barbusse, Henri, 5–6

Bardèche, Maurice, 78

Baudelaire, Charles, 4, 5, 12, 27, 29–30, 34, 38, 50, 52, 91, 97, 109, 179, 282–83

Beckett, Samuel, 39, 140

Beethoven, Ludwig van, 51

"Before the Night" ("Avant la nuit"), 28–29

belle époque, 2

Bergson, Henri, 5, 8, 205, 233, 234

Bible, 62, 202, 203, 204, 209, 211, 271

Bible of Amiens, The (*Bible d'Amiens, La*; Ruskin), 13, 15, 58–59, 60, 61–62

Bisson, L. A., 59, 60

Bizet, Geneviève Straus (née Halévy), 3

Bizet, Georges, 3

Bizet, Jacques, 3

Blanchot, Maurice, 75

Blum, Léon, 5

Boisdeffre, Raoul François Charles Le Mouton de, 85

Bonnefoy, Yves, 176

Bonnier, Gaston, 136–37

Borowitz, Helen O., 71

Botticelli, Alessandro, 143–44

Bourget, Paul, 23

Boutroux, Émile, 5, 8–9

Bouvard et Pécuchet (Flaubert), 44

Brée, Germaine, 78

Brun, Bernard, 246

Burke, Edmund, 180, 181

Caillavet, Arman de, 4

Caillavet, Gaston de, 4, 5

Calmann-Levy (publisher), 12

Captive, The (*La prisonnière*). See under *In Search of Lost Time*

carnivalesque literature, 254. See also *In Search of Lost Time—Vol. 7: Time Regained*

Carter, William, 12

cathedrals, 61–63

Chambord, Comte de, 186

Chamfort, Nicolas, 46

Chardin, Jean-Baptiste-Siméon, 70–72

Chateaubriand, François-René de, 110, 178

"Chopin," 30–31, 50

Chopin, Frédéric, 30–31

"Chose normandes." See "Norman Things"

Christianity and Christians, 126–27

Cicero, 145

"Cires perdues." See "Lost Wax"

"Clair de lune." See "Moonlight"

Clarac, Pierre, 89, 246

Cocteau, Jean, 203

"colère de Samson, La" (Vigny). See "Samson's Anger"

"Combray." See under *In Search of Lost Time—Vol. 1: Swann's Way*

Comédie humaine, La (Balzac), 108

"Comedy of High Society" ("Comédie mondaine"), 43

Compagon, Antoine, 200

Complete Short Stories, The (Proust), 29, 33

"Confession d'une jeune fille, La." See "Young Girl's Confession, The"

contingency and chance: art and, 287; contingency of real events, 99;

contingency of scientific laws, 275–76; knowledge of the self and, 126; narrator and, 279, 283, 286; Poincaré and, 281; Proust and, 228, 283–84

Contingency of the Laws of Nature, The (*De la contingence des lois de la nature*, Boutroux), 8–9

"Conversation avec Maman." See "Talking to Mama"

"Countess, The" ("La comtesse"), 104. See also *Against Sainte-Beuve*

"Critique of Hope in the Light of Love" ("Critique de l'espérance à la lumière de l'amour"), 47. See also *Pleasures and Days*

Curtius, Ernst-Robert, 23

Cuvier, Georges, 108

Cuyp, Albert, 32

Dante, 205, 206

Darlu, Alphonse, 3, 8, 12

Darwin, Charles, 210

Daudet, Mme Alphonse, 5

Daudet, Léon, 12–13, 14–15, 23

Daudet, Lucien, 12–13

"Days in an Automobile" ("Journées en automobile"), 138. See also *Pastiches et mélanges*

"Days of Reading" ("Journées de lecture"), 59, 60

De l'amour (Stendhal). See *On Love*

"Death of Baldassare Silvande, Viscount of Sylvania, The" ("La mort de Baldassare Silvande Vicomte de Sylvanie"), 35–37

Denis, Maurice, 67

Departure for a Ride on Horseback (*Le Départ pour la promenade à cheval*; Cuyp), 32

Descartes, René, 79, 235

determinism: Boutroux and, 8; genetic determinism, 104, 106; narrator and, 278, 280, 285, 288; Poincaré and, 288; Proust and, 104, 282; Stendhal and, 81

Deux chevaux de trait devant une chaumière. See *Two Workhorses in Front of a Thatched Hut*
Dictionary of Received Ideas (Flaubert), 45
"Dinner in High Society, A" (Un Dîner en ville"), 39–40
Divine Comedy (Dante), 205, 206
Dostoyevsky, Fyodor, 8, 27, 254–55
"Dream" ("Rêve"), 49. See also *Pleasures and Days*
Dreyfus, Alfred, 14
Dreyfus, Robert, 3, 5–6
Dreyfus affair, 14, 45, 85, 106, 160, 186, 214–15
Dreyfusards, 15, 252
Du côté de chez Swann (*Swann's Way*). See under *In Search of Lost Time*
Du côté de Guermantes (*The Guermantes Way*). See under *In Search of Lost Time*

Editions de la Pléiade (publisher), 24, 69, 73, 246
Einstein, Albert, 128, 281
Eliot, George, 76, 77
Emerson, Ralph Waldo, 42, 65
"Encounter by the Lake" ("Rencontre au bord du lac"), 48–49. See also *Pleasures and Days*
"End of Jealousy, The" ("La Fin de la Jalousie"), 37–38, 46
"End of the Night, The," 105–6
epistemology: meaning of, 278; modern epistemology, 288–89; narrator and, 279, 280; nineteenth-century epistemology, 288; Poincaré and, 129; Proust and, 9, 17, 108, 204
Exercices de style (Queneau), 17

Fallois, Bernard de (publisher), 18, 24, 69, 80, 89, 93–94, 99, 106
"Family Listening to Music, A" ("Famille écoutant la musique"), 49. See also *Pleasures and Days*

"Fan" ("Eventail"), 54–55
Fasquelle (publisher), 19
Father Goriot (Balzac), 183
Fathers and Sons (Turgenev), 181
"Fenêtres, Les." *See* "Windows, The"
Ferré, André, 246
Figaro, Le (newspaper), 16–17, 23, 56, 60, 138
"Fin de la Jalousie, La." See "End of Jealousy, The"
First Republic (France), 1
Flatland (Abbott), 282
Flaubert, Gustave, 23, 27, 34, 35, 98, 110–11, 114, 140
Flowers of Evil, The (*Les Fleurs du mal*; Baudelaire), 29–30, 97, 109
"Forest Scene" ("Sous-Bois"), 50. See also *Pleasures and Days*
"Fragments from Italian Comedy" ("Fragments de comédie italienne"), 42–44. See also *Pleasures and Days*
France, Anatole, 4, 11
François le Champi (Sand), 277
Freud, Sigmund, 122, 145, 203–5
Fugitive, The (*La fugitive*). See under *In Search of Lost Time*
Fumaroli, Marc, 179–81

Gallimard (publisher), 19, 20, 21
Gaubert, Serge, 78
Gaulois, Le (newspaper), 30
Genet, Jean, 209
"Gérard de Nerval," 107. See also *Against Sainte-Beuve*
Gicquel, Bernard, 34
Girard, René, 223
Gluck, Christoph Willibald, 31
Goncourt, Edmond de, 5, 249
Goncourt, Jules de, 249
Gothic Image: Religious Art in France in the Thirteenth Century, The (*L'art religieux du 13e siècle*; Mâle), 13
Grasset (publisher), 20
Gregh, Fernand, 5

Guermantes Way, The (Du côté de Guermantes). See under *In Search of Lost Time*

Haas, Charles, 20
habit: artists and, 185; determinism and, 288; habitual variations of habit, 128; memories of love and, 177; narrator and, 129–30, 193, 195, 281, 282, 288; as a Proustian theme or law, 39; sexual pleasure and 41–42; time and, 265; usual perceptions and the daily self and, 120–21, 195, 281, 282, 288
Hahn, Reynaldo, 7, 14, 17, 45
Halévy, Daniel, 1, 2, 6, 142
Hauser, Lionel, 21
Haussonville, Count d', 57
Heath, Willie, 33–34
"homme et la mer, L'." See "Man and the Sea"
homosexuality, 106. See also *In Search of Lost Time*—Vol. 4: *Sodom and Gomorrah;* Proust, Marcel
Horace (Roman satirist), 39–40
Houston, John, 133
Hugo, Victor, 53
Huxley Aldous, 23

Illiers (France), 1. See also *In Search of Lost Time; Jean Santeuil*
Imitation of Christ (Thomas à Kempis), 39
imperfect tense. See verb tenses
impressionism, 57
In Search of Lost Time (A la recherche du temps perdu): aesthetic vision or theory of, 59, 94, 95; art and music in, 49, 63–64, 108, 288; background of, 13, 15, 18–20, 28, 33; belief in science, 86; as a bildungsroman, 77, 156, 184–85, 189, 201–2, 215, 216, 247, 249, 251; characters and characterizations in, 225–26; concluding thoughts on, 278–90; conclusion of, 101; cycles of

events and characters in, 98, 246–47; death in, 36; desire for return to childhood in, 51; development and editions of, 24–25, 28, 115, 246–47; dreaming in, 235; Dreyfus affair in, 85, 87; education in, 74; fictional theory developed in, 95; friendship in, 74; grandmother in, 35; guilt in, 122–23; homosexuality in, 106, 107; human inadequacy in, 77; interpretations of, 20, 21, 269; love in, 37, 49; narrator and narrative voice in, 83, 89, 131, 155–57, 282–83; paradise in, 89; Racine mentioned in, 40; religion in, 42; reviews of, 23–24; self in, 8, 233, 234–35; setting for, 1; society in, 36, 103; snobs and egomaniacs in, 43, 56, 131–32; structure and strategies of, 34–35, 40, 55, 67, 87, 252, 265; themes of, 112, 233; time in, 64, 83, 113; universal fall in, 202. *See also* contingency and chance; habit; Vinteuil's sonata
—Vol. 1: *Swann's Way (Du côté de chez Swann)*: aristocracy and bourgeoisie in, 141–42, 146–47, 148–50; background of, 15, 17–20; Balbec (village), 133, 156; as a bildungsroman, 154; comedy and irony in, 114, 147, 148, 158; conclusion of, 152, 154; exploration of reading, writing, and art in, 131; habit and habitual deviation from habit, 129–30; history and subjectivity in, 141–42; laws in, 119–20, 121, 122–23, 126; marriage, love, and family in, 74, 81, 121–23, 142–46, 149, 151, 158; memory in, 117–21, 152–53; metaphor, allegory, and simile in, 145–46, 173; music and art in, 49, 143–44, 149–50; narrator and narrative voice in, 113–22, 140–41, 146, 150, 151, 154; narrator's

vocation and procrastination,
112–14, 123, 131, 132, 138, 150;
prelude, 118–19; reviews of, 23;
sections, 112–13; themes, 141, 158;
verb tenses in, 115–17, 118–19, 121
—"Combray": ambiguity in, 160;
chance and contingency in, 283;
church in, 62, 99, 127, 128, 129;
chronology of, 129; comedy and
irony in, 127, 133, 137–38, 139–
40; intimations of loss and evil
in, 134–36, 137, 138; intimations
of paradise in, 89, 112, 123,
127, 132, 133, 134, 136–37,
283; intimations of resurrection
and religion in, 43, 125–27, 134,
283; *Jean Santeuil* and, 73–74;
knowledge of self in, 126; lime
tea, the *petite madeleine*, and
memory in, 71–72, 124–26,
139, 243, 276, 284, 285;
literary voice in, 59; memory
in, 120–21, 123–26, 129, 177;
metaphor, allegory, and simile in,
133–35, 137, 138, 139; narrative
structure in, 92; narrator and
childhood experiences in,
65–66, 92, 99–100, 112–13, 116,
120–26, 127, 129–36, 138–40,
154, 168; narrator and writing
in, 139, 178, 283; placement in
a war zone of, 62; reality and
realism in, 139–40; relativity
in, 138–39; as a separate novel,
112; subjectivity in, 140; time
in, 123–26, 128–29, 132–33;
verb tenses in, 65–66, 125, 129;
walking routes, Swann's way
and the path to Guermantes, in,
133–39
—*female characters*: Aunt Léonie,
125, 127–28, 129; Albertine,
19–20; Berma, 157; Duchess of
(Mme de) Guermantes, 137–38,

168; Gilberte, 113, 134–35, 147,
151, 157, 158–59, 173; Mlle
Vinteuil, 42, 135–36, 171, 259;
Mme Verdurin, 143, 147; Odette
de Crécy, 37, 113, 130, 142–44,
145, 146, 147, 148, 150, 151,
152, 158, 173
—*male characters*: Bergotte, 31,
131, 158, 160; Bloch, 131;
Comte de Forcheville, 146–47;
Doctor Cottard, 147; Duke of
Guermantes, 158; Elstir, 29;
Legrandin, 131–32; M. Vinteuil,
135–36, 259; Marcel, 113; Saint-
Loup, 142; Swann, 20, 37, 49,
81, 82, 121–22, 131, 134, 141,
142–51, 157, 158, 173; Uncle
Adolphe, 139
—"Place-Names: The Name"
("Noms de pays: Le nom"), 20,
113, 151, 155, 156
—"Swann in Love" ("Un amour de
Swann"), 112, 113, 115, 120
—Vol. 2: *Within a Budding Grove*
(*A l'ombre des jeunes filles en
fleurs*), 22, 23; ambiguity in, 160;
aristocracy in, 177–79, 182–85;
art and music in, 194–96; Balbec
(village), 159, 165, 166, 174,
175–77, 195; beauty in, 176; church
in, 175–76; comedy and satire in,
161, 163, 168, 175, 176–78, 183,
184; group of girls in, 165–66,
176; intimations of paradise in,
164; intimations of the fall in, 197;
love in, 151, 164–65, 166, 168,
176, 177; memory in, 177, 195;
names in, 159, 163, 174, 175,
176–77; narrator and narrative
voice in, 151, 155, 159–67, 175–85,
194–97; narrator's vocation and
procrastination, 160, 178; positive
ideas of negative characters, 160;
reality, idealization, and deflation in,

Vol. 2 (*continued*)

175–76, 177, 184; subjectivity and
the discontinuity of the self, 164,
177, 230. *See also* habit; Vinteuil's
sonata

—*female characters:* Albertine, 165–
66; Berma, 193–94; Duchess of
(Mme de) Guermantes, 159, 163,
166, 168, 177; Gilberte (Swann's
daughter), 159, 161–62, 163,
164–65, 177; Mlle de Stermaria,
174; Mlle de Villeparisis, 177,
178–79, 181; Mme Bontemps,
163; Mme Swann, 162;
narrator's grandmother, 179,
184, 197; Odette, 162, 163, 195;
Princess de Luxembourg, 177

—*male characters:* Ambassador
Norpois, 160–61, 193; Bergotte,
160–61, 185, 195, 196; Baron de
(M. de) Charlus, 154, 177, 182–
85, 195; Duke de Guermantes,
183; Elstir, 176, 185, 195, 196;
Palmède (Mémé) [other names
for M. de Charlus], 184; Saint-
Loup, 177, 181–82, 184; Swann,
161, 163, 195; Vinteuil, 194–95,
196

—"Place-Names: The Place," 155,
175–76

—Vol. 3: *The Guermantes Way*
(*Du côté de Guermantes*), 3, 21,
23; aristocracy and society in,
55, 169–70, 171, 186–91, 193;
art and music in, 192–93, 194;
Balbec (village), 187, 189, 190,
195, 196, 197; comedy and satire
in, 170, 171, 176, 185–86, 187,
199; conclusion of, 188; Dreyfus
affair, 160; Guermantes family
and dinner party, 169, 189–92;
Guermantes townhouse, 169, 176,
189; intimations of paradise in, 168;
intimations of the fall in, 188; love

and sex in, 166–68, 169, 173–75,
191, 199; memory in, 168–69,
174, 198; metaphor, allegory, and
simile in, 173, 174; names in,
159, 168–69, 171, 174, 175, 188;
narrator and narrative voice in,
104, 154, 159–60, 167–75, 185–94,
197–99; narrator's vocation and
procrastination, 192–93; reality,
idealization, and deflation, 169–70,
171–75, 176, 188, 189, 192, 193;
religion in, 170; theater in, 193,
194; voyeurism in, 170–71

—*female characters:* Berma,
171; Duchess of (Mme
de) Guermantes, 166–74,
189, 190, 191–92, 197–98;
Melusine (fairy), 167; Mme
de Villeparisis, 172, 185, 189;
narrator's grandmother, 198,
199; narrator's mother, 173–74;
Princess of Guermantes, 171, 188

—*male characters:* Baron de (M.
de) Charlus, 154, 185–88, 189;
Duke of Guermantes, 188–89,
190–91; Elstir, 189, 190, 195;
Prince of Guermantes, 167–68;
Saint-Loup, 169, 172, 192, 197;
Swann, 188–89, 191–92

–Vol. 4: *Sodom and Gomorrah*
(*Sodome et Gomorrhe*), 21, 22, 23;
aristocracy, society and social life in,
207, 213–15, 236–37; art in, 236;
Balbec (village), 210, 213, 215, 216,
219, 228; biblical analogies in, 212;
chance in, 210–11, 216; comedy
and satire in, 200, 201, 206, 207–8,
209, 213, 216–17, 236; death and
loss in, 201, 212, 215–16; dreaming
in, 235; Dreyfus affair in, 214–15;
homosexuality in, 208–10; guilt
in, 212; intimations of redemption
in, 235; intimations of the fall in,
155, 200–202, 211–13, 214, 215,

236; knowledge in, 211, 212; love, desire, sex, and jealousy in, 201, 202, 211, 216, 220–21; memory in, 215, 228, 233–34, 235; names in, 236–37; narrator and narrative voice in, 135, 154–55, 200–202, 206, 208, 209–12, 213–17, 220–21, 233–35, 236–42; narrator's vocation and procrastination, 215–16; self in, 235; theme of, 200
—*female characters:* Albertine, 201, 202, 211, 213, 216–17, 220, 221; Andrée, 210, 221; Mlle Vinteuil, 211, 216; Mme Verdurin, 213, 214, 233, 236, 241; narrator's grandmother, 201, 211, 215, 228; Odette, 214; Princess of Guermantes, 213, 214, 215, 220
—*male characters:* Baron de (M. de) Charlus, 154, 171, 201, 207–10, 213, 214, 236; Bergotte, 214; Bloch, 215; Brichot, 236, 237; Doctor Cottard, 210–11, 236; Duke of Guermantes, 214; Elstir, 236; Jupien, 154, 171, 201, 207–8, 209–10; Morel, 214; Norwegian philosopher, 233; Prince of Guermantes, 215; Swann, 213, 215, 220
—Vol. 5: *The Captive (La prisonnière)*, 21, 23, 24; aristocracy, society, and social life in, 219–20, 224; art and music in, 235–36, 237–38, 239–44, 285–86; biblical myth in, 207; comedy and satire in, 201, 218–19, 224, 237; death and immortality in, 240–41; intimations of redemption in, 236; intimations of the fall in, 223, 237, 240, 241; love, desire, possession, and jealousy in, 211, 217, 218–20, 222–23, 224; memory in, 237; metaphors, allegory, and similes in, 221–22; narrator and

narrative voice in, 217, 218–20, 221–23, 226, 235–36, 237–38, 239–44; narrator's vocation and procrastination, 217, 218, 223, 240, 241; patriarchal society and, 207; self in, 236; weather and the seasons in, 218
—*female characters:* Albertine, 207, 211, 217, 218, 219–20, 221, 222, 226, 237, 243; Duchess of Guermantes, 218; Françoise, 218, 219; Léa, 218–19; Mlle Vinteuil, 219, 222; Mme Verdurin, 219, 220, 222, 224–25, 243; Odette, 223, 224; Princess Sherbatoff, 224–25
—*male characters:* Baron de (M. de) Charlus, 219, 220, 223, 224, 243; Bergotte, 240, 241; Morel, 219, 220, 224; Saniette, 224; Swann, 224; Vinteuil, 241–42
—Vol. 6: *The Fugitive (La fugitive)*, 21, 24; biblical myth in, 207; comedy and satire in, 201, 227, 229; contingency and chance in, 228; death in, 228; dialectical reversals in, 231; intimations of redemption and resurrection in, 233, 235, 244; intimations of the fall in, 228, 230, 231, 244–45; love, desire, sex, and jealousy in, 220, 226–27, 228, 229–30, 232; memory in, 227, 235, 244–45; metaphor and allegory in, 233; music in, 270; narrator and narrative voice, 217–18, 220, 226–32, 244–45; narrator's vocation and procrastination, 217, 218; patriarchal society and, 207; self in, 228, 230, 244; social change in, 231–32; trip to Tansonville and Combray, 246–47; trip to Venice, 230–31, 244–45
—*female characters:* Albertine, 207, 220, 226, 228–29, 230, 244,

female characters (continued)
255; Andrée, 230; Berma, 227;
Gilberte (Swann's daughter),
230, 231–33, 246; Marquise de
Villeparisis, 231; Mlle d'Oloron
(Jupien's niece), 231; Mme de
Sazerat, 231; narrator's mother,
217, 231, 244; Rachel, 231
—male characters: M. de Norpois,
231; Morel, 232; Saint-Loup,
231–32
—Vol. 7: Time Regained (Le temps
retrouvé), 24; aristocracy, society
and social life in, 251, 252, 255,
262–64, 266; Balbec (village), 249,
272, 274; carnivalesque dimension,
254–55, 259–60, 261, 263, 265,
266, 269; change in narrative
mode, 248–49; comedy and satire
in, 249, 250, 251, 255, 257, 265,
266; determinism in, 280; dialectical
reversals in, 247–48; evil in, 136;
history and historicism in, 266;
imagination in, 274; intimations
of redemption and resurrection,
249, 261, 262, 267, 268, 269–70,
272, 273–74; intimations of the
fall, 248–49, 251, 269; literature
in, 270, 284, 287; memory in,
247, 253, 161, 262–63, 272–74,
277–78; metaphor, allegory, and
similes in, 254, 264–65, 271,
273–75; narrative strategy in, 265,
282–83; narrator and narrative
voice in, 231, 247–48, 249–67,
277, 279–80; narrator's illness and
death, 286; narrator's vocation and
procrastination, 156, 248, 249–50,
262–64, 268–70, 281, 283, 286;
paradise in, 273; Paris in, 231, 251,
254, 257; past and present in, 67,
272–74, 280; Proust in, 261–62;
realism and reality in, 250–51, 265,
280; relativity in, 281; reception

given by the Guermantes, 248,
249, 263–66, 267, 269, 271–72,
277–78; reversals and inversions
in, 251, 252–53, 254, 255, 257,
258, 259–61, 262, 264, 265, 269;
self in, 126, 156, 270, 271, 276;
Tansonville and Combray, 246–48,
249, 252–53, 273; time and time
span in, 251, 265–66, 269, 272;
title of, 246, 284; World War I in,
251–54, 256–58, 261–62, 266;
writing, art, and music in, 270,
275–80, 284, 286–88
—female characters: Berma, 267;
Duchess of Guermantes, 264;
Gilberte (Swann's daughter), 163,
247–48, 251, 252–53; Mlle de
Saint-Loup (Gilberte's daughter),
267; Mme Bontemps, 252; Mme
Verdurin, 250, 251–52, 255,
256, 263, 267–68; Odette, 266;
Princess of Guermantes (formerly
Mme Verdurin), 256, 263, 268;
Rachel, 248, 267
—male characters: Baron de (M. de)
Charlus in, 136, 225, 226, 248,
249, 254, 255–59, 264, 268,
271; Bergotte, 271; Goncourt,
249–50; Jupien, 259–61, 264;
M. Bontemps, 252; Morel,
226, 248, 255, 259; Prince de
Guermantes, 262, 267–68; Saint-
Loup (Gilberte's husband), 248,
251, 253–54, 258, 262, 267;
Verdurin, 250

Jaloux, Edmond, 23
Janet, Paul, 8
Jansenism, 40, 271, 276
Jaurès, Jean, 84
jealousy, 221. See also In Search of Lost
Time
Jean Santeuil: art and artists in, 80, 131;
background of, 11, 24, 68, 69, 70,

72–73, 75; "Beg-Meil" section of, 91–93; belief in science, 86; childhood and paradise in, 88–89, 92; comedy and the comic in, 76–77, 90, 158; cycles in, 88–90; descriptions of parents in old age, 75–75; Dreyfus affair and, 85–87, 160, 215; editor in, 73; education in, 74; ethics and idealism in, 85–87; friendship in, 74; gardens in, 125; human inadequacy in, 77; love in, 37, 74, 75–76, 80–83; Marie affair (fictional political scandal), 83–87; memory in, 87, 91; narration and narrator in, 59, 72, 73–74, 75, 76–77, 82–83, 87–90, 92–93, 114; places in, 88–90; political issues in, 15, 74, 83–87; Professor Beulier in, 74; publication/editions of, 69, 73, 80, 84, 89; redemption, resurrection, and recall of time past, 87, 92, 93; religious images in, 88–89; society and social life in, 74, 75–79; structure, strategy, and time in, 75, 83, 87–88, 91–93; themes of, 56, 74, 75, 78, 88, 131; theory of ethics and writing, 79–80, 87; utopia and divine harmony in, 90–91; verb tenses in, 88–90, 92, 116; writers in, 73, 79–80, 87; writing in, 91, 92–93

Jesuits, 272

Jews, 1, 106–7. *See also* Dreyfus, Alfred

"Journées de lecture." *See* "Days of Reading"

Joyce, James, 11, 193, 203

Kafka, Franz, 11, 203

King Lear (Shakespeare), 225, 255, 256, 258, 264

Kolb, Philip, 24

La Bruyère, Jean de, 26–27, 34, 38–39, 42, 43, 45, 46, 70

La Rochefoucauld, François de, 26, 38–39, 42, 43–44, 46, 70

Lacan, Jacques, 122

Lamartine, Alphonse de, 91

Landry, Joshua, 144

Laurens de Waru, Gustave, 5

Lauris, Georges de, 18

Le Cuziat, Albert, 21

Lemaire, Madeleine, 6

Lemoine, Henri, 17

Lemoine affair, 17

"Lighthouses" ("Les Phares"; Baudelaire), 30

Littérature et conversation: La querelle Sainte-Beuve-Proust (Fumaroli), 179–81

Lorrain, Jean, 12

Lost Illusions (Balzac), 184

"Lost Wax" ("Cires perdues"), 44. See also *Pleasures and Days*

Lusignan, house of, 167–68

"Lycidas" (Milton), 65

"M. de Guermantes' Balzac" ("Le Balzac de M. de Guermantes"), 104–5. See also *Against Sainte-Beuve*

MacMahon, Edme Patrice, 152

Madame Bovary (Flaubert), 35

Magic Mountain (Mann), 22

Mâle, Émile, 10, 13, 60, 62, 128

Mallarmé, Stéphane, 11–12, 27, 31, 34, 44, 54, 55, 155–56

"Man and the Sea" ("L'homme et la mer"; Baudelaire), 50

Mann, Thomas, 11, 22

Mantegna, Andrea, 148–49

"Marine." *See* "Seascape"

Mathilde, Princesse, 56, 178

Maurras, Charles, 14–15, 23

Mayor, Andreas, 246, 265

Mazarine Library (Paris), 9

"Melancholy Summer of Madame de Breyves, The" ("Mélancolique Villégiature de Madame de Breyves"), 40–41. See also *Pleasures and Days*

Melusine, 167–68

Mensuel, Le (student journal), 5, 29

Mercure de France, 14, 17–18

"Method of Sainte-Beuve, The" ("La méthode de Sainte-Beuve"), 97, 107. See also *Against Sainte-Beuve*

Middle Ages, 170

Middlemarch (Eliot), 76

Milton, John, 65, 246

Molière (Jean-Baptiste Poquelin), 29

Moncrieff, C.K. Scott, 22, 115, 125, 177, 246

"Mondanité et mélomanie de Bouvard et Pécuchet." *See* "Social Ambitions and Musical Tastes of Bouvard and Pécuchet"

Monet, Claude, 136

Montesquiou, Robert de, 6–7, 45, 56

"Moonlight" ("Clair de lune"; Verlaine), 51

"Moonlight Sonata" ("Sonate clair de lune"), 51. See also *Pleasures and Days*

Moore, Marianne, 176

"mort de Baldassare Silvande Vicomte de Sylvanie, La." *See* "Death of Baldassare Silvande, Viscount of Sylvania"

Mozart, Wolfgang Amadeus, 31–32

Musil, Robert, 11, 203

"Mystery in Letters" ("Le mystère dans les lettres"; Mallarmé), 11, 54

myth, use of, 202–3

"Names" ("Noms de personnes"), 103–5. See also *Against Sainte-Beuve;* "Place-Names: The Name" under *In Search of Lost Time*—Vol. 1: *Swann's Way*

Napoleon, 142

Nerval, Gérard de, 109–10

Neuburger, Louise, 5

Neue Merkur, Der (literary and political journal), 23

Nietzsche, Friedrich, 46

Noailles, Anna de, 56, 61

Nolte, Ernst, 23

"Noms de pays: Le nom." *See* "Place-Names: The Name" under *In Search of Lost Time*—Vol. 1: *Swann's Way*

Nordlinger, Marie, 14, 59

"Norman Things" ("Choses normandes"), 29

"Nostalgia—Daydreams under Changing Skies" ("Regrets et rêveries, couleur du temps"), 46–52. See also *Pleasures and Days*

Nouvelle Revue française (NRF), 19, 20, 21, 110

obscurity. See "Against Obscurity"

Old Testament. See Bible

"On Flaubert's 'Style'" ("A propos du 'style' de Flaubert"), 110

On Love (*De l'amour;* Stendhal), 80–81

"On Reading," 65–66, 67, 277

Paradise Regained (Milton), 246

Paris, France, 1

Parisian Commune, 142

Parousia (second coming), 270, 272

Pascal, Blaise, 126, 222, 271

Pastiches et mélanges, 16–17, 22–23, 59–60, 61–62, 64, 138. See also "Days in an Automobile"; "On Reading"

Pater, Walter, 64

Patterson, Ian, 246

"Pédérastie," 2–3

Phèdre (Racine), 40–41, 193, 221, 227

Picquart, Georges, 85–86

"Place-Names: The Name." See under *In Search of Lost Time*—Vol. 1: *Swann's Way*

Plato, 27, 51, 79, 86, 145

Platonism, 54, 65, 274

Pleasures and Days (*Les plaisirs et les jours*), 6, 7, 8; art and artists in, 32–34, 81; comedy and satire in, 39–40, 44–45, 46, 77, 201; death in, 35–37; dedication of, 33; desire for return to childhood, 51–52;

destruction of a moral being in, 39–40; dominant theme of, 44; dreams in, 49–50; early intimations of the fall in, 201; fragments in, 42–46; ideas and narrative modes of, 38–39; metaphors in, 29–32, 44, 46; music and musicians in, 29–32, 34, 49; narratives of deaths in, 35; love, desire, and jealousy in, 37–38, 47–50, 81; nature in, 50–51; organization of complementary symmetries in, 34–35, 37; pessimism of, 34, 46–48; play of oppositions and contrasts in, 31, 32–35, 37; poetry in, 30–32, 34, 46, 52–53, 57; preface by Anatole France, 11, 12; prose poems in, 34–35, 46–53; psychological laws and, 28–29, 37, 38, 39, 41, 49; religion in, 42; stories in, 35–42; subjectivity and delusion in, 48–50, 51; summary and perspective on, 26–27; techniques and imagery in, 52. *See also* "Death of Baldassare Silvande, Viscount of Sylvania"; "Dinner in High Society, A"; "Dream"; "End of Jealousy, The"; "Fragments from Italian Comedy"; "Melancholy Summer of Madame de Breyves, The"; "Nostalgia—Daydreams under Changing Skies"; "Social Ambitions and Musical Tastes of Bouvard and Pécuchet"; "Violante or High Society"; "Young Girl's Confession, A"

Portrait of the Artist as a Young Man (Joyce), 193

possession, 38, 81–82, 144, 174–75, 216, 221. See also *In Search of Lost Time*

Potter, Paulus, 32

"Previous Life" ("La vie antérieure"; Baudelaire), 52

prisonnière, La (*The Captive*). See under *In Search of Lost Time*

Proust, Adrien (father), 1–2, 9–11, 15, 109

Proust, Jeanne (née Weil; mother), 1, 2, 10–11, 14, 15, 18, 93, 95–100, 109, 116

Proust, Marcel: acceptance of nineteenth-century "biologism," 105; ambivalence toward medicine, 199; awarded Prix Goncourt, 23; birth, childhood, school, and university years, 1, 2–10; characters and characterization by, 225, 232; as a chronicler of social change, 213; comedy and satire of, 180–81, 184, 204, 205, 213, 222; correspondence of, 24; coverage of French social life and society, 55–58, 104; as critic, 94–95; death of, 24, 284; Dostoyevsky and, 255; duels with Jean Lorrain and others, 12–13; employment of, 9; friends and social life of, 2, 3, 4, 6, 9, 12–16, 19–20; guilt and conscience of, 204; health, 10, 15–16, 19, 23, 24, 33–34, 100; idolatry, 64; imagination of, 270; influence of his writing, 180; inner life of, 3–4, 29; law of life and, 54; literary theory and descriptive aesthetics of, 94; love, desire, possession, and jealousy, 143–45, 174–75, 205–6, 221, 222, 223–24, 229–30; memory themes of, 59–60, 64, 152–53, 206, 230; metaphors, allegories, and similes of, 29–31, 44, 57, 103, 133–34, 137, 203–4, 205–7, 239; military service of, 4; negative criticism of, 179–81; omniscient narration, 230; paradise and, 32, 206; pastiches of, 42; pessimism of, 46; Plato and, 86; politics and philosophy of, 5, 8–10, 14–15, 27; process of development of, 69; psychology of, 10; recurrent themes of anguish, snobs, and lovers of, 41, 45–46, 56, 64, 74, 76, 102; redemption and, 206; relation to biblical myth, 202–07; relativity of, 138; religion and spirituality of, 1, 8,

Proust, Marcel (*continued*)
10, 21–22, 62–63, 72, 101; Ruskin
and, 58–60, 61, 62, 63–67, 93, 128;
search for transcendence of reality,
202; sensations and the past of,
102–3; sense of humor of, 22, 104;
sex and sexuality of, 10, 12, 21, 22,
106, 204; as a writer, 10–13, 15–18,
22–24, 26–28, 52–53, 68, 70, 91,
100–101; World War I and, 19–22.
See also habit; *In Search of Lost Time;*
Jean Santeuil; Pleasures and Days;
rationalism and rationalists; realism
and realist fiction
—*miscellaneous writings:* articles, 16;
Chroniques, 24, 56; essays, 6, 11,
14, 15, 16–17, 23, 30, 70; pastiches,
17; poetry, 2–3, 29, 30–31; short
stories, 28, 33; translations of
Ruskin's works, 13–14, 15;
unpublished works, 69–71.
—*views:* theory of literary criticism,
60–61; of chance and contingency,
210, 228; of the fall, 181, 203–7,
228, 232, 239; of homosexuality
and bisexuality, 28–29, 105–7,
207–10, 232; of language, 155–56;
of literature, 2, 3, 6, 11, 23–24,
27–28, 29, 44, 53–54, 67, 98, 180;
of love, 41, 71; of music and art, 7,
13, 14, 15, 29–33, 41, 51, 57, 59,
60–64, 67, 71–72, 98, 238, 239–40,
278–79; of past and present, 37,
57, 62, 64–65, 66, 67, 270, 279;
of perception and intelligence, 102;
of poetry, 52–54; of race, 106; of
reading, 65–67; of redemption, 102;
of science, 107–9, 278–79; of self,
56–57, 194, 230, 232; of suffering,
164–65; of utopia, 32, 34–36, 55,
57, 58, 90–91, 138, 159, 181, 213;
of the world and work, 238–40; of
writers, 179, 238–39

Proust, Robert (brother), 2, 10, 15, 24,
100

Queneau, Raymond, 17

Rabelais, François, 34
race, 106
Racine, Jean, 29, 40–41, 53, 193, 221,
227
Rambouillet, Madame de, 180
rationalism and rationalists, 22, 53, 80,
105, 109, 235, 270, 275, 287
"rayon de soleil sur le balcon, Le." *See*
"Sunbeam on the Balcony, The"
"Real Presence" ("Présence réelle"), 50.
See also *Pleasures and Days*
realism and realist fiction: antirealism,
288–89; Balzac and, 105; conventional
and unconventional realism, 114;
In Search of Lost Time and, 207;
modernists and, 289; Proust and, 55,
70–71, 72, 75, 80, 98–99, 265, 288–
89; realist fiction, 114, 140; surrealists,
270; *Time Regained* and, 248, 249,
250–51, 254; Tolstoy and, 35
Réflexions (Vauvenargues), 26
"Regrets, Reveries the Color of Time."
See "Nostalgia—Daydreams under
Changing Skies"
Réjane, Gabrielle, 22
"Relics" ("Reliques"), 49–50. See also
Pleasures and Days
Rembrandt, 13, 70
*Remembrance of Things Past. See In
Search of Lost Time*
"Rencontre au bord du lac." *See*
"Encounter by the Lake"
"Republic of Dukes." *See* Third Republic
"Return, The" ("Retour à Guermantes"),
99–101, 109. See also *Against Sainte-
Beuve*
Revolution of 1789 (France), 252
Revue blanche, La, 7, 11, 28, 52, 54–55

*Revue de métaphysique et de morale,
La,* 3
Revue des deux mondes, La, 13
Revue lilas, La, 3
Revue verte, La, 3
Richards, I. A., 137
Riefstahl, Madame. *See* Nordlinger,
Marie
Rimbaud, Arthur, 179
Rivers, J. E., 232
Rivière, Jacques, 20
Ruskin, John, 10, 13–14, 15, 51, 58–65,
67
"Ruskin et la religion de la beauté"
(Sizeranne), 13

Sainte-Beuve, Charles-Augustin, 5, 23,
70, 79, 93, 107–8, 178, 179–80,
181. *See also Against Sainte-Beuve;*
"Method of Sainte-Beuve, The"
"Sainte-Beuve and Balzac" ("Sainte-
Beueve et Balzac"), 97–98. *See also
Against Sainte-Beueve*
"Sainte-Beuve and Baudelaire" ("Sainte-
Beuve et Baudelaire"), 97, 109. *See
also Against Sainte-Beuve*
Saint-Hilaire, Geoffroy, 108
"Samson's Anger ("La colère de Samson";
Vigny), 206–7
Sand, George, 277
Sartre, Jean-Paul, 223
Saussine, Madame de, 55
Scenes from a Courtesan's Life (Balzac),
184
Schelling, Friedrich, 91
Schopenhauer, Arthur, 29, 46
Schumann, Robert, 31–32
"Seascape" ("Marine"), 51–52, 241. *See
also Pleasures and Days*
second coming. *See* Parousia
Sesame and Lilies (*Sésame et les lys;*
Ruskin), 13, 15, 58, 59, 65, 261
Sizeranne, Robert de la, 13

"Social Ambitions and Musical Tastes of
Bouvard and Pécuchet" ("Mondanité et
mélomanie de Bouvard et Pécuchet"),
44–45. *See also Pleasures and Days*
Sodom and Gomorrah (*Sodome et
Gomorrhe*). *See under In Search of
Lost Time*
Sodome et Gomorrhe (*Sodom and
Gomorrah*). *See under In Search of
Lost Time*
"Sonate clair de lune." *See* "Moonlight
Sonata"
Sorel, Albert, 4–5
Souday, Paul, 12, 18, 167
"Sous-Bois." *See* "Forest Scene"
"Space and Geometry" (Poincaré), 281
Spinoza, Baruch, 99
Stendhal (Marie-Henri Beyle), 80, 110,
143, 230
Stones of Venice, The (Ruskin), 14, 67
Straus, Mme Geneviève, 3, 16, 19, 20.
"Sunbeam on the Balcony, The" ("Le
rayon de soleil sur le balcon"), 96. *See
also Against Sainte-Beuve*
"Sunday at the Conservatoire, A" ("Un
dimanche au conservatoire"), 30
"Swann in Love" ("Un amour de
Swann"). *See under In Search of Lost
Time—Vol.* 1: *Swann's Way*
Swann's Way (*Du côté de chez Swann*).
See under In Search of Lost Time
Sylvie (Nerval), 109, 110
symbolism (art movement), 52–53, 54
syphillis, 35–36

Tadié (publisher), 72, 75, 80, 84, 89
Tadié, Jean-Yves (biographer), 4, 8, 12,
22
Tagore, Rabindranath, 21
Taine, Hippolyte, 107–8
"Talking to Mama" ("Conversation avec
Maman"), 96–97. *See also Against
Sainte-Beuve*

Temps, Le (newspaper), 12

temps retrouvé, Le (Time Regained). See under *In Search of Lost Time*

tenses. *See* verb tenses

Thélème Abbey, 34, 57

Thibaudet, Alfred, 110

Third Republic (France): aristocracy and, 142, 186; Dreyfus affair and, 14; monarchy and, 147; patriarchal society and, 207; political life of, 8, 9–10, 83–84; as the "Republic of Dukes," 1

Thomas à Kempis, 39

three body problem, 286

Time Machine, The (Wells), 282

Time Regained (Le temps retrouvé). See under *In Search of Lost Time*

Times Literary Supplement, 23

Tolstoy, Leo, 8, 35, 36, 38

Tonfarben, 242

tragedy, 221

Turgenev, Ivan, 181

Turner, J. M. W., 63

Two Workhorses in Front of a Thatched Hut (Deux chevaux de trait devant une chaumière; Potter), 32

Van Dyke, Anthony, 32–33

Vautrin (in *Father Goriot*), 183, 184

Vauvenargues, Marquis de, 26–27, 46, 70

verb tenses: imperfect (*imparfait*), 65–66, 88–90, 110–11, 116–17, 125; perfect (*parfait*), 66; present perfect (*passé composé*), 66, 115–16, 117, 125; preterit (*passé défini*), 115, 116–17, preterit same as absolute or historical past (*passé simple*), 66; use by Flaubert, 110–11; use by Proust,

115–17. See also *In Search of Lost Time; Jean Santeuil*

Verlaine, Paul, 29, 34, 51

Vermeer, Johannes, 15, 237, 240

Vinteuil's sonata: narrator and, 162–63, 194–95, 237, 242, 247, 284–85; Swann and, 146, 149–50

View of Delft (Vermeer), 15, 23, 237, 240

Vigny, Alfred de, 178–79, 206

"Violante or High Society" ("Violante ou La Mondanité"), 39. See also *Pleasures and Days*

Vuillard, Édouard, 67

Wagner, Richard, 28, 152, 254

War and Peace (Tolstoy), 35

Watteau, Antoine, 32, 71–72

Weber, Max, 237

Wells, H. G., 282

Wernher, Sir Julius, 17

Whistler, James Abbott McNeill, 250

Wilde, Oscar, 5, 64

"Windows, The" ("Les Fenêtres"; Mallarmé), 31

Within a Budding Grove (A l'ombre des jeunes filles en fleurs). See under *In Search of Lost Time*

Wittgenstein, Ludwig, 115, 194, 234

Woolf, Virginia, 203

World War I, 18, 19, 21, 61–62, 117, 251–54, 256–58, 261–62, 266

"Young Girl's Confession, A" ("La Confession d'une jeune fille"), 41–42, 259. See also *Pleasures and Days*

Zola, Émile, 14, 85, 108, 215